MIRROR OF WAR

THE WASHINGTON *STAR* REPORT

MIRROR OF WAR

THE CIVIL WAR

Compiled and Edited by

JOHN W. STEPP

STAR Staff Writer

and

I. WILLIAM HILL

Feature Editor, THE *STAR*

CASTLE BOOKS, INC.

"Mirror of War" by John W. Stepp and I. W .Hill

© 1961 by The Evening Star Newspaper Co.

Library of Congress Catalog Card Number: 61–17947

Printed in the United States of America

58578—T

This edition published by
arrangement with Prentice-Hall, Inc.

Foreword

This book is the result of a quick evolution of ideas rather than of any spontaneous decision to produce it.

Well in advance of the Civil War centennial The Star began the consideration of some appropriate way to recall to readers of another generation some of the outstanding events of the conflict. The Civil War was a peculiarly local story in Washington, seat of government of the Union of States, whose preservation or dissolution was at stake. As a newspaper published continuously in Washington since 1852, The Star had lived through the dark days of the crisis.

Search for ideas, naturally enough, began within Star files and they were promptly rewarding, quickly contradicting the old saying that "Nothing is deader than yesterday's newspaper." The newspapers of hundred-year-old yesterdays were very much alive, and the years of their silence gave new vigor to what they had to say. It was decided to let them retell the narrative of Washington and the war as they told it a century ago.

The method chosen was a weekly reprint of war reporting in The Star, to appear on consecutive dates corresponding generally with the centennials of the events described. Announcement of the undertaking, to continue during the four centennial years of the war, brought immediate evidence of public interest. The press section of *Newsweek* found it newsworthy and ran an item about it. This came to the attention of John Walsh, an associate editor of the publishing firm of Prentice-Hall. He came to Washington for conversations with I. William Hill, The Star's Feature Editor, who supervised the project, and John Stepp, already well on his way in assembly and arrangement of the material. He was interested and helpful. His recommendation was approved by his associates at Prentice-Hall. Thus the book, and credit to those chiefly responsible for it.

Although it contains history, this is not a history book. Its content is indicated by the title, "Mirror of War." The Star of 1861–65 was the mirror. It reflected, in its day-to-day reporting, the image of war seen by Star readers of those days. Whether the image happened to be accurate or was distorted by circumstances unknown at the time to those who projected the image is neither here nor there. This book is concerned with the image mirrored by The Star.

The introduction to this book, written by Mr. Hill, provides the setting for the narrative which follows. It contains interesting descriptive matter and comment on Washington, The Star and Civil War journalism. So the remainder of this brief foreword is by way of dedicating this book to its real authors, the reporters and editors of The Star and of many other newspapers whose contributions made possible The Star's war reporting.

For the most part, they are anonymous and with few exceptions their identity is not recorded in The Star. On a quaint monument in the Maryland hills near the battlefield of Antietam, erected by one of the war correspondents and dedicated by him to his brethren, the names of more than one hundred of them appear—including that of Crosby S. Noyes of The Star and a few others who, in one way or another, became identified with The Star. Many of those thus memorialized were doubtless contributors to The Star. This book is not dedicated to individuals, but to a group of Civil War correspondents who helped to shape the course of future journalism in the United States. They demonstrated that the gathering and reporting of news, rather than opinion, is the primary function of good newspapers. They helped change the newspapers they represented from organs of opinion to distributors of information. There were no rules on how to report a war, so they made their own. They experienced hardships and frustrations in overcoming barriers to the flow of news that still exist in many parts of today's world. Their battles with the politicians and the generals in their efforts to let the people know what was going on are memories occasionally refreshed by repetitions of history in this country today.

They lacked the facilities of communication and travel available to the latter-day brethren of the press. They lacked the disciplined craftsmanship and techniques of reporting that now, a century later, are commonplace. Judged by modern standards, much of their reporting was crude, windy, given to irrelevant personal opinion and reliance on rumors rather than verified fact.

But they did a good job with what they had. They were real newspapermen.

BENJAMIN M. McKELWAY
EDITOR, *The Evening and Sunday Star*,
WASHINGTON, D.C.

v

Contents

Introduction:

A NEWSPAPER AS THE MIRROR OF WAR

In a history book, we see the past as it sits for its portrait. The image is retouched, refined, its countenance relieved of distracting irrelevancies. A newspaper, on the other hand, recording the diverse events of any given day, mirrors the past as people saw and lived it at the time—complete with teeming detail, sometimes inaccurate, sometimes without perspective, but always with lifelike reality. A yellowing newspaper can take each of us back to relive a bygone day, almost to the point where we feel we are reading by candlelight.

With this book, the editors propose to take you back to the years 1861–1865. Their intent is to enable you to live the suspense of the Civil War by having it unfold exactly as it did for newspaper readers in the Nation's Capital a hundred years ago. Your mirror of the past is *The Evening Star,* the only surviving newspaper that covered the Civil War from its home front in Washington, D.C.

The contents of this volume are made up of the 62 biggest stories of the Civil War period direct from the files of *The Star* of the 1860s. The format for each chapter includes:

1. A brief transitionary background to keep events in perspective.

2. A reprint of *The Star's* reports on each big story beginning with the election of Abraham Lincoln and continuing through the last gunfire at sea, more than two months after General Lee's surrender at Appomattox. Where necessary for either accuracy or clarity, modern editorial notes have been inserted. As a convenience for the reader, modern headlines have been used as chapter titles.

3. Illustrations from contemporary photographers, artists or engravers. (It should be borne in mind that newspapers of the Civil War period were not equipped to publish pictures. The first news illustration ever published by *The Star* is included in this volume.)

4. Some views of the Washington homefront as it was reflected in local news items and advertisements.

But first, let's look at news gathering and the newspaper of 1861–1865, *The Star* in particular; at the Washington of that day; and at the dark clouds of impending war, as you would have viewed them all during the closing days of 1860.

Early News Gathering

Newspapers, like the means of waging war, had evolved slowly. To the earliest American editors, news was whatever information of interest came to them, however old, however inaccurate. Even by 1800, no effort had been made to go out and gather news. Newspapers were often crammed with sentimental verse, pompous essays, religious dissertations and bombastic political propaganda. News gathering, as such, began about the time of the War of 1812, but the practice grew slowly. By 1860, many newspapers still resembled the periodicals of the turn of the century.

In 1843, the first telegraph line was opened—between Washington and Baltimore. The part the telegraph was to play in developing the newspaper was not immediately apparent. New York newspapers, the most aggressive of the day, still relied on pony express, carrier pigeons, and express boats in trying to beat competitors. But by 1847 the electromagnetic telegraph was clicking away in more than a dozen cities. Telegraph transmission was expensive, however, and often inadequate for the news load.

In May, 1848, six New York newspapers, hungry for fresher news, pooled their resources to form the Associated Press, the progenitor, but a vastly different type of organization from the modern wire service of the same name. Though the organization was formed to supply the New York newspapers with wire news, at a lower pro rata cost, news was also sold at a weekly rate to newspapers in Philadelphia, Baltimore and later, Washington. As the Associated Press grew, it designated "agents" in American cities to provide news by wire. These "agents" were more distinguished by their facility in operating a telegraph than by their ability at reporting.

Newspapers buying the wire service gradually began to divide themselves into regional groups. This was because news was distributed to them on a regional basis, and regional grouping facilitated their dealing with the parent group in New York. Thus, by the time of the Civil War, there was a Philadelphia Associated Press, a Southern Associated Press, a Western Associated Press, etc. Often the word "Associated" was dropped and credits in old newspapers read simply "Southern Press" or "Western Press."

Washington, D.C. at the time of the Civil War. The large building in the left background is the Smithsonian Institute. The view is looking southeast from the vicinity of the Treasury Department.

Cattle grazing around the unfinished Washington Monument during the war.

The Washington bureau of the Associated Press was established in 1856, headed by Lawrence Augustus Gobright, who already had been the Associated Press "agent" in Washington for eight years. Gobright was to serve the Associated Press in Washington throughout the Civil War. On the night of Lincoln's assassination, Gobright was to be present when an usher at Ford's theater found the derringer with which John Wilkes Booth had shot the President.

The first reporter ever assigned to stay constantly with a President-elect was an Associated Press man: Henry Villard, who was sent to Springfield, Ill. immediately after the election of Lincoln in November 1860. Villard stayed with Lincoln until after his inauguration. When war came, the Associated Press dispatched "agents" to all battlefronts, and portions of their work are represented in this volume.

Washington and "The Star"

By 1852, four years after the founding of the Associated Press, 100 newspapers had been started in the Nation's Capital. All but four failed. Two were simply mouthpieces for the Whig administration of President Millard Fillmore. One was the traditional organ of Franklin Pierce's Democratic party. The fourth had the official job of reporting Congressional proceedings. None was a newspaper in the growing sense of what a newspaper should be.

Against this background, *The Evening Star* was born, December 16, 1852, in a small print shop eight blocks west of the Capitol. Its founder and first editor was Capt. Joseph Borrows Tate, 34, a practical printer. He founded *The Star* with the idea of making it a new kind of newspaper—one that would not represent any political party, and would publish real news, especially that of local interest.

Six months later, *The Star* was bought by William Douglass Wallach, a newspaperman, who was to remain its owner-editor throughout the Civil War. Soon after taking over, Wallach hired a young man from Maine—Crosby Stuart Noyes—as a circulation expert. Noyes very

The Civil War office of the *Washington Star,* located at 11th Street and Pennsylvania Avenue.

quickly became a reporter, however, and in the years ahead was to distinguish himself for his reporting during the Civil War. Later in 1867, with such partners as Samuel H. Kauffmann and George W. Adams, he was to buy *The Star* from Wallach. Today, *The Star* is owned by the descendants of these men.

By 1860, *The Star* had moved from its humble first home to its own building, on the southwest corner of Eleventh Street and Pennsylvania Avenue, midway between the Capitol and the President's House (the name for the White House at that time).

From this imposing building, the newspaper that appeared at 2 p.m. each weekday consisted of only four pages, the usual size of metropolitan dailies at the time. Its pages were 14 by 21 inches, six columns to a page. The type face was small and headlines were restricted to one-column width. As will be noted on pages to follow, spectacular news, instead of causing Editor Wallach to use wider headlines, only led to his writing additional decks on his one-column headlines.

In appearance, *The Star* of Civil War days still clung to British and colonial traditions. Two-thirds of its first page consisted of advertisements, many in number and small in size. Page One space left by the ads often presented sentimental fiction, verse, do-it-yourself articles, and such humor as Artemus Ward yarns.

Editorials appeared on Page Two, though editorials and news stories were sometimes difficult to distinguish. Local news, government news and wire dispatches were divided between Pages Two and Three. It was here that the big Civil War news was to be found, especially at the beginning of the war. Later, big news began to creep onto the first page. Except for an average of half a column, Page Four was given over entirely to advertisements.

Why the newspaper of a hundred years ago was so organized has been the subject of much modern speculation. It was probably the result of production problems and tradition. Two pages were printed simultaneously on one side of a sheet—Pages One and Four coming off the press first. The sheet was then turned over and Pages Two and Three were printed. But why not print the big news on the first page? The probable answer was that tradition and business practice called for advertisements on Page One. Ads could be set in type early. It seemed better to save the more open Pages Two and Three for all possible late news.

During the Civil War, all type was still set by hand, one character at a time and, amazingly, with few typographical errors. The slowness of this method was undoubtedly the reason why so many of the stories on the pages to follow will strike the reader as peculiar in comparison to modern newspaper stories. What the present day editor calls a "new lead" was apparently unheard of one hundred years ago. "New leads" meant the resetting of type. As a consequence, if a big story were breaking, the story in the old *Star* began with the first news to come in. Later news was hung on the end of that, and so on. The result is a chronological collection of developments where, in some cases, a report down the column will refute news published higher up. The format does, however, provide an element of suspense.

The Star of Civil War times was printed on a single large cylinder press—"fastest steam press south of Baltimore," the blurbs used to say. By 1862, regular editions were coming out at 2 and 4 p.m., with frequent "extras," often printed on half sheets.

The news content of *The Star* came from four sources: the Washington reporting of *The Star's* staff, including Editor Wallach and Reporter Noyes; the Associated Press wire news, with all dispatches filtering through Washington on the North-South telegraph line; correspondence to the editor, a news form that lies behind the word "correspondent" as designation for a far-away reporter; and exchanges, in which, by mutual agreement, a newspaper would clip and publish items from an out-of-town newspaper. Instances of all of these will be found in the Civil War stories.

The life of a reporter one hundred years ago was a busy one. Reporter Noyes arrived at the office at 7 a.m., dinner pail in hand. His first tasks were to prepare the crime news, no small assignment in the Washington of 1860, to write an editorial or so, clip the exchange papers, and prepare numerous one-paragraph filler items. Then he went out to visit government departments, perhaps the courts, and other news sources. When night came, there were meetings of the citizenry to provide more local news. Somewhere in between Noyes not only penned all his material (no typewriters in those days, or telephones, to help in covering stories) but read proof, supervised layout of pages, and made sure the sometimes drunken pressman got the finished product to the

Crosby Stuart Noyes, the *Star*'s ace reporter during the war.

reader. Reporter Noyes' day rarely ended before midnight. By-lines were rare a hundred years ago but undoubtedly many of the news stories in this book were written by Crosby S. Noyes.

Washington in 1860

The Nation's Capital was but sixty years old on the eve of the Civil War. Hardly a third of its sixty square miles was developed, the rest consisting of open fields. A British newsman of the time called Washington "a suburb without a city." The populated portion (60,000 souls) was concentrated in an area between the Potomac and Anacostia Rivers, and between Rock Creek and "The Boundary" (now known as Florida Avenue). Houses and buildings had just begun to have street numbers. Federal buildings were widely scattered, lending irony to the Capital's conception as "a city of magnificent distances." All streets, even Pennsylvania Avenue, were unpaved. In dry weather, they were ribbons of dust; in wet, oceans of mud.

Visitors to Washington arrived by train, steamship up the Potomac, or by one of six highways. Long Bridge, over the Potomac, connected Alexandria Road on the Virginia shore with Maryland Avenue; a sign at the Virginia end read "Walk your Horses." The other main highways into Washington crossed Chain Bridge en route from Leesburg, Va., Benning's Bridge or the Eleventh Street Bridge en route from southern Maryland; or came from Baltimore or Annapolis by the Bladensburg Road and from western Maryland by the Rockville Pike, via Tenallytown, D.C. and Georgetown.

Once in the Nation's capital, the visitor could find hotel accommodations along Pennsylvania Avenue. The two largest hotels were Willard's (still existent, but known as The Willard) and the National Hotel (later to become the headquarters for Federal Censorship of Civil War news).

William Douglass Wallach, owner-editor of the *Star* during the war.

When the 1860 visitor went sightseeing, he found the dome of the United States Capitol unfinished, and Washington Monument construction halted at a height of 125 feet, while cows grazed about its base. The red Tudor-style Smithsonian Institution looked out over a daisy-covered Mall. The President's House, so designated on 1860 maps, was unadorned by wings and office space. The most impressive structure was the Treasury building at Fifteenth Street and Pennsylvania Avenue. Also at its present site was the Navy Yard, which built ships and manufactured armaments, with the United States Marine Barracks conveniently situated close by. City Hall was on Judiciary Square, as was the blue-painted jail known as "The Blue Jug." Hains Point and the Tidal Basin, known to present-day tourists for their Japanese cherry blossoms, were nothing but a marshland where sportsmen gunned for ducks and reed birds. What is now Constitution Avenue, with its imposing buildings, was then Tiber Creek, so clogged with mud and filth as to impede barges.

When night fell, Pennsylvania Avenue was illuminated by gas, as were the finer residences, though many still relied on kerosene lamps and candles. Fires were a constant threat, and volunteer companies vied for the honor of fighting a blaze, water being conveyed from cisterns spotted along the street.

The pace of life was slow, walking being the most reliable and popular means of transportation. Horse-drawn omnibuses plied Pennsylvania Avenue. Horseback riding was for the privileged; horse-drawn hacks and carriages for the well-to-do.

Males comprised the work force both in and out of government. Women who worked had to be content with stay-at-home jobs or the lot of domestics. It was not until 1862 that the Treasury Department hired the first of what were to be thousands of "government girls." Organization activities even then were important to Washington, ever a city of "joiners." Besides trade unions, there were organized groups

7

dedicated to civic betterment, religious life, and fraternal and temperance activities. Home Front stories pertaining to most of these are included in this volume.

For entertainment in the winter, there were organized balls, music halls, uplifting lectures at the Smithsonian, and the theater (including the still-flourishing National Theater). In the summer, berry-picking festivals and picnics were popular, as were excursions down the Potomac to Mount Vernon and Fort Washington. Billiards and bowling were favorites even then, while lustier sportsmen attended horse races and cockfights. Quoit-pitching was an attraction on the lawn of City Hall.

High society managed to enjoy itself, despite the periodic inconvenience of carrying guests from carriage to doorstep because of the mud. Receptions began as soon as the midday meal was over. Evening affairs began when it was dark enough to light the tapers, and gayety often continued until dawn. Ladies' fashions were fulsome, with low necklines, floral drapery and plumage. For men, the last word in style was a high collar, bunchy neckwear, a brocaded vest, a stovepipe hat and a suit of black.

This was the Washington mirrored in *The Star* of 1860.

The Mood of the Nation

It was an era of rumor. News passed by word of mouth over a bottle of wine and, even in *The Star,* hearsay was sometimes cloaked by being credited to a "reliable gentleman," always anonymous. More and more, as 1860 neared its close, the rumors from the South were beginning to translate into factual reports.

The differences which had been pulling the North and South apart for more than three decades were reaching a point of no return. There had been no single starting point. The germ of conflict was implanted in the two sections virtually from the birth of the American colonies.

In the North and Midwest, big cities had sprung up. Manufacturing, spurred by the industrial revolution in Europe, blossomed with the cities. Railroads, extending from the Atlantic coast to the Mississippi River, laced the section together. Northern shipping handled practically all the Nation's overseas commerce. Cheap and fertile land, as well as wage-earning opportunities, beckoned to dissatisfied Europeans. The North became wealthy and powerful.

Below the northern boundary of Maryland, known as the Mason-Dixon line, the economy was of a different sort. Emphasis was on the cultivation of crops, especially cotton. Climate and simple cultivation methods favored the use of African slave labor. Only affluent whites could afford slaves, however. Thus a ruling class resembling a feudal aristocracy developed, composed chiefly of 300,000 planters who owned 3,500,000 slaves. This master class controlled state governments and Southern economy. As long as the South continued to prosper, the South's way of life was not likely to change.

So disparate had the two sections become that prewar European travellers remarked that going from one section of the United States to another was like passing into a foreign country.

The growth and influence of the North ultimately raised Southern fears that the North would dominate the central government, hence the Nation, at the South's expense. Because of this, and a belief that the Federal Union had been designed as a loose confederation of sovereign states, Southern leaders argued that the individual states had a right to conduct their own affairs.

Meantime, in the North, a feeling was growing that slavery should be abolished as a moral wrong. As early as the 1830s, European colonial powers and most Latin American countries had begun outlawing slavery. Southern slave owners were alarmed. The movement threatened their very existence. Abolition would bring economic disaster.

Over the years, both sections had fought with laws and verbiage—the North to contain slavery where it was or, better, to end it altogether; the South to protect and expand it into the new territories of the West. Northerners, moreover, were infuriated by a Supreme Court decision which held that a slave was not a citizen, and that slavery was legal anywhere in the Nation. On the other hand, Southerners were outraged by John Brown's attempted slave insurrection at Harpers Ferry, in what was still part of Virginia, an event dealt with at length in *The Star* during 1859. Southerners regarded the insurrection as a Northern conspiracy to bring violence and chaos to the South. All the while, extremists on both sides increasingly fanned the emotions of the masses.

Despite a strong sentiment to preserve the Union, dissatisfied States grew more impassioned in their cry for secession. In an earlier decade, South Carolina had toyed with the secession principle, but President Andrew Jackson had quashed the move. Now, in mid-century, the cry had gone up again with even more fervor.

The Democratic Party, the best hope for holding the Nation together, broke apart along sectional lines in the Presidential nominations of 1860. Lincoln, held by many Southerners to be a tool of the abolitionist conspiracy, was nominated by the Republicans, the purely Northern party.

All these events were chronicled in *The Star* by Editor Wallach and Reporter Noyes. Wallach was now one of the best-known figures in Washington. He was a close friend of Edwin McMasters Stanton, the attorney who was to become Lincoln's Secretary of War and a rigid censor of news dispatches. Wallach was even closer to William Henry Seward, the ex-governor of New York who was to become Lincoln's Secretary of State. Seward had often been Wallach's guest at the editor's plantation home near Cambridge on Maryland's Eastern Shore. Though a Democrat who understood and sympathized with the South, Wallach quickly and firmly aligned himself with the Union cause.

Both Wallach and Noyes were to become close friends of Abraham Lincoln. Meanwhile, in November 1860, they turned their attention to the election. *The Star* was beginning its function as the mirror of the biggest story of the Nineteenth Century.

ABRAHAM LINCOLN IS ELECTED

(Wednesday, November 7, 1860)

The *Star's* readers, we take it for granted, were not unprepared for the result of yesterday's election, for it has sought to raise no baseless hopes in their minds upon the subject; having for weeks past clearly foreseen that the defeat of Lincoln was impossible.

They have, as good citizens, now before them, the plain duty of submitting with grace to the will of the people as manifested at the ballot-box. Those who may hesitate so to do will thus prove unworthy of the high prerogative of American citizenship, which embraces obligations, it will be remembered, as well as privileges. That Lincoln has been overwhelmingly elected according to the forms of the Constitution is undeniable; and that his elevation to power in the Government under that election can no longer be opposed except by naked and palpable revolutionary means, no less apparent. Those who counsel aught but acquiescence in the result under the circumstances, therefore counsel neither more nor less than revolution; and that, too, while the South are the richest and most prosperous community under the Government of the United States, that the world contains under any government. At this moment, there is not a tithe of the want, crime and individual discontent with one's lot in life, at the South, that exists at the North. This is for the most part doubtless the result of the South's advantages of soil, climate, pursuits and institutions. What man of common sense with aught accumulated that may be endangered by revolution, will be rash enough to favor any such violent change as now proposed!

By November 8, a nearly complete tabulation of electoral votes could be published. The figures were not quite accurate, but they substantiated the initial reports and speculations.

(Thursday, November 8, 1860)

The Presidential Election.

The following statement shows at a glance how the several States have voted.

FOR LINCOLN.
Electoral Votes.

Pennsylvania	27
New York	35
Illinois	11
Connecticut	6
Massachusetts	13
New Hampshire	5
Ohio	23
Rhode Island	4
Vermont	5
Indiana	13
Iowa	4
Maine	8
Michigan	6
Wisconsin	5
Minnesota	4
Total	169

The Electoral College consists of 303 electors, of whom 152 is a majority. The Republicans have already 17 votes more than that majority.

FOR BELL.

Kentucky	12
Tennessee (probably)	12
New Jersey (fusion)	2
	26

FOR BRECKINRIDGE.

North Carolina	10
South Carolina	8
Delaware	3
Louisiana	6
New Jersey (fusion)	2
Georgia	10

The following States may be added as certain for Breckinridge, though returns have not been received from them:

Alabama	9
Mississippi	7
Florida	3
Arkansas	4
Texas	3
	65

A rally at the Lincoln home during the campaign. The tall man in the white shirt at the right of the doorway is Abraham Lincoln.

FOR DOUGLAS.

Missouri (probably)   9
New Jersey   3
                                            —
                                       12

DOUBTFUL.

Virginia 15
Maryland   8

☞ *The final official count wound up this way: Lincoln, 180; Breckinridge, 72; Bell, a surprisingly strong 39; Douglas, 12. And long before the final results were in, ominous sounds were coming from the South.* ☞

(Saturday, November 10, 1860)

The Signs of the Times.

AFFAIRS AT CHARLESTON— THE NEWS OF LINCOLN'S ELECTION.

The Charleston *Mercury* says:—"Yesterday, November the 7th, will long be a memorable day in Charleston. The tea has been thrown overboard— the revolution of 1860 has been initiated. Intense though quiet excitement prevails throughout the community. The Government officials, as our columns will show, have resigned. From early evening on Tuesday, until two o'clock the next morning, the Mercury office was crowded with anxious expectants of the news from New York. All day yesterday our bulletin board was surrounded and our office filled with a continually flowing crowd. At twelve o'clock was unfurled from our windows and stretched across the street a red flag, with the Palmetto and the Lone Star. A shout from below, and twice three hearty cheers greeted its appearance. The Association of 1860 immediately assembled, and arrangements have been made for a public meeting to indorse the action of the Legislature in the call of a State Convention to assemble as soon as practicable. The feeling on all hands is for prompt separate State action. The Federal officers who have resigned their places are expected to address the meeting to assemble as soon as the Legislature shall have acted. Charleston is not behind the State, and will play her part in the great drama now before us, as becomes her intelligence, her stake, and her civilization. On every lip is the stern cry *"Viva la liberta!"*

Washington News and Gossip.

UNWISE COUNSELS.—The Republican press of the non-slaveholding States continue the insane work of pooh-poohing the existing condition of things at the South. In this they are grievously misleading the communities in whose midst they are printed, whose interests are so closely involved in the continuance of the Confederacy intact.

. . . We need not protest the earnestness of this opinion of ours—that it is not announced for political effect. The whole course of the *Star* upon this momentous question, ever since we have regarded the Union as being in danger, involves a guarantee that we are indeed solicitous only that the South shall give the incoming administration a fair trial, instead of resorting to what it may deem necessary measures of self-protection ere its policy with reference to the slavery question may be developed. . . .

WASHINGTON HOMEFRONT, NOVEMBER, 1860.

☞ *Election excitement gripped every city of the Nation, and the excitement in Washington could be called typical.* ☞

Washington City on the Night of the Election of Abraham Lincoln.

Last night was a feverish one in Washington, we hardly need say. Long before there was any possibility of returns being received from New York City, upon which point the interest seemed to culminate, Pennsylvania avenue, Seventh street, C st. and Indiana avenue were alive with people, scurrying in hot haste from one hotel to another. There was also a crowd at the telegraph office, ready to stream off hot foot at the tail of any dispatch emerging from the office, go where it might. The bulletin board at the National Hotel was scanned with the closest scrutiny "for anything later." . . .

At the Club Rooms

The various political headquarters were of course densely jammed with partisans, and those anxious to gain any possible crumbs of information about the look of things.

The Democratic Jackson Association rooms were largely visited and had a pretty noisy crowd, which was elated and depressed by turns, as the various dispatches came in . . . A band of music was sent for and housed in the neighborhood, preparatory to the triumphal parade, but beyond a few preliminary drum taps and tunings of instruments no music was dispensed . . .

At the Bell and Everett rooms, on Seventh street, there was a good attendance, and while waiting for returns the crowd was kept entertained by lively anecdotal speeches . . .

At the Douglas rooms, on C street, we found the assemblage rather jubilant in view of the handsome Douglas vote given in Virginia. They were smoking some very good cigars . . . and were altogether a right genteel-looking crowd.

At the Republican headquarters ("wigwam"), Indiana avenue, there was an immense crowd, and the sound on approaching was that of bees swarming. Inside, the hall, like the Breckinridge rooms, fairly *stunk*—that's the word—with the fumes of bad tobacco. Pah! what a fog! . . . The news from Fairfax, Va., that the Falls Church precinct polled twelve votes for Lincoln, got up a hurrah, but generally the returns in the early part of the evening were not such as to make the Republicans particularly sunny-faced. There were rumors afloat in the room at this hour of a threatened attack upon the building by the "National Volunteers;" but, we imagine, they were scarcely credited, as it was not deemed possible that the Jackson Association would wish to add to the discredit of its late history by such a volunteer act of infamy . . .

The Election Returns at the Theatre

A large audience was assembled at the theatre last night with the double purpose, it was supposed, of witnessing the performance and hearing the election returns . . . The first of these announcements . . . was made by Joe Jefferson while performing the character of Simon Lullaby, and was received with loud cheers . . . Breckinridge, Bell and New York fusion successes were received with enthusiastic applause, while the Lincoln majorities were generally hissed . . .

The Scrimmage at Brown's

Near midnight, the crowd about the hotels had grown not only large but noisy, being made up very largely of drunken young men, "spiling for a muss." A short, light-haired chap called out vociferously for anybody to show him a d—d black Republican. A Second Ward boy, who doesn't train with the Republican Wigwam folks, we believe, but who seemed disposed to wade in just for the fun of the thing, presented himself as the identical individual sought for by Whitehead, and followed the word by a blow upon the nozzle of the latter. The adherents of the respective belligerents immediately rushed to the support of their principals, and for a few minutes there was a general tussle and fight . . .

SECESSION LEADERS HAD VOWED THAT THE ELECTION OF Abraham Lincoln would propel the Southern States out of the Federal Union. Few in the North took the warning seriously. After all, ran the general view, the same old threat had been made off and on since the early days of the Republic. Nothing would come of it this time either.

Events immediately succeeding election day hinted, however, that Northerners perhaps were studying the wrong crystal ball. Down south the immediate reaction to the election results was explosive.

South Carolina, long in the forefront of the secession movement, promptly voted large sums for arms. The State legislature could act swiftly since it had been holding open session in these days of crisis. State troops drilled to the cheers of excited throngs, "Minutemen" organizations—shades of New England in Revolutionary War days—marched and countermarched along flag-bedecked streets. The flags were not the Stars and Stripes, but the Palmetto of South Carolina. The banners were grimly inscribed: "Prepared in mind and resources—ready to give life and property."

Similar scenes flourished in the rest of the South, but most ominous of all was the purposeful action of the State governments in the lower South. One after another, South Carolina, Florida, Mississippi, Alabama and Georgia called conventions to act formally on whether the time had finally come to quit the Union. The pro-Union element in all of these States was lost in the clamor for revolutionary action. The cry was now for loyalty to State sovereignty, and freedom from the "oppression" of Yankee moneychangers, the Black Republicans, and others who would abolish slavery, the basis of most of the Southern economy.

South Carolina was the first to hold a secession convention, which opened December 17. Among the delegates were some of the State's most illustrious names—John A. Inglis, William Porcher Miles, Lt. Col. Wilmot Gibbs DeSaussure, Robert W. Barnwell, John A. Calhoun, a kinsman of the earlier great statesman; Maxcy Gregg, soldier-lawyer, and that flaming fire-eater, Robert Barnwell Rhett.

The convention was meant to be held in Columbia, the inland capital, but smallpox had broken out in the city. Lest something so undignified as a disease germ intrude on their high purpose, the delegates hastened on to Charleston, where the secession germ was most virulent of all. The mood was such as to prompt one Southerner to observe: "You might as well try to control a tornado as to attempt to stop them from secession."

SOUTH CAROLINA LEAVES THE UNION

SOUTH CAROLINA IN CONVENTION. FOURTH DAY.

CHARLESTON, Dec. 20.—The Convention met at 11 o'clock and, as usual, was opened with prayer.

The journal having been read, a resolution was offered to invite the Mayor of Charleston to a seat on the floor. After being amended so as to include the Governor of the State, President of the Senate and Speaker of the House, it was adopted.

The Chair announced the appointment of the committee to draft a summary of the causes which induced the secession of South Carolina; and also the four standing committees.

Mr. Rhett moved a resolution to appoint a committee of thirteen for the purpose of providing for the assemblage of a Convention of the seceding States and to form a constitution. Adopted.

By today's journalistic standards of presenting the heart of a story first, this account was certainly in low gear. It was printed in The Star *apparently exactly as transmitted by telegraph from Charleston and as dictated to the telegrapher by an informant who adhered to the canons of parliamentary, as opposed to journalistic, reporting. In any case, the crux of the whole earth-shaking story came in the next section of the account, and in the same quiet vein one would expect of a report on some civic group action to preserve the dogwood.*

The Ordinance of Secession.

Mr. Inglis made a report from the committee to prepare and draft an ordinance proper to be adopted by the Convention, as follows:

"An ordinance to dissolve the Union between the State of South Carolina and other States united with her under the compact entitled the Constitution of the United States of America.

"We, the people of South Carolina, in convention assembled, do declare and ordain, and it is hereby declared and ordained, that the ordinance adopted by us in convention on the 23d day of May, in the year of our Lord one thousand seven hundred and eighty-eight, whereby the Constitution of the United States was ratified, and also all acts and parts of acts of the General Assembly of this State ratifying the amendments of the said Constitution, are hereby repealed.

"And that the Union now subsisting between South Carolina and other States, under the name of the United States of America, is hereby dissolved."

The ordinance having been read, was taken up and passed by a unanimous vote of 169 members.

The vote was taken in 15 minutes past 1 o'clock. As soon as its passage was known without the doors of the convention, it rapidly spread on the streets, and the large crowd there collected evidenced their approval with immense cheering.

Mr. Miles moved that the clerk telegraph the members of Congress representing the State at Washington; which was carried unanimously.

Mr. DeSaussure moved that the ordinance be engrossed on parchment, under the direction of the Attorney General, and be signed by the president and members this evening, at Institute Hall, and that it be placed among the archives of the State.

The hour of half-past six was agreed upon as the hour to proceed to Institute Hall for the purpose of signing the ordinance.

The account then goes into the discussion that preceded the convention action. Much of it dealt with the problems the new "republic" of South Carolina would have collecting revenues and handling the mails. The delegates also oratorically flexed their sovereign muscles, as these excerpts show.

The Debate.

Mr. Calhoun.—We have pulled the temple down that has been built for three-quarters of a century. We must now clear the rubbish away and reconstruct another. We are now houseless and homeless— We must secure ourselves for storms. . . .

Mr. Gregg.—The President of the United States has thrown down the gauntlet in his message. He has said that it is his duty to collect the revenue, and he will do it. On one side the Federal government claims the right and declares the intention to

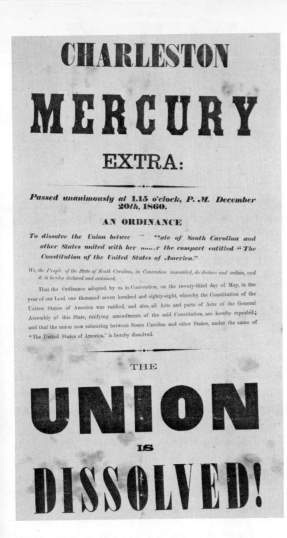

CHARLESTON
MERCURY
EXTRA:

Passed unanimously at 1.15 o'clock, P.M. December 20th, 1860.

AN ORDINANCE

To dissolve the Union between the State of South Carolina and other States united with her under the compact entitled "The Constitution of the United States of America."

We, the People of the State of South Carolina, in Convention assembled, do declare and ordain, and it is hereby declared and ordained,

That the Ordinance adopted by us in Convention, on the twenty-third day of May, in the year of our Lord one thousand seven hundred and eighty-eight, whereby the Constitution of the United States of America was ratified, and also, all Acts and parts of Acts of the General Assembly of this State, ratifying amendments of the said Constitution, are hereby repealed; and that the union now subsisting between South Carolina and other States, under the name of "The United States of America," is hereby dissolved.

THE
UNION
IS
DISSOLVED!

execute the power of collecting the revenue in our port. On the other side we have declared that we are free. I desire no compromise. . . .

Mr. Rhett.—This great revolution must go on with as little damage as possible to the country. By making the federal agents ours, the machinery will move on. The federal laws of taxation must not exist over us; we are now contending for the great principle of taxation. I trust the present system of taxation has fallen forever. . . .

Mr. Barnwell.—We have seceded from the United States and established our independence. We can't allow the United States to exercise authority over us any more. . . .

As the Convention were leaving St. Andrew's Hall, the chimes of St. Michael's Episcopal Church pealed forth "Old Lang Syne" and other airs.

And the same mood persisted long after the secession ordinance was passed and the embossed parchment copy of it prepared and signed with a flourish by the convention delegates.

Rejoicings at Charleston.

CHARLESTON, Dec. 21.—A grand procession of Minute Men is in progress to-night in honor of the secession of the State from the Federal Union. The procession embraced several thousand Minute Men, citizens, strangers, firemen and military, with music, banners and transparencies. The line is brilliantly illuminated with large locomotive reflectors, presenting quite an imposing display.

The procession formed in front of secession Hall and proceeded to the Mills House, where the band serenaded Governor Pickens. Subsequently Wm. D. Porter, President of the (State) Senate, General (James) Simons, Speaker of the (State) House, General (David Flavel) Jamison, President of the Convention, Mayor (Charles) Macbeth (of Charleston) and others received the same compliment, and returned their thanks in appropriate remarks. . . .

The city is alive with pleasurable excitement. A number of private residences, public buildings and newspaper establishments are illuminated.

Most of the populace was enthusiastic, but not all. One of the exceptions was the respected Charleston judge, James L. Petigru, a devoted Carolinian but also devoted to preserving the Federal Union. As the excitement swirled around him, he wryly observed: "South Carolina is too small for a republic and too big for a lunatic asylum." He added portentously: "They have this day set a blazing torch to the temple of constitutional liberty and, please God, we shall have no more peace."

A view of Charleston, South Carolina.

Library of Congress

WASHINGTON HOMEFRONT, DECEMBER, 1860.

☛ The sound of marching feet down south grew louder, and the people of the Nation's Capital were making up their minds on the pervading issue, Union or secession. The columns of The Star reflected this in reporting the local news of the day. ☛

"THE UNION FOREVER."—This morning a beautiful flag, "the Stars and Stripes," was hoisted upon the staff over the Perseverence engine house, in Centre Market Space, and with it a streamer, upon which was imprinted, in legible characters, "the Union forever.". . .

The Franklin Fire Company, which yesterday had their flag half-masted in respect to the memory of a venerable and respected member and esteemed citizen, today at noon ran it up to the masthead—the flag of the Union.

———◆———

WHAT COMPANY C THINKS.—Company C, Washington Light Infantry, Assembled at their armory on Monday evening. The endorsement of certain resolutions previously adopted by companies A and B, of the battalion, expressive of their determination "to stand by the Stars and Stripes so long as a shred remained," was proposed, upon which a discussion arose, when they were laid on the table by an overwhelming vote, because a clause in the constitution of the company prohibits any political discussion; . . . and for further and more potent reason that said resolutions were inappropriate under the existing affairs of the nation.

Citizens of Savannah, Georgia demonstrate before the first "flag of independence" raised by the South.

Library of Congress

South Carolina's flag, with a Palmetto tree in the upper left-hand corner.

THE COCKADES—We see in some of the avenue shop-windows the various cockades now in use for sale. We give a description of them for the benefit of our readers:

South Carolina.—This cockade is made of three layers of very dark blue cloth, notched at the edges and fastened together by a gilt button, on which the following appears in relief: In the centre is the "Palmetto," with two arrows (crossed) and fastened together at the point of the crossing with a bow-knot of ribbon. . . .

The Union Cockade.—. . . a double rosette, the centre one being of red silk, and the pendants of blue. The gilt button that fastens the whole together shows the eagle of America, surrounded by the stars of the United States.

☛ Threats of disunion and war did not occupy all the space, by any means. ☛

———◆———

A BEAUTIFUL PIECE OF WORK.—We yesterday examined a chandelier in the Vice President's room, new Senate, manufactured to order in Philadelphia. . . . This chandelier exceeds anything of the kind ever before seen in this city. It is a twelve-light burner, the material throughout being of superb gilt, artistically embellished. The body of the chandelier has three admirably designed medallion heads of Washington, and above this, there is a tripod of figures, exquisitely proportioned, symbolical of youth and immutability. Each of these figures supports a column surmounted by a finely modeled eagle, bearing the shield of our Nation. Within the space formed by the three columns stands a figure of a North American Indian, dressed in all the paraphernalia of the aboriginal warrior. Immediately above the three columns is the cornice or crowning piece of the whole work, embellished with the coat of arms of the thirteen original States.

16

As EARLY AS THE DAY AFTER LINCOLN'S ELECTION THE Federal colonel commanding the Charleston installations had been stopped by a mob as he tried to move weapons from the arsenal in the city to Fort Moultrie. Rather than roil the Charlestonians beyond endurance, President Buchanan ordered the weapons returned and the colonel shipped to a remote post in the West.

Maj. Robert Anderson was appointed to the post. The selection of this career officer was ideal. He was a Kentuckian of Virginia ancestry and his wife a Georgian. While he understood the South's viewpoint and aspirations, he was loyal to the army and intensely devoted to the Union. However, his position as combined conciliator and military commander was untenable. The Carolinians pressed unremittingly for the Federals to get out of the harbor forts—Moultrie, Sumter and Castle Pinckney—despite the fact that Maj. Anderson had precious little to vacate: less than 80 troops and four months of provisions. The forts themselves were little or no menace, being in poor repair; to make any of them defensible would require extensive construction and a garrison of at least 700 fighting men. But Maj. Anderson was firm in two resolves: to do all possible to avoid provoking hostilities, and to remain in the forts until specifically ordered to vacate them.

The major repeatedly told Washington of his pitiful military position at Fort Moultrie, his base, and had asked for reinforcements and supplies. President Buchanan, beset by divisions in a cabinet that was half secessionist, could bring himself to no clear decision. The only definite instruction the worried major could obtain was: ". . . An attack on or an attempt to take any one of (the three forts) will be regarded as an act of hostility, and you may then put your command into either of them which you may deem most proper to increase its power of resistance. You are also authorized to take similar steps whenever you have tangible evidence of a design to proceed to a hostile act."

Maj. Anderson looked around him. The land side of Fort Moultrie was wide open for assault. Public and official South Carolina was making increasingly menacing gestures at that position, in the major's mind enough to constitute "tangible evidence" of hostile designs. But there, waterlocked in the middle of Charleston harbor, sat Fort Sumter, certainly an impregnable place compared to Moultrie. Since Washington would not make a positive move, the major would.

U. S. OCCUPIES FORT SUMTER

(Thursday, December 27, 1860)

EXCITING STATE OF AFFAIRS AT CHARLESTON.
Fort Sumter Occupied by Major Anderson.
Resolution in Convention to Take the Forts.

CHARLESTON, Dec. 26, 1 p.m.—Operator's dispatch—Heavy firing in the harbor—cause unknown.

BALTIMORE, Dec. 27, 10:30 a.m.—A special dispatch to the *American,* dated Charleston this morning, says: "The Government troops have abandoned Fort Moultrie, spiked their guns, and gone to Fort Sumter, commanding the harbor. War has begun."

This is from a reliable source.

The "firing" referred to in the first dispatch may have been signal shots set off by the Federals, or the smoke from gun carriages set afire at Moultrie after the garrison left. The next dispatch dealt with positive action by the secession convention still sitting in Charleston, undertaken without reference to Maj. Anderson's move.

The Convention.

CHARLESTON, Dec. 27.—*Tenth Day*—After prayer and reading of the journal, the President announced the reason why the ordinance of yesterday was not printed in the journal.

It was immediately moved to go into secret session.

Mr. De Treville tried to get in a resolution, and commenced reading it, as follows:

Resolved, that the Governor of South Carolina be authorized and requested to take possession of Forts Moultrie and Sumter.

Here he was interrupted by a demand that the previous motion for a secret session should be put, which was done, and the motion was carried, and the Convention went into secret session.

Fort Moultrie Evacuated.

CHARLESTON, Dec. 27.—Fort Moultrie was evacuated last night. The guns were spiked, and the carriages demolished by fire. Only four soldiers were left in charge of the fort. The troops were all conveyed to Fort Sumter.

The excitement in the city is intense. It is believed that the Convention is now taking action upon the resolution in relation to taking the forts.

Note by the Washington Reporter—Military gentlemen here express the belief that Major Anderson, in changing his position, acted perhaps not by direct orders to that effect, but according to his discretion as a commander of the post by choosing the most strategic point in his jurisdiction defensible by a small force.

The Military Out.

CHARLESTON, Dec. 27, 12:30 p.m.—Maj. Anderson states that he evacuated Fort Moultrie in order to allay the discussion about that post, and at the same time to strengthen his position.

CHARLESTON, Dec. 27, 1 p.m.—Captain [John Gray] Foster, with a small force, still occupies Fort Moultrie.

The excitement is still on the increase. Several military companies have been ordered out.

Into the vacuum left by the departing Federals rushed the Secessionists.

Major Robert Anderson

Library of Congress

Anderson's garrison arriving at Fort Sumter under cover of night.

(Friday, December 28, 1860)

FROM SOUTH CAROLINA.
The Overt Act Committed — Fort Moultrie and Castle Pinckney Taken.

CHARLESTON, Dec. 28.—The Palmetto flag was raised yesterday afternoon over the custom house and post office at 5 p.m. About the same hour the Palmetto flag floated out to the breeze at Castle Pinckney, and a large military force went over last night to Fort Moultrie. The ball has opened at last.

MAJOR ANDERSON ACTED ON HIS OWN RESPONSIBILITY.

CHARLESTON, Dec. 27.—The Agent of the Associated Press has just had an interview with Captain Foster, now commanding Fort Moultrie, who says that Major Anderson acted on his own responsibility in evacuating Fort Moultrie and taking possession of Fort Sumter.

Fort Moultrie was not set on fire, as first reported. Capt. Foster and a few regulars are still there.

(Saturday, December 29, 1860)

From South Carolina.

CHARLESTON, Dec. 28.—Capt. [F. C.] Humphreys still holds possession of the United States Arsenal.

Castle Pinckney and Fort Moultrie occupied by State troops, under the instructions of the Governor of the State to hold peaceable possession of these forts, and for the purpose of protecting Government property. Castle Pinckney and Fort Moultrie were held by about twelve men, who peaceably surrendered. There was no collision and none was anticipated when the troops left the city to garrison these forts.

The excitement is now subsiding.

OFFICE OF THE ASSOCIATED PRESS, Washington, Dec. 29, 1:30 p.m.—Not a word in relation to affairs in South Carolina has been received at this office since 2 p.m. yesterday. Commercial and official dispatches in relation to business have been received as usual, so far as is known. *Reporter.*

☞ *As if to give smug summary to the chain of events,* The Star *offered this footnote—which since has proved apocryphal.* ☞

---◆---

HOW IT WAS MANAGED—We hear that on Christmas Day Major Anderson dined formally with the secession authorities—chiefs—in Charleston, and was duly carried back to Fort Moultrie by early moonlight, apparently very much overcome by the good things drinkable set before him. Those in charge of the steamer posted in the channel to watch his movements in the fort, therefore thought it would be safe for them to relax their vigilance and them-

Departure of the wives and children of the Federal garrison in Sumter.

selves take a Christmas night frolic, and in the midst of which Anderson and his force spiked Moultrie's guns and landed safely in Fort Sumter. The apparent intoxication of Anderson was but a feint to have the very effect it did have.

WASHINGTON HOMEFRONT, DECEMBER, 1860.

⚓ The significance of what was taking place in South Carolina was not lost on Washingtonians, and a new fervor for the old flag sprang up. ⚓

——◆◆——

DOWN TOWN LAST NIGHT the prevailing topic was South Carolina, as usual, only a little more so. Early in the evening a man, in a state of fever, rushed into Brown's Hotel and announced that Senator Hunter had received a dispatch from Charleston stating that the Carolinians had made an attack on Fort Sumter, and were sent back with a flea in their ear by Major Anderson's little party of men. Some few of the credulous gave ear to the story, but those better posted pronounced it to be bogus. One solitary secession cockade made its appearance during the evening, wearing a lonesome aspect, and evidently pining for sympathy that was not forthcoming. Hon. James L. Orr, one of the Sovereign Commissioners, made his appearance for a few moments in conversation with an Alabama member, looking as urbane and jovial as ever, and appearing a good deal more like a citizen than a "foreigner."

At the National [Hotel], the only thing worth notice was an animated discussion between an enthusiastic but good-humored democrat on the one side, and three or four equally even-tempered republicans on the other, as to how far slaves were "property," &c.

At Willard's, sundry anxious parties, of all political complexions, waited to catch, by hook or crook, some inkling of what was going on in the border-State caucus, then being held in the Music Hall.

——◆◆——

THE GRAND UNION BANQUET, which commences to-night in the hall over Galt's store, adjoining Brown's Hotel, promises to be a fine affair. Time and expense have not been spared in perfecting the programme. The ladies (for none but ladies could rightly conduct an entertainment like this) promise ample remuneration for all money spent, in the way of strawberries and cream, and other delicacies of the season. A band of music, of course, has been secured. Look out for the flag of *thirty-three* stars spread from the window, and you cannot miss the place.

20

THE AMERICAN FLAG, LONG MAY IT WAVE.—In these troublous times we would suggest that all who prefer union and peace to disunion and war, should raise the glorious flag of our country, and thus declare to the world their sentiments. No place is so appropriate as Washington, where the Stars and Stripes should float, an emblem of promise to all patriotic hearts, and a rebuke to treason from whatever source it comes. Let every house-top be decorated with this banner of peace, and let it float from every public building. The Smithsonian Institution, the summit of the Washington Monument [half-finished], the public Departments should all proclaim to the stranger as he passes through this city, that the fires of true patriotism are not extinguished; that the city of Washington is not inclined to desert its colors, but will maintain them as they were transmitted to us by our heroic ancestors. Again we say unfurl the Star Spangled Banner, fling it to the breeze, a beacon of hope, the light of which will cause a thrill of patriotism in every true American heart.

🖝 *Firebugs loose in the inflammable city were another cause of local concern.* 🖝

————————◆————————

INCENDIARISM AND INSURANCE COMPANIES.—The recent incendiary operations in various parts of the city have touched slightly every city insurance company. The amount of the loss is, to be sure, not very great; but the continuance of fires in the same ratio would soon eat away the capital of some of the stock companies. Three fires the night of the 5th inst. all drew upon one company; and by the fires in the West End alone, every company lost a small amount. The great want of conveniences for the speedy procurement of water in the East and West Ends has attracted attention in the City Councils, and possibly measures will be taken to remedy this defect. A resolution was offered in the lower board for the purpose of directing the Mayor's attention to the law authorizing a reward for the capture of incendiaries.

The interior of Fort Sumter. Cannons waiting to be mounted are seen on the ground at right.

Harper's Weekly

By TRANSFERRING HIS GARRISON FROM MOULTRIE TO Sumter, Maj. Anderson exploded a bomb that shook the land. South Carolinians (who had emissaries in Washington trying to coax all the Charleston forts away from Federal possession, were outraged. The drums beat louder all over the South. In Washington, President Buchanan was appalled that a mere army major, acting on his own initiative, could so rock the wandering Ship of State. Farther north, patriots cheered the major's initiative and daring.

In any case, the thing was done. Although tempted, the President could not bring himself to undo the act. His cabinet, for one thing, had recently gotten new backbone in Edwin McMasters Stanton, brilliant lawyer and unwavering Unionist. Besides, there were Northern mutterings that "Old Buck" should be impeached if he placated disunionists any further. Despite intensified pressures from South Carolina, the President at last took a solid stand for the Union. As he explained to a friend: "If I withdraw Anderson from Sumter, I can travel home to Wheatland (Pa.) by the light of my own burning effigies." Then, on December 30, he received further urging from that revered old lionheart, Winfield Scott, General-in-Chief of the Army: Reinforce Sumter!

The President finally acted. He approved dispatching a sloop-of-war loaded with more than 200 troops, equipment and supplies. But Buchanan-like, in a matter of days, he grew shaky again. Instead of a warship, an unarmed merchantman, *Star of the West,* was hired to do the job, and in utmost secrecy. Thus, what had started as a firm and open military maneuver to assert the authority of the Federal government over its own property, became only a half-hearted and furtive gesture.

The operation, moreover, was one of the worst-kept secrets of the crisis. Secession sympathizers in the North quickly telegraphed the news to South Carolina. Newspapers everywhere spilled the story to their readers. Consequently, gun batteries in the secession-held forts around Charleston harbor were ready for anything.

Star of the West was a lumbering, unglamorous vessel—with her sail masts, smokestack and sidewheels—to be paddling into history to the sound of cannon.

U. S. TROOP SHIP FIRED ON

(Thursday, January 10, 1861)

From South Carolina.
THE "STAR OF THE WEST" FIRED INTO FROM FORT MOULTRIE AND MORRIS ISLAND.

CHARLESTON, Jan. 9.—The steamer *Star of the West,* with troops to reinforce Fort Sumter, arrived off the Charleston bar at an early hour this morning, when she attempted to enter the harbor with the American flag flying, when a brisk fire was opened upon her by the garrison stationed at the light-house on Morris Island.

The guns of Fort Moultrie on the other side also opened on her, when the steamer put about and went to sea again. We have not been able to learn whether the steamer or any persons on board was injured. The belief is that no injury was sustained either by the boat or those on board.

Major Anderson, from Fort Sumter, did not respond.

The doubtful distinction of firing the first shot of what was to become the Civil War fell to a cadet of The Citadel, George E. Haynsworth, who happened to be from the inland town of Sumter, S.C. The batteries' aim was poor, however, so damage to the ship was slight and no one was hurt. Nonetheless, the skipper of the Star *quailed at the demonstration, and put back out to sea. The action spared Major Anderson from having to decide to risk bringing on general war by firing Sumter's guns to protect his own relief mission.*

Flag of Truce from Fort Sumter.

CHARLESTON, Jan. 9.—Lieut. Hall, of Fort Sumter, came over to the city about 11 o'clock this morning with a flag of truce, and repaired to the quarters of the Governor, followed by a crowd of citizens.

He was in secret communication with the Governor and council for about two hours. At two o'clock he was sent in a carriage, with the Governor's aide to the wharf, and returned to Fort Sumter.

The object of the mission is not known, but it is supposed that it relates to the firing into the *Star of the West.*

The people are intensely excited. There was no demonstration against Lieut. Hall, but the curiosity to learn the purpose of his mission is intense.

2nd. Lt. Norman C. Hall, a Michigander just out of West Point, was the youngest of the Sumter garrison.

Further Particulars.

CHARLESTON, Jan. 9.—At an early hour this morning our citizens were aroused by the loud and repeated reverberation of cannon to seaward, and a general rush was made from all parts of the city to the wharves. The excitement was intense, and the military rushed to arms for the general defense.

Twelve or fifteen [cannon] reports were heard, first from the works on Morris' Island, followed by a few shots from Fort Moultrie.

The anxiety to know the cause of the firing was intense, the whole city remaining for an hour or more

Shore batteries on Morris Island firing at the *Star of the West.*

Harper's Weekly

President James Buchanan

in suspense. There were no shots fired from Fort Sumter, and it was at once supposed to have been occasioned by the *Star of the West* attempting to enter the harbor with reinforcements to Major Anderson. Later in the day this was ascertained to be the case. . . .

🔫 *With the first three dispatches sequentially on the record, the fourth conflicted on one important detail: how far did* Star of the West *penetrate? Not knowing, the Editor could only go ahead and publish what he received with an explanatory note. The problem of conflicting reports from the front would plague editors and readers throughout the war. What follows is a perfect instance.* 🔫

THE "STAR OF THE WEST" IN CHARLESTON HARBOR.

NEW YORK, Jan. 10.—Captain [John] McGowan [Skipper of the *Star of the West*] telegraphs that the *Star of the West* has arrived and anchored safely in Charleston harbor.

(*Note by the Reporter.*—The source from which both dispatches in relation to the *Star of the West* emanated admits of but slight doubt that they are each generally correct. The interview between Lieut. Hall and the Governor of South Carolina may account for the sudden transition of affairs in that quarter. A few hours will probably elucidate the matter.)

🔫 *The newsmen in Charleston wasted no time learning the contents of the official dispatches between the commander of the Federal Fort Sumter, and the Governor of the newly seceded sovereign State of South Carolina. The reports were in print next day.* 🔫

Important from Charleston.

CHARLESTON, Jan. 10.— . . . The communication from Major Anderson to the Governor is as follows:

MAJOR ANDERSON TO GOV. PICKENS.

Fort Sumter, Jan. 9, 1861

To His Excellency, the Governor of S. Carolina:

Sir: Two of your batteries fired this morning on an unarmed vessel bearing the flag of my government. I am not notified that war has been declared by South Carolina against the United States, and I cannot but think that this hostile act has been committed without your sanction or authority. Under that hope I refrain from opening fire on your batteries.

I have the honor, therefore, respectfully to ask whether the above mentioned act—one I believe without a parallel in the history of our country or any other civilized government—was committed in obedience to your instructions? I notify you if the act is not disclaimed, that I shall regard it as an act of war, and shall not, after a reasonable time allowed for the return of my messenger, permit any vessel to pass within range of the guns of my fort.

In order to save, as far as is in my power, the shedding of blood, I beg you will have due notification of my decision given to all concerned.

Hoping, however, that your answer may justify a further continuance of forbearance on my part, I am yours, respectfully, Robert Anderson.

Reply of the Governor.

Governor Pickens, in his reply to Maj. Anderson, after stating the position of South Carolina to the United States, and declaring that any attempt to send troops of the United States into Charleston harbor, to reinforce the forts there, would be regarded as an act of hostility, in conclusion says:

"Any attempt to reinforce with United States troops Fort Sumter, or to retake or resume possession of the forts within the waters of the State, which you abandoned, after spiking the guns and doing other damage, it cannot be regarded by the authorities of this State as indicative of no other purpose than the coercion of a sovereign State by the armed force of the federal government.

"Special agents, therefore, have been off the bar

of this harbor to warn approaching vessels, armed or unarmed, having on board troops to reinforce your fort, not to attempt to enter the harbor. Special orders have been given to the commanders of the forts not to fire on such vessels until the throwing of a shot across their bows would warn them of the prohibition of the State. Under these circumstances, the steamer *Star of the West*, it is understood, this morning attempted to enter the harbor with troops, and having been notified that she could not enter, was fired into. This act is perfectly justified by me.

"In regard to your threats as to vessels in the harbor, it is only necessary for me to say that you must be the judge of your responsibility. Your position in the harbor has been tolerated by the authorities of the State, and while the act of which you complain is in perfect consistency with the rights and duties of the State, it is not perceived how far the conduct you propose to adopt can find a parallel in the history of any country, or reconcile with any other purpose of your Government than that of imposing on this State the condition of a conquered province.

"(Signed.)   F. W. Pickens
Governor of South Carolina."

SECOND COMMUNICATION FROM MAJOR ANDERSON.

Fort Sumter, Jan. 9, 1861

To His Excellency Governor Pickens:

Sir: I have the honor to acknowledge the receipt of your communication, and to say that, under the circumstances, I have deemed it proper to refer the whole matter to my Government, and intend deferring the course indicated in my note of this morning until the arrival from Washington of the instructions I may receive.

I have the honor also to express the hope that no obstructions will be placed in my way, and that you will do me the favor of giving every facility for the departure and return of the bearer, Lt. T. [Theodore] Talbot [a Kentuckian], who is directed to make the journey to Washington.

(Signed.)   R. Anderson

Gov. Pickens immediately granted the permission desired.

Lt. Talbot left Charleston last night with dispatches from Maj. Anderson to the President. He goes to Washington for instructions from the President. A party of gentlemen entertained him at the Charleston Hotel before he left.

The affair produced some excitement here, but all is now tranquil.

(*Note.*—Some doubt having been entertained of the authenticity of a dispatch received at New York yesterday purporting to be from the captain of the *Star of the West*, to the effect that he had safely entered Charleston harbor, an inquiry was sent to the agent of the Associated Press at Charleston, who replied as follows:

CHARLESTON, Jan. 10, 4 p.m.—The dispatch is false. What you have received from here in reference to the affair is strictly reliable.)

☞ *Thus did the editor resolve the conflict between the two dispatches that appeared among the earlier accounts.* ☞

WASHINGTON HOMEFRONT, JANUARY, 1861.

☞ *Not only were the big developments, such as the shelling of the* Star of the West, *of concern to* The Star, *but the editors found time and space every day to report the "little" events that were taking place on the Federal City's own doorstep.*

At the time of the Star of the West *episode,* The Star's *"Local News" columns naturally reflected alarms of war:* ☞

THE U. S. FRIGATE PENSACOLA. Lately commissioned at Norfolk, arrived at the Washington Navy Yard this morning. She was towed up here to receive her engines, which were built in this yard, and are said to be the finest specimens of machinery ever put into a war vessel in this country.

BUILDING ASSOCIATIONS.—The general uneasiness in this community as to the future of the city, has naturally had its effect on the shareholders in Building Associations, and there has been something of a stampede to "draw out," though much confidence is expressed by those having experience in such associations, that those who hold on will not regret it. . . .

FEARFUL SOULS.—Yesterday, a well-known money lender, a German, who is very uneasy about the existing state of affairs, inasmuch as it will greatly affect the value of his numerous investments, was awakened from his slumbers by the firing of the morning salute at the Columbian Armory. Too alarmed to spare time to· complete his toilet, he rushed into a neighbor's house exclaiming, "Mine Got, Misher F——, der Britches is comed, and we pe all kilt in der mornin." He was soon calmed down by his cooler neighbor, and went to work immensely relieved that the conflict was not yet inaugurated.

L T. TALBOT PROCEEDED TO WASHINGTON WITH HIS COM-
mander's report and request for instructions on the *Star of the West* incident. He later related his amazement when, on being received by
Buchanan, the President implored him—a mere lieutenant—"What
shall we do?"

That big question mark remained the hallmark of the last days
of the Buchanan administration. The effect of Federal policy—or lack
of it—was to leave the immediate decision for war or peace to the discretion of Major Anderson sitting alone on the Sumter powder-keg.

Beyond Charleston Harbor and Washington, history was mov-
ing rapidly. The same day that guns blazed at *Star of the West,* the Mississippi legislature voted to secede. Within three weeks Florida, Alabama, Georgia, Louisiana and Texas did the same. Secessionist troops
in all these States, and in Arkansas, too, were seizing forts, arsenals and
other Federal property.

Developments were ominous. Still, the majority of ordinary
people North and South wanted to preserve the Union short of war.
Their feeling was probably best represented by Congressional proposals to settle the sectional differences by compromise. A "peace convention" inspired by the Virginia legislature met throughout February
in Washington to find a solution. Nothing came of any of the attempts.

By February 23, when President-elect Abraham Lincoln arrived for his March 4 inauguration in the Federal City—secretly, after
assassination scares in Baltimore through which his route from Springfield, Ill., passed—the Federal government already was faced with a
Southern counterpart. A provisional government of the Confederate
States of America had been formed 19 days earlier in Montgomery,
Ala. In Jefferson Davis, former army officer and Secretary of War of
the United States, the Southern portion of the former Union had its
own President.

ABRAHAM LINCOLN TAKES OFFICE

(Monday, March 4, 1861)

THE INAUGURATION OF ABRAHAM LINCOLN, PRESIDENT OF THE UNITED STATES.

This important 4th day of March, 1861, dawned rather inauspiciously with leaden skies, and tornadoes of dust, which was leveled somewhat later by a slight fall of rain. As the morning wore on, however, the skies brightened and the wind lulled, auguries noted with some complacence by those who pin their faith on such omens. The streets thus early were crammed with pedestrians, ninety-nine faces out of one hundred being those of strangers. The crowd in this city is undoubtedly larger by half than on any previous occasion of the sort, but the proportion of ladies is very much smaller. Of these arrivals it is safe to say that two-thirds are Western men. . . .

The Sunday Before the Inauguration.

A day more un-Sabbath like than yesterday cannot well be imagined. A restless multitude of strangers filled the streets and swarmed about the hotels through the day and night, and at dusk the brilliantly lit up Capitol, with Senate flag flying, and the crowds pouring in that direction, had a thorough weekday look. During the day swarms of dusty looking chaps, bearing carpet-bags, wandered forlornly about the town looking for lodging.

"Uncle Abe" Didn't Go to Church.

About ten o'clock yesterday morning there was a big gathering of people on Fourteenth street, in front of the private entrance to Willards' Hotel, with the idea of getting a look at the President elect when he should emerge from that door to go to church. The jam by half-past ten had increased so much as seriously to impede travel upon the sidewalks, and the policemen stationed here had considerable difficulty in keeping a passage open for pedestrians. With each opening of the door there was a general twisting of necks, and all tall men of only moderately good looks were closely scanned as they passed out, but 11 o'clock came and passed, and no Uncle Abe. About this time it was whispered that Mr. Seward had just gone into parlor No. 6, and for a while it was thought that he would presently come out with Mr. Lincoln under his wing to escort him to church as on last Sunday. But as time passed it became probable that the visit of Mr. S. had another object, and the crowd melted away. Mr. Lincoln was not visible during the day, and the hotel talk was that the finishing touches to the inaugural [speech] and the definite adjustment of the cabinet slate was the work at hand. . . .

Al Fresco Toilet Arrangement.

Among the picturesque features of the present raid upon Washington has been the odd expedients of the houseless visitors to supply themselves with hotel accommodations after a gipsy sort of their own. Thus hundreds have lodged at night upon market stalls and lumber piles, and in the morning have assembled at the public fountains to perform their toilets, dispensing with the luxury of soap for the time being, and using pocket-handkerchiefs of dubious purity in lieu of towels. . . .

The crowd at the inauguration ceremonies before the unfinished capitol dome.

Library of Congress

President Lincoln, shortly after the inauguration.

At Willard's.

Early in the forenoon the streets in the neighborhood of Willards' were crowded by a large and excited throng, all waiting to get a peep at the President elect. The President's Mounted Guard and the Georgetown Mounted Guard were stationed on Fourteenth street, their left resting on F street, and many amusing incidents occurred caused by the efforts of military gentlemen to keep back the "free and independent," who had come there to see, and were not to be foiled. The crowd seemed to be in a very good humor, except when some official trespassed on what they consider their reserved right, when they did not hesitate to d—n them to an unlimited extent. About 11 o'clock the military formed, and the hotel took on an animated appearance—every window being crowded.

A little after 12 o'clock the word was passed along the line of the infantry on the avenue, and the cavalry on Fourteenth street, to present arms. This was handsomely done, when the President and President elect emerged from the lower (Fourteenth street) door of the hotel. They were warmly applauded, and from our position in front of the crowd we heard not a single remark offensive to the outgoing or incoming President. This argues well for the self-respect of our citizens. Mr. Buchanan looked, as usual, dignified and at his ease, and Mr. Lincoln seemed to bear his honors meekly, and to be not at all excited by the surging, swaying crowd

which surrounded him. Mr. Buchanan's private carriage was first drawn up to the entrance, but from what we could learn of the moments going on we judge that the President elect preferred to make his appearance in an open carriage, where all could see him, as one was substituted for Mr. Buchanan's closed carriage.

The President and President elect took their seats in the carriage, the military at a "present arms," and the band on the left playing "Hail to the Chief." ["Hail to the Chief," now the traditional musical introduction to the President, was written by the English composer-conductor James Sanderson, and published in the United States in 1820. It is part of a musical score written for Sir Walter Scott's "Lady of the Lake" stage presentation. First line of text goes: "Hail to the chief who in triumph advances . . ."] Senator Pearce and Senator Baker [James Alfred Pearce of Maryland, and Edward Dickinson Baker of Oregon, a personal friend of the President-elect], of the committee of arrangements, having been seated in the same carriage, it moved out to its position in the line being preceded by the company of Sappers and Miners, and flanked on the right by the Georgetown Mounted Guard and on the left by the President's Mounted Guard. There was some grumbling at this arrangement, as it was almost impossible to get a view of the President elect, which seemed to be the chief object in view with the majority of spectators. . . .

🔫 *Here,* The Star, *in the journalistic style of the day, went into detail. In 3,000 words, ALL the parade marshals and marching units were listed. The item had the virtue of plenty of names; and names made the news then as now.* 🔫

The Appearance of the Streets.

Never in the history of Washington was so immense a crowd of spectators seen on Pennsylvania avenue. From the Treasury to the Capitol, on both sides of the Avenue, from the building line to the curb-stone, myriads were packed in solid mass, in incalculable numbers. Every available window, and balcony, and house-top near the Avenue and on it was full of human forms and faces, till no room remained to stand or sit.

They Have Music in Their Soles.

Perhaps the oddest incident of the day was the following: As the civic portion of the procession passed up the avenue, there was noticed a singular sound, not easily describable—a sharp, cracking, rasping sort of detonation, at regular intervals of perhaps three seconds. The police, on the alert for air guns and other implements of assassination, walked up and down the line completely puzzled. The locale of the peculiar noise soon became narrowed down to the New England delegation, and pretty soon the facts of the case came out, creating no little amusement all around. It seems that the New England folks wear "pegged" boots and shoes pretty generally, and this season with extra heavy soles on account of the deep snows. Coming South, the unusual heat and dryness of the atmosphere here has shrunk the peg-timber in their foot-wear excessively, occasioning a general squeaking with every movement, swelling in the aggregate, when the delegation was keeping step in line, to a volume perceptible in the pauses of the Marine Band for several blocks. "Treasons" and "stratagems" cannot be chargeable on men with so much music in their soles (Shakspeare), and perhaps they don't care a darn for the "spoils" either. . . .

The Closing Hours of Congress.

The doors of the Capitol were guarded by a strong force of special police, who admitted none except members, officers of the House and Senate, and ladies. When the reporters of the House charged on the police and passed in, about every third man about the doors suddenly became a reporter, and the *expose* of the ignorance of some was exceedingly refreshing. No persons were admitted into the galleries of the House, so Congress had its closing shouts and yells of "Mr. Speaker," &c., all to itself. A few disconsolate ladies watched from the windows of the passages around the galleries the forming of the military companies in front of the platform, and whiled away their time in listening to the half audible confusion in the Hall.

The Picture Machine.

Mr. Geo. Stacy, an enterprising photographer from New York, having obtained permission, had erected a stand in the east grounds of the Capitol, about a hundred yards from the scene of the inauguration, from the summit of which he had mounted an immense photographic lens, and during the ceremonies was busily engaged taking impressions of the crowd. . . .

The Ceremonies at the Capitol.

Crowds gathered about the Capitol early this morning, and retained their position there through all the hours until the arrival of the procession, lest they should lose the opportunity of a footing within hearing and seeing distance of Mr. Lincoln during the delivery of the Inaugural. . . .

On the arrival of the President and President elect they entered by the north door of the north wing of the Capitol, and proceeded to the President's room. . . .

The Diplomatic Corps and Justices of the Supreme Court entered the Senate Chamber a few minutes before the President elect.

After a short pause, those assembled in the Senate Chamber proceeded to the platform on the central portico of the Capitol. . . .

All being in readiness, the oath of office was administered to the President elect by the Chief Justice [Roger Brooke Taney] with much solemnity; and on the conclusion of the President's address . . . the President, accompanied by the Committee of Arrangements, proceeded to the President's house.

THE INAUGURAL.

Shortly after 1 o'clock p.m., Mr. Lincoln commenced delivering his Inaugural Address in a clear voice, reading from printed copy, interspersed with numerous manuscript interlineations. . . .

❧ The Star *at this point carried the entire text. The President, immediately on finishing the address, handed his type-sheet copy, with his handwritten changes, to The Star's reporter, Crosby S. Noyes. The address itself, firm yet conciliatory toward the "dissatisfied fellow-countrymen" of the South, has been printed and reprinted thousands of times. Suf-*

The scene at the inauguration of Jefferson Davis in Montgomery, Alabama.

Library of Congress

President Jefferson Davis

fice it here to quote the closing paragraph, one of the most poignant of all Lincoln's utterances:

". . . I am loth to close. We are not enemies, but friends. We must not be enemies. Though passion may have strained it must not break our bonds of affection. The mystic chords of memory, stretching from every battlefield and patriot grave to every living heart and hearthstone all over this broad land, will yet swell the chorus of the Union when again touched, as surely they will be, by the better angels of our nature."

EDITORIAL.
(Tuesday, March 5, 1861)

THE INAUGURAL.—In this city there are no two opinions relative to the ability of President Lincoln's inaugural. All regard it as being a State paper of great force of reasoning; while all friends of the Union of all parties assent to most of its conclusions. The few disunionists left among us to-day—nine-tenths of them having made themselves scarce here since Saturday night last—of course fail to see propriety in its exposition of the President's obligation to execute the laws of the land as far as he has power so to do. However, it was not to be expected that those who recognize right in secession, integrity in wholesale robbery, and virtue in perjury where the oaths broken were merely taken to maintain the authority and integrity of the United States, can or will realize that the head of the Government rests under any obligations whatever that make his duty conflict with the success of the schemes of the disunion conspirators. . . .

The Inauguration Day account appeared as one continuous story, filling all six columns of page 3, the choice "hot-news" page in those days. It amounted to a vast grab bag of details. Mixed among items dealing with the parade and the Inauguration itself were incidentals about the crowd, preparations and such. Here are some of the sidelights culled from the non-stop full page story:

Dusting the Route.

Saturday night, about a hundred men, in small parties, were at work removing the dust from the main avenue between the Capitol and the President's Mansion. The work was not completed that night, so extensive a one did it prove, but was entered upon again last night, and finished. Yesterday little heaps of mud and dust were piled in the carriage-way, awaiting the resumption of the work.

A Temperance Crowd.

It is noticed by some of our bonifaces that the crowd of strangers now flooding the city, whether from the tightness of the times or the prevalence of Maine-law principles, do not liquor up to any appreciable extent. Probably such another "cold-water army" was never assembled here. The hack drivers and porters also complain that the new-comers are mainly of the carpetbag order, rely on "shank's mare" as a means of locomotion about town, and exhibit mental throes of the deepest on being called on to disburse a quarter dollar.

Eccentric Visitors.

Inauguration time inevitably brings to this city a number of oddish people, some decidedly crazy, and some about half-and-half. Where they burrow during the four years interval we know not, but as sure as Inauguration Day comes around, they are on hand here, bristling with eccentricities and idiosyncrasies.

[One] attracted great attention, and before and after the ceremonies held forth to quite a crowd of listeners. His topic was the degeneracy of the age and the wickedness of rulers.

Arrival of Roughs and Plugs.

Yesterday Baltimore contributed her full quota of roughs and plugs, who came in by the turnpike and railroad, as they were enabled to travel. Their identity was soon demonstrated, for with their first drinks on reaching the city they began to belch out their rallying cries, notoriously Baltimorean. This morning a fresh squad came in, and they may cause some annoyance here before the city is well rid of them.

The Old Soldiers.

Soldiers of 1812 met at the City Hall, numbering about one hundred and twenty, but as the major portion of them were old men and feeble, it was decided that they do not appear in the procession, not being able to stand the fatigue of the march.

Special Duty on the House Tops.

The Washington Rifles were detailed for special duty, in full uniform. The special duty of this company was to occupy the tops of several prominent buildings along Pennsylvania avenue, in squads, and overlook the procession as it passed.

On the Watch for Assassins.

Though the reports that an attempt would be made to shoot Mr. Lincoln while delivering his Inaugural was not seriously credited, it was thought advisable to omit no precaution to frustrate any such plot; and, accordingly, the police in front of the Capitol were noticed preventing the assembling of any suspicious looking individuals in compact masses by passing amongst them ever and anon.

Smart Detectives.

The Baltimore and Philadelphia detectives brought on here to spot rogues visiting this city for plunder at inauguration time, seem to have confined their labors chiefly to sampling liquors at our drinking shops, etc. etc. A drunken party of them entered a well-known Cyprian establishment on Thirteenth street, south of the avenue, last night, pioneered by one of our own police, and possibly they quartered for the night. The city, we presume, will foot the bill.

WASHINGTON HOMEFRONT, FEBRUARY, 1861.

☞ *Less than a week before the Inauguration, officials of Washington City received an exclusive insight into the nature of the lanky man from Illinois who would be the 16th President of the United States.* ☞

LOCAL NEWS.

Interview of the City Authorities with Mr. Lincoln.

The city authorities yesterday [February 27], after their farewell interview with Mr. Buchanan, proceeded to Willard's Hotel to welcome the President elect to the city. On arriving at the Hotel, they were ushered into one of the parlors, and in a few minutes it was announced that Mr. Lincoln was ready to receive them. Marching up the stairs in double file, the party with the rear brought up by the Chief of Police . . . were introduced into the presence of our future President. Mayor [James Gabriel] Berret, having been introduced to Mr. Lincoln . . . proceeded to address him as follows:

Mr. Lincoln: As the President elect, under the Constitution of the United States, you are soon to stand in the august presence of a great nation of freemen, and enter upon the discharge of the duties of the highest public trust known to our form of government, and under circumstances menacing the peace and permanency of the Republic, which have no parallel in the history of our country. It is our earnest wish that you may be able, as we have no doubt you will, to perform the duties in such a manner as shall restore peace and harmony to our now distracted country, and finally bring the old ship of State into a harbor of safety and prosperity, thereby deservedly securing the universal plaudits of the whole world. I avail myself, sir, of this occasion, to say that the citizens of Washington, true to the instincts of constitutional liberty, will ever be found faithful to all the obligations of patriotism, and as their chief magistrate, and in accordance with the honored usage, I bid you welcome to the seat of Government.

Mr. Lincoln replied as follows:

Mr. Mayor: I thank you, and through you the municipal authorities of this city who accompany you, for this welcome. And as it is the first time in my life, since the present phase of politics has presented itself in this country, that I have said anything publicly within a region of the country where the institution of slavery exists, I will take this occasion to say that I think very much of the ill feeling that has existed and still exists between the people in the section from whence I came and the people here, is dependent upon a misunderstanding of one another. I therefore avail myself of this opportunity to assure you, Mr. Mayor, and all the gentlemen present, that I have not now, and never have had, any other than as kindly feelings towards you as to the people of my own section. I have not now, and never have had, any disposition to treat you in any respect otherwise than as my own neighbors. I have not now any purpose to withhold from you any of the benefits of the Constitution, under any circumstances, that I would not feel myself constrained to withhold from my own neighbors; and I hope, in a word, that when we shall become better acquainted —and I say it with great confidence—we shall like each other better. I thank you for the kindness of this reception.

LINCOLN'S ACCESSION AS CHIEF OF WHAT WAS LEFT OF the National State altered Federal policy not a whit. The new President, like his predecessor, intended to play a waiting game. So it seemed to the world at large when the inaugural dust had settled.

Buchanan, through befuddlement or design, had permitted his administration to make endless concessions to the maverick Southern States in the interests of preserving the peace, and perhaps the Union, too. Lincoln also was willing to make concessions. But, pondering his duty, he had committed himself publicly and to his own conscience "to hold, occupy and possess" the property of the Federal government.

Fort Sumter was one of these properties.

Many powerful advisors, preferring peace-at-almost-any-price, urged against such stubbornness. Though he wavered at first, Lincoln's line of conviction held. Major Anderson, the President determined, would be reinforced, despite the powerful gun batteries menacing the fort, and despite the certain wrath of South Carolina and her restless sister states.

Fort Sumter symbolized the Union. And, as a President before him had growled, "Our Federal Union, it must be preserved."

On April 6, an assortment of men-of-war, tugs and supply ships steamed out of the North to save the symbol. This was to be for keeps, not another ill-starred endeavor like *Star of the West*.

Five days later as the first of the relief force approached Charleston Harbor, a patrician officer with a melodious name issued an ultimatum to Fort Sumter in the name of the new Confederacy.

Brig. Gen. Pierre Gustave Toutant Beauregard, Confederate States of America, demanded of Major Robert Anderson, United States of America: Surrender, or else!

The major refused the general.

SUMTER ATTACKED; WAR BEGINS

(Saturday, April 13, 1861)

CONFLICT AT CHARLESTON.

Immense Excitement.

Bombardment of Fort Sumter.

THE FIRE RETURNED BY MAJOR ANDERSON.

CORRESPONDENCE BETWEEN GENERAL BEAUREGARD AND MAJOR ANDERSON.

TWO GUNS AT FORT SUMTER SILENCED.

BREACH IN THE FORT REPORTED.

Arrival of U.S. Ships of War off the Bar.

CHARLESTON, April 12.—The excitement prevailing here for several days past rose to the very highest pitch this morning, when it was ascertained that war had been actually commenced and Fort Sumter attacked by the forces of South Carolina.

It appears that the fire was opened on Sumter about four o'clock this morning with considerable spirit from the batteries on Sullivan's Island (where Fort Moultrie is situate), Cummings' Point, Morris Island, and other points.

Major Anderson returned the fire, and a brisk cannonading has been kept up throughout the day up to the hour of sending off this dispatch.

We have no information from seaward yet with regard to the movements of the United States vessels outside.

The militia are under arms, and the whole of our population are on the streets. Every available space facing the harbor is filled with anxious spectators.

LATEST FROM SEAT OF WAR.

CHARLESTON, April 13, 10 o'clock a.m.—The bombardment is being continued at intervals on the Confederate States' side. A shell is thrown into the fort every twenty minutes.

It is supposed that Anderson is resting his men, as he is not responding.

Three vessels-of-war are reported outside, but the weather is boisterous and they cannot get in.

The floating battery works well. [This was an incongruous looking rig erected near Moultrie to augment the proper shore batteries.]

Troops are hourly arriving. Every inlet on the coast is fully guarded.

CHARLESTON, April 13, a.m.—The cannonading is going on fiercely from all points, from the vessels outside the harbor, and all along the coast. Fort Sumter is on fire.

Later from Charleston.

CHARLESTON, April 13, 10:30 a.m.—At intervals of 20 minutes the fire was kept up all night on

Fort Sumter bursts into flame under the pounding of Confederate artillery.

Harper's Weekly

The people of Charleston crowd the rooftops to watch the bombardment.

Fort Sumter. Anderson ceased to fire in return at 6 p.m. All night he was engaged in repairing damages and protecting his barbette guns. He commenced to return his fire this morning at 7, but seems to be greatly disabled.

The battery on Cummings Point does Sumter great damage.

At nine this morning a dense smoke poured out from Fort Sumter, and the Federal flag is at half mast, signalling distress. The shells from Fort Moultrie and Morris Island fall into Anderson's stronghold thick and fast. They can be seen in their course through the air from the Charleston battery.

The breach made in Sumter is on the side fronting Cumming's Point. Two of its portholes are breached into one, and the wall from the top is crumbling.

Three vessels, one of them a large-sized steamer, are over the bar, and seem to be preparing to participate in the conflict.

🖝 *These were the warships* Harriet Lane *and* Pawnee *and the chartered merchantman,* Baltic. *The warship* Pocahontas *arrived much later, and another, the* Powhatan, *never did show up owing to a confusion in orders. Tugboats, which were to have carried troops through shallow water to the fort, wound up in places far from Charleston.* 🖝

The fire of Morris Island and Fort Moultrie is divided between Sumter and the ships of war. The ships have not as yet opened fire.

Later.

An explosion occurred at Sumter. A dense volume of smoke was seen suddenly to rise, and Anderson ceased his fire for an hour. His flag is still up. It is thought the officers' quarters in the fort are on fire.

Another Dispatch from a Private Source.

CHARLESTON, April 13.—The batteries on Sullivan's and Morris Island are shelling Sumter with extraordinary effect. Cumming's Point batteries are widening the breach on that side. The fire inside the Fort is still going on. Anderson has suspended his fire. There have been two explosions in Sumter this morning.

Still Later.

CHARLESTON, noon.—The ships are in the offing, quietly at anchor. They have not fired a gun. The entire roofs of Anderson's barracks are in a vast sheet of flame.

The shells from Cumming's Point are bursting in and over the doomed fortress in quick succession, but the Federal "flag still waves" at the masthead. Major Anderson appears to be solely occupied in putting out the fire.

The fire on Sumter is as regular as ever, and every shot seems to tell. We anxiously look for Anderson to haul down his flag.

The Very Latest.

CHARLESTON, April 13.—Two of Anderson's magazines have exploded. Occasional shots are fired on him from Fort Moultrie, while the Point Cumming's battery is doing the heavy work. The exploded magazines are thought to be the lesser ones.

The greatest excitement prevails here. The battery, wharves, steeples, and every available place are packed with people. The ships are in the offing, and have not aided Anderson; and it is now too late, as it is past high water, and it is believed they cannot come over the bar.

🖝 *The fort was isolated from help. The South Carolinians were determined. It was all over soon, but there was no Sunday newspaper, and Star readers had to wait over the weekend for further news.* 🖝

THE SURRENDER OF FORT SUMTER.

No One Killed!—Several Wounded.

CHARLESTON, April 13, 1 p.m.—Anderson's flag and mast are down—supposed to have been shot away.

The Federal flag has again been hoisted. William Porcher Miles, under a white flag, has gone to Sumter.

Anderson has hauled down the Federal flag and hoisted a white one.

The batteries have all stopped firing, and two boats with Confederate flags are on their way to the fort.

Fort Sumter has surrendered. The Confederate flag has been hoisted. No one of the garrison, or Confederate force, as far as is known, has been killed.

Three fire companies of our city are now on the way to the fort to extinguish the conflagration before it reaches the great magazine.

CHARLESTON, April 13, 9:50 p.m.—The news of the unconditional surrender of Fort Sumter has just arrived. Ex-Senator [James] Chesnut, Ex-Governor [John Lawrence] Manning, and William Porcher Miles [a leading Secessionist] have just arrived.

In two thousand shots which were fired by Fort Sumter, none of the Confederate troops were hurt.

Bells are ringing out a merry peal, and the Charlestonians are engaged in every demonstration of joy.

It is estimated that there are nine thousand men under arms on the islands and in the neighborhood.

The correspondent of the *Associated Press* has just had an interview with William Porcher Miles [who had visited the fort], who states, in the most positive terms, that no one was killed at Fort Sumter. This is reliable, and puts to rest all reports to the contrary. . . .

THE FLEET AT CHARLESTON.

CHARLESTON, April 13.—A boat from one of the vessels outside has communicated with General Simmons [Brig. Gen. James Simmons, South Carolina militia], in command of the forces at Morris Island, and made a request that one of the steamers should be allowed to enter port for the purpose of

Library of Congress

General Beauregard

taking away Major Anderson and his command. An arrangement was agreed to by the parties to stay proceedings until nine o'clock to-morrow.

SOME PARTICULARS OF THE SURRENDER.

CHARLESTON, April 13.—Hostilities for the present have ceased, and victory belongs to South Carolina, with a display of a flag of truce on the ramparts of Fort Sumter.

At half-past one o'clock the firing ceased, and an unconditional surrender was made. The Carolinians had no idea that the war was at an end so soon. . . .

The visitors [to the fort] report that Major Anderson surrendered because his quarters and barracks were destroyed, and because he had no hope of reinforcements. The fleet lay idly by for thirty hours, because they could not help him. Besides, his men were prostrated by over-exertion. . . .

Within Fort Sumter everything but the casements is an utter ruin. The work looks like a blackened mass of ruins. The wall looks like a honeycomb. Near the top is a breach as big as a cart. . . .

STILL LATER.—Fort Sumter has just been turned over to Gen. Beauregard. Major Anderson was allowed to fire a salute in honor of his flag.

The appearance of Fort Sumter soon after its surrender.

Fifty guns were fired from the barbettes and casements. [During this salute a gun burst, killing one Union artillerist—the sole death of the entire Sumter engagement.] Major Anderson is now embarking upon the *Isabel.* Their leave-taking is a thrilling scene. They sail direct to New York. . . .

🔫 *The* Isabel, *a Charleston steamer, ferried the garrison to the* Baltic *for the voyage home. It would be South Carolina's last concession to the North for a long time.* 🔫

EDITORIAL.

(Saturday, April 13, 1861)

THE COLLISION AT SUMTER.—As was anticipated, Beauregard on informing the Oligarchic authorities at Montgomery that the Government had declined to permit Anderson's command to starve in Sumter, after their violation of their pledge to permit him to procure provisions in Charleston, was ordered to bombard Sumter forthwith ere the appearance of the unarmed steamer bearing provisions in the harbor, and that of the fleet to put them into the fort by the military power of the Government if they were not allowed to land them peaceably. See our columns elsewhere for what has subsequently occurred there.

All Union men everywhere will agree with the *Intelligencer,* which this morning points out the fact that the Oligarchy have commenced hostilities under circumstances in which they will be likely to find no justification in the judgment of those who are *not* anxious to "fire the Southern heart" in order to precipitate the border States into association with their usurpation—the purpose for which war has so clearly been inaugurated. If there had previously existed in the minds of any a shadow of doubt of the fact that it was long since determined at Montgomery to inaugurate the war thus at the very first moment after Beauregard could possibly make himself strong enough to venture the attack, surely the circumstances transpiring at Charleston from the 6th inst., when the notification of the stoppage of his supplies was given, to the firing of the first gun yesterday must dispel it.

But we have no room to-day for comments on these so pregnant occurrences.

WASHINGTON HOMEFRONT, APRIL, 1861.

🔫 *In Washington the week Fort Sumter was bombarded,* The Star *reported that the local military was on the move, and non-military affairs seemed to be taking a turn for the worse:* 🔫

THE VOLUNTEER MILITARY OF THE CITY MUSTER TO THE DEFENSE ON THEIR HOMES AND FIRESIDES.—As we went to press the volunteer companies were responding to the call of the War Department for volunteers to defend the city of Washington from assault. In the case of some of the companies a portion of the members declined to take the oath required by the Department of all soldiers mustered into the United States service, and the deficit in the ranks of said companies thereby brought them below the standard requirement as to numbers, and they were not received by the Government.

The following is the form of the oath administered to the volunteers who were mustered into the service of the United States yesterday. . . .

"I, _____ _____, do solemnly swear that I will bear true allegiance to the United States of America; and that I will serve them honestly and faithfully against all enemies or opposers whatsoever; that I will obey the orders of the President of the United States, and of the officers appointed over me, according to the rules of the armies of the United States; so help me God. . . ."

◆

THE FLOOD IN THE POTOMAC— WHARVES SUBMERGED AND PROPERTY DESTROYED.—On Sunday morning the storm which had been so long threatening commenced, and with the exception of a few hours on Monday, has been pouring down upon us an incessant flood, transforming gutters into respectable rivers, and the Potomac into a surging sea. At first the water rose but slowly in the [Tiber] canal and river, as the earth drank it in almost as fast as it fell, but yesterday forenoon it began to make encroachments upon the banks, and soon overflowed all the lowlands along the shore. . . .

The water on the Maryland side of the Anacostia is said to be very high, and on the Virginia shore the damage to the Orange and Alexandria and the Washington and Alexandria Railroads, it is said, will cause a temporary suspension of travel. . . .

◆

THOSE SNAKES AGAIN.—Mention was made in yesterday's *Star* of a report that a couple of copperhead snakes had been found in a mail bag received from Florida, at the Dead Letter Office. We are informed by an officer of the Dead Letter department, that the said snakes, as stated, never came in the Dead Letter department, but that some time ago two living copper snakes arrived at the City Post Office in a mail bag, and were instantly killed; and that these two snakes, each more than three feet long, were seen by some of the officers of the Dead Letter department.

A delegation of Charleston dignitaries inspects the interior of the fort after its surrender.

THE CANNONADE IN CHARLESTON HARBOR ECHOED loudly throughout the North.

The day after Major Robert Anderson lowered the Stars and Stripes and marched his command out of Fort Sumter, President Lincoln issued a proclamation. (*The Star* ran it verbatim.) He proclaimed:

"Whereas the laws of the United States have been for some time past and are now opposed . . . by combinations too powerful to be suppressed by the ordinary course of judicial proceedings . . . I . . . hereby do call forth the militia of the several States of the Union, to the aggregate number of Seventy-five Thousand, in order to suppress said combinations, and to cause the laws to be duly executed."

It was, in effect, a declaration of war against the Southern Confederacy.

Within 48 hours, 12 of the Northern States eagerly agreed to meet their troop quotas. Agreeing to furnish troops for Federal service was one thing. But delivering them to the "seat of war"—as Washington was then regarded—would, in the light of all circumstances, take some doing.

Washington, that first week after Sumter, seemed a Union island crumbling in a sea of secession. The residents themselves were as divided in cause as the Nation itself. The city's feeling of naked isolation grew more intense. On April 17, the Commonwealth of Virginia—just across the Potomac from the Federal city—cast its formidable lot with the Confederacy. To show that the Old Dominion meant business, Virginia militia captured Harper's Ferry forthwith. This was the Federal arsenal town on the Potomac above Washington in what is now West Virginia. Abolitionist John Brown had created a stir there 18 months before with his abortive raid to free slaves.

Virginians clamored for an immediate march on Washington.

Surrounding the Capitol, on the north bank of the Potomac, Maryland seethed. Another of the slaveholding "border" States, Maryland was torn between secessionism and unionism. Baltimore and Annapolis, especially, were felt to be shaky for the Union cause. These were the two centers through which troops from farther north would have to pass to protect the Capitol.

When the first of Washington's defenders—a company of Army regulars and about 400 unarmed Pennsylvania militia—arrived the evening of April 18, they brought ominous news from Baltimore. A disunionist mob had jeered and thrown cobblestones at them as they passed through the streets.

Next day, a dapper well-armed Sixth regiment of Massachusetts volunteers—the first of a contingent commanded by Brig. Gen. Benjamin Franklin Butler—arrived in Baltimore by rail.

U. S. TROOPS ATTACKED IN BALTIMORE

(Friday, April 19, 1861)
BLOODSHED IN BALTIMORE.
The Troops Fired Into— Several Killed.

BALTIMORE, April 19.—There has been terrible bloodshed here to-day. The last portion of the Seventh [actually the Massachusetts Sixth Infantry Regiment] were attacked and several were killed. The Governor [Thomas H. Hicks] has proclaimed martial law. It is believed that the railroads will continue to convey all the troops for the Government. The Governor has issued an order to preserve the peace at every hazard.

(Second Dispatch.)

It is as yet impossible to say with certainty what portion of the troops were attacked. They had displayed a white flag as they marched up Pratt street, but were greeted with showers of stones. The Mayor [George William Brown] with the police preceded them. The streets were blocked up by an immense crowd. The soldiers finally turned and fired on the mob and several were wounded. The wounded have just gone up the street in carts. It is reported there is dreadful work at the depot. [The troops were in the process of transferring from the Philadelphia to the Washington Depot—about one mile apart.]

(Third Dispatch.)

BALTIMORE, April 19.—At the Washington Depot an immense crowd had assembled. The rioters attacked them there, and the military fired upon them. Several were wounded. It is said four were killed on each side.

The city is in the greatest excitement.

Martial law has been proclaimed, and the military are rushing to their armories.

The railroad track is said to be torn up outside the city, and parties have threatened to tear up Pratt street bridge.

As the military passed along Pratt street a perfect shower of paving stones rained on their heads.

The cars have left for Washington, being stoned as they left. From *The Evening Star,* Saturday, April 20, 1861:

PROGRESS OF THE WAR.
The Massachusetts Volunteers Arrive Here.

From the hour at which the *Star* went to press yesterday, conveying intelligence of the attack at Baltimore on the Massachusetts troops on the way hither for the defense of the Federal City, until the arrival of the train bringing them, this town was very much

Baltimore mobs attacking Massachusetts volunteers.

New York troops debarking in Washington.

excited, and the streets were blocked up at every corner. Gradually, as the hour for the train to arrive drew near, a crowd formed at the railroad depot, completely encircling the building. About 5 o'clock p.m. the whistling of the engine, as it approached the city, measurably relieved the feeling of solicitude that had begun to manifest itself, as it gave assurance that the railroad track was not torn up, as had generally been apprehended. Presently an engine bearing a signal flag rounded the bend at H street, and came up to the depot. The engineer, in reply to the thousands of questions put, replied that the train containing troops was following.

In about five minutes the regular passenger train arrived, and immediately following it the extra train containing the military. One of our volunteer companies had walked out to the H street curve, and as the train rounded the point, gave three hearty cheers for the men of Massachusetts. The train stopped just outside of the depot, and the troops disembarking, formed in a column, and marched through to New Jersey avenue, and thence to the Capitol, entering the rotunda by the East Portico. They were followed by the crowd which had now swelled to several thousands, who cheered the troops vociferously as they passed up the street. They were dressed in full winter uniform, with knapsack strapped to their back over their grey overcoats, and presented a thoroughly soldierly appearance. After halting for a while in the rotunda, the men were taken to their quarters in the new Senate chamber and the adjoin-

ing rooms. Orders were then passed along the line to stack their arms and lay aside their knapsacks, but no man was allowed to lay off his overcoat, or in any way embarrass his movements in case of an alarm. Having eaten nothing but part of a soldier's ration since ten o'clock Thursday night, the troops were nearly exhausted, and on being filed into the galleries, immediately sank down upon the cushioned seats, and forgot their fatigue and hunger in refreshing sleep. No arrangements had been made for their suppers, and consequently it was very late before any got their suppers.

Beneath The Star's *account of the Baltimore riots, attention was called to an historic event:*

The Anniversary of the Battle of Lexington.

A remarkable coincidence is connected with this [Baltimore] affair. Yesterday, the day on which Massachusetts shed the first blood in the defense of our Capitol, was the anniversary of the battle of Lexington, in which she shed the first blood for liberty.

WASHINGTON HOMEFRONT, APRIL, 1861.

Alarm over the desperate state of Washington's defenses was indicated by some paid notices in The Star *the week Sumter fell:*

ONE HUNDRED VOLUNTEERS wanted for service in the District of Columbia. Apply to the corner of Tenth and E, old Medical College, first floor.

NOTICE—All persons desirous of joining Company B, National Guard, will meet THIS EVENING, at 7½ o'clock, at No. 600 H street, between 4th and 5th sts.   By order
                                        Capt. P. H. King.

ATTENTION.—All German citizens are requested to attend a meeting on THURSDAY, the 18th instant, at 7½ o'clock, at Mr. Gerhardt's Hotel, for the purpose of organizing a military company.

EDITORIAL.

(Tuesday, April 16, 1861)

UNACCOUNTABLE.—Nothing could more strongly illustrate the madness which rules the hour than the fact that a considerable number of citizens of Washington, some of them holders of real property, are rabid Secessionists. They know that the object of the leading Secessionists has been and is to destroy the Union forever; they know that the value of their own property and that of their friends and neighbors depends on the preservation; yet all their sympathies are with those who seek not only the ruin of their country, but also their individual ruin. Surely none of them can be so infatuated as to believe that in the event of a final separation of the Union into a Southern and Northern Confederacy, Washington will be the seat of government for either. Why then should any true Washingtonian sympathize with the disunion cause? What have they to gain by the ruin of their country and their city? What but ruin to themselves?

Is it not *unaccountable?*

☞ *Elsewhere in the paper, other advertisements showed there was still a normal side to life.* ☞

Female Education.

THOSE parents who wish their daughters to receive a thorough and systematic education, where their physical training will receive daily and special attention, under the most approved system of Calisthenics and Gymnastics, are respectfully invited to visit the Union Female Academy, corner Fourteenth st. and New York av.

MR. & MRS. Z. Richards,
                                        Principals.

LINCOLN AS HE IS.
          STEEL ENGRAVED PORTRAIT.
          The best Portrait yet published of
HON. ABRAHAM LINCOLN (with whiskers)
          AT FRENCH & RICHSTEIN'S,
          NO. 278 PENNA. AVENUE,
                    Washington, D. C.
          Trade supplied at low prices.

A rascal met a pretty, innocent girl in the cars on Wednesday, and induced her to go to Chicago to see the sights. In a walk around the city the villain took her to a disreputable house, under pretense of seeing some friends, and left her, promising to return in the evening. Depravity has its depths, and that of the keeper of the house was not the lowest; a few words with the girl showed her the facts, and she had the honor to inform the police of the entrapping, and the girl was rescued.

National Archives

The rotunda of the capitol building shelters Washington's defenders.

A S APRIL WANED, TROOPS WERE GATHERED IN FORCE TO protect the Northern Capital perched perilously on the Southern Confederacy's edge.

Pro-secessionist Marylanders were burning railroad bridges north of Baltimore to keep the Yankee soldiers north of the Mason-Dixon Line, which separated the "Free State" from Pennsylvania. But reinforcements were getting through, nevertheless. Washington's apprehensive government and citizens could now relax a little.

The arrival of the troops, however, posed a new and immediate problem for President Lincoln: whom to appoint to command the assembling army? Two candidates came instantly to mind: Col. Robert Edward Lee and Brig. Gen. Joseph Eggleston Johnston. Both were West Pointers. Both had fought with skill and gallantry as U.S. Army officers in the Mexican War of 1846–48. Before that, Joe Johnston had carried the Stars and Stripes against the Indians in the 1832 Black Hawk War in the Upper Mississippi Valley, and in Florida's Seminole War of 1835–43. Robert E. Lee served the same colors as superintendent of the U.S. Military Academy from 1852–1855. Four years later, he led the Federal force which put down John Brown's insurrection at Harpers Ferry.

Both, in short, were old soldiers of the Old Flag. Johnston, in April 1861, held high rank as Quartermaster General of the U.S. Army. Lee, colonel of the 1st U.S. Cavalry that crucial month, also ranked close to the top. Of Lee, Winfield Scott—aged, debilitated, but fiercely loyal General-in-Chief of the Army at the outbreak of the Civil War—expressed his regard in this fashion: "He's as true as steel, sir! True as steel!"

Besides being outstanding military men, Johnston and Lee were also proud Virginians. It wasn't long before they made plain where their hearts were.

MANY OFFICERS LEAVE THE UNION

(Tuesday, April 23, 1861)

Department News.

ARMY OFFICERS RESIGNED.—Gen. Joseph E. Johnston, Quartermaster General, Col. Robt. E. Lee, 1st Cavalry . . . Capt. W. L. Cabell, Assistant Quartermaster, Lt. J. B. Hood, 2d Cavalry . . . Lieut. L. L. Lomax, 1st Cavalry, Brevet Lieut. Col. J. B. Magruder, 1st Artillery, Lieut. G. B. Anderson, 2d Dragoons . . . Lieut. J. Marmaduke, 7th Infantry, Capt. Sam Jones, 1st Artillery, Bvt. Lieut. Col. John H. Winder, 3d Artillery . . . have resigned in the course of the last two or three days.

COL. ROBERT LEE, LATE OF THE U. S. ARMY.—We hear that this gentleman, who resigned yesterday, has been urged to repair to Richmond to take a command of the entire militia of the State. If he yields to this request, we take it for granted that the public will hear no more of Governor Letcher's efforts to effect an assault upon Washington City, insomuch as he knows well that to prove in the least effective, a very different military organization, equipment, &c., must exist among its assailants than such as those proposing to assail it now have.

The day The Star published these terse items, Lee accepted the offer of Gov. John Letcher to command all Virginia State troops. Five days earlier, Lee had declined an informal offer of the Union army command. Johnston, on heading South, was promptly appointed a major general of Virginia troops and placed in command of newly captured Harpers Ferry. It had been with real anguish that both officers left the Union service through loyalty to their native State, rather than devotion to the secession cause.

Lee, soon to become commander of the Confederacy's Army of Northern Virginia, was to prove "worth an army in himself." Johnston later was to be distinguished as one of the most skilled and tenacious defensive generals in modern warfare.

Of the other officers, The Star listed in its portentous little story, the following would become Confederate general officers of note:

William Lewis Cabell, Western theater combat leader; John Bell Hood, one of the "fightingest" of all at the head of his Texas Brigade and larger commands; Lunsford Lindsay Lomax, combat commander in the East; John Bankhead "Prince John" Magruder, combat leader in the East and West; George Burgwyn Anderson, to die fighting at the head of his troops; John Sappington Marmaduke, to be captured fighting in the West; Samuel Jones, artillerist and military department chief in the West and South; John Henry Winder, to become notorious as a supervisor of Federal prisoners of war.

Naval officers, as well, were leaving the Union. Among them, The Star noted in a separate news item, was Commodore Franklin Buchanan, Commandant of the Washington Navy Yard. As a Confederate naval captain, Marylander Buchanan would skipper the ironclad Merrimac, a ship that would live on in naval annals. *

General John B. Magruder

Photographic History of the Civil War

General John B. Hood

General Robert E. Lee

EDITORIAL.

(Tuesday, April 23, 1861)

THE MILITARY AND NAVAL RESIG-
NATIONS OF YESTERDAY.—It is well for the
public service that the military and naval officers
who yesterday came to the conclusion to resign, have
quit the service of the United States. If those gentlemen felt conscious that they could no longer serve
the United States with the spirit of loyalty with
which honorable men should be impressed, in their
late positions, it was but their duty to the Government to decline longer to wield its trusts. We have
no word of reproach for them because they failed
to leave the service sooner; because knowing well
that they have with great reluctance, indeed, resigned, even at this late day. We, however, deprecate
their course in resigning at all; because still enter-
taining the lively hope that the difficulties of the
times will be settled without a serious collision with
arms, though under the impression that their failure
to remain true to their flag at this time is likely
greatly to encourage those to wage vigorous war who
are striving to consolidate the South by making war
on the Government of the United States. The 4th
of July rapidly approaches, when the whole subject
matter is, by express action of the President, to be
remitted to arbitrament different from that of the

sword. In the meanwhile, the Government here will
be duly prepared to respond to any course of action
which Congress may lay down for it. If ere then
those who are in arms against it do not force it into
active war, we see no reason whatever to believe
that it will resort to it; its war policy being, until
Congress directs, only to repel force with force.

WASHINGTON HOMEFRONT, APRIL, 1861.

🖝 *Now that war was a reality, the editors felt it
was time to benefit their readers with an appropriate
glossary.* 🖝

WAR TERMS.—A casemate is a stone roof to a
fort, made sufficiently thick to resist the force of
cannon balls, and a casemate gun is one which is
placed under a casemate. A barbette gun is one which
is placed on the top of the fortification. An embra-
sure is the hold or opening through which guns are
fired from fortifications. Loop holes are openings in
walls to fire musketry through.

❖

PREPARATIONS FOR BATHING.—Yester-
day afternoon, a large party of the soldiers stationed at the Capitol threw a dam across the Tiber,
just above New Jersey avenue [near the Capitol],

where they intend to enjoy the luxury of an evening bath hereafter. The water is already quite deep, and will make an excellent place for a good wash.

THE SEVENTH REGIMENT AS M.C.'s.— The members of the Seventh Regiment [New York] seem determined to keep things moving. They yesterday took possession of the seats in the Representative Hall, improvised a Speaker, and held a spirited session, in which the speech-making and business proceedings are said to have been of the richest order.

PENNSYLVANIA AVENUE TO BE CLEANED BY WHOLESALE.—A machine for this purpose invented by our fellow-townsman, Mr. James P. Ellicott, was exhibited in front of the Patriotic Bank, on Seventh street, yesterday afternoon, in the presence of the Water Commissioners. It consists of a doubly perforated pipe, surmounted with a cap, and laid the entire length of the street and in the center of the same connected to the water mains by suitable regulators, so that any desirable amount of water can be thrown upon the street to either wash or irrigate it at pleasure. Much admiration was expressed with its performance, and the Water Commissioners seemed satisfied of its effectiveness for general use.

WASHINGTON BANK NOTES.—The banks of this city have in circulation, in all, an aggregate of but fifty thousand dollars. The stockholders are known to be worth millions of dollars in the aggregate, while it is not disputed that in law every stock-

Library of Congress

General Joseph E. Johnston

holder is bound in the whole amount of his property for the redemption of the notes of the bank in which he owns stock. We submit, therefore, that there is no substantial reason whatever for the panic that exists among persons in trade here upon the subject of receiving District notes. We hear that a poor woman was actually charged twenty per cent by a butcher in market this morning, for changing her only money, a Washington $5 bank note—a piece of shameless extortion, indeed; the note being intrinsically worth its face in gold, so far as security for its eventual redemption in gold is concerned.

T̲HE CONFEDERATE STATES CONGRESS ON MAY 6, 1861, formally recognized that a "state of war" existed between South and North. But as a shooting war it wasn't much. Since Fort Sumter and the bloodshed in Baltimore, combat had flared at only two points.

At Philippi, in the upper part of western Virginia, 1,500 Confederates clashed with 4,000 Federals of Brig. Gen. George Brinton McClellan's command, on June 3, 1861. In the engagement—hardly more than a skirmish—the Southerners were so thoroughly routed that the incident was branded the "Philippi races." Total casualties came to less than 20. The main effect of Philippi was to cement western Virginia to the Union, and make something of a hero of Gen. McClellan.

A week later, near Federal-held Fort Monroe on the peninsula formed by the York and James Rivers in Tidewater Virginia, a more ambitious fight took place. At Big Bethel, a few miles from historic Yorktown, the attacking Federals failed to make the most of their four-to-one numerical advantage over 1,400 Confederates, and were driven back to their fort with 76 casualties. Big Bethel's claim to fame: it was the first land "battle" of the Civil War.

While it is true that men were being killed and wounded, the April-June period is principally conspicuous as one of political and military preparation for an Armageddon that Americans sensed was coming, but whose vast dimensions and tragic costs were only dimly suspected. In that interim:

"Solid-South" Arkansas and divided Tennessee entered the Confederacy, swelling the Confederate community to 11 states. Maryland's secessionist element was stifled—at least along the northern access to Washington—by troops and the legislature's anti-secession vote. Divided Kentucky's Governor Beriah Magoffin proclaimed a state of armed neutrality.

Federal property was still being seized bloodlessly at points as far apart as Missouri and North Carolina. There were countermeasures, too. Brig. Gen. Nathaniel Lyon and his Federals forced Gen. Sterling Price and his command from Jefferson City, Mo. The garrison at Gosport Navy Yard, Norfolk, partly foiled the Confederacy when it burned the installation and scuttled a number of its own ships. The steamer *Merrimac* was among them.

Lincoln, in a new proclamation, extended the coastal blockade to include Virginia and North Carolina with the original seven seceders. And lest it seem an empty gesture, the harbors of Charleston, S.C., Savannah, Ga., and Mobile, Ala. were each patrolled by a warship.

Soldiers were being concentrated in great masses. Wherever they collected, illness and death stalked through their ranks. Realizing this less dramatic consequence of warfare, compassionate and far-sighted people made preparations on the humanitarian front.

One of them was Dorothea Lynde Dix.

WOMEN TO SERVE AS HOSPITAL NURSES

(Tuesday, April 23, 1861)

We understand that Miss Dix, of New York, the well-known philanthropist, has offered her own services, and the services of a large number of experienced nurses, to President Lincoln, in case they may be needed.

Sixtyish Miss Dix had indeed earned the characterization "well-known." A driving, tough-spirited crusader in an era that cried for many social reforms, she had devoted the better part of her life to improving care and facilities for paupers, criminals and lunatics. Among other things, she caused some 30 insane asylums to be built in states which hadn't ever had any.

Now, like hundreds of other deeply concerned women, she turned her energies toward easing the pain and discomfort the new citizen-soldiers were encountering in military life.

Her proffer to the government was certain to receive thoughtful attention for another reason. Two months earlier, she had notified authorities of a plot to kill President-elect Lincoln as he passed through Baltimore en route to his inauguration. Her warning may have saved his life.

(Tuesday, June 11, 1861)

The News Here.

EMPLOYMENT OF WOMEN AS NURSES FOR THE ARMY HOSPITALS.—The Secretary of War has addressed a letter to the Surgeon General, in which he says that during the present war, the forces being made up chiefly of volunteers, public sentiment and the humanity of the age require that the services of women as nurses should be made available in the general hospitals, where, except in a very humble capacity, they have heretofore been excluded. As many carefully selected women are in training in various cities of the loyal States, it is the order and wish of the department that women be adopted or substituted for men now in the general hospitals, whenever it can be effected, and that only such women as have received previous training for this purpose be accepted as nurses, except when these can no longer be had. And it is ordered that none be received except those who have presented their applications to a lady appointed by the department to preside over the volunteer women nurses, and who shall have sole authority to select and accept nurses, requiring their age to be above thirty, with certificates of character and capacity.

Miss Dix has been appointed superintendent of the women nurses, with the exclusive authority to accept such as she may deem properly fitted for the service. The transportation, subsistence, and wages of such nurses as may be accepted here are to be paid from such moneys that would be expended in the wages and support of men nurses, or are derived from the usual resources of hospital services.

Dorothea Dix, organizer of the Women's Nurse Corps.

Clara Barton, who pioneered the work of women nurses.

☞ *Two days before the War Department announced its decision to man military hospitals with women, an organization known as the United States Sanitary Commission had been formed. Operating independently but by sufferance of the government, the commission served to unify the efforts of women's volunteer aid societies which had mushroomed all over the North. It gave attention to the health and welfare of the troops, and its attacks on poor equipment, supplies and facilities, led to remedial action that vastly improved health and morale in camps and on the battlefields.*

Woman's emergence from the seclusion of the home to participate in war was an extension of the example set by Britain's Florence Nightingale in the Crimean War of 1853–56. Miss Nightingale's achievements notwithstanding, American military authorities accepted the concept resentfully and reluctantly. But American womanhood was determined.

Typical of these women was a middle-aged spinster, Clarissa Harlowe Barton. Massachusetts-born "Clara" Barton—who would some day found the American Red Cross—was among the women in Washington who hastened to minister to the troops that had fought through the Baltimore mobs.

The soldiers' reaction to such womanly attention was mirrored in a news item: ☞

(Thursday, June 25, 1861)

RESOLUTION OF THANKS.—The wounded soldiers of the Sixth Massachusetts Regiment now in the Infirmary here, held a meeting yesterday morning at which resolutions were adopted, tendering their heartfelt thanks to the officers, surgeons and Sisters of Mercy of the Infirmary, for their gentle and sympathetic attention to them; to the ladies who called upon them on their arrival with proffers of willing hands and humane hearts to add to their comfort and well-being; and to all who have visited and given them their sympathy and the warm grasp of a friend's hand. . . ."

☞ *Womanly energy was to find other wartime outlets. The Star came up with this item involving a Southern lady, and handled it with a chuckle:* ☞

(Wednesday, June 12, 1861)

An exchange says: "A lady who has just reached Memphis from Cincinnati, writes to her sister that she carried through, upon her person, forty pounds of powder, 10,000 percussion caps, and eight revolvers." What a "person" she must have!

WASHINGTON HOMEFRONT, JUNE, 1861.

☞ *War was no longer exclusively a man's affair. By a similar token, the editors of* The Star *were well aware that their readership included a large body of women. To twit the ladies, this "humorous"—and proper—jingle was run on page 1:* ☞

RATHER SHORT.—The Boston *Traveller* states that most of the shirts made by the ladies of Boston for the volunteers are from four to six inches *too short!*

> Like a man without a wife,
> Like a ship without a sail,
> The most useless thing in life
> Is a shirt without a—proper length.

☞ *And "Victory Gardens" were in vogue even then, with garden weeds apparently the greatest nemesis on that front.* ☞

Kitchen and Fruit Garden.

The rapid growth induced by the favoring weather usually experienced this month, may be yet more hastened by proper cultivation. Keep down the weeds, keep the soil loose—these are the golden rules of gardening.

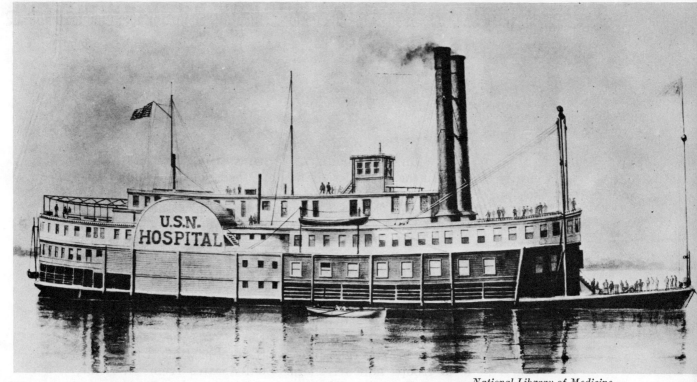

The U.S.S. *Red Rover,* the first hospital ship, was equipped with such innovations as elevators and operating rooms.

ASPARAGUS.

Discontinue cutting from the bed, where the gathering began early. Keep down all weeds, and allow the plants to grow—the feathery stalks will be an ornament to the garden.

CORN.

Plant Stowell's Evergreen, or other sweet varieties, to keep up a succession for late use. Keep well hoed and free from weeds. . . . (etc.)

Then there was the inescapable advertisement appealing to milady's vanity and purse.

LADIES, ATTENTION!—Those Bonnets, Hats, Flats and other fancy goods of Mrs. R. G. Etchison's (which have been delayed on account of the obstruction of the Railroad between this city and New York), has just arrived. If you will call soon you will find a beautiful assortment of new Spring goods, which will be sold very cheap owing to the times. Remember it is No. 12 Pennsylvania avenue, between Eighth and Ninth streets, No. 12.

THE ANTAGONISTS, BY MIDSUMMER OF 1861, WERE clearly aligned. In the Confederacy's camp stood South Carolina, Mississippi, Florida, Alabama, Georgia, Louisiana, Texas, Virginia, Arkansas, Tennessee and North Carolina. Considered "safe" for the Union was all of New England, the Midwest, California and Oregon, as well as three of the border "slave-States"—Maryland, Delaware and Kentucky. In addition, a large part of Virginia west of the Allegheny Mountains, far away from slaveholding Tidewater Virginia, had moved to form its own government, which swore allegiance to the Union. Missouri, another border State, was open to contention, and the scene of organized fighting. A fiercely pro-Union officer, Gen. Nathaniel Lyon, was elbowing Confederates under Gov. Claiborne Jackson and Gen. Sterling Price around the State. By the end of June, Lyon's potpourri of loyal troops had driven the Confederates from St. Louis, Jefferson City and Boonville. The sound of firearms elsewhere was intermittent and scattered.

During the relatively quiet pause after Fort Sumter, both North and South were feverishly engaged in mobilizing their resources. The North had a vast preponderance in both manpower and material. The total population of the 23 Northern and border States was 22 million. These numbers would be swelled during the war years by immigrants from overseas (nearly half a million would take up arms for the Union). Industry north of the line, formed roughly by the Potomac and Ohio Rivers, was going full blast; food was plentiful, and the banking system strong. The Union, moreover, had an active merchant marine and navy, and a railroad system that was the marvel of the world.

Though it gave the Southerner small pause at the outset of the war, the Confederacy's population consisted of only 10 million, one-third being Negro slaves. Its industry was poorly developed in an economy lop-sided with agriculture. The maritime fleet was small, the rail facilities limited—with little industrial output to expand either.

The fighting man of the South was probably the Confederacy's greatest asset. The boast that any one Southerner could lick any three to five Yankees in battle would prove to be an exaggeration. But Johnny Reb was led by many brilliant officers from the very beginning of the war. The combination, despite 2-to-1 numerical odds, gave the Confederate government confidence in its policy of destroying the Northern will to fight to a finish.

In the hope that the war could be made short and glorious, both sides fanned their resources and inventiveness to white heat. Refinements were made in conventional arms. Brand-new weapons were devised. Confederate engineers, for example, worked on an iron-plated battle ship that barely showed above water. Yankee craftsmen designed something similar on their own drawing boards.

President Lincoln especially was receptive to devices which showed promise of making the conflict short and decisive. Prof. Joseph Henry, secretary of the Smithsonian Institution, brought one such new gadget to the President's attention. It was a gas-filled balloon, big enough to take men aloft to observe the enemy's military movements.

Prof. Thaddeus S. C. Lowe—an ''aeronaut,'' they called him—had been experimenting with balloons for some time. In fact, just eight days after the South Carolinians started lobbing shells into Fort Sumter, Prof. Lowe took off under one of his big gas-bags from Cincinnati, Ohio. He wanted to prove that upper air currents moved from West to East, and his theory was correct. When he came down nine hours and 900 miles later, he found himself in the Carolinas, under arrest as a Yankee spy, and threatened by mobs. Fortunately for Prof. Lowe and the future of aeronautics in the United States, a reputable citizen stepped forward to vouch for him as a scientific investigator who had made a similar ascent from Charleston, S.C., less than a year before. After the authorities sent him back north, Prof. Lowe bragged that he was the first prisoner of the Civil War.

Prof. Lowe wanted to interest President Lincoln in the possibilities of his hydrogen-filled silken sacks. With Prof. Henry looking encouragingly on, Lowe tried some preliminary runs from the Smithsonian grounds in mid-June. Then he took his rope-shrouded silks and wicker basket to the foot of Capitol Hill, near what is today the apex of the Federal Triangle, and started up his portable gas generators.

BALLOON FOR SPYING IS SHOWN

(Wednesday, June 19, 1861)

The News Here.

A SUCCESSFUL AND IMPORTANT EX-
PERIMENT.—For some time past preparations
have been making to introduce balloons into the
service of the United States, for the purpose of
making observations of hostile camps, entrenchments, military movements, &c. Yesterday afternoon, the first practical experiment to that end was
made in the grounds surrounding the Columbia Armory, in this city. Professor Lowe, the balloonist,
had charge of it, and succeeded admirably. The balloon (a very fine one) ascended several hundred
feet, and was held at the desired altitude by a stout
cord. Mr. Lowe was accompanied in the car by the
Messrs. Geo. H. Burns and Charles Robinson, teleg-
raphers, and two telegraph wires, attached to the

One of Lowe's balloons ascends with a passenger at
a military installation.

United States Army

battery worked in the War Department, connected
with a small field telegraphing instrument worked
by Mr. R. The distance between the instrument
thus elevated and the battery was about half a mile.
The altitude attained permitted the observer to
note everything below for many miles with great
distinctness. The following dispatch was transmitted
to the President when the balloon was at its greatest
altitude to which it was deemed necessary to permit
it to ascend:

Balloon Enterprise.
(Washington, D.C., June 18, 1861)

To the President of the United States:

This point of observation commands an area near
fifty miles in diameter. The city, with its girdle of
encampments, presents a superb scene. I have pleasure in sending you this first dispatch ever telegraphed from an aerial station, and in acknowledging
indebtedness to your encouragement, for the opportunity of demonstrating the availability of the
science of aeronautics in the military service of the
country. T. S. C. Lowe.

It was regarded questionable before that experiment was made, whether unknown atmospheric in-
fluences might not prevent the due operation of elec-
tricity in working the telegraph at a high altitude;
which did not prove to be the case, as the communications between the operators at the two ends of
the wires was as perfect as though they had been
suspended over the usual poles within fifteen feet of
the earth's surface.

Doubtless with the aid of powerful telescopes, the
use of this balloon will enable the commander of a
force to inspect thoroughly the interior of the works
opposed to him, and to know instantly any movements of troops of the enemy; and that, too, without the slightest danger to those making the observations and transmitting the required intelligence
on the lightning's wings. It will be remembered that
to the balloons used by the French in the late Italian
campaign no telegraphing apparatus was undertaken
to be attached; that achievement having been left
to American genius and enterprise, as explained
above.

BALLOON ASCENSION.—Considerable curiosity was excited this morning by the ascension of Prof. Lowe's balloon from the grounds of the President's House. The Professor spent some time taking up his friends and others fond of aerial rides, who enjoyed a fine view of the surrounding encampments.

Not everyone was impressed with Prof. Lowe's demonstrations, as the following item indicates. Records failed to show how high he managed to ascend around Washington. Lowe claimed a maximum altitude of 23,000 feet on his Cincinnati to South Carolina flight.

The Balloon Arrived and Tested—So Far It Accomplishes Nothing.

(Correspondence of the *Star*—per pony express.)

TAYLOR'S TAVERN, Fairfax County, Va., June 24—*Editor of The Star:* Professor Lowe reached this point with his balloon at about 10 a.m. yesterday. At 12 m. he attempted an ascent, but the wind was too high, and he gave up the experiment until it lowered. At 6 p.m. he tried it again, and claimed to have ascended perhaps five hundred feet. Yet he could see nothing that indicated the presence of the enemy except a huge cloud of dust in the direction of Fairfax Court House, caused he thought by the maneuvering of a considerable body of the enemy's cavalry. He could not even distinguish the Court House village. I saw him make the experiment, and do not think he went up more than two hundred feet. I expect he forgot to bring along a sufficiency of cord to make his balloon serviceable. In a still later ascension at 10 p.m., I hear he failed to see any camp fires. . . . I trust General McDowell [Irving McDowell, commander of the Federal army south of the Potomac at the time] will have him get more cordage, so that the balloon may attain an elevation of 1,000 feet, and may also send a competent *military* observer with the Professor. Such an observer will doubtless be able to render a much more satisfactory account of what is visible in a military way from the balloon, than the Professor himself can.

The Lincoln Administration must have been impressed for Prof. Lowe was named chief of aeronautical engineering of the Army. He was the first to send telegraph messages from the air to the ground, and the first to take aerial photographs—all this in addition to his claim of being the first pris-

National Air Museum, Smithsonian

Professor Thaddeus Lowe

oner of the Civil War. Lowe's inventive mind also created an ice-making machine and various innovations in providing gas for heat and illumination. Although his service as a military balloonist during the next two years was appreciated and applauded, Prof. Lowe got into wrangles with the military, and quit. He retired with his dreams until his death in 1913.

WASHINGTON HOMEFRONT, JUNE, 1861.

The Chief Executive had plenty to worry about for the Nation. The lesser folk of the Federal City had a lot on their minds, too.

PRESIDENT LINCOLN VISITS THE CAMPS.—Yesterday President Lincoln, accompanied by Secretaries Cameron and Chase [Simon Cameron, War; Salmon P. Chase, Treasury], paid a visit to the camps over the river, where they were received with great enthusiasm. The party spent some time in examining the fortifications, and left highly pleased with the completeness and perfection of the arrangements for defense.

Citizen-soldiery filled the town. Many of the boys lacked a sense of responsibility, especially with their weapons. This letter to the editor was typical of a long series of firearms episodes.

MORE "CARELESSNESS" IN THE USE OF FIREARMS!—*Editor, Star:* Last night, near 11 o'clock, while sitting near my chamber window en-

joying the luxury of the day's papers, a bullet came whizzing through the open casement and in such provoking proximity to my noggin as to cause me to involuntarily abbreviate the distance between my chin and shoulders. The bullet aforesaid did no harm except to slightly mar 'he beauty of a nicely papered wall, and somewhat startle your humble servant. Of course the whole thing was "accidental," and I freely pardon the offender whoever he may be; but please, my dear fellow, don't do so any more. If you must play such tricks, a little warning if you please, and I may be able to contribute something to your sport.
J.M.K.

PLOT TO BLOW UP THE LONG BRIDGE.—Two secessionists were arrested by members of the Third New Jersey Regiment . . . at Hunter's Landing, near the Long Bridge. They had in their possession four kegs of powder, a bundle of fuses, and a package of matches. They had taken a boat, and were moving in the direction of the further draw of the Long Bridge, it is supposed with a view to blowing it up. A sergeant of the regiment overheard them essaying their plans. . . .

THE OTHER DAY, a lady in a hack drove up to the door of Mr. Selby Scaggs' house, in the country, in the absence of Mrs. S., and ringing the bell, desired to see her. On learning the lady was absent, the stranger handed the servant a bundle, and directed it be given to Mrs. S. on her return. She left hastily in the hack, and the servant immediately afterwards discovered the bundle to contain a strap-

ping big white boy baby, about two weeks old. Mr. Scaggs expresses his decided disapprobation of the whole proceeding.

BATHING PLACES.—The soldiers arriving during the hot weather are anxious to find bathing places as soon as possible, in order to relieve themselves of the dust which accumulates upon them in misery until it is removed by a refreshing bath. Unfortunately, many take to the canal [Tiber] for this purpose, ignorant of the fact that it is hardly more than a drain for the most populous portion of the city, into which all the sewers empty; and that by bathing there between sunrise and sunset they are violating a law of the city. A few rods further, near the Washington Monument, is an excellent bathing place, where all may bathe safely; the good swimmer and the beginner may have their own sport, without injury to themselves or shocking the delicacy of anyone, providing they select the proper times—the early morning and after sunset.

DIDN'T PAY.—Last night a chap of secession sympathies rather put his foot into it at the corner of Thirteenth and G streets. As a squad of soldiers were quietly passing by, he called out loud enough for them to hear: "There's some of you Union men, I suppose; a pack of d—d hounds!" The soldiers very coolly walked into him and gave him a very severe thrashing, from which he escaped by begging, "For God's sake, gentlemen, let me up, and I'll run." They let him up, and he exhibited a specimen of fast travelling . . .

Balloon being filled with gas in preparation for an ascent.

United States Army

ABRAHAM LINCOLN HAD ACTED SWIFTLY AND POSITIVELY when the Federal authority was challenged by cannonade at Fort Sumter. He called out the militia of the loyal States, ordered a blockade of Southern seaports, and played free and fancy with the sacred privilege of *habeas corpus*. Eyebrows were raised by many concerned over the strictly legal aspects of Executive action. But the Government and the multitudes of the North were too busy preparing for the threat to the Union to worry much at the moment over legal technicalities. Still, the questions could not be ignored.

Consider, for example, the President's suspension of the writ of *habeas corpus*. The issue first arose when, in the early hours of May 25, a Marylander, suspected of disloyalty to the Government, was arrested by the Federal army, and jailed in Fort McHenry, a landmark of American freedom. The man's lawyer rushed to Chief Justice Roger Brooke Taney of the United States Supreme Court, who conveniently lived in Baltimore. Justice Taney granted the attorney's plea for a writ that would free his client, at least long enough for a court inquiry into the legality of the arrest. Gen. George Cadwalader, a Pennsylvania lawyer now in uniform and commanding the Fort, brushed aside the Chief Justice's order. In succeeding weeks, Baltimore's police chief and four police commissioners were also locked up on suspicion of secessionism, and their pleas for freedom ignored. At these events the White House only shrugged. After the Baltimore riots of April, the Government was taking no chances getting troops through to Washington.

For authority to make the April call for troops, the Administration had to burrow into old statutes. The legal beagles came up with the Militia Act of 1793, last used by President Washington to quell the Whisky Rebellion of 1794. President Lincoln felt it suited present needs.

Imposing a blockade of Southern seaports raised another neat legal point. Blockade in its traditional usage meant that a state of war existed, and that the belligerent which proclaimed it was entitled not only to close enemy ports and seize enemy ships, but to seize neutral vessels trafficking with blockaded ports. Despite these implications, the Federal Government insisted, for other purposes, that it was not technically at war with the Confederacy—but was merely trying to put down an armed insurrection.

The President was aware he was treading on delicate ground, and felt he must offer some justification to the country. He chose a special session of Congress, which he had called April 15, for his opportunity. The date was July 4, 1861.

LINCOLN ASKS CONGRESS TO BACK HIM

(Friday, July 5, 1861)

☞ *With no introduction—or "lead"—at all,* The Star *launched directly into the message text, topped with a small-type headline:* ☞

THE PRESIDENT'S MESSAGE.

Fellow-citizens of the Senate and House of Representatives: Having been convened on an extraordinary occasion, as authorized by the Constitution, your attention is not called to any ordinary subject of legislation. . . .

Soon after the first call for militia, it was considered a duty to authorize the commanding general, in proper cases, according to his discretion, to suspend the privilege of *habeas corpus,* or, in other words, to arrest and detain, without resort to the ordinary processes and forms of law, such individuals as he might deem dangerous to the public safety. This authority has purposely been exercised but very sparingly. Nevertheless the legality and

President Lincoln

Library of Congress

propriety of what has been done under it are questioned; and the attention of the country has been called to the proposition that one who is sworn to "take care that the laws be faithfully executed," should not himself violate them. Of course some consideration to the questions of power, and propriety, were given before the matter was acted upon.

The whole of the laws which were required to be faithfully executed, were being resisted, and failing of execution in nearly one-third of the States. Must they be allowed to finally fail, even had it been perfectly clear that by the use of the means necessary to their execution some single law, made in such extreme tenderness of the citizen's liberty, that practically it relieves more of the guilty than the innocent, should, to a very limited extent, be violated? To state the question more directly, are all the laws *but one* to go unexecuted, and the Government itself go to pieces, lest that one be violated? Even in such a case, would not the official oath be broken, if the Government be overthrown, when it was believed that disregarding the single law would tend to preserve it? But it was not believed that this question was presented. It was not believed that any law was violated.

The provision of the Constitution that "The privilege of the write of *habeas corpus* shall not be suspended unless when, in cases of rebellion or invasion, the public safety may require it," is equivalent to a provision—*is* a provision—that such privilege may be suspended when, in cases of rebellion or invasion, the public safety *does* require it. It was decided that we have a case of rebellion, and that the public safety does require the qualified suspension of the privilege of the writ, which was authorized to be made. Now it is insisted that Congress, and not the executive, is vested with this power. But the Constitution itself is silent as to which, or who, is to exercise the power; and, as the provision was plainly made for a dangerous emergency, it cannot be believed that the framers of the instrument intended that, in every case, the danger should run its course until Congress could be called together; the very assembling of which might be prevented, as was intended in this case, by the rebellion . . .

56

. . . This issue embraces more than the fate of these United States. It presents to the whole family of man the question whether a constitutional republic or democracy—a government of the people by the same people—can or cannot maintain its territorial integrity against its own domestic foes. It presents the question whether discontented individuals, too few in number to control administration according to law in any case, can always, upon the pretenses made in this case, or on any other pretenses, or arbitrarily without any pretense, break up their government, and thus practically put an end to free government upon the earth. It forces us to ask: "Is there, in all republics, this inherent and fatal weakness? Must a government, of necessity, be too strong for the liberties of its own people, or too weak to maintain its own existence?" . . .

The seceders insist that our Constitution admits of secession. They have assumed to make a national constitution of their own, in which of necessity they have either discarded or retained the right of secession as they insist it exists in ours. If they have discarded it, they thereby admit that on principle it ought not be in ours. If they have retained it by their own construction of ours, they show that to be consistent they must secede from one another whenever they shall find it the easiest way of settling their debts, or effecting any other selfish or unjust object. The principle itself is one of disintegration, and upon which no government can possibly endure. . . .

He expressed his view of the nature of the conflict.

This is essentially a people's contest. On the side of the Union it is a struggle for maintaining in the world the form and substance of government whose leading object is to elevate the condition of men— to lift artificial weights from all shoulders; to clear the paths of laudable pursuit for all; to afford all an unfettered start, and a fair chance in the race of life. Yielding to partial and temporary departures, from necessity, this is the leading object of the government for whose existence we contend.

I am most happy to believe that the plain people understand and appreciate this. It is worthy of note that while in this, the government's hour of trial, large numbers of those in the army and navy who have been favored with the offices have resigned and proved false to the hand which had pampered them, not one common soldier or common sailor is known to have deserted his flag.

Great honor is due to those officers who remained true, despite the example of their treacherous associates; but the greatest honor, and most important fact of all, is the unanimous firmness of the common soldiers and common sailors. To the last man, so far as known, they have successfully resisted the traitorous efforts of those whose commands, but an hour before, they obeyed as absolute law. This is the patriotic instinct of the plain people. They understand, without an argument, that the destroying of the government which was made by Washington means no good to them.

Our popular government has often been called an experiment. Two points in it our people have already settled—the successful establishing and the successful administering of it. One still remains—its successful maintenance against a formidable internal attempt to overthrow it. It is now for them to demonstrate to the world that those who can fairly carry an election can also suppress a rebellion; that ballots are the rightful and peaceful successors of bullets; and that when ballots have fairly and constitutionally decided, there can be no successful appeal back to bullets; that there can be no successful appeal, except to ballots themselves, at succeeding elections. Such will be a great lesson of peace: teaching men that what they cannot take by an election, neither can they take it by a war; teaching all the folly of being the beginners of a war. . . .

The message drew to a close. Its flavor became personal.

It was with deepest regret that the executive found the duty of employing the war power in defense of the government forced upon him. He could but perform this duty or surrender the existence of the government. No compromise by public servants could, in this case, be a cure; not that compromises are not often proper, but that no popular government can long survive a marked precedent that those who carry an election can only save the government from immediate destruction by giving up the main point upon which the people gave the election. The people themselves, and not their servants, can safely reverse their own deliberate decisions.

As a private citizen, the executive could not have consented that these institutions shall perish; much less could he, in betrayal of so vast and so sacred

Chief Justice Roger Brooke Taney challenged Lincoln's arbitrary seizure of citizens under war powers.

a trust as the free people have confided to him. He felt that he had no moral right to shrink, nor even to count, the chances of his own life in what might follow. In full view of his great responsibility he has, so far, done what he has deemed his duty. You will now, according to your own judgment, perform yours.

He sincerely hopes that your views and your actions may so accord with his, as to assure all faithful citizens who have been disturbed in their rights of a certain and speedy restoration to them, under the Constitution and the laws.

And having thus chosen our course, without guile and with pure purpose, let us renew our trust in God, and go forward without fear and with manly hearts.

Before it adjourned, in a month's time, the special session would approve and legalize all the President had done since March 4, and vote money and powers to carry on.

EDITORIAL.

(Saturday, July 6, 1861)

THE MESSAGE.—There exist no two opinions here with reference to the message sent to Congress yesterday. That is, among the Union men in the Federal Metropolis. Without distinction of political party, by all here whose hearts are in the preservation of the Union, its statement of the facts involved in the present state of things is recognized as truthful to the letter, and its views of the policy to be pursued as being wise, humane and eminently patriotic. The entire absence of political partizan feeling characterizing it cannot fail to strengthen the cause in which it was written; inasmuch as it embraces irrefragable proof that he (President Lincoln) has done no more in the premises than his plain duty to his charge, and that he proposes only to use the military power of the Union for the restoration and preservation of the rights and liberties of all its citizens as they were enjoyed previous to the denouement of the oligarchy's conspiracy, and to that end only. . . .

The message, though promulgated under circumstances that might almost justify the manifestation of indignant hostility to the South on the part of the Government, breathes a spirit of frank kindness to and confidence in the people of the South, which will sooner or later tell with powerful effect upon the Southern popular mind. . . .

WASHINGTON HOMEFRONT, JULY, 1861.

Celebrating the Fourth of July in mid-19th Century America normally was exuberant, as befitted a people hardly more than three generations removed from their independence from the Old World. But a subdued air surrounded the Fourth in Washington in 1861. Perhaps the hot wind of war swirling just across the Potomac River had something to do with it.

THE CELEBRATION OF THE DAY YESTERDAY.—The national aniversary was celebrated in a manner of peculiar but striking interest here yesterday. The usual excursions, pic-nics, display of fire-works, &c, were wanting; but in place of this there were such scenes as the parades of armed and drilled volunteers in bodies of twenty or thirty thousand strong—reviews in which the conspicuous object to which each military and civic eye were turned in passing was the towering form of the commander-in-chief of the national forces, General Winfield Scott; public addresses, in which the speakers were the distinguished men who form Mr. Lincoln's cabinet; and flag-raisings, in which the chief magistrate of the United States elevated the Stars and Stripes to their proper commanding position. . . .

THE REVIEW.

The scene at the point of review, as regiment after regiment of handsome, well-drilled troops passed in apparently endless succession, was inspiriting and brilliant in the extreme. Crowds of well-dressed people occupied all the positions favorable for sight-seeing along Lafayette Square and the President's grounds. President Lincoln and his Cabinet, and Private Secretaries Nicolay and Hay, with General Scott and a brilliant staff of officers, were seated upon a platform upon the avenue, nearly in front of the White House. The platform was gratefully shaded by the broad folds of the American flag, and bore other emblems appropriate to the day . . .

Numerous incidents of the parade, of the most interesting character, might be mentioned had we space to-day, but one we must allude to, so striking was it.

As the Garibaldi Guard (regiment) filed past the canopy in which the President, Gen. Scott, and other distinguished civilians and Generals were, each man of the whole thousand drew from his hat or breast the green sprig which so strikingly ornamented them, and threw it towards and in many instances upon the person of the veteran hero of Lundy's Lane and Cerro Gordo, while from the head of each company there was a beautiful bouquet of natural flowers thrown into his lap in the same manner.

The President and General Scott review arriving troops in front of the White House.

A. Waud—Library of Congress

ONE OF THE FIRST INVASIONS OF THE SOUTH IN THIS war took place in plain view of the White House and the half-built monument to George Washington. It occurred on May 24, 1861. The Federal Government, considering itself too close to the "seat of war" for comfort, sent troops across the creaky bridges of the Potomac to occupy Arlington Heights. Simultaneously, a waterborne force seized the First President's old haunt, Alexandria. Among the homes physically occupied was Arlington House, built by John Parke Custis, stepson of Washington, and more recently the residence of Robert E. Lee, late of the United States Army.

The movement was made with but one incident of note: the death of the first Union officer of rank in the Civil War. Col. Elmer Ephraim Ellsworth, commander of the New York "Fire Zouaves," met his end indulging in the kind of heroics that endeared men to their age. Armed with a reputation as long-time head of the dashing precision-drill teams then so popular in the country, Ellsworth charged into an Alexandria hostel to tear down a secessionist banner flying above the roof. The proprietor shot him dead in the act (and himself was killed on the spot). The death of the colonel, a friend of Lincoln, was spread for days across the pages of *The Star* and newspapers all over the North. The public went into mourning over Col. Ellsworth's heroism, and he was buried from the White House.

Of rather more consequence, the slopes across from the Federal City were secure at last. Brig. Gen. Irvin McDowell, a big Ohioan whose biggest previous line command had been as a lieutenant in the Regular Army, was in command of the Federal field forces around Washington. The first job he set himself was to try to mold the random assortment of untrained volunteer units into a semblance of an army. He had barely started when a clamor arose in the North. People—particularly those who ran newspapers—counted large numbers of troops in Washington who, they pointed out, weren't fighting anyone except each other in tavern brawls. Get them moving, they demanded. "On to Richmond!" rang the cry.

McDowell paled, but the White House cocked an attentive ear. After all, nearly three months had elapsed since Sumter, and the Union had yet to aim a decisive blow at the rebellion. Besides, the enlistments of the "90-day wonders" who had signed up for the President's initial militia call, would soon expire. McDowell was ordered to march.

His route was out the Warrenton pike toward Centreville and the railhead at Manassas Junction, 30 miles deep in Virginia. There, Beauregard—the Confederacy's "hero of Fort Sumter"—had concentrated some 20,000 troops. McDowell, with a numerical superiority of around 15,000, was expected to crush this force and, indeed, sweep "On to Richmond.'' Other Confederates were not far away. Joe Johnston, with 11,000, was at Winchester in the Shenandoah Valley, 30 miles from Manassas. He had abandoned Harpers Ferry in mid-June, leaving that ravaged arsenal town to be occupied by a fumbling major general of Pennsylvania volunteers, Robert Patterson, commanding 18,000 Federals. Patterson's assignment was to move farther into the Valley of Virginia and keep Johnston busy while McDowell smashed Beauregard. It would all be over, the amateur strategists figured, before Brig. Gen. Theophilus Hunter Holmes, North Carolina, could bring up his 3,000 men from Aquia Creek to help ''Old Bory.''

It seemed like a holiday picnic, that hot July day, when McDowell's columns tramped out of the Washington fortifications and down the dusty pike into Virginia. Silken flags, which their ladies back home had stitched, floated gaily above the regiments. Uniforms of every design and color set off the glint of musket barrels in fantastic fashion. And mixed into the gaudy spectacle—and the sweat and the thirst and the choking dust—were civilians out for the fun. There were Congressmen and their ladies in carriages, sutlers with wares to peddle exorbitantly from their carts, vicarious adventurers on horseback, ordinary folk on foot. The enthusiasm was tremendous.

But the troops themselves were untrained greenhorns. Just about as green as their erstwhile brothers waiting on the far side of the muddy creek called Bull Run.

SOUTH ROUTS UNION AT BULL RUN

(Monday, July 22, 1861)

Particulars of the Closing Conflict and Defeat, by an Eye Witness.

THE STAMPEDE OF TEAMSTERS, SPECTATORS, AND DEMORALIZED SOLDIERS.

THEY ARE FORCED BACK TEMPORARILY.

(Special Correspondence of *The Star*.)

Editor Star: I left Washington for Centreville and Bull Run on Sunday morning. . . . Between Fairfax Court House and Centreville we began to meet carriage loads of civilians, newspaper men, Congressmen and others, just from the scene of conflict, and who, in elated terms shouted to us the news of a glorious victory as they whirled past on their way to Washington with the joyful tidings. "Three batteries taken," "The enemy driven upon Manassas Junction," was heard in a continuous buzz for miles, and until we arrived at the singular spur or elevation which shoots up so commandingly and known as Centreville. Climbing to the earthwork erected here we could see clouds of smoke and dust to the left, to the centre, and to the right, indicating active infantry and cavalry movements going on, but the artillery was quiet for the time. This was about 4 p.m., or shortly before.

Confederate fortifications near Centreville after evacuation. Logs were propped up to simulate cannons.

Library of Congress

A singular lull as to information of what was going on below and beyond was noticeable for a few minutes. Then the perturbed faces of some sweaty newcomers from nearer the scene of conflict showed that something was going wrong. The army wagons that had advanced beyond Centreville began to make a retrograde movement towards Fairfax Court House "to get them out of the way," it was said, but as squads of dust-begrimed, exhausted, spiritless looking soldiers began to arrive from the battlefield and hurry forward in the same direction, an uneasy feeling began to pervade the gathering of spectators. Our reserve columns, however, commenced to form steadily on the right of the Centreville height indicating that a stand would be made there, however the odds might go in the valley below.

. . . The stream of demoralized soldiers who filled the roads and overflowed into the fields on the way towards Fairfax Court House began to look like a stampede, especially as many civilians, from Washington and elsewhere, who had come out in private carriages to see the fight, began to turn their horses' heads homewards; putting whip to their horses with such activity that not a few were wrecked by the way, from coming in contact with the heavy army wagons.

Senators Chandler, Wilson, Wade, and other members of Congress, somewhat later set their faces Washingtonwards with gloomy faces.

Some desultory artillery firing was occasionally heard, but it was evident that the day's work was over, and that the enemy, however successful in his bushy converts, was either not able or courageous enough to follow and engage our columns in the open fields for that night at least. Passing along the road to Fairfax Court House we saw the carriageway completely strewn with different articles thrown away by soldiers and teamsters. The panic among the teamsters was increased by an accidental explosion of some cartridges, and they, apparently thinking the enemy was upon them, hastened to throw away bags of grain, blankets, barrels of provisions, knapsacks, spades, &c., which were broken by the heavy wheels and presented the most singular medley im-

Children play at Sudley Ford where the Federal flanking movement crossed.

aginable. It is estimated that not less than $5,000 worth of grain was thus thrown away within a distance of four or five miles. In many instances the drivers cut the horses loose from the vehicles when there was a block, and hurried on. Some of them actually pricked their horses with bowie knives to accelerate their speed.

The squads of demoralized soldiers were meanwhile adding their quota to the panic, by throwing away guns, knapsacks, canteens, &c., and by trying to mount upon and into private carriages, as a means of escape. . . .

🐚 *That rout was the main news story of the day, played at the top of a column on Page 2, the principal news page of* The Star *at the time. Who the "special correspondent" was, nobody knows—maybe someone specifically sent out, perhaps just a friend of the editor's doing him a good turn. He must have known his way around Washington for he recognized the Messrs. Zachariah Chandler of Michigan and Benjamin Franklin Wade and Henry Wilson of Massachusetts, the Abolitionist fanatics, as they headed back to the capital.*

As to the battle itself, McDowell's plan was sound. Part of his army distracted the Rebels on his left along Bull Run, while another feinted farther upstream along Warrenton pike at the Stone Bridge. The main effort was a wide flanking movement designed to roll up the Rebel left. The massive flank maneuver proved too much for his raw recruits, however. The timing and execution went haywire. As a

result, the Confederates knew what to expect and, though as inexperienced as the Federal troops, were ready for it.

One thing the Union commander had not reckoned with was the presence of Johnston. Owing to the feeble gestures of Patterson in the Shenandoah Valley, Johnston had been able to forget the threat there. Marching his men over the Blue Ridge, he entrained them on the Manassas Gap Railroad and sped them to the battlefield in time to take a decisive part in the action. This, incidentally, was the first tactical use of the rails in a conflict.

The fight itself had begun in earnest around 8 a.m. that Sabbath. It was a see-saw melee bravely fought, but with only spotty coordination in the armies of either side. Despite the blunders and the confusion, the Federals, sweeping across the pike and up Henry House Hill, seemed to have success in their grasp until mid-afternoon. At that point, Johnston and Beauregard, demonstrating their capacity to cooperate, swung men from a far wing of their army to hit the Henry Hill Federals hard in their right flank. The spirit went out of the Union troops, and disintegration began.

Battle reports flowed into The Star *all day Sunday, a non-publishing day. Many were outdated by the swiftness of events, but they supplied personal touches to the great, muddled conflict. Here is a sample of one of the earlier dispatches. Although out-of-date when published, it was news from the front, so* The Star *gave it prominence on Page 2 on Monday.* 🐚

Ruins of the bridge over Cub Run where the Federal retreat from Bull Run turned into a rout.

THE BATTLE AT BULL RUN.

(Associated Press Account)

FAIRFAX COURT HOUSE, July 21.—The following dispatch has been received:

CENTREVILLE, July 21, a.m.—We have successfully outflanked the enemy. At half-past two o'clock this morning the various regiments about Centreville were formed for a march. At three o'clock they were in motion in the direction of Perryville, leaving Bull Run to the left. . . . At Gen. McDowell's headquarters, three miles beyond Centreville, the greater part of the army moved to the right to avoid a bridge some distance beyond, said to have been undermined. . . .

The 69th New York regiment was assigned the post of honor in the advance. The members of this regiment have agreed unanimously to serve, although their time of enlistment is now out. All the New York regiments will follow this example. The moving of the grand army was an imposing sight. For five hours one steady column of troops passed through Centreville.

Particulars of the Battle—
Severe Fighting.
Great Loss of Life.

The Secretary of War received a dispatch announcing that fighting was renewed at Bull Run yesterday morning. Our troops engaged the enemy with a large force, silenced their batteries, and drove the secessionists to the Junction [Manassas] with great slaughter. The firing was heard in this city, from the direction of Bull Run, from 11 till about 3 o'clock. After a cessation till nearly 5 o'clock, the sound was again heard, and the reverberating of cannon was still audible at seven o'clock.

A gentleman who arrived last night says that at 3 o'clock in the afternoon the Second and Third New Jersey Regiments were ordered to march forward from Vienna. . . . Other troops were hurrying forward to the scene of hostilities, and there was much military excitement and bustle in all the camps. . . .

The time element in the above item was garbled. That's just one of the things readers had to contend with.

Incidents of the Battle.

A poor little drummer boy was cut completely in two by a canister shot which struck him just under the arms. A piercing "Oh!" emitted in childish treble, the soldiers who were near him say, was a sound that will ring in their ears for life.

Among the disasters of the day were two very serious ones from the firing into each other by mistake, of our own regiments. The Eighth New York Regiment was badly cut up thus by either the Fourteenth or Twenty-fifth Regiments of the same State. The Sixty-ninth New York Regiment had one company destroyed almost to a man by a fire from our own forces. . . .

Later Particulars of the Battle.

. . . The panic was commenced in a light battery commanded by a fat lieutenant. He was proceeding under orders to flank one of the enemy's batteries, when a detachment of their cavalry made a dash at them. Instead of unlimbering and essaying to receive the charge with grape or canister, he turned and instantly fled, leaving two of his pieces on the field. . . .

Aside from encouraging the Confederacy in its cause, and shocking the North into the realization that this was to be no easy war, Bull Run served an important purpose: officers who would hold positions of high command went through their first ordeal in modern warfare. Thomas Jonathan Jackson "stood like a stone wall" with his Virginians. Also on the field—to select a few—were James Ewell Brown Stuart, "Beauty"; James Longstreet, "Old Pete"; Jubal Anderson Early, "Jubilee"; Richard Stoddert Ewell. And on the Union side, William Tecumseh Sherman, "Cump"; George Gordon Meade, "Old Snapping Turtle"; Ambrose Everett Burnside, he of the gorgeous sidwhiskers; Oliver Otis Howard; William Buel Franklin. Some would not live to see the end of the war. Some would be disgraced by it. Others would become heroes still hallowed in the Nation's history.

Later in the week, as further reports and observations kept dribbling in from the battlefield, this comment on the conduct of officers and men appeared in The Star. _It seemed an apt summary._

(Wednesday, July 24, 1861)

Latest from the Seat of War.

NEWS FROM OVER THE RIVER.

Bravery of Our Volunteers.

Officers of the regular army who participated actively in the engagement at Bull Run, speak in the highest terms of the bravery and coolness of the soldiers composing our volunteer force and of their cheerfulness under the trying circumstances of want of proper food and rest previous to the battle, some of them having marched many miles and been without anything to eat except dry bread for more than **twenty**-four hours. With good officers they would be **equal** to any troops in the world, but some of them complain very much of the incompetence of those set over them, and well they may, if it be true as we hear it stated, that numbers of commissioned officers were among the first men to arrive in Washington. That the majority of the officers, however, are in every way worthy of their positions, there can be no doubt. The victory was certainly with us until late in the afternoon, although only eight or ten regiments out of fifty were engaged, and to show how badly frightened the secessionists were, we need only state that many of our troops, too exhausted to travel, returned to Centreville after the cavalry which attempted a pursuit was repulsed, and that these Fed-

General Irvin McDowell, commander of Federal troops at Bull Run.

eral troops slept here all night, and formed and left at 9 o'clock next morning, up to which time not a man had dared to cross Bull Run in this direction. As a Federal officer observed, the rebels were the worst scared men he ever saw, "except our own troops."

EDITORIAL.

(Monday, July 22, 1861)

THE GREAT BATTLE OF YESTERDAY.

Elsewhere in the _Star_ will be found an account of as many of the incidents as we have been able to get in type in time for the issue of to-day.

Our army suffered a heavy reverse, but by no means such an overthrow as panic-stricken civilians and the soldiers who fled in advance of the retreat imagine and allege.

The great body of our troops are slowly retreating to-day in remarkably good order, recovering most of the munitions, baggage, &c., thrown away by those stricken with the panic. . . .

The army will again occupy the positions from which it started out last week, in and around the intrenchments and forts constructed for this city's security on the other side of the Potomac.

In the belief of General Scott they are impregnable, and this city is as secure from the enemy as it was a fortnight ago, quite—notwithstanding yesterday's disasters at a point twenty-eight or thirty miles from us.

We may not inappropriately add that at 4 p.m. yesterday, the victory was clearly ours. The retreat

One of Professor Lowe's balloons snagged in a tree en route of Bull Run battlefield.

movement is ascertained to have been caused by an accidental and trifling panic in one of the regiments, to which it spread from confusion among its own teamsters. . . .

WASHINGTON HOMEFRONT, JULY, 1861.

☜ The city could have no doubt that something fearful was going on across the Potomac. ☜

FOR THE SEAT OF WAR.—Dr. A. J. Borland, of this city having volunteered his services to the Government, was this morning furnished with a pass . . . , and started for the seat of war, to render professional aid to the wounded.

———◆———

THE STEAMERS to Alexandria are suspended from their regular trips to-day, by order of Government, which doubtless needs them for transportation of munitions of war, &c.

AMBULANCES.—Two long trains of ambulances crossed the Long Bridge into Virginia yesterday.

———◆———

ATTENTION, DISTRICT VOLUNTEERS!—You were mustered out of service before the war fairly began. You did your duty, and your whole duty. But shall we now fold our arms in inglorious ease, while our brethren are in the field fighting our battles for us? Never——never! Let us seize upon our arms and share their fate. I propose that the District Volunteers, and all true men who are disposed to join us, organize immediately and apply to the Government for arms and offer to fight in our country's cause, until the enemy are driven from our vicinity. We should raise a brigade of volunteers in the District in two days.

I have the honor to remain, your friend and fellow-citizen,

Edward C. Carrington.

The Confederate Black Horse Cavalry charges on the battlefield of Bull Run.

Bull run was a fight the Union commander knew he wasn't ready for, and certainly did not want. Nonetheless, the defeat was so shattering, the public shock so great, that McDowell had to lose his command. His subsequent wartime career turned out equally inauspicious.

The dust had hardly settled over the battlefield before McDowell's successor was found. George Brinton McClellan was a pint-size, 35-year-old officer with a Napoleonic complex. Not only was he ambitious, but he was convinced that he was the best qualified man in the Union to lead it on to glorious victory. McClellan had been graduated second in his class at West Point, and performed gallantly in the Mexican War. In the interim between wars, he had returned to civilian life, achieving success as a railroad executive. When the Civil War began, he wasted no time getting back into a uniform with a major-general's stars, in the Ohio volunteers. Shortly installed with the same rank in the Regular Army, he was named head of the Department of Ohio. It was in this capacity that he crossed from Ohio into Western Virginia, and for the past few weeks had the Confederates on the run from Philippi, Rich Mountain and Carrick's Ford. All were relatively minor engagements. But in the eyes of Lincoln, who first met McClellan in his law practice days, here was a man who was moving the Rebels in the right direction—southward. Most important to the Union cause at the moment, McClellan possessed a sure talent for organization, and for inspiring troops to believe he was as great as he thought he was.

At the time "Little Mac" was taking over the principal army of the East, Maj. Gen. John Charles Fremont assumed command of the newly created Western Department, based at St. Louis in agitated Missouri. This was Fremont, the "Pathfinder" of Northwest exploration fame. That his reputation as a military commander would never begin to match his explorer's renown became evident from the start.

Nathaniel Lyon, the vigorous Union general who had been pushing Missouri's Confederates around for nearly three months, was getting farther and farther away from his St. Louis base. He had kept going on Fremont's assurances that he would be properly supported. But lately, it seemed, the "Pathfinder" was too busy for military business. He had found political paths to explore while wearing the authority of the army uniform. One such venture was a proclamation to free the slaves of disloyal citizens of his department. Lincoln quickly slapped him down on that one.

Meanwhile, Lyon was on his own—and characteristically undaunted. The little general had concentrated his nearly 6,000 troops at Springfield, Mo. The town was athwart the route of some 11,000 militia and volunteers of Louisiana, Arkansas and Missouri, moving up from the southwestern corner of the latter State. They were headed by a Missourian, Maj. Gen. Sterling Price, and a Texan, Brig. Gen. Ben McCulloch. Lyon felt he should strike soon. An equal number of Confederate forces were near enough to throw in with Price and McCulloch, and two-to-one were bad enough odds. So Lyon headed South to a point near where the main road crossed Wilson's Creek, about 10 miles from Springfield. Here he divided his force, trying a looping flank movement similar to McDowell's at Bull Run. The flanking force was under Colonel Franz Sigel, refugee from the German Revolution of 1848. The plan was aimed at putting a fatal squeeze on the Confederates.

UNION GENERAL DIES IN BATTLE

(Tuesday, August 13, 1861)

ANOTHER GREAT BATTLE IN MISSOURI.

General Lyon Killed!

Just as we go to press this afternoon, the War Department has received the following dispatch from General Fremont:

St. Louis, Mo., Aug. 13

To the Secretary of War.

Gen. Lyons' Aide reports an engagement with severe loss on both sides. Gen. Lyons killed. Col. Siegel is in command. He is moving back in good order from Springfield towards Rolla.

Note.—Rolla is 120 miles by railroad from St. Louis. Ample reinforcements have been promptly sent by Gen. Fremont from St. Louis, and ordered from Ohio and Indiana.

Colonel Seigel is evidently aiming to draw the enemy after him into the center of Missouri, where they can be taken at greater disadvantage than upon the border of Arkansas, near which this engagement occurred.

His march from Springfield to where he would be joined by the forces sent to him by Gen. Fremont, is probably not more than fifty miles.

☞ *This was probably an exaggerated interpretation of Sigel's flank march. Note also the spelling difficulties the correspondent, telegrapher or typesetter —or all three combined—had with the names "Lyon" and "Sigel."* ☞

(Wednesday, August 14, 1861)

Important from Missouri.

THE ENEMY REPULSED WITH TERRIBLE LOSS.

Particulars of the Death of General Lyons.

ST. LOUIS, Aug. 14.—The following is a *verbatim* report of that brought by special messenger to General Fremont:

Early Saturday morning Gen. Lyon marched out from Springfield and came up with the enemy . . . four miles southwest of Springfield, where they had taken a strong position. Gen. Lyon fired the first gun . . . when the battle immediately commenced.

A severe cannonading was kept up for two or three hours, when the fire . . . proving too severe for the enemy, they gradually fell back towards their encampment on Wilson's Creek. Lyons' cavalry on the left flank, and Siegel's artillery on the right, then began a terrific attack, which spread slaughter and dismay in the ranks of the rebels, pursuing them to their camp.

Shells from (James) Totten's artillery set fire to their tents and baggage wagons, which were all destroyed.

A Louisiana and a Mississippi Regiment seemed to suffer most, and were almost annihilated.

Sometime in the afternoon, while Gen. Lyon was leading his column, his horse was shot under him. He immediately mounted another, and as he turned around to his men, waving his hat and cheering his men on to victory, he was struck in the small of the back and fell dead to the ground. The command then devolved on Gen. Siegel.

The pursuit was continued until nightfall, when our little army rested for the night in the enemy's encampment.

Sunday morning General Siegel, fearing the enemy might recover and attempt to cut his command off from Springfield, fell back on that city. . . . Then fearing the great numbers of the enemy might

General Ben McCulloch

69

General Sterling Price, in command of the rebels at Wilson's Creek.

induce them to get between him and Rolla, Siegel concluded to fall back on Rolla with his prisoners, trains, and meet reinforcements.

At the time of the departure of the messenger the enemy had not been seen, and it is probable Seigel has not been disturbed on his march.

Ninety rebels were captured, including a Colonel of distinction, the messenger not remembering his name. The sword and horse of McCulloch were among the trophies.

Reinforcements were on the way to Rolla, and Gen. Siegel and his army may be considered safe.

🔫 *One hundred years later, it is all but impossible to learn what the* Star's *telegraphic news sources were. Whether the word from Wilson's Creek via St. Louis was supplied by a news service, or whether the paper got its dispatches from the War Department, is uncertain. The route of the battlefield report from the far corner of Missouri was negotiated by horseback, in any case. Communications, in short,*

Colonel Franz Siegel

were shaky, and the distance was great. Small wonder that newspaper editors could do little, such as sending a telegraphed inquiry, when discrepancies showed up in dispatches—like whether Lyon had been shot in the front or back. 🔫

(Thursday, August 15, 1861)
The Battle in Missouri.

ROLLA, MO., August 13.—The following additional account of the battle at Springfield is furnished by an eye-witness who left Springfield on Sunday morning and came here on horseback. Our army marched out of Springfield on Friday evening only 5,500 strong, the Home Guard remaining at Springfield. The army slept on the prairie a portion of the night. About sunrise on Saturday morning we drove in the outposts of the enemy, and soon after the attack became general.

The attack was made in two columns by Gens. Lyon and Sturges (Samuel Davis Sturgis)—Gen. Siegel leading a flanking force of about one thousand men, with four guns, on the north of the enemy's camp.

The battle raged from sunrise until one or two o'clock in the afternoon. The rebels in overwhelming force charged Totten's battery three distinct times, but were each time repulsed with great slaughter.

General Lyon fell early in the day. He had previously been wounded in the leg, and his horse shot under him.

The Colonel of one of the Kansas regiments having become disabled, the boys cried out to Gen. Lyon, "General, you come and lead us on." He did so, and at once put himself in the front. While thus cheering his men on to the charge, he received a ball in his left breast, and fell from his horse. He was asked if he was hurt, and replied, "No, not much," but in a few minutes expired without a struggle.

Gen. Siegel had a very severe struggle, and finally lost three of his four guns. His artillery horses were shot in the harness, and the pieces disabled. He endeavored to haul them off with a number of prisoners he had taken, but was finally compelled to abandon them, first, spiking the guns and disabling the carriages.

About 1 o'clock the enemy seemed to be in great disorder, retreating and setting fire to their train and baggage wagons. Our forces were too much fatigued and cut up to pursue, and so the battle may be considered a drawn one. . . .

Gen. Siegel marched back to Springfield in good order, after perfecting his arrangements, gathering the baggage, and blowing up what powder he could not carry, and destroying other property which he did not wish should fall into the hands of the enemy.

Our troops left Springfield on Sunday night, and encamped 30 miles this side of that place, the enemy not pursuing. The only hostile demonstration observed during the day being the firing of muskets at the rear guard.

Gen. Seigel is confident that he could have held Springfield against the force he had engaged, but was fearful of reinforcements to the enemy from the southwest, and that his line of communication to Rolla would be cut off unless he fell back.

Gen. Lyon began the attack upon the receipt of intelligence that the enemy was expecting reinforcements from Gen. (William Joseph) Hardee's column, which was approaching from the southeast.

A portion of the artillery of the enemy was admirably served, and their infantry fire was also very severe.

It is thought that Gen. Seigel fell back no further than Lebanon, where reinforcements would reach him.

☞ *The North had another hero to join Ellsworth. Newspapers, including* The Star, *paced the public through the mournful measures of laying Lyon to his final rest. The battle which killed him rated as another Union loss. But it was a victory, too. Wilson's Creek contributed largely toward discouraging any further serious menace to Missouri by the Confederates. The border State lying in strategic proximity to the country's great central waterways—the Missouri, Mississippi and Ohio—was nearly safe for the Union.* ☞

WASHINGTON HOMEFRONT, AUGUST, 1861.

☞ *The build-up of McClellan's army had a tremendous impact on Washington life as volunteers poured into the city in an endless stream to be trained and organized for duty. Among the local signs of the times was a news item involving a "White House" that bore no relation to the Executive Mansion that had been popularly known as THE White House since the time of the War of 1812, when the British burned it, and its sandstone exterior had been given a coat of white.* ☞

THE WHITE HOUSE.—This title has been applied to the large building recently erected at the depot for the accommodation of arriving troops, and has already become an "institution" in that vicinity. This building was constructed of the Inauguration

ball-room material, and is well adapted to its intended use. The entrances are large and almost innumerable, the floor is of planed pine well joined. The building is nearly 300 feet in length, and about 40 feet wide, and well lighted with gas. In one end three baths, twelve feet wide and four feet deep, have been constructed, into which Potomac water is introduced, and the manner in which the dusty volunteers splash about therein, after a long ride over the road, is peculiarly refreshing, even to a spectator. . . .

THAT PUMP.—The attention of the authorities is called to the condition of the pump on North Capitol street, between B and C, it having been out of order several days, thereby compelling residents of the neighborhood to go several squares to get inferior water. The pump is continually racked by soldiers from the depot in their efforts to get water, and is consequently being rapidly used up.

☞ *The following item left no doubt as to the sentiment held for Northern men disinclined to join the ranks.* ☞

The Cold Shoulder.

The Northern papers seem to be unanimous in declaring that the popular reception of either officers or men returning home by getting off from their military engagements upon this or that excuse, is anything save cordial. It should therefore be known to all disposed to sneak out of the service, that on reaching their homes they are sure to be marked men.

General Nathaniel Lyon, commander of Federal forces at Wilson's Creek.

71

THE THROES OF ORGANIZING AND MANEUVERING FOR POSItion still occupied most of the attention of the armies North and South that August. The policy of the Confederate Congress, two weeks after the start of war, was to stand on the defensive against "coercion," or the invasion of rights and property. The position was consistent with the South's wish to conduct no Northern aggression, but only to be left alone to pursue its separate way. The core of Federal policy, of course, permitted no such separatist pursuit. As long as the Rebels chose to stay on the defensive, the Yankees intended to take the initiative wherever possible. The offensives in Missouri and Western Virginia (where Robert E. Lee had now gone to stop Yankee inroads) manifested Federal policy. Epitomizing the Confederate aim, there stood Joe Johnston, commanding an army of 40,000, ensconced behind breastworks around Manassas, while nearby Washington and Maryland swayed, probably ripe for an invasion plucking.

The respite from large-scale military action during the long pause after Bull Run also gave both Governments a chance to tidy up civilian affairs. There were colossal headaches on the homefronts.

Davis' Congress looked hopefully toward the border slave States of Delaware, Kentucky, Maryland and Missouri. It authorized raising volunteer troops there. And financial rigors were setting in. The Congress voted to issue paper money, the notes to be payable six months after a peace treaty, presumably victorious.

The manifold problems of President Lincoln in this period included a consistent and considerable leakage of Northern war materials into Dixie. He issued a proclamation that all commercial intercourse with the 11 "insurrectionary" States would be herewith banned, and the materials confiscated. (The very next day, his point was underscored. A story in *The Star* reported the seizure near Washington of two wagonloads of medical supplies bound for Richmond from Baltimore.) Lincoln and his aides were also examining naval strategy—blockade—as the best means of stifling the South's short-winded economic life.

In the first four months of the war, the Federal coastal blockade had existed mostly in theory. The Federals at the start had but 42 ships available for any kind of duty. Of these, only four could be spared to patrol nine major harbors and their passages: New Orleans, La.; Wilmington, N.C.; Mobile, Ala.; Savannah, Ga.; Charleston, S.C.; Apalachicola, Fla.; Galveston and Brownsville, Tex.; and Cape Hatteras, N.C. These were scattered along 3,500 miles of seacoast stretching from Mexico to Hampton Roads, Va., the nearest Federal base to the blockading squadrons. Most, being at river mouth, had numerous entry channels. As a consequence, 9 of every 10 ships succeeded in running the blockade through the first year of the war. Among them were the Rebel raiders—privateers which the North indignantly branded as pirates, and which preyed annoyingly on Yankee commerce.

One major flaw in the blockade armor was Hatteras Inlet on the stormy shores of North Carolina. Forts Hatteras and Clark shielded the inlet, allowing Confederate traders and privateers to slip through almost at will. Critical as the Confederacy's own shipping and supply problems were, every cargo-filled craft that could get out and back through Hatteras meant new life. Once behind the protective barrier of the outer coast, the ships had their choice of ports. They could cross Pamlico Sound and sail up the Neuse River to the railhead city of New Bern, or up the Pamlico River to Washington. By heading North across Albermarle Sound and traversing the canal through Dismal Swamp, they could reach bottlenecked Norfolk, Va., by its back door.

Lincoln and his cabinet concluded that this loophole had to be stopped up. Furthermore, Hatteras in Federal hands would enable the fleet to set up a new anchorage hundreds of miles closer to blockade operations than Hampton Roads. The army and navy would join in an amphibious assault, the first in modern warfare. Maj. Gen. Ben Butler would be in charge. Flag Officer Silas Horton Stringham, another New Englander (from Connecticut), would command a motley fleet that included seven men-of-war and two chartered vessels carrying 900 soldiers and Coast Guardsmen. Also in the entourage was the flat-bottomed canal boat *Fanny,* which had one gun and no business being there except that she might be useful in shallow water.

The task force pulled out of Hampton Roads past the salutes and waving kerchiefs of Fortress Monroe on August 26, and headed down the Atlantic.

HATTERAS WRESTED FROM REBELS

(Saturday, August 31, 1861)

INTERESTING FROM FORTRESS MONROE.

BALTIMORE, August 31.—The steamer which arrived at this port to-day brings the following information from Fortress Monroe, dated yesterday:

The gunboat *Iroquois,* from the blockading fleet off Savannah last evening, reports having heard heavy cannonading when off Hatteras inlet, and also that she spoke a brig which had met the Federal fleet. No other intelligence has been received here of the formidable expedition which left Fortress Monroe several days since.

One of the Confederate prisoners, retained for some days at Old Point (Comfort), expressed the opinion that the Federal vessels would be blown up by submarine batteries which Commander Maury has placed in Hatteras Inlet and other assailable points on the Carolina coast. . . .

(Monday, September 2, 1861)

BRILLIANT UNION VICTORY!

Capture of Fort Clark and Fort Hatteras and 630 Prisoners!

Fifteen Confederates Killed and 30 Wounded!

U. S. FLAG SHIP MINNESOTA
August 30, 1861

Major General John E. Wool,
Commanding Department of Virginia.

GENERAL: Agreeably to your orders, I embarked on the transport steamers *Adelaide* and *George Peabody* 500 of the Twentieth Regiment New York volunteers, Col. Webber commanding; 220 of the Ninth Regiment New York volunteers, Col. Hawkins commanding; 100 of the Union Coast Guard, Capt. Nixon commanding, 60 of the United States Artillery, Lieut. Larned commanding, as a force to operate in conjunction with the fleet, under the command of Flag Officer Stringham, against the rebel forts at Hatteras Inlet.

We left Fortress Monroe on Monday, at 1 o'clock p.m. The last ship of our fleet arrived off Hatteras Inlet about 4 o'clock Tuesday afternoon. Such preparations as were possible for the landing were made in the evening, and at daylight next morning dispositions were made for an attack upon the forts by the fleet, and for the landing of the troops.

Owing to the previous prevalence of southwest gales, a heavy surf was breaking on the beach. Every effort was made to land the troops, and after about 315 were landed, including 55 marines from the fleet and the regulars, both the iron boats upon which we depended were swamped in the surf, and both flatboats stove; and a brave attempt made by Lieut. Crosby, of the U. S. Army (serving with the Army as port captain at Fortress Monroe), who had volunteered to come down with the steam-tug *Fanny,* belonging to the Army, to land in a boat from the war steamer *Pawnee,* resulted in the beaching of the boat, so that she could not be got off. It was impracticable to land more troops because of the rising wind and sea. Fortunately, a 12-pound rifled boat gun, loaned us by the flag-ship, and a 12-pound howitzer were landed, the last slightly damaged. Our landing was completely covered by the shells of the *Monticello* and the *Harriet Lane.* I was on board the *Harriet Lane,* directing the disembarkation of the troops, by means of signals, and was about landing with them at the time the boats were stove.

We were induced to desist from further attempts at landing troops by the rising of the wind, and because, in the meantime, the fleet had opened fire on the nearest fort (Clark), which was finally silenced, and its flag struck. . . .

In fine, General, I may congratulate you and the country upon a glorious victory in your department, in which we captured more than seven hundred men . . . and four stand of colors, one of which had been presented within a week by the ladies of Newbern, North Carolina, to the North Carolina Defenders.

By the goodness of that Providence which watches over our nation, no one of the fleet or army was in the least degree injured. . . .

I have the honor to be, very respectfully, your obedient servant,

Benj. F. Butler,
Major General, U. S. Army, Com. Volunteers.

Federal troops carry out amphibious assault on Hatteras Inlet.

The Humbug Maury Disposed Of.

🎺 This was the form in which word reached Washington on the victory. The "news" account consisted almost entirely of Butler's 3,000-word report, with attached memoranda, to his chief. It did not make for lively reading. But with detail and authority it told the story of how the fleet shelled the outgunned forts into submission by noon, August 29, the second day of the attack. The biggest hazard encountered by the little land force was the fire from the fleet. Butler was rather pleased with himself, as indicated by the conclusion of his report.

Imagine a reporter asking an enemy prisoner what he thought was going on—and then getting it into the paper. The informant at least had an idea of the work of Matthew Fontaine Maury. The former Federal naval officer, who had remained loyal to Virginia at the outbreak of war, experimented extensively with submerged "torpedo" mines as harbor defenses. An international pioneer in the sciences of hydrography and oceanography, he was acknowledged by the world as a scientist of the highest caliber. 🎺

That transparent humbug and trickster, Lieut. Maury, who managed to achieve a foreign reputation by unblushing thefts upon the labors of abler but modester men than himself—Professors Henry, Bache, Espey and others—is likely now to be estimated at his true value, at least by the Confederates, who were credulous enough to put faith in his pretensions to the extent of believing that by his wonderful submarine batteries and other kickshaws he could blow up sky-high any of Uncle Sam's vessels that might seek an entrance into Hatteras Inlet. The result of the expedition from Fortress Monroe will doubtless set secesh to cogitating upon the value of the Maury "Harbor Defenses," more particularly as to that of the similar "masheens" of his in Elizabeth and James Rivers.

🎺 A follow-up story, based on prisoners' accounts, gives a graphic picture of the hardships of the Southern soldier. 🎺

Admiral Silas Stringham, commander of the Federal fleet at Hatteras Inlet.

Matthew F. Maury, inventor of the Confederate water mines used at Hatteras.

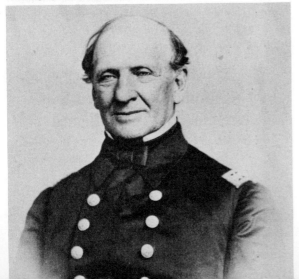

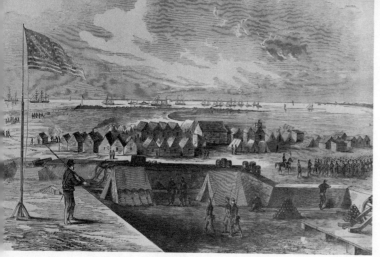

Fort Hatteras as seen from the ramparts of Fort Clark.

(Tuesday, September 3, 1861)

Interesting Particulars of the Surrender of the Hatteras Forts.

A short time before the surrender of Fort Hatteras about three hundred of the rebel garrison had taken refuge in the bomb-proof magazine, which was so crowded that several fainted, and when a shell struck and penetrated it, a panic ensued which the officers could not control. Within ten minutes afterwards, our shots meantime raining in upon them, the white flag was run up. During this time most of the casualties occurred. The prisoners manifested great surprise at falling into Uncle Sam's hands, from whose grasp they had believed themselves perfectly secure. The rank and file were equally astonished to find that they were fed and sheltered instead of being slaughtered in cold blood.

The officers felt keenly the miscarriage, and did not hesitate to say that North Carolina had got a severe blow. All manifested great anxiety to know what was to be done with them, and were assured that they were going among better friends than they had at home, and where they would receive full rations regularly. The last consideration seemed to afford great satisfaction to the privates. When the capitulation took place, the provisions of the garrison were running very low, consisting principally of salt junk and molasses.

The rebels' shells were filled with sand. But few fuses were found in the fortress. The shells were supposed on shipboard to be rifled shot, owing to the sand. The powder in the fort was of a poor quality. There was a large number of percussion caps, rebel make. The copper was not water-proof, and they were very poor.

About half the prisoners had been in the fort for three months, with little pay. They complained of hardships.

The arms were mostly altered from flint to percussion locks. They were of very poor quality. But two companies were fully uniformed, the rest were in citizens' clothes. There was a separate corps of Coast Guard, recently organized into regiments, under Col. (James Green) Martin, one of the most prominent North Carolina lawyers.

A number of the defenders were from the country, having volunteered since the arrival of the fleet, consisting of substantial men, planters, ship owners, tar boilers, proprietors. Some of the soldiers said they had enlisted to avoid being impressed; others didn't hesitate to express the hope that the war would speedily close, adding that it was "a bad business."

When the prisoners were taken on board the *Adelaide* the call for water was universal, and their thirst appeared unquenchable. All the ice on board was used up in a twinkling. The prisoners said they had had no water fit to drink since they had been in the fort. They were perfectly exhausted, and could lie down anywhere for a nap.

The hospital was poorly supplied. The wounds, without exception, were caused by the explosion of bombs, and were of a horrible description. They bled but little, in consequence of the searing from hot shell. . . .

When the white flag appeared, cheer upon cheer went up from the fleet. Our tars, who had entered into the contest with their whole soul, regarded the captives as their game, which they bagged with utmost enthusiasm. One gunner, who lost his ramrod overboard, was in the water after it in a jiffy. He returned with it before he was missed, swearing that he wasn't going to have his gun disgraced for want of a rammer. . . .

WASHINGTON HOMEFRONT, SEPTEMBER, 1861.

☞ *Sensational news was going the rounds, and on the fourth of the month. It was based on the latest triple-distilled hearsay, but the editors were so excited they indulged in the rarity of putting a fat headline on a "local" news item.* ☞

HIGHLY IMPORTANT!
The Rumors of the Death of Jefferson Davis Confirmed.

At a late hour last night, a branch of the Government received a dispatch from a reliable party in

Louisville, notifying it that those in that city understood to be in close communication with Richmond, were satisfied of the correctness of the rumors of the death of Jefferson Davis, that had reached Louisville from Nashville, on the night before.

We have to add that at 10 a.m. to-day a party reached here from Manassas Junction, which point he left on Monday night last. He has more than once previously brought correct information from that quarter, and therefore we place reliance in his statement of the fact that, on Monday morning, information reached there by telegraph that Jefferson Davis died at 7½ a.m. (of that day); and that ere his departure (from the Junction) those persons there who could raise a piece of crape, had, each, donned it, on account of the death of Davis.

P.S.—As we go to press, similar information reaches Washington from still another source, embracing the further news that the immediate cause of his death was "congestive chills."

In the course of the day on Monday last the Confederate flags at some of the points on the Potomac were put at half-mast.

Jeff, of course, still had a long life ahead of him. Possibly one of his especially bad attacks of dyspepsia or neuralgia had laid him low and started tongues flapping. Nevertheless, The Star *persisted in repeating the story at intervals for days—one of which read like this:*

Library of Congress

General Benjamin Butler, commander of the Federal troops during the Hatteras assault.

THE REMARKABLE CASE OF J. D.—There is no doubt that Jefferson Davis is dead—dead as herrings that are red—but it certainly *is* singular that he is able to go on issuing proclamations as usual. As they say down on the Eastern Shore, dying is not so unhealthy as it used to be.

Troops land at Hatteras Inlet.

Library of Congress

THERE HAD BEEN A TIME DURING THE SPRING OF 1861 when the Federal Secretary of State, politically muscular and convinced that he—rather than that man from Illinois—would run the Government, tinkered with the idea of making war with Britain and France. This, reasoned William Henry Seward, would end the Nation's troubles. Nothing like an old-fashioned foreign war to close the ranks at home. Lincoln fortunately let it be known who was boss and burst his Secretary's dream bubble. One war at a time was enough.

Before the year was out, however, the North would reach the brink of a second war—all because a Yankee naval captain believed in acting first and letting others worry about the aftermath.

The Hatteras victory, meanwhile, was being succeeded by events that moved tolerably well for the Union. Lee's campaign to recapture what McClellan and others had won in Western Virginia had failed. The mountain people were closer than ever to forming their own State—Kanawha, or West Virginia, whatever it would be called. Derided by his ill-wishers in the South, Lee was now assigned to a distant command responsible for the coasts of Florida, Georgia and South Carolina. The good, gray aristocrat seemed to be fading from prominence. Brig. Gen. Ulysses Simpson (actually, Hiram Ulysses) Grant seemed, on the other hand, to be rising from obscurity. A West Point graduate who had later run afoul of the bottle, Grant had resigned his commission to struggle with civilian life. But the war had brought him back to the colors. He now commanded the Federal area around the mouth of the Ohio River. His troops, in September, occupied Paducah, Ky., driving out the Confederates of Brig. Gens. Gideon Johnson Pillow and Benjamin Franklin Cheatham. Grant's gains were short-lived. Maj. Gen. (and Episcopal Bishop) Leonidas Polk showed up with reinforcements and drove him right back out of Belmont. But Grant had shown he knew how to give the command, "Forward!"

Kentuckians were coming to a boil. Polk had put the kettle on when he occupied Columbus and Hickman in September. In a swift answer, the Federals sent Brig. Gen. George Henry Thomas to organize loyal troops at Camp Dick Robinson in the Eastern part of the State. Confederates, under the over-all command of Gen. Albert Sidney Johnston, took Bowling Green with Brig. Gen. Simon Bolivar Buckner at their head. Behind Brig. Gen. Felix Kirk Zollicoffer, they dispersed Unionist Kentucky troops from Barboursville. A more familiar name cropped up in headlines around this time—Robert Anderson, Union "hero of Fort Sumter." He was now a brigadier general charged with organizing Kentucky troops throughout his native State.

Action at sea continued vigorously. The Confederacy's privateers and blockade-runners were still operating with near impunity from points South of Cape Hatteras. The Federal fleet was taking measures to shut off these outlets. Part of this process was the capture of Ship Island, astride the coast of Mississippi. In November, a joint force, under Brig. Gen. Thomas West Sherman and Flag Officer Samuel Francis Du Pont, blasted and took over the two forts guarding Hilton Head, harbor entrance to Beaufort, S.C. The day after Hilton Head fell, the Federal Government entered its greatest international crisis of the war.

Up to this point, the Confederate States Government had failed, by informal means, to gain recognition by foreign powers. It would now dispatch two ministers plenipotentiary—"commissioners" —overseas to do the job. James M. Mason, descended from the celebrated Masons of Virginia, would treat with Britain for aid and comfort to the Confederacy. John Slidell, a lawyer in what used to be the French colony of Louisiana, would approach France. With their aides and Slidell's voluminous family, they scurried through the Charleston blockade one rainy October night, and succeeded in reaching Cuba, the first goal of their journey. The party left Havana November 7 aboard the British mail packet *Trent* bound for St. Thomas. On that British possession they would board ship for London. Their intention was no secret. Among those who got wind of the plan was Capt. Charles Wilkes, former explorer of the Antarctic now commanding the Federal warsloop *San Jacinto*. Wilkes pondered the intricacies of sea law. One thing was clear: in wartime a neutral ship carrying dispatches for the enemy could be captured by that enemy's opponent. But what about the question the lawbooks did not answer: could a neutral ship carrying human emissaries of the enemy be captured and its "live dispatches" seized?

Ruled Sea-dog Wilkes to his own satisfaction: yes! The *San Jacinto* turned her rudder to intercept the *Trent* in a narrow channel 230 miles east of Havana.

U.S. SEIZES REBEL ENVOYS ON ENGLISH SHIP

(Saturday, November 16, 1861)

THE SEIZURE OF MESSRS. MASON AND SLIDELL.

The Particulars of Their Capture.

THE PRISONERS GO DIRECT TO FORT WARREN.

The United States steamer *San Jacinto,* cruising in the Bahama channel on the 8th November, in the forenoon, overhauled the English mail steamer *Trent,* and placed her under her (the *San Jacinto*'s) guns.

Lieut. Fairfax was ordered on board the *Trent* to ascertain if Messrs. Slidell, Mason, McFarland and Eustis were on board; with directions, in case he

The *San Jacinto* halting the British steamer *Trent.* Mason and Slidell were taken aboard the *San Jacinto.*

National Archives

found them there, to cause them to be brought on board the *San Jacinto.*

They were found there, and declined to go on board the U.S. steamer unless force was used; whereupon Lieut. Fairfax placed his hand on Mason's shoulder, and with other assistance, quietly took him to the *Trent*'s gangway, and from thence into the *San Jacinto*'s boat.

Mr. Slidell making a similar assertion of his purpose, was taken to the gangway and carried on to the *San Jacinto*'s boat in the same way.

They were all well treated on Captain Wilkes' ship, which immediately started for the United States with her important prisoners, reaching Hampton Roads yesterday—Friday—morning.

Capt. Wilkes sends to the Navy Department voluminous papers on the affair, including written statements concerning their capture, from all the male prisoners named above.

☞ *George Eustis and James E. MacFarland were the commissioners' secretaries. All four were packed off to prison at Fort Warren, outside Boston.* ☞

(Tuesday, November 19, 1861)

WHAT WILL ENGLAND DO?

Since the capture of Messrs. Mason and Slidell, many persons have been anxiously enquiring what will England do? What she will do is uncertain, but what she *ought* to to is very sure. The British Government should direct Lord Lyons to return the thanks of her Majesty to the United States Government for its forbearance in not having seized the Steamer *Trent,* brought her into port and confiscated ship and cargo for an open flagrant breach of international law in suffering the agents of enemies at war with the United States to come on board, and for carrying official papers and despatches of the enemies of the United States. By all writers and jurists the conveyance of hostile despatches is regarded as an illegal assistance afforded to a belligerent of the most injurious, hostile and noxious character. . . .

This principle has been enforced by the British Government for nearly a hundred years with inflex-

Captain Charles Wilkes, commander of the *San Jacinto*.

ible severity against every maritime power. Carrying the enemy's despatches has often been declared by that government as an act of the most noxious and hostile character. . . .

By the Queen's Proclamation, in May last, the British Government acknowledged the rebel States to be Belligerents, to wit, enemies of the United States Government, making war upon it. The hour that proclamation was made, British ships, by their own principles of international law were bound under penalty of seizure and confiscation to abstain from carrying despatches or doing any act that favored the Confederates, because in time of war such act would be noxious and hostile to this Government. But instead of observing such conduct, British vessels have become the daily vehicles of Confederate communication. It was time for an end to be put to his unneutral conduct. . . .

🖝 *The hopes of the South were raised. Maybe the commissioners in a Yankee jail would do the Confederacy more good than having them negotiating abroad.* 🖝

(Thursday, November 21, 1861)
Latest News from the South.
THE RECEPTION OF THE NEWS OF THE CAPTURE OF SLIDELL AND MASON AT NORFOLK.

NEW YORK, Nov. 20—A special dispatch to the *Tribune,* dated Fortress Monroe, yesterday, says that Lieut. Warden states that the intelligence of the arrest of Mason and Slidell had caused great excitement among the rebels at Norfolk, with some rejoicing at the prospect of retaliation by England.

John Slidell

🖝 *The all-important reaction from Britain came after the time lag caused by the breadth of the Atlantic. A steamer crossing then took about two weeks.* 🖝

(Monday, December 16, 1861)
Highly Important from England.
ARRIVAL OF THE STEAMER "EUROPA."

Great Excitement over the Mason and Slidell Affair—A Queen's Messenger Sent with Dispatches to Lord Lyons to Demand the Restoration of the Persons of the Southern Envoys— Views of the British Press.

HALIFAX, Dec. 15.—The *Europa* arrived here to-day from Liverpool, on the 30th ult., and Queenstown on the 2d inst., where she was detained until Monday, by order of the British government. She has the Queen's messenger on board, with dispatches for Lord Lyons.

———◆———

LONDON, Dec. 1.—*The Observer* states that the government will demand from President Lincoln and his Cabinet the restoration of the persons of the Southern envoys to the British government.

Yesterday afternoon after five o'clock her Majesty held a Privy Council at Windsor Castle. Three of her Majesty's ministers, including the First Lord of Admiralty and Secretary of State for War, traveled from London to Windsor by special train to be present. Previous to leaving town, the three ministers had attended a Cabinet council at Lord Palmerston's official residence.

The *Observer* says a special messenger of foreign affairs has been ordered to carry our demands to Lord Lyons, and will proceed by packet from Queenstown to-day. The public will be satisfied to know that these demands are for an apology, and to insist on a restitution to the protection of the British flag of those who were violently and illegally torn from that sacred asylum.

The Observer adds: "There is no reason why they should not be restored to the quarter-deck of a British Admiral at New York, or Washington itself, in the face of ten or twelve men of war, whose presence in the Potomac would render the blustering Cabinet at Washington as helpless as the *Trent* was before the guns and cutlasses of the *San Jacinto*. It is no fault of ours if it should come even to this."

Arrangements for increasing the force in Canada are not yet complete, but in a very few hours everything will be settled. In the meantime a large ship, the *Melbourne,* has been taken up and is now being loaded with Armstrong guns, some 80,000 Enfield rifles, ammunition and other stores at Woolwich. It is not impossible that this vessel will be escorted by one or two ships of war. The rifles are intended for the Canadian military, and strong reinforcements of field artillery will be dispatched forthwith.

The *London Times'* City article of the 30th says: "The position of the Federal States of America is almost identical in every commercial point of view with that which was occupied towards us by Russia before the Crimean War. Russia had a hostile tariff while we looked to her for a large portion of our general supply of breadstuffs, but there is this peculiarity in our present case, that the commencement would be by breaking up the blockade of the Southern ports, at once set free our industry from the anxiety of a cotton famine, and send prosperity to Lancashire through the winter. At the same time we shall open our trade to eight million in the Confederate States who desire nothing better than to be our customers.

"At a privy council on Saturday an order was issued prohibiting the export from the United Kingdom, or the carrying coastwise, of gunpowder, saltpetre, nitrate of soda and brimstone."

The *Times* has no hope that the Federal government will comply with the demands of England. . . .

It was regarded when the *Europa* left that there was a hopeful look, and consols and cotton (stocks) had slightly improved but, after digesting the tone of the American press, a reaction set in, and fears were entertained that the Washington government would justify the act.

James Mason

The English journals were very bitter and hostile, continuing to treat the affair as an intolerable insult. . . .

Old and ailing General-in-Chief Winfield Scott was vacationing at the time. However, he took pains to help get his government out of a jam.

(Thursday, December 19, 1861)

Warlike Preparations—Troops Under Orders for Canada—Letter from Gen. Scott.

By the steamship *Jura*, at Portland from Liverpool and Londonderry on the 6st inst. (whose arrival we announced yesterday), the following has been received:

The excitement relative to the Trent affair continued abated (sic). The stock market was more heavy and unsettled than ever.

The United States Consul at Paris had communicated to the French papers a letter from General Scott, in which he declared there is no truth in the report that the Cabinet had ordered a seizure of the Southern commissioners, even under the protection of a neutral flag. He was quite ignorant of the decision of his Government, but says it is necessary to preserve good relations between America and England; and England, he hopes, will agree on a solution of the question whether the prisoners were contraband or not. If they were agents of the rebels, he says it will be difficult to convince even impartial minds that they were less contraband of war than rebel soldiers or cannon. In conclusion, General Scott expresses his conviction that a war between America and England cannot take place without more serious provocation that at present given.

Lord Lyons, the British Ambassador.

The London *Star* thinks that Gen. Scott's letter will receive a hearty response in England as a message of peace.

The *Times* says that Gen. Scott, like his countrymen, is rather inclined to disavow the conception of the outrage than to repudiate it, now that it has been done.

It is reported that rebel and federal privateers are cruising at the entrance of the English channel.

It is said that the Admiralty have ordered two ships to proceed immediately to the West Indies to act as convoy to mail steamers.

(Saturday, December 28, 1861)

The Settlement of the Mason and Slidell Affair.

Subjoined will be found an abstract of the correspondence between the Governments of Great Britain and of the United States in relation to the question of international law raised by the proceeding of Capt. Wilkes; and of the representations made on the same subject by the Government of France, and the reply of Mr. Seward in answer to these representations.

The correspondence opens with a communication from Mr. Seward to Mr. (Charles Francis) Adams, our Minister to England, under date of November 30, in which, after mentioning the Trent affair, he says:

"It is to be met and disposed of by the two Governments, if possible, in the spirit to which I have adverted. Lord Lyons has prudently refrained from opening the subject to me, as I presume waiting instructions from home. We have done nothing on the subject to anticipate the discussion; and we have not furnished you with any explanations. We adhere to that course now, because we think it more prudent that the ground taken by the British Government should be first made known to us here; and that the

discussion, if there must be one, shall be had here. It is proper, however, that you should know one fact in the case without indicating that we attach importance to it, namely, that in the capture of Messrs. Mason and Slidell on board a British vessel, Capt. Wilkes having acted without any instructions from the Government, the subject is therefore free from the embarrassment which might have resulted had the act been specially directed by us.

"I trust that the British Government will consider the subject in a friendly temper, and it may expect the best disposition on the part of this Government."

On the same day (Nov. 30), Earl Russell, Her Britannic Majesty's Secretary for Foreign Affairs, writes to Lord Lyons, reciting the circumstances under which he understood the capture of these parties to have been made, and proceeds to characterize it as an outrage on the British flag, and, after expressing the hope and belief that it had not been authorized by our Government, adds:

"Her Majesty's Government, therefore, trust that when this matter shall have been brought under the consideration of the Government of the United States, that Government will, of its own accord, offer to the British Government such redress as alone could satisfy the British nation, namely: the liberation of the four gentlemen and their delivery to your lordship, in order that they may again be placed under British protection, and a suitable apology for the aggression which has been committed. . . .

Lord Lyons, in acknowledging (Dec. 27) the receipt of Mr. Seward's communication, says:

"I will, without any loss of time, forward to Her Majesty's Government a copy of the important communication which you have made to me.

"I will also without delay do myself the honor to confer with you personally on the arrangements to be made for delivering the four gentlemen to me, in order that they may again be placed under the protection of the British flag.

"I have the honor to be, with the highest consideration, sir, your most obedient humble servant,

LYONS."

⚓ *While Seward agreed to Her Majesty's demand to release the captives, he refused to offer formal apology as "not called for." Mason and Slidell were released back to the "protection of the British flag" January 1, 1862, and resumed their sensationally interrupted journey to Europe from Provincetown, Mass. Anglo-American relations soon got so friendly that the Federal Government permitted British reinforcements to land and cross New England to enter Canada since the St. Lawrence River was frozen.* ⚓

Secretary of State William Seward

WASHINGTON HOMEFRONT, NOVEMBER, 1861.

🔫 *From time to time since rising to high command in the Union army, McClellan would treat himself and the flag-waving civilians to military "spectaculars." Here was one that took the homefront, if not the battlefront, by storm.* 🔫

THE GREAT REVIEW.

Everybody in Washington went over to-day to see the great review at Bailey's Cross Roads, but owing to the length of the route prescribed (via Ball's Cross Roads) and the costiveness of narrow passage ways at the Long Bridge draws, and the stockade, it was half a day's work to get to the point of review. Many who went were sitting for hours in their vehicles at the bridge waiting for the slow current to move on.

Gen. McClellan, with a brilliant staff, and escorted by several regiments of cavalry with a full cavalry band, proceeding by the same route (Long Bridge, Ball's Cross Roads and Munson's Hill), did not reach the ground until quarter past 12 M.

On his arrival he received a salute and salvos by battery; and as he rode along the line in review, the roars of cheers that were sent up from seventy-five thousand throats of his army were nearly as deafening as the thunders of artillery.

The scene at this time was imposing in the extreme—a scene to be remembered for a lifetime; as General McClellan with his full staff and accompanied by President Lincoln and Secretaries Cameron and Seward, on horseback, dashed rapidly along past the immense bodies of infantry, cavalry, and artil-

lery, extending for miles in the open fields between Munson's Hill and Bailey's Cross Roads.

Following upon this review, the marching review of the troops would take place, not probably to be finished until nightfall, such were their numbers.

The divisions of Generals McDowell, (George Archibald) McCall, (Samuel Peter) Heintzelman, (William Buel) Franklin, (Louis) Blenker, (William Farrar "Baldy") Smith and Fitz John Porter were on the ground, including eighty regiments of infantry, seven of cavalry and twenty batteries of artillery, altogether in the neighborhood of seventy-five thousand men.

How many spectators were present, cannot be estimated now, but they may be reckoned by scores of thousands.

🔫 *Washington Police, a busy lot these days, had their hands full, and some statistics show just how busy they were.* 🔫

———◆———

ANOTHER ASSAULT ON THE POLICEMEN.—Last Saturday, patrolman Garrett, of Seventh Ward police, was attacked by a number of marines, while in the vicinity of Tin Pot alley. Notwithstanding the number against him, he succeeded in fighting his way through, and, with several patrolmen and good citizens who came to his assistance, secured the arrest of the three principals, Isaac Harris, John Cuff, and ____ Donaldson, and they were sent to jail for court by Justice Stratton.

Garrett was but slightly hurt, but Harris, the leader of the party, had his head severely cut, and a finger knocked off in his fight with Garrett, who used his staff like an old hand. Garrett is a partner of Larcombe, the patrolman who was so seriously injured by soldiers in the same locality last week.

Her Majesty, Queen Victoria

84

OLD FUSS AND FEATHERS'' SCOTT WAS OUT OF THE picture. Youth, in the form of the self-esteemed McClellan, had replaced him, after considerable conniving, as chief of the whole Union army. The succession had occurred two months before. Yet here it was 1862, and McClellan was still drilling and organizing, organizing and drilling —and making no motions at the Confederates.

A public shout for action again assailed the President's ears. Concluding he had better act on his own, he issued what he called General War Order No. 1. He ordered that on George Washington's next birth date all Union forces, land and sea, would advance on rebeldom. The order must have been issued, too, as an admonishment to McClellan. For, aside from the impracticability of launching an all-fronts assault with his scattered, poorly connected forces, he could read the dispatches. McClellan could see that other forces were advancing, even if his own were not.

Ambrose Burnside, now a brigadier general, was moving an invasion fleet of 65 vessels, commanded by Flag Officer Louis M. Goldsborough. The destination was Roanoke Island, key to the offshore waters of North Carolina and the inland waterways to Norfolk, Va. The fleet would pass through newly-won Hatteras Inlet and win its main prize, plus a few on the mainland. Commanding the Confederates was Brig. Gen. Henry Alexander Wise, Governor of Virginia at the time of John Brown's incendiary raid on Harpers Ferry more than two years before.

Farther West, in Kentucky, the Federals had just won engagements at Middle Creek and Prestonburg under Col. James Abram Garfield, one day to be President of the United States; and at Mill Springs (Logan's Crossroads) under Brig. Gen. George Thomas, who was already showing classic steadiness in combat and winning the devotion of his men. These encounters were minor, however, in comparison with what was brewing in the West. Parts of an old plan were being revived. It was a legacy left by ''Fuss and Feathers,'' who had devised it shortly after the start of the war. A grand strategic scheme, it was called the ''Anaconda Plan.'' Many had derided it because it wasn't scaled to end the war in a couple of weeks. In those hopeful days people were too impatient to wait while a long-drawn-out operation like ''Anaconda'' was effected. Its concept was to constrict the Confederacy in snake-like fashion by blockading Southern seaports and seizing the South's big inland artery of commerce and communication, the Mississippi River. Now, in January, the blockade was well under way, and the second element of ''Anaconda'' was being readied.

Brig. Gen. Don Carlos Buell, Ohioan commanding the Department of Ohio, was the one who brought Scott's old plan to life again.

Maj. Gen. Henry Wager Halleck, successor to Fremont as commander of the Missouri area, approved it. (Among other things, it seemed a likely way to advance his fortunes in Washington.) The actual work would be done by that stubby little brigadier, Grant, in conjunction with an equally aggressive Navy captain, Andrew Hull Foote. Among Foote's preliminary problems was to overcome Halleck's obsession for red tape in order to build and equip a fleet of iron-clad river monsters, called gunboats, never before seen around the upper Mississippi.

All at last was set. On February 2—almost simultaneous with the launching of an even stranger ironclad, the *Monitor,* at the East coast town of Greenpoint, Long Island—Foote's motley assortment of iron gunboats and wooden troop transports steamed from Paducah up the Tennessee River toward the heartland of the South.

TWO REBEL STRONGHOLDS TAKEN

(Friday, February 7, 1862)

Telegraphic.

Great Victory in Kentucky.
FORT HENRY TAKEN!!

The following thrilling dispatch has been received just as we go to press:

CHICAGO, Illinois, Feb. 7.—FORT HENRY IS TAKEN.

☞ *This was a frequently recurring instance where important dispatches were so skimpy that the newspaper headline was longer than the story itself. Slight error in the headline, in this instance, too. The scene was in northwest Tennessee close to the border of, but not in, Kentucky.* ☞

Second Edition.
Three O'Clock P.M.

OFFICIAL ACCOUNTS OF THE SURRENDER OF FORT HENRY, WITH TWENTY CANNON AND SEVENTEEN MORTARS.

THE BATTLE BETWEEN THE FORT AND UNITED STATES GUNBOATS.

Commodore Foote Hands Over the Fort and Prisoners to the Army.

The Navy Department, at two p.m. to-day, received the following highly important dispatch:

U. S. FLAG STEAMER CINCINNATI,
Off Fort Henry, Tennessee River, Feb. 6, 1862.
HON. GIDEON WELLES, Sec'y Navy:

The gunboats under my command—*Essex*, Commander (William D.) Porter; *Carondelet*, Com'r Walter; *Cincinnati*, Commander Stenabel; *St. Louis*, Lt. Com'dg Paulding; *Conestoga*, Lt. Commander Phelps; *Taylor*, Lieut. Com'dg Gwinn, and *Lexington*, Lieut. Com'dg Shirk—after a severe and rapid fire of one hour and a quarter, have captured Fort Henry, and have taken General Lloyd Tilghman and his staff and 60 men as prisoners.

The surrender to the gunboats was unconditional, as we kept an open fire upon them until their flag was struck. In half an hour after the surrender I handed the fort and prisoners over to Gen. Grant, commanding the army, on his arrival at the fort in force.

The *Essex* had a shot in her boilers, and after fighting most efficiently for two-thirds of the action, was obliged to drop down the river, as I hear that several of her crew were scalded to death, including the two pilots. She, with the other gunboats, officers and men, fought with the greatest gallantry.

The *Cincinnati* received 31 shots, and had one man killed and eight wounded—two seriously.

The fort with twenty guns and seventeen mortars was defended by Gen. Tilghman with the most determined gallantry.

I will write as soon as possible.

I have sent Lieut. Commanding Phillips and three gunboats after the rebel gunboats.

A. H. Foote, Flag Officer.

Federal gunboats shelling Fort Henry.

NOTE.—The rebels had a sustaining force of some 15,000 (as believed here this morning) hovering around Fort Henry to sustain it.

That this force has either been routed by Gen. Grant (who was cooperating with Commodore Foote's gunboats) or ingloriously fled before Grant's army, leaving the fort to its fate, is plain from the fact that G. stood ready and able to receive the fort and prisoners from the commodore half an hour after the latter had taken them.

See elsewhere in to-day's *Star,* many interesting particulars concerning Fort Henry, and the great importance of taking it, &c.—under the head of "THE MOVEMENT UP THE TENNESSEE RIVER."

☞ *The victory could be claimed almost exclusively by Foote. After dropping Grant's troops off about three miles downstream for a land assault on the Fort, the flag officer moved ahead and started the attack with his superior cannon. The foot soldiers were impeded by flooded low ground. Brig. Gen. Lloyd Tilghman, one of Maryland's Tilghmans, surrendered to Foote about an hour before Grant was able to come up. The Confederate had actually been fighting a delaying artillery action to enable the infantry garrison of about 3,000 to escape into the stronger fortifications of Fort Donelson, some 13 miles away on the Cumberland River. Grant's force of about 15,000, swelled by a division headed by Brig. Gen. Lewis Wallace (who would one day write a novel about Ben Hur), headed for Donelson Feb-*

ruary 11. At the same time, part of Foote's fleet steamed on up the Tennessee as far as Muscle Shoals, near Florence, Ala., while the gunboats went down the Tennessee, into the Ohio, and on up the Cumberland toward the next objective. ☞

(Saturday, February 15, 1862)
FORT DONELSON.

This forenoon a dispatch reached the General-in-Chief here from Gen. Halleck at St. Louis, announcing the investment of Fort Donelson with a force of 50,000 men, aided by the noble fleet of Commodore Foote, and anticipating its speedy reduction. Gen. Halleck says that Pillow, Floyd and Buckner are in it, with a force of 15,000 men, and he is evidently of opinion that his arrangements to cut them off from reinforcements will surely be successful. How any portion of the rebel army in Fort Donelson can possibly escape death or capture, is past us to divine.

Parties who came up by the Old Point (Comfort) boat say it was reported at Norfolk yesterday that Fort Donelson had been captured.

Latest from Fort Donelson.

Just as the second edition of the *Star* of to-day goes to press, a dispatch from General Halleck's headquarters has reached here addressed to Senator Thompson, saying—"Fort Donelson is taken, with 15,000 prisoners, and Floyd among them."

Troop transports on the Tennessee River.

National Archives

B-4853

General Simon Buckner, who surrendered Donelson.

Commodore Andew Foote, commander of the Federal gunboats.

At 2½ p.m. no dispatch verifying the above had reached the headquarters here, where its truth, however, was not regarded as being improbable.

Our latest positive advices from Fort Donelson are up to 12 o'clock on the night of the 13th, when it was confidently believed by our officials that the question of the surrender of the place was one of hours only. So we are inclined to believe this good news is true.

☞ *The news was not only true, it was sensational enough to place in the middle of Page 1.* ☞

(Tuesday, February 18, 1862)

SURRENDER OF FORT DONELSON.

Desperate Fighting—Federal Loss 400 Killed, 800 Wounded—15,000 Confederates Taken Prisoners— 65 Pieces of Artillery and 20,000 Stand of Arms Captured.

CHICAGO, Feb. 17.—A special dispatch to the *Times* dated Fort Donelson, Feb. 16 says: Fort Donelson surrendered at daylight this morning. We have taken Generals Buckner, Johnson, Bushrod, and 15,000 prisoners, also 3,000 horses.

Generals Pillow and Floyd, with their brigades, ran away on steamers during the night, without letting Buckner know their intentions.

Gen. Smith led the charge on the lower end of the works, and was first inside the fortification. The Fort Henry runaways were all here bagged.

The prisoners are going on board the steamers for Cairo.

Our loss is heavy, probably 400 killed and 800 wounded. We lost a large percentage of officers, among them Lieut. Col. Erwin, of the 20th Illinois;

White, of the 31st, and Smith, of the 48th. Cols. John A. Logan, Sawyer and Ransom are wounded.

Major Post, of the 8th Illinois, with two hundred privates, are prisoners, and have gone to Nashville, having been taken on the night before the surrender in a skirmish.

The enemy's loss is very heavy, but not as great as ours, as they fought behind intrenchments, whilst our brave fellows had nothing to shelter them from the iron storm.

We should have taken them by storming on Saturday if our ammunition had not given out in the night.

McClernand's division, composed of Generals Oglesbie's, Wallace's and McArthur's brigades, suffered terribly. They were composed of the 8th, 9th, 11th, 18th, 20th, 29th, 30th, 31st, 35th, 38th and 49th Illinois. Gen. Lew Wallace, with the 11th Indiana, 8th Missouri, and some Ohio regiments, participated in the assault.

Taylor's, Willard's, McAllister's, Schwartz's and De Casse's batteries were in the fight from the commencement.

THE LAST STRUGGLE— THE ASSAULT.

The enemy turned our right for half an hour, but our lost ground was more than regained.

Gen. Lanman's (Jacob Gartner Lauman's) brigade, of Gen. (Charles Ferguson) Smith's division, was the first in the lower end of the enemy's works, which was done by a charge of bayonet.

As nine-tenths of the rebels were pitted against our right, our forces on the right were ready all night to recommence the attack on Saturday morning; they were met on their approach by a white flag, Gen. Buckner having sent early in the morning a dispatch to Gen. Grant, surrendering the works. The outworks of the fort extended some five miles.

General U. S. Grant

The Trophies.

The rebels lose 48 field pieces, 17 heavy guns, 20,000 stand of arms, besides a large quantity of commissary stores, &c.

The Enemy Demoralized.

The rebel troops are completely demoralized, and have no confidence in their leaders, as they charge Pillow and Floyd with deserting them.

What Our Troops Endured.

Our troops, from the moment of the investment of the fort on Wednesday last, lay on their arms night and day—half the time without provisions, all the time without tents, and a portion of the time in a heavy rain storm.

Grant, with about 27,000 men, directed his assault against the landward fortifications and rifle pits, while Foote blasted away with his gunboats. The latter took considerable punishment from Donelson's artillery, and was himself wounded. Grant's command, under Brig. Gens. John Alexander McClernand, Wallace and Smith, was having hard going against 21,000 Confederates. The Confederates' three-way command setup contributed largely to the cave-in. The officers—Pillow, Buckner and Brig. Gen. John Buchanan Floyd, former governor of

Arkansas and War Secretary under President Buchanan—couldn't agree whether to stay or leave. Floyd and Pillow decided to leave with about a fourth of the troops, delegating the doubtful pleasure of commanding Donelson to Buckner. Col. Nathan Bedford Forrest, seeing things were getting untenable, got permission to gallop out with his men. And contrary to the opening paragraph of the above dispatch, the two officers, Johnson and Bushrod, weren't captured at all but got away to fight many another battle.

THE SURRENDER—RECEPTION OF THE NEWS AT ST. LOUIS—GREAT REJOICING.

ST. LOUIS, Feb. 17.—Fort Donelson surrendered at 9 o'clock yesterday morning to our land forces. Several gun boats were present at the time.

An immense amount of war material is among the trophies of the victory.

Floyd skulked away during the night before the surrender.

The gunboat *Carondelet,* Capt. Walker, which arrived at Cairo this morning with the news, brought a large number of our wounded to the Paducah and Cairo hospitals.

This city is wild with excitement and joy. The cheering news was read at the Union Merchants' Exchange, creating the most intense enthusiasm. The "Star Spangled Banner," "Flag of our Union" and "Red, White and Blue" were sung by all present with enthusiasm; after which, they marched to headquarters, some 1,200 or 1,500 strong, where three rousing cheers were given for Gen. Halleck and Com. Foote.

Gen. Halleck appeared at a window and thanked the people for their hearty demonstrations, and said: "I promised, when I came here, with your aid, to drive the enemies of our flag from your State. This has been done, and the enemy is now virtually out of Kentucky, and soon will be out of Tennessee."

More cheers for the Union were given, and the Star Spangled Banner was repeated, and then the crowd dispersed. . . .

Although the demand for "unconditional surrender" had been made heretofore by other Union officers—as recently as Foote at Fort Henry—Grant's specification of these unbending terms caught public fancy. Utter jubilation, as well as the fact that the first letters matched the initials of his given name, forever associated unconditional surrender with Grant. As a victory, it was far-reaching, breaking the center of the Confederacy's western line, forcing A. S. Johnston to pull back out of Western Tennessee and Kentucky, and setting the stage for the drive down the Mississippi that was now sure to come. ✑

WASHINGTON HOMEFRONT, FEBRUARY, 1862.
THE VICTORIES.

Salutes were fired last night, this morning, and at noon to-day at the arsenal and navy yard here in honor of the successes of our arms.

✑ *Meanwhile, the social life of the Nation's capital was not to be outdone by the drama of war. On the eve of Fort Henry's capture, the White House was the scene of a gala event.* ✑

The Entertainment at the White House Last Night.

Jupiter Pluvius, who has reigned (and *rained*) so imperiously for so many weeks, despite the prayers and anathemas of military men, and forward-movement-folk generally, kindly consented to abdicate for

a brief season—there being a lady in the case—and on last night permitted the visitors to the White House to repair there under genial skies and lighted by a bright moon.

The cards of invitation were lettered thus:

> THE PRESIDENT AND MRS. LINCOLN,
> request the honor of
> . . . .
> company on Wednesday evening,
> Feb. 5th, at 9 o'clock

These were received at the door by the janitors; and parties minus the precious bits of paste-board "who had left their cards at home" or were "sure it would be all right," were rigorously excluded or kept a good while in probation.

By ten o'clock the arrivals were thick and fast, and from that hour until midnight the East Room presented a brilliant spectacle indeed.

The President and Mrs. Lincoln occupied the center of the room, no formal presentations being made to them, but the guests on arriving advanced to pay their respects to each.

The deck of a Federal gunboat.

In other parts of the room and in the adjoining rooms various celebrities held court also, their various localities being designated by the crowds that eddied around them.

Gen. McClellan, whether stationary or promenading with Mrs. McClellan or Miss Marcy, was thus lionized. Tall, Englishy Senator Sumner had his circle, and Gen. Fremont and "Jessie," on their appearance in the rooms, were immediately surrounded by their admirers. Sturdy, soldierly looking Mc-Dowell, conversing in English and French with equal facility, was not only the object of respectful attention from his fellow countrymen (who believe in him despite Bull Run), but was made much of by the Diplomats and foreign element of the gathering generally. . . .

At eleven o'clock, the President taking the daughter of Senator Browning, of Illinois, upon his arm, entered upon the promenade, and Mrs. Lincoln followed with Senator B.

A sense of duty to lady readers admonishes us to mention that Mrs. Lincoln was tastefully dressed (according to the verdict of lady authorities present, and who are sure to be rigid enough critics in such matters) in white satin, with black lace flounces, perhaps half a yard or more in width, the flounces festooned up with white and black ribbon. She wore pearl ornaments, and a handsome Parisian head-dress with bunches of crape myrtle, &c., and with bouquet to match.

Having passed through the rooms in promenade, the President led off in the direction of the supper-room, and the guests following were struck with admiration by the scene presented.

The celebrated caterer, Maillard, of New York, who has been here in person for some days, with his head waiter, Charles Hartmyer, and others of his force—waiters, cooks, artists in confectionery—had evidently exerted himself to give Washington a taste of his quality, and the tables were loaded with the products of his genius. The supper was, in many respects, the most superb affair of the kind ever seen here.

At the west end of the table was a war device, a helmet (sugar) supported by figures and with waving plumes of spun sugar; next came a tasteful basket; next a hermitage, followed by a temple surmounted by the Goddess of Liberty; then Chinese pagodas, Roman temples, cornucopias, fountains with spray of spun sugar and surmounted by stars; and then the good American frigate "Union," with guns, sails, flags, smoke stack and all, complete in sugar, and the whole supported by star-and-stripe-draped cherubs.

Fort Pickens loomed up in sugar on a side table, surmounted, however, by something more eatable than barbette guns, in the shape of deliciously prepared birds, and similar "chicken fixins." . . .

There was a superb *pate de foi gras* inviting the respectful attention of gourmands, and other delicacies and luxuries in such profusion that the joint attack of the thousand or more guests failed to deplete the array. Champagne and other costly wines and liquors flowed freely in hospitable emulation with the enticing blandishments of the edibles. . . .

HAD GEORGE WASHINGTON BEEN AMONG HIS COUNTRY-men on February 22, 1862—the 129th anniversary of his birth—he might have suffered a broken heart. His nation was torn in half, yet both parts pledged faith to his memory. North and South, two peoples and two governments honored the "father" of their countries with oratory, parades, flag-waving. In the South, for that matter, there was something special to offer. On this anniversary day the Confederate States of America would inaugurate its own President, heading a new and permanent government wholly separate from the old United States of America which Washington had helped bring into being. The ceremony, moreover, was in Richmond, capital of Washington's native State, and, since May 29, 1861, the seat of the new Confederation of States.

Jefferson Davis, with his powers as Chief Executive of the South, felt he had to act fast. It was no secret that McClellan, with his huge and well-trained army, planned to descend the Potomac River and Chesapeake Bay, and strike at Richmond by way of the peninsula between the James and York Rivers. Within two weeks of his inauguration, Davis proclaimed martial law in the Confederacy's capital. He called up Robert E. Lee from the South's lower reaches to help protect the Richmond defenses. Joe Johnston and his army in Northern Virginia were ordered back from Manassas to form defenses along the South bank of the Rappahannock River—another bulwark for Richmond.

Up in Yankeedom, that metal cheese-box, the *Monitor,* was being prepared for a voyage to Hampton Roads, Va. The Yankees had a stirring song to cheer their patriotic spirits. Its lyrics had appeared, anonymously, in the *Atlantic Monthly* that February under the title "Battle Hymn of the Republic." The author, Miss Julia Ward Howe, daughter of a Boston preacher, had been inspired to write the piece during a visit to the war camps of Washington the year before. "Battle Hymn" was a morale booster much as "Bonnie Blue Flag" was down South.

It was war on the homefront as well as the battlefront. But where, just now, was the "clash of arms?" The reader would have to look far west in an area which maps of the time could detail only as scattered pinpricks, vague trails wandering across the rivers with Spanish-sounding names. Beyond Texas, in the New Mexico-Arizona territory, Confederate and Union interests were also at stake. On February 21 that part of the Civil War frontier burst into flame.

TEXANS DEFEAT FEDERALS IN NEW MEXICO

(Monday, March 10, 1862)

IMPORTANT FROM NEW MEXICO.

Desperate Battle Ten Miles South of Fort Craig—Great Loss on Both Sides.

DENVER CITY, Friday, March 7, via Julesburg, Saturday, March 8.—The following news was received here to-day by military express:

A desperate and terrible battle lasting all day, took place at Valverde, ten miles south of Fort Craig, on the 21st of February. The fight was probably resumed again on the 22nd.

The loss is great on both sides.

Both parties claim the victory.

A regiment of New Mexicans, commanded by Col. Panton, ran away.

Capt. McRae, who had charge of our artillery, and every one of his command, were killed at their post, and their cannon was taken by the rebels.

Kit Carson was within 15 miles of Fort Craig.

Firing was heard from his direction, with what result was not ascertained at the time the messenger left.

General E. S. Canby, the Federal commander.

Library of Congress

☞ *Big news with sparse details must have caused many an ulcer among newspaper editors of the time. The dispatch reporting the battle of Valverde was routed by telegraph, horseback and—who knows?—maybe even gila monster over the remote trails from Albuquerque and Santa Fe, New Mexico, through "Denver City," Colo., St. Louis and on East. As quickly as the shaky communications system allowed. The Star published the news. But the time lag was considerable.* ☞

(Friday, March 14, 1862)

Telegraphic News.

LATER FROM FORT CRAIG.

Bloody Fight between Texan Rebels on the Rio Grande and a Portion of the Federal Troops under Col. Roberts—The Mexican Volunteers become Panic-Stricken and the Rebels Gain the Day.

ST. LOUIS, March 13.—*The Republican* has advices from Albuquerque, New Mexico, to February 23d, giving details of a recent battle at Fort Craig. The fight commenced on the morning of the 21st between a portion of our troops under Col. Roberts, and the enemy across the Rio Grande, with varied success, until two o'clock. Col. Canby then crossed the river in force with a battery of six pieces under Capt. McCray (McRae) of the cavalry, but detailed in command of the battery. He had also a small battery of two howitzers. The enemy are supposed to have had eight pieces. The battle was commenced by the artillery and skirmishers, and soon became general. Towards evening most of the enemy's guns were silenced. They, however, made a desperate charge on the howitzer battery, but were repulsed with great loss.

Capt. McCray's battery was defended by Capt. Plimpton's company of United States infantry and a portion of Col. Pinos' regiment of Mexican volunteers. The Texan rebels charged desperately and furiously with their picked men, about 600 strong. They were armed with carbines, revolvers and seven-pound bowie knives. After discharging their carbines at close distance, they drew their revolvers and reached the battery amid a storm of grape and canister.

The Mexicans of Pinos' regiment now became panic-stricken, and ingloriously fled. Captain Plimpton and his infantry bravely stood their ground, and fought nobly till more than one-half of their company were numbered with the dead. With his artillerymen cut down, and his supports reported killed, wounded or flying from the field, Capt. McCray sat down calmly and quietly on one of his guns, and with revolver in hand, refused to fly or desert his flag. He thus fought to the last, and gloriously died like a hero, the last man by his guns.

The Texans suffered terribly in the charge. Many of our officers distinguished themselves. Maj. Donaldson, who was the chief aide of Col. Canby, acted bravely, and was conspicuous in every part of the field. His horse was wounded, but the Major was not injured.

Kit Carson, in command of a regiment of volunteers, deployed as skirmishers, did good service during the action, and behaved well. We have to name the loss of Lieutenants Michler and Stone, who, like Captain McCray, nobly and bravely maintained the honor of our flag to the last. Many other officers were wounded. Our loss is about 200 killed and wounded. That of the enemy is believed to be much greater. The greatest confidence is reported in Col. Canby, and if the volunteers will do their duty, the Texans will yet be ignominiously driven from New Mexico.

☞ *Reading the reports from the Rocky Mountain country, it was next to impossible to find a pattern of campaign. The word that seeped through did, however, give the impression that a small but vicious war was going on a thousand miles West of the Mississippi River. It involved struggles for forts and towns isolated on the far frontier. Confederates and Federals alike had to contend, not only with each other, but with extremities of weather, problems of water and food supply, and the unpredictable nature of the Indians, where the Apaches, Comanches and Kiowas still resented the intrusion of whites.*

The current campaign involving Valverde was to prove the most ambitious of the war in that theater of operations. It had started the previous July when Texas Col. John R. Baylor with a motley crew of Confederates headed up the Rio Grande River from San Antonio. He captured Fort Fillmore, just across the westernmost border of Texas, as well as the numerically superior Federal force which had evacu-

General Henry Hopkins Sibley, commander of rebel troops.

ated the fort. This accomplished, Baylor claimed the area South of Albuquerque and West to California as the Confederate Territory of Arizona. He also pronounced himself governor.

Baylor's force soon was joined at Fort Bliss, Tex., by troops under Brig. Gen. Henry Hopkins Sibley. Once again the Confederates moved up the Rio Grande to firm their claim to the land as Confederate. Sibley's campaign reached its high tide at Valverde, where the Confederates defeated Federal troops operating from nearby Fort Craig under Col. Edward Richard Sprigg Canby and aided by the celebrated Indian fighter, Col. Christopher (Kit) Carson. Colorado and New Mexico units combined with U.S. Regulars to oppose Sibley. ☞

(Wednesday, April 16, 1862)

The Latest by Telegraph.

ANOTHER UNION VICTORY.

CONFIRMATION OF THE BATTLE AT APACHE PASS.

KANSAS CITY, April 14.—*Hon. E. M. Stanton, Secretary of War:* The Fort Union Mail brings confirmation of the battle of Apache Pass. Our loss is 150 killed, wounded and missing. The enemy acknowledge their loss to be from three to four hundred killed and wounded. Ninety-three rebels were taken prisoners, thirteen of whom were officers. Our forces

Colonel Kit Carson, the Indian fighter, fought against the rebels.

captured and burned sixty-four wagons laden with provisions and ammunition, killing 200 mules.

The Texans attacked our battery four times, the last time coming within forty feet of our guns, but were repulsed with heavy loss. Col. Slough is encamped at Bernal Springs, forty miles from Fort Union. The Texans fell back to Sante Fe. Col. Canby, with 1,000 regulars and Kit Carson's regiment, are reported within three days' march of Col. Slough; and Col. Slate is on the Jornida with reinforcements for the enemy.

(Tuesday, April 29, 1862)
MORE UNION SUCCESSES IN NEW MEXICO.

The following was received here to-day:

KANSAS CITY, April 2, 8 p.m.—*Hon. Edwin M. Stanton, Secretary of War:* Through Sante Fe mail, with dates to the 12th, has arrived.

Col. (John P.) Slough and Gen. Canby formed a junction at Galesto (Galisteo, New Mex.) on the 11th. Major Duncan, who was in advance of Gen. Canby's advance guard, encountered a large party of Texans, and routed them.

Major Duncan was slightly wounded.

The Texans were thirty miles south of Galesto, in full flight from the Territory.

No doubt is entertained of the speedy capture of Sibley's command, as they are entirely destitute of everything.

After winning at Valverde, the Confederates bypassed Fort Craig and aimed for Albuquerque and Santa Fe, which the Federals abandoned in March. Canby's Federals, moving North from that fort, plus others from Fort Union under Slough, now outnumbered the Confederates 2,600 men by two-to-one. Sibley hastened back down the Rio Grande to his starting point at Fort Bliss. When he learned that Federal Col. James Henry Carleton was marching more reinforcements of Regulars through the Rockies from California, he abandoned Fort Bliss and backed up all the way to San Antonio. Except for skirmishing and scouting activities, the Rocky Mountain territory would remain quiet, and secure for the Union, the rest of the war.

(Thursday, May 1, 1862)
The Troubles of the Overland Mail.

SALT LAKE, April 29.—The report attributing the overland mail difficulties to the employees of the company is entirely destitute of foundation. Persons with whom we are personally acquainted have been in the fights with the Indians. On the 17th, in Mr. Fowler's division, the agent and nine men, with two coaches with the mails, were attacked by the Indians near Split Rock. Six Mail men were wounded and compelled to abandon the mails, coaches and animals. The Indians afterwards burned Plant's Station. The wounded party left Pacific Springs night before last. The telegraph operator at Pacific Springs and another person had a fight with some Indians, and narrowly escaped. Their animals were hit several times with arrows. The station-keeper at Green river was killed a few days since while endeavoring to protect mail property. Thus far four employees of the company have been killed. Although the greater part of their stock is gone, the employees remain. A force is being raised in this city by Brigham Young, under the authority of the President, for the protection of the route.

WASHINGTON HOMEFRONT, FEBRUARY, 1862.

ANNIVERSARY OF WASHINGTON'S BIRTHDAY—It is noticeable that the observances in honor of the natal day of Washington, a day which it seems was to have been equally honored in the capital of the loyal and the rebellious States, should in both cities be clouded by calamity. While loyal citizens here rejoice in the successes which have attended the Federal arms both in the East and West, they recognized with submission the chastening hand of Providence, which has brought affliction in the family of our chief magistrate. In Richmond, the inauguration of the ruler they have set up, will necessarily be of a gloomy character, for those who commenced, and have carried on the unholy war against the Government must, in the reverses which they have recently sustained, see "the beginning of the end."

The day was ushered in here by the ringing of bells, and the firing of salutes from the navy yard and arsenal, and the guns in the fortifications about Washington echoed and re-echoed the booming throughout the day. The national flag was displayed from all the public buildings and most of the private residences in and about Washington. The illumination, which would have been a general one through-

out the District if it had not been for the death in the President's family, will be only partial.

THE FUNERAL OF WILLIE LINCOLN.— The Departments were all closed to-day in consequence of the arrangements for the funeral of William Wallace, second son of President Lincoln. His remains were placed in the Green room at the Executive mansion, where this morning a great many friends of the family called to take a last look at the little favorite, who had endeared himself to all the guests of the family. The body was clothed in the every-day attire of youths of his age, consisting of pants and jacket, with white stockings and low shoes—the white collar and wristbands being turned over the black cloth of the jacket. The countenance wore a natural and placid look, the only signs of death being a slight discoloration of the features.

J
UST AFTER THE BEGINNING OF THE WAR, FEDERAL COM-
modore Charles S. McCauley, head of Norfolk Navy Yard, had done
a messy job—from the Union standpoint—of spoiling things to the advantage of the secessionist Virginians. Seemingly, said one observer,
the old commodore was "stupefied, bewildered and wholly unable to
act." Encouraging his state of indecision were a staff and work force
with strong secessionist tendencies who had little desire to keep Federal
ships and shore facilities out of Southern hands. In the resulting confusion, only part of the shore facilities was destroyed by the departing
Federals. The flames that had been set among the ships in the Navy
Yard had been destructive, but much that was left could be salvaged.
Among the remains were the hull and machinery of the steam frigate
Merrimack.

The ship had been named for the Merrimack River—not the
town of Merrimac—in northeastern Massachusetts. In the newspaper
accounts of her career, the "k" in *Merrimack* would be dropped, although official Navy usage would preserve the "k." However, the
spelling problem mattered little to the Confederacy. The weird new
craft being shaped from the one-time frigate would bear the name
Virginia. Anyone since earliest colonial times could spell that.

Whatever her name, the ship had been pulled out of the mud
at Norfolk, and under the direction of Stephen Russell Mallory, Secretary of Navy, CSA, was being rebuilt with iron rails and plates protecting her sloped sides. She would ride only a few feet above water. So
constructed, and sporting a ram on her prow and cannons around her
sides, she could devastate the wooden-hulled ships blockading Norfolk
harbor at Hampton Roads. She might even menace Federal shipping
farther afield.

The remodeling of the *Merrimac,* with all its implications,
was not lost on the Lincoln administration. After a slow grinding of
executive and legislative gears, the Federal Government concluded that
it should devise a counter-weapon forthwith. John Ericsson, a Swedish-
born marine engineer, was called in. An inventor of refinements in naval
armament, and innovator of screw-propelled warships, Ericsson developed the weirdest of all his naval creations. So strange was the product
that it would be derisively branded as "Ericsson's Folly," and "cheese-
box on a raft." The ship he sold the Government rode even lower in
the water than the *Merrimac.* It was constructed entirely of metal, and
the small area that showed above water made a very difficult target.

The Confederate iron-clad emerged from her berth up the
Elizabeth River on Saturday, March 8, and commenced wreaking the
havoc among the Federal ships in Hampton Roads that Secretary Mallory had intended. Panic spread through the Federal Command all the
way to Washington. Next day, none too soon, Ericsson's folly, the
Monitor, creased the waves off Norfolk.

UNION WINS IRONCLAD BATTLE

(Monday, March 10, 1862)

THE LATEST FROM OLD POINT.

Arrival of the Federal Iron-Clad Gunboat Monitor— She Is Attacked by the Merrimac, Jamestown and Yorktown

(OFFICIAL)

March 9, 7 p.m.—The telegraph line to Fortress Monroe was completed this evening, and the following dispatch has just been received by the government:

FORTRESS MONROE, March 9, p.m.—The Ericsson iron-clad gunboat *Monitor* arrived here last night. Early this morning she was attacked by the three vessels, the *Merrimac, Jamestown* and *Yorktown*. After a five hours' contest they were driven off—the *Merrimac* in sinking condition.

Two lieutenants commanded in the battle of revolutionary craft: Catesby Roger Jones on the Confederate iron-clad; John Lorimer Worden on the Monitor. *Flag Officer Franklin Buchanan had been in command of the* Merrimac *during the Saturday duck-shoot among Federal ships. Wounded during that action, he turned the ship over to Jones. Worden had charge of the* Monitor *during most of the Sunday engagement but, when disabled, he handed command over to Lt. S. D. Greene.*

The Official Dispatches.

The Merrimac *Retires from the Fight in a Sinking Condition—Efficiency of the* Monitor—*The Frigate* Minnesota *Safe.*

March 9, p.m.—The following was to-night received by Maj. General McClellan from Major General Wool, dated—

FORTRESS MONROE, March 9th, 6 p.m.—Two hours after dispatch to the Secretary of War last evening the *Monitor* arrived. She immediately went to the assistance of the *Minnesota,* which was aground, and continued so until a few minutes since.

Early this morning the *Monitor* was attacked by the *Merrimac, Jamestown* and *Yorktown.* After a five hours' contest they were driven off and the *Merrimac* was towed by the *Jamestown, Yorktown* and several smaller boats towards Norfolk, no doubt for the purpose, if possible, to get her in the dry dock for repairs.

The *Minnesota* is afloat, and is being towed toward Fortress Monroe.

DISPATCH FROM ASSISTANT SECRETARY FOX.

The following dispatch was also received last night:

The *Monitor* (foreground) and the Confederate *Merrimac* blazing away at close range.

Library of Congress

FORTRESS MONROE, March 9—6:45 p.m.— *G. Welles, Secretary of the Navy:* The *Monitor* arrived at ten o'clock p.m. last night, and went immediately to the protection of the *Minnesota*, lying aground just below Newport News. At seven a.m. to-day the *Merrimac*, accompanied by two wooden steamers and several tugs, stood out towards the *Minnesota* and opened fire.

The *Monitor* met them at once and opened her fire, when all the enemy's vessels retired, excepting the *Merrimac*. These two iron-clad vessels fought, part of the time touching each other, from 8 a.m. to noon, when the *Merrimac* retired. Whether she is injured or not it is impossible to say.

Lieut. J. S. Worden, who commanded the *Monitor,* handled her with great skill, assisted by Chief Engineer Stimers. Lieut. Worden was injured by the cement from the pilot-house being driven into his eyes, but, I trust, not seriously. The *Minnesota* kept up a continuous fire, and is herself somewhat injured. She was removed considerably to-day, and will probably be off to-night.

The *Monitor* is uninjured, and ready at any moment to repel another attack.

G. V. (GUSTAVUS VASA) FOX,

Assistant Sec. Navy.

☞ *On another page the same day,* The Star *supplied further details as more information came in from Fort Monroe.* ☞

Particulars of the Naval Engagements of Yesterday and the Day Before!

At 2½ p.m. to-day we learned the following particulars of the naval engagements of yesterday and the day before. Viz.:

At 10 a.m. (Saturday) the enemy's vessels were discovered coming out from Norfolk and James River. Capt. (John) Marston, senior officer on the station, then ordered the *Minnesota*, Capt. (Gersholm J.) Van Brunt, to get under weigh.

Two tugs aided Captain Marston's ship, the *Roanoke* (whose steam power was injured). The *Merrimac* was then seen coming from Sewall's Point towards Newport News, accompanied by several rebel gunboats.

The *Roanoke* was with difficulty towed towards the enemy, but her broken shaft made her progress slow.

The *Merrimac* immediately attacked the *Congress* and *Cumberland,* particularly the latter.

The *Minnesota* grounded at about 7 miles from Fortress Monroe. The *Roanoke* pressed forward. On getting in sight of the *Cumberland,* it was evident she was sinking.

The *Merrimac* was then joined by the *Jamestown* and *Yorktown* iron-clad rebel steamers, from James River—both of which attacked the *Congress.*

The latter surrendered at 10 minutes past 4 p.m., in consequence of being aground, and therefore unable to bring her guns to bear on them.

The *Roanoke* about then got aground. As soon as the tugs pulled her off, they went to the *Minnesota's* aid, hoping to get her off also.

At 5 p.m. the frigate *St. Lawrence,* in tow of the *Cambridge,* passed up above the *Roanoke,* the *Minnesota* being then aground and engaged with the *Merrimac.*

The *St. Lawrence* also grounded, but the *Cambridge* got her afloat. The *St. L.* being unable to render the *Minnesota* assistance, returned down the harbor.

The enemy's batteries at Sewall's and Pig Point opened fire on all our vessels as they severally went up and returned—the *Minnesota, St. Lawrence, Roanoke, Cambridge* and *Mystic;* striking the *St. Lawrence* and the *Mystic.*

The crew of the victorious *Monitor* at leisure on its deck.

Captain Franklin Buchanan, commander of the *Merrimac.*

The range proved too great for our guns, but those of the battery went far over our ships.

At 7½ p.m. it was discovered that the *Congress* had been fired by the rebels, and she continued to burn until 1 a.m., when she blew up.

At 8 p.m. (a mistake—the actual time was 2 a.m.) (Sunday) the *Monitor* arrived, and Capt. Marston instantly ordered her to the assistance of the *Minnesota.*

Yesterday morning the *Merrimac* renewed the attack on the *Minnesota,* and was promptly taken in hand, to her surprise, by the *Monitor.*

The fight, which soon became a close quarters one, continued for several hours; the *Monitor* going around the *Merrimac* and hammering on her like a cooper around a cask.

Finally—near evening—the *Merrimac* abandoned the contest, running back towards and past Sewall's Point.

When last seen, the *Merrimac* was apparently in tow of her consorts, her crew being on her upper deck, as she disappeared.

It is not doubted by Lieut. Worden that she is seriously crippled.

The *Minnesota* had about 5 killed and 9 or 10 wounded—no officers among either.

The *Cumberland* had her Chaplain (probably) drowned, Master's Mate Harrington and 20 men killed, and about 130 drowned, including some 50 who were wounded.

Acting Commander Joe Smith, Jr. (Commodore Joe Smith's son), of the *Congress,* was killed. Paymaster Buchanan was her only officer not taken prisoner. None of the rest of her officers were killed or wounded. It is not known yet how many men she had killed or wounded.

Lieut. Morris (who is safe) fought the *Cumberland* until she sunk—which she did with her flag flying—a worthy son, indeed, of a glorious naval sire (Commodore Henry W. Morris).

The *Monitor* had not a man killed—Lieut. Worden, her commander, only being wounded on her. His eyes and face are badly but not dangerously powder burned.

Capt. Radford, the commander of the *Congress,* happened to be absent on a court martial, and thus escaped capture.

☞ *Two old-style ships had been lost, but the Federal Government had the means to stop the new menace. The* Star *could afford a complacent editorial comment.* ☞

The Cumberland and Congress.

The loss of two sailing war vessels is of no importance whatever to the service, except so far as the loss of officers, men and material of war on board

Lieutenant John Worden, commander of the *Monitor.*

John Ericsson, inventor of the *Monitor*.

them is concerned. For a contest with modern ships they were worse than useless, though as against anything but iron-clad vessels such as attacked them, they might have been efficient, employed as they were, simply to lay at anchor before the entrance of rivers.

☞ *Realizing the value of undersea craft in waging war,* The Star *devoted two full columns on Page 1 of its March 12 edition to a treatise on the* Monitor, *its features, its inventor, and the historic engagement. The story began:* ☞

The Great Naval Engagement.

The Ericsson Iron-Clad Steam Battery,
    The Monitor.
    The test of this steam battery with the iron-clad steamer *Merrimac,* and her success in crippling the rebel steamers *Merrimac, Jamestown* and *Yorktown,* give full warrant of her efficiency as claimed by her distinguished builder, Captain Ericsson. It will be

remembered that she was built under an agreement with the Government to accept her if her trial *"before the batteries of the enemy"* should prove her capable of all that was claimed by her inventor. Most opportunely has she arrived to check the arrogance of the rebels, and to drive back, in a disabled condition, their boasted master batteries, and, in the language of a dispatch from the Assistant Secretary of the Navy, Captain Fox, "she stood ready last night to meet anything that floats. . . ."

WASHINGTON HOMEFRONT, MARCH, 1862.

☞ *Innovations were being demonstrated right in Washington City, too.* ☞

THOSE IN THE SECRET, Viz.: Prominent army and naval officers, Senators, Congressmen and ourselves, witnessed a sight last night the most beautiful ever displayed to our admiring gaze.

Major (Albert James) Myer, founder and head of the Signal Department, whose services are so pre-eminently useful, even necessary, to the Army and Navy, last night submitted to a final test a night signal. The brilliant colors and changing hues formed a *tout ensemble* worthy of a Fourth of July celebration.

Of course, we are not in the secret as to the interpretation of the signals; none but Major Myer's officers are; but we are justified in saying that with these new signals, called asterisks, signaling can be done as unerringly by night as by the day flag system now in use, and which is so simple and effective in character—itself the invention of the major.

No army in the world is so thoroughly equipped as our own, and its signal department is superior to that of any other foreign service; and this is entirely owing to the earnest, one-idea, labious Major Myer, who has seized on every adjunct to render his department aid. To-day we may say it is perfect.

☞ *Oops! said* The Star *next day.* ☞

ERRATUM.—Our types yesterday made Major Myer's new signals to be "asterisks" instead of "asteroids"—as written.

WHILE MC CLELLAN DAWDLED IN THE EAST, THE WAR was blowing hot in the Ozark region of Arkansas and Missouri. Brig. Gen. Samuel Ryan Curtis, successor to Nathaniel Lyon, the slain Union hero of Wilson's Creek, had menaced Springfield, Mo., with about 11,000 troops, in February. Sterling Price, with his 8,000 Confederates, had backed off into northwestern Arkansas to await the arrival of help. This came out of the snow and mud in the form of 9,000 more troops from Maj. Gen. Earl Van Dorn, Ben McCulloch and Brig. Gen. Albert Pike. Pike, with Stand Watie—the only Indian to become a Confederate brigadier—headed an unmartial assortment of Cherokees, Choctaws, Chickasaws, Creeks and Seminoles. The opposing forces collided March 6 at Pea Ridge, near Elkhorn Tavern, Ark. When the smoke from the two-day struggle—more confused than most—had lifted, McCulloch was dead and the Confederates were retreating to the Arkansas River. Across Missouri to the East, Federal Maj. Gen. John Pope just one week later captured New Madrid. The town, combined with a nearby fortress called Island No. 10, kept Federal river traffic from passing southward on the Mississippi.

These, however, were only sideshows of the big campaigns that President Lincoln hoped were developing. The President was trying hard to get something military off the ground in the East at least. His most vexing problem in that respect was the Union's fair-haired boy general. General-in-Chief of the Army McClellan simply did not seem to want to get moving, although the army he now held poised around Washington was massive, well-equipped and well-trained. Presidential patience wore thin—so thin that on March 11 McClellan was stripped of his authority as General-in-Chief and designated as head of the Potomac Department only. That way, it was hoped, the general would feel sufficiently unencumbered to launch at least one offensive.

The Richmond Government was certain the Federals would be coming its way any day now. To be ready, President Davis proclaimed martial law in the counties below the Confederate capitol fronting Chesapeake Bay and the lower James River where invasion could be expected. The area around Norfolk was another likely invasion beachhead. Fort Monroe and Hampton Roads, opposite Norfolk on the north side of the James River estuary, was the obvious base for all Union operations southeast of Richmond.

The all-important question, where, was still unresolved by the Davis cabinet when the leading units of McClellan's 112,000 troops left Alexandria March 17 and steamed down the Potomac River.

Robert E. Lee, now serving as military advisor to President Davis, thought he knew where the blow would come. It was to be the first of many correct diagnoses Lee would make of McClellan's intentions.

McCLELLAN LAYS SIEGE TO YORKTOWN

(Monday, April 7, 1862)

OUR ARMY NEAR YORKTOWN.
Ship Point and Other Positions in Our Possession.
THE CASUALTIES THUS FAR.

The Fortress Monroe boat to Baltimore brings information from the neighborhood of Yorktown up to Saturday afternoon. Ship Point had been taken by our troops, and other places on the route formerly occupied by the rebels.

Some skirmishing and cannonading had taken place between the outposts of the enemy and our forces, in which the following casualties were said to have occurred:

Killed—Edward Lewis and Charles L. Lord, of 3d Massachusetts battery, and John Reynolds, of 4th Rhode Island battery.

Wounded—Timothy Donohue, in hand; Freeman Karring, leg; and Chas. Tucker, contusion of chest —all of 3d Mass. battery. Sergeant Jos. Wade, company C, in arm; Cyrus Wilcox, company C, pieces of shell in leg; and C. W. Peck, company F, in leg—all of sharpshooters.

Our men are in good spirits and ready for any contest.

(Tuesday, April 8, 1862)

VERY LATEST FROM GEN. McCLELLAN'S ARMY!

Despatches from Fortress Monroe up to 5 p.m. yesterday embrace the latest intelligence received there relative to the progress of Gen. McClellan's army upon the peninsula lying between the James and York rivers.

Elsewhere this afternoon we publish full and interesting particulars in that connection up to the close of the day before yesterday.

At five p.m. yesterday it was known at Fortress Monroe that throughout the day General McClellan had been engaged at long range with the Yorktown fortifications, though the engagement was not a brisk one, the firing on both sides being occasional. No casualties to speak of on our side were known at Fortress Monroe to have occurred up to the hour (5 p.m. yesterday) when this information left there.

It is evident that Gen. McClellan is proceeding as methodically and surely with his work in hand on the Peninsula, as Commodore Foote and General Pope proceeded with theirs, at Island No. 10.

We doubt not, however, he will make much shorter work with his, as Yorktown can hardly hold out forty-eight hours longer.

Capture of a rebel lunette near Yorktown.

Library of Congress

Colonel Hiram Berden, who commanded Federal sharpshooters during the Peninsula Campaign.

So this was McClellan's big operation against Richmond. Despite a numerical advantage of around two-to-one, "Little Mac" had decided to lay old-fashioned siege to old Yorktown. While the Federal commander was fiddling with his overcautious plans, the Confederates, on Lee's advice, were calling in reinforcements from all over Virginia and constructing fortifications closer to Richmond. Even so, when the Southern army was all present and accounted for on the peninsula, it numbered no more than 60,000. This figure, through faulty intelligence work, would be magnified many times by McClellan during the campaign. For details on the start of the "drive" The Star had to rely on its newspaper clipping service and a Philadelphia competitor.

(Tuesday, April 8, 1862)
The Fight at Yorktown.

A forward Movement—Incidents along the Route—Shelling Entrenchments.

(Sanctioned by Major General John E. Wool, Commanding Department of Virginia.)

The correspondent of the Philadelphia *Inquirer* writes:

FORTRESS MONROE, April 6.—Friday, the 4th inst., was the day fixed for the movement on to Yorktown. Gen. McClellan and staff arrived at Fortress Monroe on Wednesday on board the steamer *Commodore.* The troops were full of enthusiasm and longed for an advance movement. They, the soldiers, have great confidence in Gen. McClellan.

On Friday morning, about daylight, the grand army struck tents, and commenced the march "onward to Richmond." Gen. (Samuel Peter) Heintzelman's *corps de armee* moved up through Great

Bethel—the direct route to Yorktown. After leaving the camp, some miles beyond Hampton, the advance struck across New Market bridge, along a most beautiful and romantic road.

As we stood at New Market bridge we saw a full brigade of Philadelphia troops pass, viz.: 3d Pennsylvania Cavalry, Colonel (William Woods) Averell (formerly Young's Kentucky Cavalry); Colonel Owens' (Joshua Thomas Owen) 60th Pennsylvania; (DeWitt Clinton) Baxter's Fire Zouaves, and the celebrated California regiment.

A company of (Col. Hiram) Berdan's Sharpshooters took the advance, with the 4th Michigan and the 14th N. York, and the 3d Pa. Cavalry in the extreme advance.

The first place of note along the road was "Rosedown," a beautiful and unique dwelling. We saw the proprietor, Mr. W. Russell, standing at the gate, his slaves carrying water for the wearied soldiers. Mr.

A captured rebel battery at Yorktown.

A line of Federal mortars at Yorktown.

R., as usual among all we came to, expressed Union sentiments, and complained that the rebels had burned down all his fences, and disturbed him generally.

About one-half mile beyond this is a place called Halfway House. This is about twelve miles from Yorktown. This is a hard-looking corner—dilapidated old buildings and negro quarters, as usual, with the largest part of the house on the outside in the shape of chimneys.

After leaving this delectable place, we heard the booming of a gun. The troops shouted—the horses pricked up their ears—all were anxious to push on at a double-quick. The officers checked them. York river could be distinctly perceived some distance on the right.

It was now half-past one o'clock. The men were wearied, yet anxious to proceed. The discharge of heavy riddled pieces became numerous. The enemy seemed to respond briskly with a very heavy piece, as the sound of the discharge seemed sullen and heavy.

We soon perceived Allen's 5th Massachusetts Battery banging away at a very formidable earthwork. A short time previous to this, the 3d Pennsylvania Cavalry drove in the Rebel pickets. Griffin's Battery was also unlimbered in range. The 14th New York, companies B and A of Berdan's Sharpshooters, were advancing towards the batteries. There being no further response from the enemy, after firing some sixteen shells, the column advanced along a winding road made by the Rebels around Howard's Mills. After getting to the top of the hill, batteries could be seen all around. It was a very formidable stronghold. The enemy retreated. Major Phillips had command of the Rebel cavalry. He left everything behind—meat on the fire cooking. They were somewhat surprised at the rapid advance of the Union forces.

The 2d and 8th Mississippi occupied the above fortifications, and called the place Camp Misery.

General Heintzelman and General (Fitz John) Porter arriving, made a house in the center of these fortifications the headquarters of this corps.

The Union army bivouacked in the rebel camp "Misery" preparatory to an early start.

The March to Yorktown.

The army, under the immediate command of General McClellan, left camp at daylight, the advance being as far as Cockeysville. Soon after starting, the heavens became black with large, heavy clouds, giving evidence that we were to march through a heavy shower of rain. Very soon it began to rain, flooding the roads—especially those through the woods—so as to be almost impassable. The infantry pushed on, overcoming all obstacles. The cavalry and artillery dashed on pell-mell through, all anxious to get ahead. General McClellan and staff were but a short distance behind the advance.

About 10 o'clock, on the morning of the 5th, the booming of the first gun was heard. It electrified the whole line. Overcoats, blankets, haversacks, &c., were thrown away by the anxious soldiers, each regiment vying with the other to be first in. The roads became terrible for locomotion the further we advanced; mud holes, ruts, sloughs, &c., seemed to go far towards making up the road.

The line of battle was formed about 10 o'clock, Berdan's Sharpshooters in the advance. As the various columns arrived on the ground, they at once began to take their respective positions. Gen. Porter's Division had the center, Gen. (John) Sedgwick the extreme right, Gen. (Charles Smith) Hamilton and Gen. ("Baldy") Smith the extreme left.

A heavy pine forest intercepted the troops, except occasional clearings, which gave a distinct view of the enemy's entrenchments. These entrenchments seemed to be of the first-class style, and mounted with heavy guns, supposed to have come from the Norfolk Navy Yard.

Soon after the firing commenced, the enemy recognized Gen. Porter and staff, and at once opened upon him with shell, one of which burst within twenty feet of the General.

The fight was carried on almost entirely with artillery, with the exception of Berdan's Sharpshooters. Weeden's Battery opened first, followed by Martin's on the left. Soon Griffin's Third Rhode Island and Fifth Massachusetts were in position, and the battle commenced in earnest. The discharges were rapid on the Union side, answered, at intervals, by the enemy.

The first man struck was J. Reynolds, of the Rhode Island Battery. Poor fellow, he was struck with a piece of shell. Two of Col. Sam Black's men were next hit by a round shot—a thirty-two (pounder)—tearing the knapsack off one man. One was wounded slightly; while the other was mortally wounded.

The heaviest firing commenced at half-past twelve; Morell's brigade, on the left, advanced within three-quarters of a mile of the entrenched enemy.

The sharpshooters, with their telescopic rifles, kept the enemy away from their guns. They crept within half a mile of the rebels. For one hour they did not reply, our sharpshooters popping them off as soon as they attempted to load.

At one o'clock Capt. Martin's battery had two men killed, five wounded, and three horses dead. The two men killed were named Lewis and Lord.

Three of Berdan's Sharpshooters were at this time wounded, and one killed—a man from New Hampshire. He was shot through the forehead by a musket ball. Lieut. Colonel Ripley killed the man who shot him, thus avenging his death. Mr. Way, of company C (Berdan's) was shot in the arm, a bad flesh wound; Corporal Pech, shot in the leg; Mr. Wilcox, of company C, bruised by a shell.

About seven o'clock Allen's 5th Massachusetts relieved the 4th Rhode Island, the Rebels all day, when opportunity offering, trying to shell out the sharpshooters, without avail. Griffin's Battery received no loss, although batteries at their side lost several.

During the day the Rebels fired a small piece of ordnance, of one-inch bore, rifled, at the Berdans.

After Griffin's battery was brought into action it silenced three guns of the Rebels.

The artillerists acted nobly during the whole engagement. They took their position, and maintained it until ordered to move.

D. H. Phelps, of company H, Berdan's Sharpshooters, was brought in about dusk, wounded in the shoulder by a piece of shell.

Butterfield's and Martindale's brigades acted nobly during the day—both reclining on their arms, within range of the enemy's guns throughout the day.

Heavy firing closed with the day; but during the night the pickets occasionally could be heard banging away, far in advance.

Prof. Lowe at the close of the day, sent his balloon up, for the purpose of a reconnaissance.

A Federal artillery park at Yorktown harbor.

The Day After the Battle.

SUNDAY MORNING, 8 o'clock.—There is no heavy firing, but an occasional shot by the pickets; apparently no response by the enemy. The report is they are changing the location of their guns, and have two gun-boats on the York river.

If it were not for the picket firing, no one would imagine that a battle was raging. The morning is beautiful and clear, and the birds are warbling forth their spring notes. The men stand ready for the action. As yet nothing important has been done apparently.

Lieut. Libby, of the 4th Maine, was shot in the arm. He had been out for some stragglers, when he was attacked by two men.

Sunday morning, 9 o'clock.—The enemy are commencing to evacuate their batteries on the right.

A group of British officers observing the Federal campaign on the Peninsula.

General McClellan and his wife.

🔫 *Yorktown alone would occupy McClellan's attention for nearly a month before his immense army began grinding up the Peninsula closer to Richmond. The general's methods in the field would underscore Lincoln's earlier comment in a moment of anguished frustration: "He has got the slows!"* 🔫

WASHINGTON HOMEFRONT, APRIL, 1862.

🔫 *The* Star, *in an outburst of patriotic indignation, was engaged in a hassle with a clergyman as the month opened.* 🔫

THE NON-PRAYING CLERGY.—Below will be found a communication from Rev. Morsell (pastor, Washington's Christ Church), defining his position and giving a variety of reasons for omitting the prayer of thanksgiving for the success of Union arms.

The communication is courteous in tone and in keeping with the clerical cloth up to the concluding paragraph, which betrays a spice of "original sin." Our reverend correspondent advises us to "Study to be quiet and to mind our own business." My dear sir, we have had just such advice tendered us for years by all sorts of people who find publicity as to their doings unpleasant, from the big contractor, engaged in the "shoddy" business, down to 3-cent policy dealers, and the Dick Swivelers whose chronic "mistakes of a night" bring them up at the watch-house for safe keeping.

But seriously, what sort of wares would newspaper folks turn out if they acted on the precept of our correspondent? Would he, for instance, care to read a paper conducted on the "quiet" "mind your own business" plan? We dare say not.

The labored excuses for the omission of the prayer will strike the reader as altogether inconclusive, we think:

Mr. Ed. Star: I regret very much the necessity of a reply to (an) article in your paper.

A communication from a correspondent signed "East End," and your editorial comments, have rendered this communication necessary. It is correct in the denial of the statement "that I did read the prayer of thanksgiving for recent victories, and deliverance from the terrors of siege and blockade."

In reply to your editorial comments, as I presume them to be, I state that I am no secessionist, in feeling or theory. I have never held it as a right, but on the contrary, I have always thought the whole theory to be a grievous wrong, and I think that its history is its best comment as to its nature. I most distinctly avow that it is no part of my creed. I am not disloyal. Loyalty is with me a principle which does not depend on the rise and fall of parties, the coming in or going out of administrations. It is the acknowledgement of a supreme power according to our Constitution, resting in the executive, legislative and judiciary departments. As supreme, it extends over individuals, and no "State allegiance" can exempt the citizen from the obligation of obedience.

You have not given my reasons for the omission of this prayer. In justice to myself and congregation I will state these reasons:

First. It was addressed to a portion and not the whole of the clergy of the diocese. It cannot be affirmed that the reasons for thanksgiving for victory did not apply as fully to other portions, as it did to us. So far as this thanksgiving was necessary, if it was prudent to omit it elsewhere, it might be prudent to omit it here. I conceived that prudence did require its omission.

Secondly. I have endeavored to keep these agitating topics entirely out of our congregation, in sermons and prayers. There is enough of war—preaching and war—praying (preying) abroad in the land, to satisfy the most intense craving after such exciting topics of discussion.

A circumstance which occurred during the civil war in Scotland in the life of Archbishop Leighton may not inappropriately be introduced here. It was required of the ministers to preach to the "times." When the question was addressed to Robert Leighton he answered, "If all the brethren preach to the times may not one poor brother preach for eternity?" Let this, then, be my answer to all complainants. I would reserve my pulpit to preach and pray for eternity. I am a man of peace and an advocate of peace, and, thank God, its humble messenger. When this war is over we have a prayer of thanksgiving "for restoring public peace at home" exactly applicable to the condition of things in our country, and I would that I could use it to-morrow. This prayer has been selected by the united wisdom of our ecclesiastical authorities as appropriate for such occasions, and I presume that there is not a clergyman in the diocese who would not rejoice to have an opportunity of using it.

This explains my reasons for the omission of the prayer of thanksgiving for victories. It is my independent judgment, and I do not know whether it expresses the opinions of my congregation or not. They are in no wise responsible for its omission, and, consequently, not to be censured. Loyalty to the church is the best guarantee of loyalty to the State, and the past history of our church has been invariable in its testimony against all intermeddling with political subjects on the part of its ministers. She would rather allay than excite the passions of men, and as a minister at her altars, I have most faithfully discharged my duties as a clergyman and citizen by its omission. "Study to be quiet, and to mind your own business," is a precept worthy of a conspicuous place in your editorial sanctum.

Yours, respectfully, &c., J. Morsell.

WITH THE FALL OF FORTS HENRY AND DONELSON IN the center of his western defense line, Albert Sidney Johnston pulled his Confederates southward out of Kentucky and Tennessee. He drew a new defense line along the East-West railroad that ran from Memphis, on the Mississippi River, across northern Mississippi and Alabama. This railroad formed a junction at Corinth, Miss., with a North-South rail line that extended from Mobile, Ala., to Columbus, Ky. Corinth was a vital strategic point to possess. When he learned the Federals were massing in upper Tennessee to campaign for the town, Johnston spent most of March calling in Confederates from all over the area to defend it. In this concentration, the commanding general brought his immediate command back from Nashville. Maj. Gen. Braxton Bragg came up with troops from the Gulf Coast. Brig. Gen. Daniel Ruggles moved his force in from Louisiana. And the fighting bishop, Leonidas Polk, was ordered back from Columbus, leaving only enough strength to block the Mississippi at Fort Pillow, Tenn., and New Madrid and Island No. 10 in the southeastern corner of Missouri. Federal Maj. Gen. John Pope was menacing those positions on the Confederate-controlled river. Among the corps commanders bracing for the next fight were Brig. Gen. John Cabell Breckinridge, Vice President in the Buchanan Administration, and Presidential candidate of Southern Democrats in the election of 1860. Maj. Gen. P. G. T. Beauregard was now in the West as second-in-command to Albert Sidney Johnston, a post he formerly held in the East under Joseph Eggleston Johnston. (The two Johnstons were unrelated. Beauregard may have wished he had never heard of either.)

The Federal plan of attack on Corinth called first for establishing a base on the Tennessee River around Savannah, Crump's Landing and Pittsburg Landing, all within about 15 miles of each other, near the southern border of Tennessee. On the eve of the movement, Grant had been relieved as head of the main force, despite his victories at Henry and Donelson. He had incurred the petty displeasure of Halleck, the Western Department chief, who handed Grant's command to C. F. Smith. However, when Smith suffered a foot infection which was to kill him, Grant was reinstated. His force consisted of divisions under McClernand, Sherman, Lew Wallace, William Harvey Lamb Wallace, Stephen Augustus Hurlbut and Benjamin Mayberry Prentiss. At the same time, Buell with his separate command was ordered forward from Nashville, which he had occupied when Johnston vacated, to join Grant's army.

Within hours of the time McClellan began his long crawl up the Virginia peninsula toward Richmond, the contenders near Corinth were preparing for battle—the Federals with around 60,000 effectives, the Confederates with about 40,000.

The Confederates would strike first, on April 6, near a little country church four miles inshore from Pittsburg Landing. The church was called Shiloh.

REBEL GENERAL DIES IN SHILOH CARNAGE

(Wednesday, April 9, 1862)

Latest from Tennessee.
BATTLE AT PITTSBURG.

Attack of the Rebels on our Troops at Pittsburg Landing—Retreat of the Rebels with Considerable Loss—The Opposing Armies Approaching Each Other.

CHICAGO, April 7.—A special dispatch to the Chicago *Times* says that on Friday evening, the 4th inst., our forces at Pittsburg Landing, on the Tennessee river, were attacked by two rebel regiments, with two pieces of artillery and a large force of cavalry. Our forces formed in line of Battle, but the enemy only fired one round and then commenced retreating. We returned the fire and killed a large number. They only killed one of our men.

It is supposed the rebels were making a reconnaissance, but finding a larger number than they expected, they beat a hasty retreat. Ten prisoners were taken.

Further from Pittsburg Landing.

(SECOND DISPATCH)

Hon. E. M. Stanton, Secretary of War: The enemy attacked our works at Pittsburg, Tennessee, yesterday, but was repulsed with a heavy loss. No details are given.

H. W. Halleck, Maj. Gen.

The following message was received by the Secretary of War last evening:

On the 6th inst. the rebels, in overwhelming numbers, attacked our forces at Pittsburg Landing, Tennessee. The battle lasted from morning until late in the afternoon, and resulted in the complete defeat of the rebels, with heavy loss on both sides. Gen. Grant is following up the enemy. Gen. Buel has arrived in Tennessee. Two divisions of his army were in the battle.

Further from Southern Tennessee—A Great Battle and a Great Victory.

CHICAGO, April 8.—A dispatch from one of Gen. Grant's staff says: "We have fought and won the hardest battle ever fought on this continent."

This dispatch is dated Pittsburg Landing, April 6.

🔫 *The Union claims to victory were premature. On that Sunday, April 6, when the battle commenced, Grant's forces were spread out in camping formations with virtually no protective works. As a result the Confederate attack, by Hardee and Bragg, took*

The battle of Shiloh; a rebel waves a signal flag from the rooftop.

United States Army

General U. S. Grant

the Federals by surprise. Sherman's and Prentiss' hastily organized line took the brunt of the assault. The Union line quickly disintegrated and—except for pockets of fierce resistance like that formed by Prentiss' Division—reeled back. Nightfall, exhaustion and serious losses led the Confederates to suspend action after driving forward three miles, almost to Pittsburg Landing itself. The whole Union army was now in a potential trap formed by two creeks and the Tennessee River. Grant, who had been at Savannah at the outset, hurried to the field. He saw the desperate situation and ordered in reinforcements, including the first contingent of Buell's tardy army, which had been plodding over rain-sogged roads from Nashville. During the night, two Union gunboats, anchored safely in the river, tormented the depleted Confederates. ⚓

(Wednesday, April 9, 1862)

Thrilling Details of the Great Battle.

THE ENEMY'S LOSS ESTIMATED FROM THIRTY-FIVE TO FORTY THOUSAND!

UNION LOSS FROM EIGHTEEN TO TWENTY THOUSAND!

Terrible Fight During Sunday and Monday.

Desperate Attempt of the Enemy to Drive the Union Forces into the River.

(Special Telegram to the *Star*)
NEW YORK, April 9, 1862.—*Editor Star:* The New York *Herald* of this morning has an extra con-

taining the following particulars of the great battle at Pittsburg Landing:

PITTSBURG (via Fort Henry), April 9, 3:20 a.m.—One of the bloodiest battles of modern times has just closed, resulting in the complete rout of the enemy, who attacked us Sunday a.m.

The battle lasted until Monday at 4:35, when the enemy commenced their retreat, and are still flying towards Corinth. They are pursued by a large force of our cavalry.

The slaughter on both sides is immense.

The Union loss in killed, wounded, and missing is from 18,000 to 20,000. That of the enemy is estimated at from 35,000 to 40,000.

I give you the best account from observation, having passed through the storm of action for the two days it raged.

The fight was brought on by a body of three hundred of the Twenty-Fifth Missouri, the right of Gen. Prentiss, attacking the advance guard of the rebels, supposed to be pickets of the enemy, in front of the camp.

The Rebels immediately advanced on Gen. Prentiss.

Our forces soon formed into line. Hurbert's (Hurlbut's) division was thrown forward to support the center, when a desperate conflict ensued.

At 5 p.m. the Rebels forced our left wing back so as to occupy full two-thirds of our camp, and were fighting their way forward with desperate courage in their efforts to drive us into the river, and at the same time heavily engaged our right.

Gen. Grant and staff, who had been recklessly riding along our lines the entire day amid a storm of bullets, now rode from right to left, inciting our men to stand firm until reinforcements could cross the river.

The gunboats *Lexington* and *Tyler,* which lay a short distance off, kept raining shell on the rebel forces. Thus the contest raged till night.

During the night Major General (Lew) Wallace arrived and took position on the right; and Gen. Buell's forces from the opposite side and Savannah, now being conveyed to the battle ground, the entire right of Gen. Nelson's division was ordered to form on the right (left); and the forces under Gen. Crittenden were ordered to his support early in the morning.

Second Day's Battle.

The battle of the second day raged with various successes and repulses until 5 p.m., when the whole rebel army was in full retreat to Corinth, with our cavalry in hot pursuit. Gen. Buell followed the retreating rebels, driving them in splendid style.

We lost a number of our forces prisoners yesterday, among them General Prentiss, who was reported as being wounded.

Among the killed on the rebel side was their chief General, Albert Sidney Johnston.

It is further reported that General Beauregard had his arm shot off.

Captain Carson was killed by a cannon ball.

The above is a synopsis of a much longer dispatch in the *Herald* this morning, from its special correspondent, who was himself in the battle throughout its duration.

☞ *Johnston, who many had predicted would be the greatest of Southern generals, was mortally wounded by a shot in the leg in mid-afternoon of the first day. His command devolved on Beauregard, who was not hurt—despite what the news accounts said. Prentiss and his men had held on gallantly, although surrounded by the attackers. The remains of the division surrendered after hours of defending the position which would afterward be known as the "Hornet's Nest." W. H. L. Wallace was killed near here.*

With the fresh divisions of Brig. Gens. Lew Wallace, William Nelson and Thomas Leonidas Crittenden on the field, Grant ordered a counter-attack early Monday morning. The assault regained most of the lost ground after fighting as bloodily desperate as that of Sunday. Beauregard finally ordered a general Confederate withdrawal to Corinth when he learned that afternoon that an expected 20,000 reinforcements under Maj. Gen. Earl Van Dorn could not cross the Mississippi from Arkansas in time to help at Shiloh.

The Federals gave pursuit on Tuesday, but they were halted six miles from the battlefield by a fierce attack by Bedford Forrest's cavalry. ☞

(Thursday, April 10, 1862)
LATE NEWS BY TELEGRAPH.
Further Particulars.
Death of Gen.
A. Sydney Johnston Confirmed.

The following was received by the Secretary of War last evening:

"Gen. A. Sydney Johnston's body was left on the battlefield, and is in our possession, as well as the bodies of a large number of other prominent rebels."

Gen. Johnston was held by many to be the ablest officer in the whole rebel service, and his loss, with

the wounding of Beauregard (should that prove true) will leave them without any officer in whom the army have any confidence in the field. It has been erroneously stated that Gen. Johnston had "just entered upon his duties as commander-in-chief of the whole rebel forces under the appointment of Jeff. Davis." This is a mistake. Gen. Lee is the officer thus designated by Jeff. Davis, but the selection has not met with much favor in Dixie, Lee being held to be a "slow coach."

☞ *Both sides claimed victory at Shiloh. In proportion to the size of the armies, losses were about even: 13,000 Federal, nearly 11,000 Confederate. The fact remains that the Confederates failed, as they intended and nearly succeeded, to destroy the Union forces. They continued, on the contrary, to drop deeper south, leaving that much more of the Mississippi vulnerable to Federal seizure.*

Lincoln, at this time, was developing an ever firmer faith in his Western field commander, Grant. Despite the general's detractors, who blamed the near-defeat at Shiloh on his deficiencies, the President observed: "I can't spare this man; he fights." ☞

WASHINGTON HOMEFRONT, APRIL, 1862.

☞ *The editorial writers were becoming a bit peevish over the delays experienced in getting news from the battlefront. However, they seemed understanding about the whole situation.* ☞

The gunboats *Tyler* and *Lexington* supporting the Federal troops.

Library of Congress

General Albert S. Johnson

EDITORIAL.
(Friday, April 11, 1862)
The Great Battle.

Persons around us are wondering why the Government here has not, up to this time, received more official information concerning the battle of Pittsburg Landing.

The reason is plain enough. Such reports would only come here through Gen. Halleck, to whom they would be made by Generals Grant and Buell. Gen. Halleck being himself on the way from St. Louis to Pittsburg Landing, cannot be easily reached by telegraph, or easily find an opportunity to telegraph to Washington from some point on his line of travel.

Nevertheless, the expected and so eagerly desired dispatches from him may arrive here at any moment. We trust they may do so before the *Star* goes to press to-day.

☞ *Then there was the tawdry side of life in Washington.* ☜

THE SHOOTING OF BLADEN.—*Sunday Work.*—Alfred Turner, who is charged with shooting Louis Bladen on the 13th instant, and whose death we noticed yesterday, had a hearing before Justices Giberson and Clayton yesterday afternoon —John L. Smith, esq., appearing for the prosecution, and J. E. Norris, esq., for the accused. Quite a number of witnesses were examined, from whose evidence the facts may be stated as follows: On Sunday, the 13th instant, Turner and others started to go a fishing, and Bladen, who had his gun along with him, went in company; and after spending some time fishing and shooting robins, they all started towards Turner's house. Bladen, on the way, put caps on the gun several times, and snapped it at the others. When they reached Turner's the gun was loaded and fired off. McDonald and Turner went into dinner together, leaving Bladen outside. Bladen afterwards came in and got his dinner, and went out and sat down by a tree. While Bladen was sitting against the tree, Turner came to the door and picked up the gun and placed a cap on it, which did not go off. He put the same cap on a second time, and holding it towards Bladen at a charge, snapped it, when it went off, and the load took effect in Bladen's face. Turner, seeing that he had shot Bladen, exclaimed, "My God, mother, I've shot Louis; I did not know it was loaded!" The mother came out, and Alfred held Bladen while his mother wiped the blood from his face. One of the witnesses testified that a few minutes previous to the affray he saw Bladen with powder in his hand, as if in the act of loading the gun; and another who was with Turner testified that he (T.) did not load it. The boys were all on good terms, although one witness testified that about last Christmas he heard Turner say that if Bladen got in his way he would shoot him.

After hearing the evidence the justices decided to hold Turner to bail in the sum of $300 to answer a charge of assault and battery, resulting in death.

The Fourteenth Wisconsin Regiment charges the rebel position during the second day.

THE MISSISSIPPI RIVER, NORTH AMERICA'S GREAT CHANnel of inland commerce, had been denied to Northern access since hostilities began. Aware of the Mississippi's economic and military significance to both the North and itself, the Confederacy choked it off from a point just below the mouth of the Ohio River southward 1,000 river miles to New Orleans and the delta on the Gulf of Mexico. Among many strong points created along the shores were three that seemed impregnable: Island No. 10, across from southeastern Missouri; Vicksburg, Miss., farther downstream, and the forts guarding the Mississippi's mouth. Union strategy called for reducing all the strong points, and the project had been launched at the upper end of the bottleneck. In March and early April, Flag Officer Foote (of Henry-Donelson note) separately and in collaboration with John Pope's army, captured first New Madrid, then Island No. 10, just upstream from that Missouri town. Six thousand Confederates and much booty were taken with the bastion.

In the interval immediately following the island's fall, Federal land forces—aside from the sluggish performance on the Virginia Peninsula—were engaged in several spectacular activities. On April 11, Brig. Gen. Ormsby McKnight Mitchel swooped into Alabama, seizing Huntsville and a 100-mile stretch of the Memphis and Charleston Railroad. Next day, another Mitchel-inspired operation threw a scare into upper Georgia. Twenty-one disguised Union soldiers, headed by a Kentucky spy, James J. Andrews, made off with a Confederate locomotive, "The General," at Big Shanty. However, their aim of destroying bridges and rails between Atlanta and Chattanooga didn't materialize. Pursued in another engine by equally intrepid Confederates, the raiders were captured. Eight, including Andrews, were tried and executed. Six of the survivors would ultimately receive the first Congressional Medals of Honor.

The Confederate Government had been jumpy enough before that episode. Martial law had been proclaimed by President Davis a short while before. Looking to their limited manpower, the Confederates had passed their first draft law for men between the ages of 18 and 35.

At sea that month, the Federal navy was recapturing coastal forts long since occupied by Southern forces. Fort Pulaski on the Savannah, Ga. harbor approaches, was one of these. More immediately significant was the naval bombardment commenced April 18 on Forts Jackson and St. Philip, for these were the Confederate strongholds astride the mouth of the Mississippi, 25 miles below New Orleans. The blasts heralded the second portion of the campaign to snatch the great river from the South. What Foote and Pope had started on the upper reaches was now being inaugurated on the lower by Flag Officer David

Glasgow Farragut and Comdr. David Dixon Porter, in conjunction with that seasoned army amphibian, Ben Butler.

The task of Porter's mortar-carrying boats was to shell the two forts to a pulp while Butler's force moved on them from the opposite side. Farragut would take his vulnerable wooden ships up to New Orleans as soon as the forts were crippled. The mortars couldn't do all that was expected of them. But Farragut steamed ahead anyway—past enemy land guns, gunboats and a variety of water obstacles, including barges that had been purposely set afire to trap him.

The fleet arrived off New Orleans April 25. Owing to the absence of all but sea communications with the expedition, the people back home didn't know what was going on until travelers brought back copies of Southern newspapers.

NEW ORLEANS SURRENDERS
TO FARRAGUT

(Monday, April 28, 1862)

Later from Old Point.
The Fleet Pass the Mississippi Forts.
NEW ORLEANS SURRENDERED.

BALTIMORE, April 28, (from Fortress Monroe, April 27.)—A boat containing four black men and a white man arrived this morning from Portsmouth.

They report that the *Merrimac* will come out soon.

A despatch in yesterday's Richmond papers, received by flag of truce, dated Mobile, Friday, says that the Union gunboats passed Fort Jackson and Phillip at 4 a.m. on Tuesday, and at 1 p.m. were before New Orleans.

A rumor was current in Norfolk last night that the city (New Orleans) had surrendered. But few troops were at Norfolk or in that vicinity.

It was rumored there that Tatnall (Capt. Josiah Tattnall) had been removed from command of the *Merrimac.*

Important from the South.
Great Excitement at Norfolk in Expectation of an Attack by Burnside.
THE STEAMER MERRIMAC.

PHILADELPHIA, April 28.—The N. York *Times* of to-day has the following special despatch:
FORTRESS MONROE, April 27.—It is stated by contrabands that the most intense excitement exists around Norfolk, and there is great fear of an attack by Burnside. Nearly all the troops have gone to the South Mills, to repel any advance he might make.

The contrabands state that the new prow of the Merrimac is twelve feet long, of wrought iron, and steel pointed.

Many citizens are leaving Norfolk.

The fall of New Orleans is conceded by every one.

Fugitive slaves brought rumors and newspapers from the South—hardly the most authoritative of news sources. But what other was there?

The News Confirmed
Through Another Source.

HEADQUARTERS DEPARTMENT RAPPA-HANNOCK, April 27.—*Hon. E. M. Stanton, Secretary of War:* I have just returned from the camp opposite Fredericksburg. I was told that the Richmond *Examiner* of the 26th (yesterday) had been received in town announcing as follows:

"New Orleans is taken. Great destruction of property and cotton and steamboats. Steamboats enough were saved to take away the ammunition. There is great consternation among the inhabitants."

Irwin McDowell, Major General.

Even major-generals were reading the Rebel press and passing the word along to the Yankee War Department in official military dispatches.

The Federal fleet passing the forts of New Orleans.

THE FALL OF NEW ORLEANS CONFIRMED.

The following dispatch from the Agents of the Associated Press at Fortress Monroe reached here last night:

FORTRESS MONROE, April 28.—A flag of truce to-day took dispatches and letters to the Federal prisoners at the South. No papers were received.

The telegraphic operators having left New Orleans, there is no further news from there. The operators attempted to return, but found the city occupied by the Federal forces.

There is no other news.

From General Wool.

The following has been received at the War Department:

FORTRESS MONROE, April 28.—*Hon. E. M. Stanton, Secretary of War:* The news of the occupation of New Orleans by our forces is confirmed to-day. No further news.

John E. Wool, Major General.

🔫 *Since Gen. Wool did not bother to name the source of his "confirmation," one suspects he was still reading the Dixie papers. Editorially,* The Star *wondered the same day what had really happened on the lower Mississippi, and pumped reassurance into its own veins:* 🔫

NEW ORLEANS AGAIN.

Some of those around us are doubting the reliability of the news of the appearance of our Gulf fleet in the Mississippi opposite New Orleans, and the simultaneous abandonment of the city by the rebel military, that has come to us through Virginia newspapers. There need be no apprehension whatever relative to its truth. Its effect upon the Southwestern troops serving in Virginia is calculated to be too disastrous to their cause to admit the possibility of its publication in Secessia unless it were useless to try to conceal it from the public there.

That we are in full possession of New Orleans is therefore positively true. The United States having the entire command of the waters surrounding it can hold it at will with not more than five thousand troops, our navy there being worth a garrison of a hundred thousand men to that end. We have no space in which to explain in detail how and why the presence of a small naval force in the river and about the lake is likely to be so much more effective there than elsewhere, further than to say that for two hundred miles, it is approachable by a land force from up the country over a strip of land nowhere more than half a mile wide, as level as a parlor floor, and without any shelter of dense foliage. In the rear of this strip is a swamp utterly impassable for troops, of varying width and capable of being made a deep and wide lake any where and at any time by half an hour's labor with half a dozen shovels. No army could march down the coast strip mentioned above with our gunboats raking it; while without a naval force superior to ours in that quarter no army could menace the city from the rear—via Lake Pontchartrain and the shell road. Under these circumstances, to take it, is to assure its possession, we command "the situation" in Louisiana almost as thoroughly as at this moment in New York.

🔫 *The writer spoke with the authority of one who may have vacationed on the delta in a happier time. He succeeded in convincing himself of the soundness of his views, for on the following day* The Star's *headline screamed:* 🔫

LATEST FROM NEW ORLEANS.
The City Certainly Ours.

(Per Telegraph from Baltimore.)

BALTIMORE, April 30 (from Fortress Monroe, April 29).—The flag of truce from Norfolk to-day brought down the wife and family of Parson Brownlow, and also Mrs. Maynard, wife of Mr. Maynard, the member of Congress—the party consisting of four ladies, two gentlemen, and six children—all from Tennessee. They bring a report that all the Union families of Tennessee have been ordered, by proclamation, to leave within 36 hours. Eighteen hundred Union men left for Kentucky a week ago last Friday. Of a party of 400 attempting to leave, 100 had been killed.

There can be no doubt of the capture of New Orleans. The southern newspapers speak of it in a most dismal strain, and demand that the mystery of the surrender of the city shall be explained.

The *Day Book* (Norfolk) in an editorial says that the fall of New Orleans is by far the most serious reverse of the war. "It suggests (it declares) great future privations to all classes of society; but most to be lamented of all, it threatens army supplies."

The raising of meat and bread, instead of cotton and tobacco, is earnestly recommended by the disconsolate editor.

The Richmond *Dispatch* of yesterday says that when the enemy's (Union) fleet arrived opposite the city, Gen. (Mansfield) Lovell refused himself to surrender it, and fell back to Camp Moore, after destroying the cotton and stores. The iron-clad Mississippi was burnt to prevent her from falling into the hands of the enemy. Nothing was said about the Louisiana, but it is supposed she was scuttled. Rumor says she was sunk at the first fire.

Camp Moore is at Tangipature (Tangipahoa), 78 miles from New Orleans, on the railroad to Jackson, Miss.

The following are the latest dispatches in to-day's Virginia papers:

"MOBILE, April 27.—The Yankee Commodore Farragut promised the Mayor's Secretary, who visited the fleet by a flag of truce, to make a renewed demand for the surrender of the city, but had not done so up to this hour—5 o'clock. Our ship, the McRae, came up from the forts under a flag of truce, with forty of our wounded, who communicated with the Federal flag-ship, but the result is unknown. It is rumored that the Federals refused to permit her to return. The rumor that Fort Pike had been evacuated and blown up is unreliable.

In a conference held with one of the Federal officers, after the correspondence between Mayor Monroe and Commodore Farragut, the officer left, declaring he would shoot down the flag on the City

Admiral David G. Farragut, who commanded the New Orleans assault fleet.

Hall if not hauled down; and actually brought his ship within range, but has not fired thus far.

It is reported that French and English men-of-war are below, and have entered their protests against shelling the city.

It is believed the Yankee vessels are short both of provisions and ammunition.

The city (New Orleans) is remarkably orderly, but the excitement is immense, and the feeling of humiliation deep.

———◆———

"RICHMOND, April 28.—The following official dispatch was received this morning by Adjutant

The angry citizens of New Orleans opposed the landing of the surrender delegation from the Federal fleet.

General Mansfield Lovell, who commanded New Orleans.

General Cooper, from Gen. Lovell, dated Camp Moore, April 27:

"Forts Jackson and St. Philip are still in good condition and in our hands. The steamers *Louisiana* and *McRae* are safe. The enemy's fleet are at the city, but they have not forces to occupy it. The inhabitants are staunchly loyal.

—————◆—————

"MOBILE, April 28.—The forts on Lake Pontchartrain were all evacuated on the 25th. We have sustained considerable loss in supplies and dismantling, but not destroying, our guns at Fort Pike. All the buildings were burned, including the telegraph office, and the operator has gone to the limits of the city to open an office, if possible. All our gun-boats on the Lake have been burnt by our own people. The Mobile boats, *Whitman Brown* and several others, are running troops, stores, and ordnance to Monacheck; after which, we fear, they will be burnt. The Yankee fleet were at Ship Island, and are again returning to that station."

🗡 *Official word of the victory did not reach Washington for publication until May 8. New Orleans was defenseless, and Farragut received its surrender from civilian authorities. The Yankees were greeted* with open hostility by the residents. In the days to come, Ben Butler, as military governor, would learn how hostile. In seeking to stabilize living conditions, he would find his occupation force spat upon. In exasperation, he would order New Orleans ladies who affronted the flag and his troops to be treated as common street-walkers. This order would earn him the epithet, "Beast Butler," and sufficient disapproval even in the North to cause his removal later in the year.*

This was all aftermath. The important fact was that the Federals had now penetrated the Mississippi River defenses from both North and South. The squeeze from both directions was getting closer to Vicksburg. 🗡

WASHINGTON HOMEFRONT, APRIL, 1862.

🗡 *Something "new," something "different" in consumer products? The 19th Century American consumer was getting that pitch from the advertiser, much as his counterpart gets it today. The advertising, in this instance, didn't deal with anything as exotic as fluorides, vitamins or detergents. It concerned that simple staple, bread.* 🗡

AERATED BREAD.

REQUA & CO.,
96 LOUISIANA AVENUE

This bread is always uniform in quality, keeping moist for many days, never souring, and is much more healthful and nutritious than fermented bread.

It is warranted free from all deleterious ingredients, and is manufactured by the only true process, being raised without fermentation.

It is highly recommended by scientific men and physicians throughout the country, and by the medical faculty of London, as also by all the leading physicians of this city.

The PECULIAR FEATURES of this Bread are:—

1st. It is perfectly LIGHT without the aid of any noxious ingredient. Hence it never becomes *sour,* but remains always sweet, pure, palatable and healthy.

2d. It is perfectly CLEANLY—the flour being rebolted, and the dough kneaded by machinery and drawn through faucets into pans, so as not to come in contact with the hand.

THE SHENANDOAH VALLEY OF VIRGINIA, ONE OF THE world's most beautiful and productive areas, lies on a southwest-northeast axis between the barriers of the Blue Ridge Mountains on the east and the Alleghenies on the west. One hundred years ago, when the United States was at war with itself, the strategic importance of this river valley was rivalled by only one other—that of the Mississippi. Their value differed.

The Mississippi River, being navigable, served as an artery for commercial and military transport. The Shenandoah as a river was valueless in that respect. But the valley through which it wandered was immensely fertile. In the possession of the Confederacy, it could supply endless quantities of food and raw material for the cause. Possession, further, gave the Southern armies a sheltered runway extending directly into the vitals of the North. By this route—if the preset defensive policy of the Confederate Government would ever change—the eastern half of Pennsylvania could be taken, and with it such railroad, political and population centers as Harrisburg and Pennsylvania. Baltimore and Washington could be isolated, or even attacked directly, by crossing through the Blue Ridge passes near Manassas, Va., Hagerstown and Frederick, Md. Conversely, the direction of the Valley slanted away from the main Federal objective in the East—Richmond. The main Federal purpose in that area, therefore, was to block the Valley of Virginia as a road for Confederate conquest.

Thomas Jonathan Jackson, former professor at Virginia Military Institute in the Valley town of Lexington, realized at an early date the value of forthright action along the Shenandoah. "Stonewall"—as he had been known since his stand pat position around Bull Run—had a serious handicap, however: he commanded too few troops. Although he had been able to seize Romney in the lower Valley early in 1862, an advance by Federal Maj. Gen. Nathaniel Prentiss Banks forced Jackson to vacate both Romney and his headquarters town, Winchester, in March. By that time, Jackson had a new mission. He was to keep the Federals preoccupied in the Valley to prevent their joining McClellan's anticipated assault on Richmond. Mission in mind, he attacked Banks at Kernstown. But he underestimated the size of the enemy, and he was drubbed. Jackson retreated up the Valley, little knowing the consternation his Kernstown fight had caused in Washington. There, Lincoln and his advisors had concluded he was attacking from strength and had to be caught.

By May, McClellan was getting none of the help he demanded for his Peninsula campaign. McClellan's hosts never would be reinforced from this source. Jackson that month had about-faced in the upper Valley. He was once more marching his "foot cavalry" back down the roads along the Shenandoah toward Banks and whatever other Federals might be there.

STONEWALL JACKSON ROUTS FEDERALS

(Saturday, May 24, 1862)

FROM BANKS' COLUMN.

A Repulse at Front Royal.

This forenoon the War Department received the following dispatch:

STRASBURG, May 21, 1862.—*Hon. Edwin M. Stanton, Secretary of War:* Colonel Kenley's command of infantry and cavalry has been driven from Front Royal with considerable loss in killed, wounded and prisoners. The enemy's force is estimated at five or six thousand. It is reported as fallen back on Front Royal. It probably occupies that place this morning.

N. P. BANKS, Major General.

(NOTE.—The force of Col. Kenley consisted of a single regiment of infantry and a single squadron of Michigan cavalry, and numbered, in all, from 1,000 to 1,100 men. A subsequent dispatch from Strasburg brings intelligence that the rebels certainly occupy Front Royal to-day. Thus the direct railroad communication with the main body of Gen. Banks' force (via Manassas Junction) is temporarily cut off. The bridge at Front Royal will probably be burned again, before Gen. Banks can repossess the point, which we take it for granted he will do as soon as he can march to it. Front Royal, it will be remembered, is on the Manassas Gap Railroad, between Manassas Junction and Strasburg, and some forty-five miles from the Junction.—*Ed. Star.*)

☞ *Front Royal was a Federal rout. The 1,000 troops of Col. John Reese Kenley's 1st (Union) Maryland was attacked by the full force of Jackson's 16,000, which ironically included the 1st (Confederate) Maryland. Banks with 7,000 at nearby Strasburg retreated to Winchester where Jackson smashed into him on May 25.* ☞

(Monday, May 26, 1862)

LATE NEWS BY TELEGRAPH.

Important Official Dispatch from General Banks.

He Crosses the Potomac in Safety at Williamsport, with his entire force, trains and all.

WILLIAMSPORT (Md.) May 26.—*To Hon. E. M. Stanton, Secretary of War:* We believe that

The charge of the First Maryland Regiment at Harrisonburg.

our whole force, trains, and all, will cross in safety. The men are in fine spirits, and crossing in good order. The labor of last night was fearful. The enemy followed us last night on our march, but has not made his appearance this morning. The news of your movements South has unquestionably caused them to look for their safety. Your dispatch was read to the troops this morning, amid the heartiest cheers.

N. P. Banks, Maj. Gen. Com'dg.

Banks, having lost Winchester, was now on the "safe side" of the Potomac River. Farther up the Valley, Fremont was laboring over the Alleghenies from the west toward Strasburg. Brig. Gen. James Shields' division, detached from McDowell at Fredericksburg, was heading from the opposite direction for a junction with Fremont. The scheme, as devised in Washington, was to cut off Jackson before he could retreat back up the Valley. Meanwhile, "atrocity" reports floated into the Federal City.

(Tuesday, May 27, 1862)

Our Troops Fired upon by the Women of Winchester.

OUR SICK WOUNDED IN THEIR COUCH.

BALTIMORE, May 26.—Reports from Williamsport say that as our troops retreated through Winchester, the women fired upon them with pistols from the doors and windows, and that the sick left in the hospitals were most brutally treated and some of them wounded.

The Star, at this point, got in on the military masterminding act.

EDITORIAL.

(Thursday, May 29, 1862)

THE SITUATION.

Up to noon to-day there was no later news in Washington from either Union Army than that published this morning. A dispatch from the Upper Potomac reached here last night, saying that there were signs that Jackson's force, instead of retreating out of the Valley at double-quick time, still lingered in the vicinity of Charlestown. This cannot possibly be true; as Jackson knows well that to do so even for forty-eight hours would inevitably result in the destruction or capture of his whole force. The fact that little information of his movements after fighting Banks at Winchester has been received here, satisfies us that he has certainly retraced his steps almost precisely as he came east—the route by which

Library of Congress

General Stonewall Jackson

his movements would be least exposed to Union observation, and least liable to interception. Nevertheless, if Fremont has done his duty, he must to-day be intercepted in his retreat, at or about Stanardsville.

(Saturday, May 31, 1862)

FROM FRONT ROYAL.

Our Army in Repossession There.

Capture of 150 Prisoners and 11 Rail Road Cars.

A dispatch received this morning at the War Department states that a brigade of our troops, preceded by four companies of the Rhode Island cavalry under Major Nelson, entered Front Royal yesterday morning, at 11 o'clock, and drove out the enemy, consisting of the 8th Louisiana, four companies of the 12th Georgia, and a body of cavalry.

Our loss is eight killed, five wounded, and one missing, all from the Rhode Island Cavalry.

We captured six officers and one hundred and fifty privates. Among the officers are Capt. Beckwith West, 48th Virginia, First Lieut. Gemmell, 8th Louisiana; Lieuts. J. K. Dickson and Waterman, 12th Georgia.

We recaptured eighteen of our troops taken by the enemy at Front Royal a week ago, among whom are Major Wm. F. Collins, 1st Vermont cavalry; George H. Griffin, Adjutant 6th New York cavalry; Lieut. Duryea, 8th New York cavalry; and Frederick Tarr, Adjutant Maryland infantry.

We captured a large amount of transportation, including two engines and eleven railroad cars. Our

Pennsylvania Bucktails assault part of Jackson's army near Harrisonburg.

advance was so rapid the enemy was surprised, and therefore not able to burn the bridges across the Shenandoah.

A dispatch from the Associated Press reported gives the names of our killed as follows, all of the Rhode Island cavalry: Captain William P. Ainsworth, Corporal John C. Babcock, Corporal D. B. Barnard, Edward K. Barnard, Cyrus A. Brackett, Calvin Cushman, Ben. Lashure and E. B. Allen.

The loss of the enemy is not yet ascertained, but is said to be large, as our cavalry cut in among them in splendid style.

EDITORIAL.

(Monday, June 2, 1862)

The Situation in the Valley.

It is plain that Jackson already finds the region of his recent fillibustering too hot to hold him, and that he is accordingly popping around in it like a quill of quicksilver in a hot shovel. The last information we have with reference to his last particular position is down to noon yesterday, when it was believed at Harper's Ferry that having started on his retreat up the Valley, he "saw snakes" about Winchester, or a vision of something else so distasteful to him as to make him 'bout face and retreat precipitately back in the direction of the Potomac. In the present state of affairs there it is not proper for us to explain in detail the probable circumstances of the strait in which Jackson probably finds himself. The *Star's* readers will recollect that on hearing of his surprise of Kenley and attack on Banks, we ventured the opinion that while they certainly proved his boldness, the result of his movement would by no means serve to prove his discretion as a commander.

But Jackson did manage to slip through the pincers that Fremont and Shields were supposed to snap on him. Not only had his army eluded the Federals, but also a seven-mile-long wagon train of captured Federal supplies and 2,000 prisoners. But the safety of the retreating army depended now on the small forces, such as Brig. Gen. Turner Ashby's, which must outdo themselves in heroic rear-guard action.

(Tuesday, June 10, 1862)

IMPORTANT FROM THE MOUNTAIN DEPARTMENT.

Milroy in Full Pursuit of Jackson's Force.

THE REBEL GENERAL ASHBY KILLED!

The following was received at the War Department this morning:

"HEADQUARTERS ARMY IN THE FIELD, *Harrisonburg*, June 7, 9 p.m.—*Hon. E. M. Stanton*,

Secretary of War: The attack upon the enemy's rear of yesterday precipitated his retreat. Their loss in killed and wounded was very severe, and many of both were left on the field. Their retreat is by an almost impassable road, along which many wagons were left in the woods, and wagon loads of blankets, clothing and other equipment are piled up in all directions.

During the evening many of the rebels were killed by shells from a battery of Gen. Stahl's (Julius Stahel) brigade. Gen. Ashby, who covered the retreat with his whole cavalry force and three regiments of infantry, and who exhibited admirable skill and audacity, was among the killed.

Gen. (Robert Huston) Milroy made a reconnaissance to-day about seven miles on the Port Republic road, and discovered a portion of the enemy's force encamped in the timber.

J. C. Fremont, Major Gen'l Com'dg.

☞ *Ashby fell May 30 near Harrisonburg. A week later, in the last rear-guard battle of the campaign, Jackson himself took on the pursuing Federals of Fremont and Shields and, despite numerical odds, turned them back at Cross Keys and Port Republic. Now came the Federals' turn to retreat back down the Valley.* ☞

(Saturday, June 28, 1862)
RESIGNATION OF GENERAL SHIELDS.

We notice General Shields upon our streets to-day in citizen's costume, a fact which seems to confirm the statement by northern papers of his resignation.

General Fremont.

Maj. Gen. Fremont has declined to serve under the orders of Major Gen. Pope, and has accordingly been relieved of the command of the corps to which he had been assigned by the President.

He still holds his commission of Major General, and hence may be assigned to duty elsewhere.

FROM THE VALLEY OF SHENANDOAH.

Information from the Shenandoah Valley, received from other than official sources, leads to the belief that Jackson's rebel troops have not in force returned from the point at which they were last seen by our troops. The speculations concerning him are various, and among them is one that he is repairing damages and preparing to secure the wheat and rye crops of the valley, which are represented to be

General John C. Fremont

very good. The reports about the enemy occupying the country between Manassas and Strasburg, in any force, are untrue. There may, however, be rebel pickets at settlements heretofore temporarily occupied by our troops.

☞ *Where was Jackson, indeed? The Union armies would find out toward the end of June.* ☞

WASHINGTON HOMEFRONT, MAY, 1862.

☞ *There was turmoil in the Shenandoah Valley and new fears for the safety of the capital. Now with major fighting in progress on the Peninsula below Richmond, a dreary spectacle once again was unfolding in Washington, which had seen nothing comparable since last July's battle at Bull Run.* ☞

ARRIVAL OF MORE SICK SOLDIERS FROM YORKTOWN.—The steamer *Louisiana,* Capt. Pearson, arrived at the Sixth street wharves, from Fortress Monroe, about 12 o'clock yesterday, with 213 more of the sick soldiers from Yorktown. Dr. A. H. Smith, of the 43rd New York regiment, is in charge of them, and reports their condition quite comfortable. They will be taken to hospitals at once.

We learn that most of the wounded on the Peninsula have been sent to Northern cities per ocean steamers. Those sent here are the sick, of which about 1,600 have arrived. But few wounded are sent here.

Many touching scenes are to be witnessed at the wharves where the sick soldiers are being landed. Several of the invalids are apparently at death's door with consumption, and in some instances the relatives or friends of the sufferers are present to soothe the last hours of the dying ones. The silent, unobtrusive agony of the young wife of one of these

General James Shields

doomed ones was noticed yesterday with feelings of deep sympathy by all who witnessed it; and a big-hearted citizen as he passed her was seen to hastily slip a piece of folded paper in her hand, and move off rapidly without looking back. On being opened, the slip was found to enclose one of Uncle Sam's "greenbacks," of a generous denomination.

Roundsman Brock, of the Seventh Ward, ascertained that the vendors of eggs, fruits, &c., to the invalid soldiers at the wharves, were charging exorbitant prices, gave them a hint yesterday that speedily caused them to come down to fair prices, very much to the gratification of the poor fellows who had been so scandalously imposed upon.

Several of the sick have died since the boats arrived, among them J. A. Steel, of the 64th New York, who died on the *Arrowsmith* on Thursday night. The body of this young man was taken off the boat and laid on the wharf, where it was suffered to remain until this morning before it was removed. We learn that this delay was occasioned owing to the case having been reported to the wrong officer. A young man named J. W. Kelly, belonging to the 5th New Hampshire, died on the same boat last night, of typhoid fever; previously to his death apparently reviving, expressing a wish to see his father, and requesting his comrades to send word to his relatives of his death.

John Borst, of the 103d Pa., died on the *Louisiana* on Thursday night, on the passage up, and as soon as the boat landed the surgeons accompanying the boat (E. S. Walker, of the 34th, and A. F. Smith, of the 4th New York) made the necessary arrangements and had him buried with the usual honors. One of the wounded secesh prisoners died on the *Kennebec* last night of typhoid fever and was buried to-day. His name or regiment we were unable to learn.

The soldiers have all been removed from the boats to the various hospitals, the most of them being taken to the Mount Pleasant and General (Judiciary Square) Hospitals. Most of the cases are of typhoid and are thought to be not dangerous, although there are some dozen or more who cannot recover. The surgeons who accompany the boats assure us that these men are all in the army of the Potomac who are so sick as to be unfit for duty, and that they will not amount to $2\frac{1}{2}$ per cent. of the whole army.

Drawing by Frank Vizetelly

Stonewall Jackson leads his men in prayer between battles.

STONEWALL JACKSON HAD DROPPED OUT OF SIGHT IN THE Valley of Virginia, and the Federals there welcomed the respite. Events in the great valley of the Midwest gave the Union cause more comfort. The Confederates had fallen back before a leisurely "drive" that came as an aftermath of the Shiloh campaign. Corinth, Miss., had been abandoned by Beauregard, and occupied in early June by Halleck's Federals. "Old Bory," pleading ill health, resigned his command shortly afterward. Bragg was now in charge, his Confederates newly based at Tupelo, Miss. In consequence of the withdrawals ever southward, Fort Pillow, Tenn., was evacuated. Memphis, an "open city" under the terms of warfare, had surrendered later, following the defeat of the Rebel gunboat fleet by Yankee gunboats on the Mississippi in plain view of the fascinated citizens. Toward the end of June, the pugnacious Farragut had bombarded Vicksburg, Miss., and sailed his fleet on up the Mississippi past the belching guns of that fortress city.

The backward movement was being duplicated by the Confederates in the East. Maj. Gen. Benjamin Huger had abandoned Norfolk in May to join forces with the Richmond defenders. Aged Maj. Gen. John Ellis Wool simply moved across the harbor from Fort Monroe, his command, and occupied Norfolk and Suffolk both. With no navy yard to call home, the *Merrimac* was destroyed by its own men, lest it fall into Federal hands.

Just across the James River from these scenes of Confederate withdrawal could be seen the biggest troop concentration of all the war theaters. On the Peninsula between Fort Monroe and Richmond, Joe Johnston's defenders of the Confederate Capital totaled 85,000, as against McClellan's 100,000. This was the largest concentration of military forces ever recorded in the Western Hemisphere, up to that time. The Federals had captured Yorktown and Williamsburg early in May. McClellan's oversupplied caution, and a constant misapprehension that he was outnumbered, had made the process maddeningly slow. Deceptions by the Confederates fed his apprehensions. Not until May 31 was the first pitched battle fought. Fair Oaks and Seven Pines, a pair of hamlets which overlooked the steeples of Richmond, provided the battleground. It was a bloody but indecisive battle. Its greatest significance was that Robert E. Lee took command of the forces which would live in history as the Army of Northern Virginia. Johnston had been seriously wounded and would not regain prominence until more than a year later.

During the three weeks after the battle, both armies maneuvered for position. During this period, one of the most spectacular episodes of the war took place. Jeb Stuart was ordered out to probe the Federal lines north of Richmond. He did more than that. In his characteristic devil-may-care style, he led 1,000 cavalry troopers completely around McClellan's army, a distance of 150 miles, with practically no loss. When he made his triumphant entry into Richmond, the capital went wild, and the rest of the South was enthralled. Stuart's ride had another effect. Since it had cut across McClellan's supply route from White House, on the Pamunkey River, McClellan promptly shifted his supply base from White House to the more secure Harrison's Landing on the James River.

The time for a showdown arrived June 25. The week-long carnage that ensued would afterward be known as "The Seven Days." During the struggle, Jackson appeared with his "foot cavalry," called East from the Shenandoah. He would prove strangely ineffectual in the tangled fighting around Richmond. Also, the Confederate defenders would suffer heavier casualties than the Federal "invaders" in the battles of Oak Grove, Mechanicsville, Gaines' Mill, Garnett's and Golding's Farms, Savage's Station, White Oak Swamp and Malvern Hill. It would be months—even years—before the contests could be accurately reconstructed and assessed.

Newspaper accounts reflected the uncertainty over what had actually taken place on the Peninsula in the climactic stage of the campaign, but the sum of the battlefield reports carried clear implications as July dawned.

McCLELLAN CAMPAIGN BOGS DOWN

(Thursday, July 3, 1862)

OUR ARMY NOT DEFEATED!

We have later information from the Peninsula just before the second edition of to-day's *Star* goes to press.

It is obtained for the most part from an intelligent and reliable gentleman who left General McClellan's headquarters on Tuesday evening last at 4 p.m. He assures us that we have lost in the almost a week's fighting but little or no material—no guns (cannon) of any kind.

Our total loss in killed, wounded and missing is generally set down at from 10,000 to 12,000; certainly not more than 15,000.

All our wounded and sick were safely brought off the field to the new position except those at Savage's Station, north of the Chickahominy.

In no one instance were our forces driven by the enemy; retiring only under orders from one position to another, in going to the new line selected for our occupation.

The Richmond papers of Monday that had been received admit a Rebel loss up to Saturday night, of 25,000 killed, wounded and missing, including Stonewall Jackson and R. Barnwell Rhett, killed on Friday.

General Henry W. Halek

Library of Congress

The whole movement was most admirably conducted, and is regarded by the army as a complete success, and our loss, though heavy, is not more than half that of the rebels, by admission of their papers. . . .

Throughout the action of Monday and Tuesday our men were cheering at all points, the whole army being in excellent spirits.

The canteens of the rebels were filled with a mixture of gunpowder and whisky.

Throughout the action of Tuesday, in progress when our informant left, the enemy were repulsed and beaten everywhere; fighting as though their energies and material were well nigh exhausted.

The fight of Tuesday was principally an artillery duel, in which the gunboats occasionally participated.

The rebels claim to have taken 5,000 prisoners. This includes our large number of sick and wounded left, with surgeons, north of the Chickahominy on Friday.

Newspaper readers confronted with such battlefield dispatches must have been totally mixed up. If the Union army was not being defeated, why was it now moving back down the Peninsula? As for some of the lesser details: Jackson, of course, was not killed, and R. Barnwell Rhett, the South Carolina politician, never got into the army. The reference to the rebel soldiers drinking gunpowder and whiskey as a battlefield bracer must have aroused indignation down South. The Tuesday, July 1, action referred to was the battle of Malvern Hill, where Federal artillery took a horrifying toll of Confederates sweeping up the open slopes. Here again, "victory," and yet a later report published the same day stated:

WAR DEPARTMENT, July 3—1:25 p.m.—A dispatch from General McClellan, just received at the War Department, dated from Berkely, Harrison's bar, July 2, 5:30 p.m., states that he has succeeded in getting his army to that place, on the bank of the James River, and had lost but one gun, which had to be abandoned last night (Tuesday), because it broke down. That an hour and a half ago the rear

The battle of Malvern Hill, as seen from the Federal position.

of the wagon train was within a mile of camp and only one wagon abandoned. That we had a severe battle yesterday (Tuesday) and beat the enemy badly, the men fighting even better than before. The men are in good spirits. The reinforcements sent from Washington have arrived.

E. S. Sanford, M. G.
(Brig. Gen. Edward Sewall Sanford, McClellan aide de camp.)

🔫 *A clue to the real state of affairs was in that dispatch. McClellan was directing his forces back to Harrison's Landing, his base. On the same day, an earlier report came straight out and used a word which the North dreaded to read: "retreat."* 🔫

(Thursday, July 3, 1862)
Telegraphic News.
FROM GENERAL McCLELLAN'S ARMY.

Four Days' Fighting—Gen. McClellan Falling
Back—Engagement on James River—
The Rebels Shelled by the Gunboats—Gen.
Magruder a Prisoner.

FORTRESS MONROE, July 1.—4 o'clock p.m. —A gunboat just arrived at Fortress Monroe from the scene of action yesterday, ten miles above City Point. That division of our army has been fighting four days, and have retreated about seventeen miles. The fight of yesterday was most terrific, the enemy having two or three to our one. The battle commenced with our land forces, and, after about four

hours' fighting, our gunboats got in range, and poured into the rebels a heavy and incessant fire. This fire the rebels stood about two hours and then retreated.

Our troops have captured, notwithstanding their disadvantages, a large number of artillery pieces and 2,000 prisoners, among whom is the rebel Gen. Magruder. The place where this last action took place is near Turkey Creek.

The retreat of the enemy last evening was with great disorder, and their loss has been very heavy—much greater, it is thought, than ours. Still I have nothing definite in regard to loss. In the retreat forced upon Gen. McClellan by the superior numbers of the enemy, I learn that he had to spike his siege guns and leave them on the field after burning the carriages—the nature of the soil rendering it impossible to move them.

In the retreat many of our sick and wounded were necessarily left behind.

There are, of course, innumerable reports and rumors here, but I send only what appears to be authentic.

🔫 *But McClellan and the people around him apparently kept whistling in the dark.* 🔫

(Saturday, July 5, 1862)
All Right on the Peninsula.

The following telegram was received to-day (July 5th) at the War Department, from an officer of high rank and character in Gen. McClellan's army:

ARMY OF THE POTOMAC, July 4.—The newspaper reporters having all skedaddled, to prevent the people of the country being frightened to death, I will simply state that at 12 m. to-day a National salute of 34 guns was fired at the headquarters of each army corps, and all the bands are playing National airs.

The men are in first-rate spirits, and the General is just starting to visit all the troops. The newspaper reporters and others who have gone to the rear don't represent the army of the Potomac. We can't be beaten, and what is more we won't be beaten.

We are all right, and always have been. If they will send reinforcements enough to fill up our losses of sick, killed and wounded, we will take Richmond from this point.

Don't believe any stampede reports you hear; there is no truth in them. Secesh is smashed up, and as soon as we can get rested and get supplies and a few more men, we can use them up completely.

This is a glorious Fourth of July for us—all right. We hear nothing of Secesh to-day. Don't fear for the army of the Potomac.

In conclusion I would just state that the Provost Marshal General found it unnecessary to order reporters to the rear, they having all skedaddled of their own accord.

☜ *The derogatory reference to newspapermen indicated something further: army censorship had worked well during the Seven Days' Battle. Reporters were severely curbed in their efforts to get stories out—which explains the piecemeal, vague and conflicting accounts that appeared in the papers* *back home. The St. Louis* Republican *later editorially explained: "There has been so much confusion in the reports of correspondents, respecting the movements and plans of our army before Richmond, that great difficulty has been encountered by all who attempted to make clear to themselves its position and the significance of its moves."*

Probably the most accurate appraisal of what had gone on came from Jeff Davis himself, courtesy of a Richmond paper, which printed this text: ☜

(Monday, July 14, 1862)

Important from Richmond.
Address of Jeff. Davis—Admission of Gen. McClellan's Masterly Movement.

(From the Richmond Dispatch of Tuesday)
JEFF. DAVIS ADDRESS TO THE ARMY.

President Davis, in consideration of the recent triumphs to our arms, has issued the following address to the officers and men who participated in the series of sanguinary battles:

Richmond, July 5th, 1862

To the Army in Eastern Virginia:

Soldiers—I congratulate you on the series of brilliant victories which, under the favor of Divine Providence, you have lately won, and as the President of the Confederate States, do heartily tender to you the thanks of the country; whose just cause you have so skillfully and heroically served. Ten

The battle of Fair Oaks.

days ago, an invading army, vastly superior to you in numbers and in the material of war, closely beleaguered your Capital and vauntingly proclaimed its speedy conquest; you marched to attack the enemy in the entrenchments; with well directed movements and death-defying valor you charged upon him in his strong positions, drove him from field to field over a distance of more than thirty-five miles, and, despite his reinforcements, compelled him to seek safety under the cover of his gunboats, where he now lies cowering before the army so lately derided and threatened with entire subjugation. The fortitude with which you have borne toil and privation, the gallantry with which you have entered into each successive battle, must have been witnessed to be fully appreciated; but a grateful people will not fail to recognize you and to bear you in loved remembrance. Well may it be said of you, that you have "done enough for glory;" but duty to a suffering country and to the cause of constitutional liberty,

claims from you yet further effort. Let it be your pride to relax in nothing which can promote your future efficiency; your one great object being to drive the invader from your soil, and carrying your standards beyond the outer boundaries of the Confederacy, to wring from an unscrupulous foe the recognition of your birthright, community, independence.

(Signed)   JEFFERSON DAVIS.

McClellan had a new plan for taking Richmond. Provided he got still more reinforcements, he proposed to get at the city by crossing to the south side of the James River and moving up via Petersburg. The Lincoln Administration was getting out of patience, however. A grave suspicion was dawning that McClellan never would be an aggressive field commander. The first assault on the Confederate capital would have to be written off as a failure, and the search renewed for a soldier who could really take charge of the fine Army of the Potomac.

The wounded and sick in the Federal field hospital at Savage Station, Virginia.

WASHINGTON HOMEFRONT, JUNE, 1862.

☞ *In the absence of clear news from the Peninsula, wild rumors filled the air in Washington.* ☞

A MISCHIEVOUS CANARD.

Last night the town was considerably excited by a mischievous rumor to the effect that there had been heavy fighting on the Peninsula, and that McClellan had met with a bad reverse. Such rumors have usually been put in circulation by Secesh, but the present one was traced to an employee at the Capitol, who stated it on the authority of Members of Congress. There was not a word of truth in the story, and it seems to have been set afloat in a spirit of revenge by some of the junketing marplots who were so deservedly set to the right about by Gen. McClellan, on their endeavor to penetrate to his front, on their late visit to the Peninsula.

A Vignette from the War Department: A PROMPT PUNISHMENT.

One who was present states the following as the particulars of a scene at the War Department yesterday:

Secretary Stanton was transacting business with various parties in his usual rapid, vigorous style, when a surgeon entered, and giving his name, said: "I understand that some charges have been entered against me."

Mr. Stanton, (selecting a document from a pile on his table.)—"Yes, sir. You are here charged with shamefully neglecting a detachment of sick and wounded soldiers sent to this city under your care. Are the facts stated in this paper true?"

Surgeon, (reading.)—"Partly so, sir. The time of my arrival is incorrectly stated."

Stanton—"Is it true that on your arrival you went to a hotel and got your supper, leaving the wounded men in the cars?"

Surgeon.—"It is, sir."

Stanton.—"And that you afterwards went to bed at the hotel, leaving the soldiers yet uncared for in the cars?"

Surgeon.—"It is, sir."

Stanton.—"Then, sir, you are dismissed from the service;" and adding some further words expressive of his utter detestation of such acts of neglect of suffering soldiers on the part of those specially delegated to care for them, the Secretary turned to a clerk and ordered the dismissal to be at once written out; and the delinquent, crushed and humbled, left the room, crying like a child.

———◆———

BASE BALL.—*National vs. Washington.*—The first match game of the season (and the only one Washington ever engaged in) was played yesterday afternoon between the abovenamed clubs, on the finely situated grounds of the National. The game resulted in favor of the Nationals, by a majority of forty runs.

On the part of the Nationals, Ned Hibbs' batting was superb, he making five home runs; while Walden took care of all balls which came in his region, and made several very fine catches.

On the part of the Washingtons, Messrs. Sharretts and Marr, as catcher and pitcher, were also excellent. Johnson on the first, and McIntire on the second bases, played well. Potter, as short, was very active, and with McHaren did some fine fielding. The following is the score:

Innings.	1	2	3	4	5	6	7	8	9
Washington	3	5	1	1	3	1	5	2	1
National	1	9	10	8	8	3	5	10	8

Home runs—Ned Hibbs, 5, Gorman, 3, Whiting, 3; French, 1; Johnson, 1.

Scorer for the National—R. N. Cronin.

Scorer for the Washington—A. J. West.

Umpire—Mr. J. Clark, of Brooklyn, N. Y.

☞ *Final score, probably determined with the aid of a comptometer: the Nationals 62, the Washingtons, 22.* ☞

THE NORTH HAD QUITE ENOUGH ON ITS HANDS TRYING to put down the Southern "insurrection." Although victories had been won in the middle western theater, progress was slow and uncertain. In the East, defeat still piled upon defeat for the Union forces. In the midst of these vexations, a new one arose in a wholly unexpected quarter. An Indian insurrection exploded in August on the northwestern frontier: the Dakota Sioux were rampaging in Minnesota.

Under an 1851 treaty with the United States, these Sioux had sold their tribal lands in Eastern Minnesota for $3 million, payable annually over 50 years. Around 6,000 Indians were involved, so the agreement amounted to the handsome sum of $10 annuity for each Sioux. The treaty also set aside a one-million-acre reservation for the tribesmen to occupy. It was located along the Minnesota River in the western part of the State, between New Ulm and Big Stone Lake.

Many of the Sioux and their tribal chiefs had long been unhappy over what they regarded as a cheap sell-out to the paleface government. Furthermore, perhaps nine-tenths of their number wanted no part of the white man's attempts to Christianize them and train them to be farmers. They were Sioux, and in the tradition of their ancestors they were hunters and fighters—especially as long as there were Chippewas around to fight.

Other incursions of the whites rankled. Small as their annuities were, the Government often was late in paying. And when payday came, white traders and sharpsters invariably were around to claim the money for settling Sioux debts. One claim alone amounted to $145,000. It was made by former Gov. Henry Hastings Sibley, a lawyer representing a fur company which did business with the Sioux. Of one $475,000 lump-sum payment set aside by the Government for the Sioux, less than one-third was actually received by them. The rest paid off claims, whether fraudulent or just.

In July, 1862, their annuity payment was late again. Trade agencies on the reservation, compounding the Indians' woe, refused to extend credit during the delay. Resentment welled up in the Sioux. Then, as it happened, four rowdy young braves went marauding around the settlement of Acton on Sunday, August 17. On a dare that he was afraid of white men, one of the companions shot a settler to death. With blood on their hands, all four went berserk and murdered two more men, a woman and a girl.

Rushing back frantically to the reservation, they confessed their crime. Two reactions set in among the tribal factions. Some of the chiefs, fearing war with the white man, favored surrendering the culprits and taking the consequences. But there were hot-heads, too, among the fighting Sioux. The *Star* told the story, for the most part, in an extended series of dispatches strung together on Page Two.

BLOODY SIOUX RISING QUELLED

(Monday, August 25, 1862)

The Massacre by Indians in Minnesota.
FIVE HUNDRED WHITES MURDERED.

ST. PAUL, MINN., Aug. 22.—Parties from the Minnesota River reached here last night. They state that the scouts estimate the number of whites already killed by the Sioux at five hundred. This opinion is based upon the number of bodies discovered strewed along the road and by the trails of blood. It is believed that all the missionaries have been killed. The civilized Indians exceeded their savage brethren in atrocities.

Mr. Frenier, an interpreter who has spent most of his life among the Indians, volunteered to go alone among them, trusting to his knowledge of them and his disguise, to escape detection. He dressed himself in Indian costume and started on his journey. He arrived at the upper agency at night. The place was literally the habitation of death. He visited all the houses and found their former occupants all lying dead, some on the doorsteps, and some inside their habitations; others were scattered in the yards and in the roads. He went to the house of the Hon. J. R. Brown, and recognized every member of the family. They numbered eighteen in all, and every one of them had been brutally murdered. At Beaver creek he found that fifty families had been killed outright. At every house he went into he recognized the dead bodies of nearly all the former inhabitants of the place.

Among the dead bodies he recognized at the agency were the following: N. Githens and family, Dr. Wakefield and family, John Eddens and family, John Moyner, Edward Moyner, Rev. Dr. Williams, Rev. Mr. Briggs and two missionaries.

Ex-Governor Sibley is now marching to the relief of Fort Ridgely. He reports that the Sioux bands are united together to carry out a concentrated and desperate scheme, and says that he will be only too happy to find that the powerful bands of the Yanktons and other tribes have not united with them.

Mr. Frenier writes to Gov. (Alexander) Ramsey on the 21st instant, saying that he left Fort Ridgely at two o'clock that morning. There were then over 2,000 Indians at the fort, and all the wooden buildings there had been set on fire, and were burning. Mr. Frenier thinks that other tribes are joining the Sioux, and that they will present a formidable array.

A reliable letter dated Glencoe, 21st inst., says that the injury done by the stampede of the settlers is immense, and that such another scene of woe could hardly be found in the South as in McLeod, Meeker, and the northern part of Sibley and other counties in Minnesota. In St. Paul and the adjoining country all the available horses are being gathered together, and all sorts of weapons will be used by willing hands for immediate and summary vengeance upon these blood-thirsty Indians.

🖝 *The horrifying news was slow getting out of St. Paul, the nearest telegraph connection, 165 miles east of the trouble. State authorities and newspapers did not want to spread alarms when it might turn out that the reports were just another Indian "scare." By August 22, four days after the Acton*

A Sioux attack on a Minnesota settler.

Fort Ridgely under siege by the Sioux.

incident, refugees were already streaming into the capital, and the worst fears were realized. The warmongering element among the Sioux—principally a chief named Red Middle Voice—had prevailed in the tribal councils. For four days since Acton, warriors had fanned out from the reservation, slaughtering and torturing unarmed settlers just north of the Minnesota River. Women and children were murdered and defiled. Many were taken captive. The leader of the uprising was Little Crow. Born near the site of St. Paul, when it was a hamlet called Pig's Eye, Little Crow had been a peaceable Sioux, even toward the hated Chippewa nation. But he agreed, very likely under pressure, to sanction war against his better judgment that the Sioux couldn't win. 🔫

CHICAGO, Aug. 23.—The St. Paul (Minnesota) *Pioneer,* of the 20th instant, says it is thought that the Indians have been induced to commit these outrages by Indians from Missouri and Secession traitors of that State, and that when Major (Thomas J.) Galbraith left the agency on Friday evening everything was quiet. The Indians had received their goods and had all disappeared, apparently satisfied with the Major's promise to send for them as soon as the money arrived to pay them their annuities. The first attack of the Indians was made on the house of Mr. Baker, on Sunday last, near the town of Acton, and thirty miles from Forest City, in which three white men and one woman were killed. On Monday morning an attack was made on Redwood, and at the time the messenger left there a number of persons had been killed. After the messenger had crossed the river he saw the Indians firing into the traders' stores and other buildings. He estimated the number of Indians engaged in the

firing at one hundred and fifty. He also stated that messengers had arrived at Fort Ridgely with money to pay off the Indians the sums due them.

The St. Paul *Press,* of the 21st inst., says that several loads of panic-stricken people from Currer and Sibley counties arrived in town last night, principally women and children. They were greatly excited, and gave exaggerated accounts of the Indians who were marching on Shaska county. They also say that the towns of St. Peter, Henderson and Glencoe have been burned. A private letter received in this city to-day, from St. Paul, dated the 20th inst., says that it seems to be the general opinion among the best informed of our citizens that these Indian troubles originated with the cursed secessionists of Missouri.

Major Galbraith was told by one of the Indians that there are now in arms ten thousand of the Sioux tribes, besides other tribes from Northern Missouri.

🔫 *Reports from the terror-stricken fugitives were conflicting when not downright incoherent. The one that the Confederacy had incited the Sioux was never given real credence. However, the Indians were aware of the Federal government's preoccupation with the "big war," and apparently counted on it as a distraction which would keep troops from being sent to punish them.* 🔫

ST. PAUL, Minn., Aug. 23d—9 p.m.—Antoine Frenier, the distinguished Indian scout, got through the Indian lines into Fort Ridgely, and brought back the following to Gov. Ramsey:

"FORT RIDGELY, Aug. 21—2 o'clock p.m.— We can hold this position but little longer unless we are reinforced. We are being attacked almost every hour, and unless assistance is rendered we cannot hold out much longer; our little band is becoming exhausted and decimated. We had hoped to be reinforced to-day, but as yet can hear of no one coming."

T. G. Sheehan, of Company C, 5th Minnesota volunteers, commands the post.

Gov. Sibley cannot reach there with his 1,200 troops until to-morrow, when a day of reckoning for the Indians will be at hand.

☞ Fort Ridgely, at the south end of the reservation, was not so much a fort as a collection of buildings. It was here that most of the settlers fled for safety. At no time during those first days when murder ran riot was the fort manned by more than 180 troops. At one point, after a relief force had been ambushed, as few as 26 soldiers were there. Ex-Gov. Sibley's relief column was inordinately slow getting to Fort Ridgely. The call for help had been made by an army private, who galloped the 165 rugged miles to Fort Snelling, near St. Paul, in 18 hours. Meanwhile, settlers armed with squirrel guns, pitchforks and anything else they could lay hands on, hurried to beleaguered Ridgely from nearby communities: Glencoe, Mankato, Henderson, South Bend and Le Sueur. ☞

(Saturday, August 30, 1862)
FROM MINNESOTA.

Fight with the Indians at New Ulm.

ST. PAUL, Minn., Aug. 28.—Ten whites were killed and fifty-one wounded at the fight on Saturday. The Indians fought bravely and recklessly. Their loss was considerable.

On Sunday our small force, under Major Flan-

Little Crow, leader of the Sioux.

drew (Charles E. Flandrau), finding that they could not stand another attack, withdrew to Mankets (Mankato), leaving the town to the mercy of the Indians. It is reported that between 500 and 600 Indians were in the fight.

Col. Sibley's command probably reached Fort Ridgely yesterday.

The adjutant general of Minnesota issued an order to the commanding officers to seize all horses and means of transportation necessary, on giving receipts to their owners.

The massacre does not seem to be confined to one locality, but spread over a vast amount of territory. It is reported that 46 families had all but two persons killed at Lake Spitik (Shetek), 60 miles southwest of New Ulm; but these reports are undoubtedly exaggerated, many persons having fled or secreted themselves, who are probably supposed to be killed.

The entire number of Sioux Indians in Minnesota is about 7,200, of whom 1,500 are warriors. Gov. Ramsey, in a proclamation, gives assurance that no apprehension need be felt for the safety of the thickly-settled parts of the State. The force sent against the Indians is believed to be more than sufficient to drive them into Missouri. Gov. Ramsey, however, has called an extra session of the Legislature, for the 9th of September, to provide means of defense.

☞ The New Ulm fight, in which a third of the town was destroyed, took place August 23. Five days later, Sibley reached Fort Ridgely. During the next month, his campaign, after frustrating an ambush at Wood Lake, would end the worst of the uprising. Of the hundreds of Indian leaders who fled, Little Crow would be slain by a settler. Of those who stayed to be captured, 306 would be tried and sentenced to be hanged. President Lincoln, lawyer that he was, took time from his Civil War problems to note that the trial evidence against most of the convicted Sioux was unconvincing. He commuted the sentences of all but 38, who were hanged at Mankato the day after Christmas, 1862.

The Sioux uprising received only sketchy coverage in newspapers east of the Mississippi River. There was more important war news to report. But the insurrection ranks as the bloodiest Indian massacre in Western frontier history. The most conservative estimate of slain settlers is 800. Some estimates of the dead go as high as 2,000. No one will ever know, because in the course of the slaughter, no less than 40,000 Minnesotans fled east, many never to return. ☞

General Henry Sibley

WASHINGTON HOMEFRONT, AUGUST, 1862.

☜ *Long had The Star, as a matter of policy, deplored rowdyism, drunkenness, and the whole spectrum of sin and vice in the wartime Federal capital. It was probably for this reason that the editors gave Page One prominence, August 26, to a Chicago correspondent's appraisal of one aspect of Washington life.* ☞

WASHINGTON'S GAMBLING SALOONS.

(Correspondence of the Chicago *Tribune*)

I intimated in my last that I had been investigating various aspects of Washington life and operations, among which was that feature known as Banking, and the gambling hells of Washington are the most noted on the continent, both in numbers and magnitude. The best customers to these establishments are the members of Congress, although, since the war broke out, and has confined the "chivalry," with their corpulent pocket-books, south of Mason and Dixon's, the heaviest income of the hells has been cut off, and at present their business seems mainly confined to officers, who, in full uniform, and at all hours of the day and night, throng the apartments of the Faro and Roulette dealers.

A ring at a doorbell, and a reconnaissance through its grated upper half by a stalwart negro, then up a pair of stairs through an ante-room, and we stand in the carpeted, elegant jungles of the modern "tiger." There are two wide, lofty rooms, divided by folding doors, both dazzling with light, softly carpeted, decorated with elegant and voluptuous paintings, and seemingly just the spot where poor, tired humanity would come to get a foretaste of Eden, and recuperate for the stern battles of life. In the first room is a sideboard, upon whose shelves are rows of elegant decanters, through which blushes the purple stand, or flashes the crystaline extract of the juniper—*Anglice*, gin.

In this room is also a Roulette table, which, as we enter, is vacant, and in the other room is a Faro table, around which are gathered a half-dozen men, so absorbed in the game that, were Gabriel to rock the earth with a blast from his trumpet, they would never hear it.

The room, by the way, is interesting from reminiscence. Here, not long since, the presiding genius was John C. Heenan—the fighting, dissolving love of the fair Adah Isaacs Menken; and here, not many weeks ago, an aspiring paymaster from Maryland succeeded in investing in one night the trifling little sum of twenty-seven thousand dollars.

I won't describe the game, for what little, if any, is not known about it in Chicago, is not known anywhere else, even in this city of iniquity—Washington.

Behind the table sits the dealer—long in finger, white in hand, and with the inevitable cluster of brilliants sparkling from digit and shirt bosom. He is grey-eyed, pock-marked, resolute, and yet pleasant in appearance, with a breadth of shoulder and a depth of chest that show him to be no mean man in case of an exchange of fistic courtesies.

On his right stands a captain, playing with half-dollar checks, and investing one at a time, evidently a loser; for, as his check is raked down, he follows it with a sigh, and, I doubt not, a curse upon the capriciousness of fortune. He has but a half dozen checks—in a minute or two they are gone; and after going to a corner and examining an empty pocket-book, he returns and stands moodily watching the game.

Next to him is a thick-set young man, who, with something less than a bushel of ten and twenty dollar checks at his side, is with the most perfect *nonchalance* betting from one to five hundred dollars upon his cards, and winning or losing without the slightest change of countenance. But he is lucky; every card that he bets on wins, until after a half hour he loses three or four times in succession, and then, with the remark, "My luck is changing, I reckon I'll quit," he counts over his checks to the dealer, who cooly, as if it were a matter of five cents, pays over to the lucky individual $3,700, in one hundred dollar three per centum coupons of the United States Treasury notes. Thrusting the immense pile of paper in his coat pocket, the gentleman rises, takes a cigar and a drink at the sideboard, and then, with a "good night, gentlemen," he walks out.

The dealer proceeds unconcernedly, while I, dazzled at such results, draw out a solitary five and de-posit it upon the king. In just three seconds the claws of the tiger cover my lonely and long-treasured five, and I see it no more; and, I may add, I have not seen it since.

During the two hours that I was in the establishment some five or six thousand dollars changed hands.

There are some five or six first class establishments of the kind in Washington, besides any quantity of lesser note. They are well known to the police, and in fact everybody else, but are not disturbed.

Execution of the convicted thirty-eight Sioux Indians.

MCCLELLAN'S GENERALSHIP AT THE GATES OF RICH-
mond had been poor, but not so calamitous that he would be stripped
of his shoulder insignia. The general still held the allegiance of most
of the homefront and the devotion of his troops. Though he remained
a commander, his command was shrinking. Throughout August, his
Peninsula forces were being shifted piecemeal back into Northern Virginia on orders from Washington. The high command—mainly the
President—had earlier showed its dwindling faith in McClellan in more
significant ways. A couple of Western generals had been called east.
One of them, Henry Halleck, was named general-in-chief of all the
Union armies. The other, John Pope, was given command of a brand-
new organization, the Army of Virginia. Halleck had been at least
nominal director of the campaigns that had conquered Fort Henry and
Donelson, pushed the Confederates back at Shiloh, and eased them out
of Corinth. Pope (with a big assist from the Navy) was the captor of
Island No. 10.

Lincoln wanted generals who could win and hoped he had a
couple in Halleck and Pope. He was on surer ground when, in the same
reshuffle, he promoted Ulysses Grant to head the Armies of the Tennessee and the Mississippi.

Pope got his Eastern career off to a bad start by delivering
a pompously condescending address to his new subordinates. The text
appeared in *The Star,* and it soon circulated throughout the city and
the army. Pope pointed out that he hailed from the Western armies,
where they saw only the backs of their enemies. He said he did not wish
to hear any more of this defensive talk "so much in vogue amongst you."
The Easterners—who ranked second to none in courage and ability—
boiled.

Early in August, Pope made aggressive gestures, taking his
army south near the Rappahannock River headwaters. He would aim
for Richmond from the Northwest, while McClellan's Federals were
being withdrawn from the Southeast. The Confederate capital, though
still jubilant over the repulse of McClellan, looked anxiously to Lee,
their hero of the Seven Days. Lee acted audaciously: he split his army
in half. Stonewall Jackson with his 17,000, headed northward, passing
to the west of Pope's growing army. Brushing aside Banks' corps of
8,000 in the Battle of Cedar Mountain, "Old Jack" circled wide. He
next emerged from Thoroughfare Gap in the Bull Run Mountains above
Warrenton, and, cutting across the Federal rail supply line, descended
on Pope's supply base at Manassas Junction, August 26. The hungry,
tattered Rebels had a high time looting the Yankee base. The supplies
they couldn't cart off, they burned. Then they headed back toward the
mountains that drew their name from Bull Run.

By this time, it dawned on Pope that something serious was going on behind him. On August 27, he moved back toward Manassas, expecting to find and trap Jackson there. He found what was left of his supply base, but no Jackson. A brush with Jubal Early's covering force, which Jackson had left to his rear, led Pope to believe he had "Old Jack" on the run toward the mountains. He had no idea that Jackson had "run" only as far as a good position a little West of Centreville. Nor did he know that Lee, with Longstreet and the rest of the Confederate army, was heading east out of the Bull Run Mountains, directly at his slowly gathering Federals.

The surroundings where the two armies met were familiar to many on both sides. The scene was the pleasant, though partially ravaged countryside around the creek where men by the hundreds had fallen in battle just a short year before.

CONFEDERATES WIN AGAIN
AT BULL RUN

(Saturday, August 30, 1862)
THRILLING NEWS FROM THE BATTLE FIELD!!

A Terrific Battle Yesterday, Lasting from Daylight Until Dark.

THE ENEMY DRIVEN FROM THE FIELD.

Our Loss not less than 8,000: that of the Enemy at least twice that.

Headquarters Field of Battle, Groveton, near Gainesville, Aug. 30, 5 a.m. Major General Halleck, General-in-Chief:

We fought a terrific battle here yesterday, with the combined forces of the enemy, which lasted with continuous fury from daylight until after dark, by which time the enemy was driven from the field, which we now occupy. Our troops are too much exhausted yet to push matters, but I shall do so in the course of the morning, as soon as Fitz John Porter's corps comes up from Manassas.

The enemy is still in our front, but badly used up. We have lost not less than eight thousand men killed and wounded, and from the appearance of the field, the enemy lost at least two to one. He stood strictly on the defensive, and every assault was made by ourselves.

Our troops behaved splendidly. The battle was fought on the identical battle field of Bull Run, which greatly increased the enthusiasm of our men.

The news just reaches me from the front that the enemy is retreating towards the mountains. I go forward at once to see.

We have made great captures, but I am not able yet to form an idea of their extent.

John Pope,
Major General Commanding.

Note by the Editor of the Star: We have positive information that Pope came up with and attacked the enemy again, a few minutes past 9 this morning. Fitz John Porter by that time had probably arrived on the field, from Manassas, seven miles off only.

Our impression that the heaviest of the fighting of yesterday was by McDowell and Sigel, in the vicinity of Thoroughfare Gap, was perhaps erroneous, judging from the above dispatch from General Pope.

Federal artillery fording the Rappahannock near Cedar Mountain, Virginia.

The remains of railroad rolling stock left by Confederates at Manassas Junction after evacuating the town.

The only possible line of even temporary retreat for Jackson, that we can perceive, is over the Warrenton turnpike towards the Rappahannock; as McDowell and Sigel are probably between him and Thoroughfare Gap, through which he would be compelled to go if seeking to proceed east. Fitz John Porter's command, which embraces some of those recently with Burnside, is very strong, we take it.

By to-morrow morning, as slowly as he may be moving, Franklin ought to be within supporting distance of Pope with a large force—sufficient, with Fitz John Porter's, to make mince meat of any possible reinforcements the enemy may get.

On the whole, as we stated a day or two since, the prospect now is rendered doubly sure that there will soon be few rebels in arms in Virginia.

P. S.—At 12.30 p.m. the firing stopped, we learn from parties just down from Fairfax county. We trust the fact means a surrender of the rebels, and do not see how it can mean aught else.

The railroad was regularly run this forenoon from the town of Warrenton to Bristow. So it is already clear that the only damage remaining to be repaired (to the railroad) is to rebuild the Bull Run and Rappahannock bridges. The former should be completed to-night—the latter may be in four or five days.

🖝 *Pope couldn't get over the notion that Jackson was high-tailing it to the Bull Run Mountains. Actually, Jackson's corps was firmly planted behind a partly completed railroad grade north of the Warrenton pike near Groveton. He was waiting for the rest of Lee's army which even then, August 29, was pouring through Thoroughfare Gap to join him on the battlefield. The "military expert," who appended*

the editor's note to Pope's confident dispatch, obviously was under the happy delusion that McDowell and Sigel had closed Thoroughfare Gap both to a retreat by and reinforcements for Jackson. McDowell, in fact, had wanted to block the Gap road, but Pope refused. 🖝

(Monday, September 1, 1862)

The Battle of Saturday Last.
THE HOTTEST OF IT LATE IN THE AFTERNOON.
The Rebel Gen. Ewell Killed and Stonewall Jackson Badly Wounded.

The great battle of Saturday last, on the south side of Bull Run, could hardly be called an engagement until perhaps five p.m., when the action became general. By six p.m., the enemy, who had managed to break through Thoroughfare Gap in the course of the afternoon, with the whole of his reinforcements, massed his troops so heavily upon Pope's left wing, under McDowell, supported by Fitz John Porter, as to drive that back half a mile, with great loss. There it made a stand, successfully checking the further advance of the enemy until night put a stop to the battle.

Finding his men and horses that had been in the engagement completely worn out for the time being, General Pope, when the battle ceased, threw his whole force upon the east bank of Bull Run (continuing to hold the crossing of that stream on the direct road between Centerville and Manassas), and posted his army on the slope of the ridge stretching down to Bull Run. That is to say: covering the slope for a space of about twelve miles in length and two and a half miles broad. General Franklin, with his fine division, had reached him by an early hour yesterday, and in the course of the day he was joined by the whole army corps of General Sumner.

Yesterday evening, General Banks joined him also, with his whole corps. That is, without the loss of a man, in executing his orders to fall back after having so completely destroyed the railroad and its paraphernalia from Manassas Junction towards the Rappahannock, as to render it impossible that it might be used by the enemy for any purpose whatever. It is not proper for us to mention the extent of the reinforcements which Franklin, Sumner, Banks —and last night, Couch, with his division—have carried to Pope. They are sufficient, however, to make up ten fold for his losses in the battle of Saturday, when he doubtless fought the whole force of Rebels.

So there need be no apprehension, we take it, that he will not be a match for them when the next shock of battle comes off. The fact that the enemy did not seek to renew the engagement yesterday, ere Pope's reinforcements arrived, augurs either that he has suffered so much in the four days fighting, and is so short of munitions, food, &c., as to be incapable for the time being of taking advantage of his success of the day before, or was preparing for a flank movement, against which Gen. Pope is surely on his guard.

The fact that he fired cut-up railroad iron for cannon balls, and that his men are living on hard crackers and coffee made of roasted wheat, lead to the impression that inability is at the bottom of his inactivity of the day, and indeed until 9 a.m. to-day, to which time the engagement had not been renewed. . . .

The rebels lost General Ewell, killed; General Jackson, badly wounded, and indeed a larger proportion of generals and other field officers killed and wounded than we did, except of the corps of McDowell, that stood the brunt of the day's engagement.

At noon to-day we had been able to gather no particulars of the situation in addition to those mentioned above, from which we conclude that all is yet well in the front.

Stonewall Jackson actually was unhurt, but Ewell lost a leg.

THE FIRST APPEARANCE OF THE ENEMY ON THE LEFT.

The Passage of Longstreet and Jackson Through Thoroughfare Gap.

Up to 1 o'clock on Saturday, the fighting was so light that it was thought there would not be any serious action for the day. A cavalry reconnaissance of four regiments, including the Michigan Cavalry, sent from the left to ascertain if the enemy were attempting a flank movement, discovered nothing to indicate their presence, but on returning to the left and after taking position, the enemy suddenly made their appearance in immense numbers in a wood in front, and so near that their faces could be distinguished.

The Federal troops under General Pope break and run from the Bull Run battlefield.

A. Waud—Library of Congress

At the same point a battery was suddenly wheeled into position and fired at the cavalry. The first shell struck in front of the cavalry, and ricochetted high over to a field in their rear. The second shell burst over their heads, when they fell back to cover of a hill. Stuart's cavalry presently appeared in large force, coming on a charge. The Confederate cavalrymen were armed with costly English shot guns, which they held at the breast and fired (both barrels at once) as they approached on the charge.

Our cavalrymen repelled the charge by a dash with their sabers, and the enemy fell back to the shelter of the woods, rallied superbly and returned again to the charge, and were again repelled. The enemy's infantry now opened upon our cavalry, compelling it to retreat. About the same time, our left wing was repulsed, and fell back with considerable loss.

Two lines of pickets effectually prevented the stragglers from moving off, and the center and right wing stood so firmly as to prevent the enemy from gaining any substantial fruits from their first successes.

Our soldiers who had been in the thickest of the fight, on the conclusion of the action fell down on the ground, too much exhausted to seek shelter or food, and slept where they were through the night, despite the falling rain.

Their hardships were increased by the want of water, as every spring and well was naturally drained to supply such a host, and many cheerfully paid twenty-five cents for a canteen full. Others drank the muddy water from the sloughs where thousands of horses had passed through.

The fact that not only Jackson, but Longstreet and Ewell, got through Thoroughfare Gap successfully, has caused some surprise, as it is stated that a regiment of men can hold the Gap against all comers, as it is narrow, and the road through it one in which it would be impossible for the enemy to unlimber a gun at the defensible points.

It is stated that Longstreet's advance, a single regiment of sharpshooters, was driven back (shelled) by a detachment sent out for that purpose; but that, from some cause, this force of ours was subsequently withdrawn, and the gap left open for Longstreet to pass through unchallenged.

Prisoners state that Gen. Lee was personally in command on Friday and Saturday.

A gentleman who left Fairfax Court-House yesterday evening at half-past six o'clock says that at that time reinforcements and ammunition were pouring into the Federal lines. This gentleman assisted

General John Pope, Federal commander at the second battle of Bull Run.

in caring for the wounded in the vicinity of the Bull Run bridge. About 1,000 of our wounded were there.

During yesterday there was no general fight, but simply skirmishing, and the rebels made no attack, but employed themselves by throwing shells from under cover of woods, from which they could not be induced to come out.

🔫 *Unfortunately for the reading public, the climactic phase of the fighting took place Saturday, and The Star did not publish on Sundays. The Confederate reinforcements referred to were Longstreet's corps, which made a shambles of the Federal left flank while the right flank was trying to dislodge Jackson. As hinted in the news story—sketchy even on Monday due to the customary confusion of battle —Pope was leaving the field to the Confederates and retreating to Washington, even though reinforcements were pouring in from Alexandria and Aquia Creek. These were troops transferred from the Peninsula.* 🔫

(Tuesday, September 2, 1862)
Latest from the Front.
PARTICULARS OF THE ENGAGEMENT LAST EVENING.
THE ENEMY HANDSOMELY REPULSED BY GEN. RENO.
Rebel Loss Severe.

We have reliable information from the front up to 9 a.m. to-day. The engagement of last evening, mentioned elsewhere in to-day's *Star*, was heaviest opposite the position of the gallant Gen. Reno, (about two miles north of Fairfax Court House,) who repulsed the enemy handsomely, and with severe rebel loss.

We however regret to have to add that in the course of the fight there, Brigadier General Isaac I. Stevens was killed. As yet, no particulars of his death have reached Washington.

After their repulse by Reno, the enemy declined renewing the engagement for the day, and had made no attempt to do so up to nine o'clock this forenoon.

At that hour, in the execution of the change of front, which we anticipated on account of the flank movement of the rebels, a large portion of our army had been massed in and around Fairfax Court House. Our right was at or in the vicinity of Flint Hill; the Court House being our center.

The impression last night and this morning at the front was that, foiled by Reno in his demonstration upon the Little River turnpike, the enemy had moved further around towards Vienna.

Our army, we may add, is in excellent order to-day.

P.S.—We hear that since 2 p.m. rather heavy cannonading in the front—in the direction of Fairfax Court House—has been heard here.

This was the battle of Chantilly, or Ox Hill, in which Federal forces under Maj. Gens. Isaac Ingalls Stevens, Philip Kearny and Jesse Lee Reno discouraged an attempt by Jackson to sweep around the whole army and trap it between Fairfax and Centreville.

THE KILLED AND WOUNDED.

Major Barney, who saw Gen. Kearney at 1 p.m. Monday, assures us that Gen. K. is not wounded or hurt, and that Gen. Hatch is but slightly hurt. A spent ball passed through his thick felt hat and flattened on his head, stunning him for a time.

The rumor that Gen. Fitz John Porter was killed, is unfounded. His name probably was confused with that of Col. Porter, of Pa., reported mortally wounded.

Gen. Sigel was only slightly wounded.

Col. W. L. Brown, 20th Indiana, killed in the late battle at Manassas, was brother of the Rev. Dr. Brown, pastor of Bridge street Presbyterian Church, Georgetown; and of Rev. J. C. Brown, D.D., chaplain of the 48th Indiana, who recently died of camp fever, contracted while in Alabama with his regiment. The family was from Ohio. . . .

Newspapers never ran out of conflicting reports from the battlefield.

(Wednesday, September 3, 1862)

Death of Brig. Gen. Kearney—His Body brought to Washington—Arrival of the Remains of Col. Fletcher Webster—Gen.

Negro refugees pass into northern lines after Confederate victory at Bull Run.

Stevens' Body in Alexandria—Gen. Taylor's Remains sent Home.

Brig. Gen. Kearney was killed in the fight of Monday afternoon. His body was brought to this city last evening. It will be embalmed and sent north.

The remains of the gallant Col. Fletcher Webster arrived in this city last evening in charge of Quartermaster Wood. The body is being embalmed, and will be sent to Boston immediately.

Gen. Stevens' body arrived in Alexandria yesterday. It will be embalmed and sent north to-day. Gen. Stevens was killed, while at the head of his brigade, by a Minie ball, which penetrated the brain. At the time he was shot, he was bearing in his hands the colors of a regiment, the color sergeant of which had been killed. His death was instantaneous.

The remains of Gen. (George William) Taylor, which had been embalmed, also passed through Washington yesterday, *en route* for the North.

The bodies of Generals Kearney and Stevens, and that of Col. Webster, were recovered from the enemy under a flag of truce.

The death of Stevens and Kearny was a severe loss. They were esteemed as two of the most promising field commanders in the Federal army. Reno, too, would soon be killed in action.

Latest from the Front.
THE MOVEMENT EFFECTED WITHOUT LOSS.
OMINOUS SILENCE OF THE ENEMY.
Jackson Gone Up the River.

By nine o'clock last evening the whole of the army of Gen. Pope had reached the position it had been determined it should assume for the present before the staunch fortifications on the south side of the Potomac, in our front. In their march of the day from the immediate vicinity of Fairfax Court House the enemy of course did their best to harass our rear with an occasional round of shell, which, however, did no damage. Everything was brought hither in good order and condition, the army being in a far better condition to renew the contest of last week at a moment's warning, than we anticipated.

Ere they reached this immediate vicinity, we hear, Major General McClellan had, in accordance with the general order of yesterday, (published elsewhere in to-day's *Star*,) issued an order assuming the chief command of the aggregated army (Pope's and Burnside's) thus assembled for the defence of the capital.

This morning it seems to be certain that the mass of the enemy that followed our army from the Rappahannock to this vicinity are directing their march somewhat up the river, being already in some force about Leesburg, and in larger force between there and the Chain Bridge, as though about to make a demonstration at the ferry opposite Poolesville, Md. . . .

Order, by the by, is rapidly being brought out of the comparative chaos that invariably follows a week of such action and marching as our troops were lately engaged in. . . .

The condition of the Army of the Potomac may have been chaotic, but defeated troops were neither routed nor destroyed, as Lee had intended and nearly accomplished. Though Pope's army numbered some 18,000 more than Lee's 55,000, Lee's audacious generalship had paid off. The Confederates, moreover, had fought as a whole army; the Federals only as parts of an army whose full strength Pope never used at one time.

WASHINGTON HOMEFRONT, SEPTEMBER, 1862.

On the heels of defeat at Bull Run, an anxious capital prepared for the worst.

*Headquarters Military District of Washington
Washington, D. C., Sept. 3, 1862.*

In pursuance of the order of the Commander-in-Chief to form military organizations of the clerks in the civil Departments of the Government, the clerks in the several Bureaus will forthwith assemble, and appoint a committee of three (3) from each Bureau on organization.

These committees will assemble at these headquarters this evening at eight (8) o'clock.

By command of Brig. Gen. (James Samuel) Wadsworth.

John P. Sherburne, Ass't Adj't General.

A camp of instruction for soldiers has been established at the Annapolis Junction. Numbers of tents have been put up for the accommodation of those under instruction. A New York regiment arrived on Monday last, and more were expected.

SHUTTING THE DRINKING HOUSES.

The order of the Military Governor directing all the drinking places of the District to be closed after to-day, is designed to meet the emergency of the present excited state of our population, already worked up to a high pitch by the recent battles, without the addition of liquid stimulus.

As soon as the city cools down again, the restriction will be removed, we hear; it not being the purpose of General Wadsworth to interfere further with our citizens than may be absolutely necessary in the military exigencies by which we are surrounded.

He will permit no liquors to be sold here in any quantity for the time being; the penalty being the instant confiscation of all found on the premises where sold.

Passes.

No persons are allowed to visit Alexandria without a proper pass.

No civilians are allowed passes to go to the battle-field or to Pope's army.

Passes are required from persons crossing the bridges and ferries.

No huckster wagons are allowed to go to camps over the river without passes.

No liquors are allowed to pass over the river unless with a pass.

ANSWERING THE CALL.

At noon to-day, about fifty surgeons, representing the counties of Dauphin, York, Berks, Lycoming, Franklin and Fulton, accompanied by about eighty nurses, arrived in the city for the purpose of offering their services in caring for the sick and wounded in the present emergency.

Delaware also sent a delegation of one hundred and twenty-seven surgeons; all of whom are stopping at Willards'.

First, RICHMOND SAVED. NOW THE ENEMY WHIPPED again just outside Washington, and falling back to the Yankee capital's forts. Good days had, indeed, come to the Confederacy. Even in the West, a scene of past defeats, Bragg's Confederate army had crossed the Tennessee River at Chattanooga, cutting through Tennessee for an invasion of Kentucky. These bright autumn days for the Confederacy had witnessed a battle at Richmond, Ky., where Kirby Smith's men overwhelmed the Federal defenders. In September, the Confederate forces would be menacing not only Louisville, Ky., but Cincinnati, just across the Ohio River.

On the Federal side, Pope had had enough of Lee, and Lincoln had had enough of Pope. The general was packed off to a newly created Department of the Northwest, in part of which the Sioux were still misbehaving. Panic again clutched at Washington's throat. Lee, with what was said to be overpowering numbers, was only 30 miles from the Federal City. Federal troops were concentrating around the city in great force. But who was the man to lead them? In desperation more than confidence, the President selected George Brinton McClellan once more.

Lee, meanwhile, did not intend to sit still while the Federals regrouped and prepared to take the initiative. With the daring that was becoming his hallmark, he pressed swiftly on farther north. Daring, backed by his hard-fighting Army of Northern Virginia, was Lee's best weapon to overcome the strength of his opponents. He marched for Maryland. To enter Maryland would not be "invasion." The Free State was a sister State of the Confederacy, kept under the "despot's heel" by armed might. Lee intended to liberate her. And if he were fast enough and diligent enough, he could win a crushing victory which might impel the North to sue for peace. Failing that, a decisive battle won in Maryland—or Pennsylvania—should heighten the Confederacy's prestige abroad. Perhaps Great Britain, France and other European sympathizers would then, at last, ally themselves with the Southern cause.

September 3, the Army of Northern Virginia moved forward through Leesburg. Once again, as before Second Bull Run, its commander undertook the hazard of dividing his army. After occupying Frederick—and getting a less than enthusiastic reception by the "liberated" Marylanders—Lee sent Jackson's corps alone across the Potomac River. His mission was to capture Martinsburg and Harper's Ferry, held by Federal arms. The other half of the army, Longstreet commanding, then left Frederick and crossed the Catoctin Mountains and South Mountain. According to Lee's plan, Longstreet's corps would be joined by Jackson's in the valley beyond South Mountain as soon as

Jackson had secured Martinsburg and Harper's Ferry. The combined force of 55,000 troops would then aim for Hagerstown—even Pennsylvania—possibly whipping the Federal army along the way.

McClellan knew nothing of this as he moved his army of 80,000 from Washington to Frederick. Nothing, that is, until by a colossal piece of luck a copy of Lee's plan of action fell into his hands. McClellan drew plans to catch the Confederates at their weakest spot in the valley beyond South Mountain. At that point an old McClellan ailment set in: hypercautiousness. He was more than deliberate in approaching the South Mountain passes pointed at Sharpsburg in the void that separated Longstreet near Hagerstown, and Jackson at Harper's Ferry. The Confederates saw his design and delayed him at the passes. This gave Jackson time to bring all his corps—except A. P. Hill's division—up to Sharpsburg.

The Confederates formed an arc around the town. Their backs were against the Potomac River. One end of their line rested on placid Antietam Creek when the Federal assault began.

WAR SOARS TO NEW FEROCITY
AT ANTIETAM

(Thursday, September 18, 1862)

Telegraphic News.

Another Great Battle.

Success of the Union Army—Awful Carnage
on Both Sides—Gen. Longstreet Wounded
and a Prisoner—Gen. Hooker Wounded.

HAGERSTOWN, (via Harrisburg) Sept. 17.—
A battle took place to-day between the army of the
Potomac and the rebels. Our right wing rested on
Sharpsburg, and our left this side of Antietam creek,
near Porterstown. The rebels are said to be falling
back to Harper's Ferry, much worried and dispirited.

The bridge reported destroyed by the Federal
forces was a canal bridge at or near Williamsport.
The destruction of this bridge is considered of great
importance, as it impedes the rebels in bringing up
their supplies.

(Second Dispatch.)

HARRISBURG, Sept. 17.—Information from the
seat of war received here indicates that this has been
an eventful day in Maryland. At the latest advices
everything was favorable. Gen. Longstreet was reported killed and (Daniel Harvey) Hill taken prisoner.

(Third Dispatch.)

HAGERSTOWN, (via Harrisburg,) Sept. 17.—
A great battle has been fought, and we are victorious.
The carnage on both sides has been awful.
Gen. Longstreet was wounded and is a prisoner.

Later.

HARRISBURG, 10 p.m.—A dispatch has just
been received at headquarters from Hagerstown
which says: "We have achieved a glorious victory."
Gen. Longstreet was not killed, but is wounded
and a prisoner.
Gen. (Joseph) Hooker was wounded in the foot.
No particulars have been received yet.

151

The battle took place near Centerville, on Catoctin
(Antietam) creek.

🔫 *It was the vexing problem of time lag. Although
Sharpsburg was only 70 miles from Washington, the
handiest telegraph connection—since Harper's Ferry
was in Confederate hands—was from Hagerstown
to Harrisburg, Pa , thence southward through Baltimore to Washington. Details were scant and largely
garbled—except for the fact that a mighty battle
was being fought, and the Federals were at least
holding their own. Readers, by this time surely, were
getting a little skeptical of dispatches and headlines
that proclaimed Union victory. And not until later
was it learned that "Old Pete" Longstreet was
neither wounded or captured, and that the battle was
closest to Sharpsburg, rather than the nearby hamlets of Porterstown and Centerville, Md.* 🔫

President Lincoln visits headquarters on the Antietam battlefield. At his right is Detective Allan Pink-
erton and on his left is General John McClernand.

Library of Congress

Antietam battlefield. The haze in the distance is the smoke rising from the actual fighting. Dimly seen at left center and right center are Federal artillery reserves. (This is, perhaps, the only existing combat photograph of any Civil War battle.)

Library of Congress

(Friday, September 19, 1862)

The War in Maryland.

Full Particulars of the Battles of Tuesday and Wednesday—The Result Considered a Decided Union Success

HEADQUARTERS, Tuesday Evening, Sept. 16. —During this afternoon information was received at headquarters showing that the enemy were recrossing the river and concentrating their forces on the ridge of hills outside of the town of Sharpsburg to within three miles of the main body of our army. Jackson left Harper's Ferry this morning—his troops commencing to arrive during the afternoon. When it became evident that Gen. Lee was disposed to engage our forces in battle at this point, Gen. McClellan sent for Franklin's corps and (Darius Nash) Couch's division, who were about seven miles distant, on the other side of Elk Ridge.

There was considerable artillery firing during the day on both sides, resulting in our having about forty men killed and wounded. Among the seriously wounded was Major Arnedst, of the 1st New York Artillery, who was struck in the side by a piece of shell.

The disposition of the troops for the impending battle was as follows: Gen. (Edwin Vose) Sumner's corps, with Banks' division, to occupy the center; Gen. Hooker's corps, with the Pennsylvania Reserves, and Franklin's corps, on the right, and (Fitz John) Porter's corps on the left of Sumner, and Burnside on the extreme left, with the view of turning the enemy's right flank. Gen. Pleasanton supported the centre with 2,500 cavalry and four batteries.

Gen. Hooker in the afternoon crossed Antietam Creek, and took a position on the hills facing Sharpsburg and three miles to the right of Keetsville (Keedysville). His troops got into action about dusk, which lasted two hours, during which the enemy were driven about half a mile, with considerable loss. The Pennsylvania Reserves, who were in the front, suffered much.

The night was occupied in getting the troops in their respective positions, while ammunition trains and ambulances were forwarded to their respective commands.

THE BATTLE OF WEDNESDAY.

WEDNESDAY EVENING, Sept. 17.— p.m.— This has been an eventful day in the history of the rebellion. A battle has taken place, in which the Army of the Potomac has again been victorious, and which exceeds in extent any battle heretofore fought on this continent.

At the dawn of day the battle was renewed on the center and right by Generals Hooker and Sumner, who, after a sharp contest of two hours, drove the enemy about one mile. The rebels rallied shortly, and with terrible loss regained most of the ground. At this time the fearless and indomitable Gen. Hooker received a shot in the ankle and was carried from the field. The command of his troops now devolved upon Gen. Sumner. Gen. (Israel Bush) Richardson, commanding a division, was severely wounded at the same time (and soon died of the wound).

Gen. Sumner, determined to retake the lost ground, ordered the troops to advance, which they did with a will, driving the rebels before them with great slaughter. They not only retook the ground but drove them a quarter of a mile beyond. In this action Gen. (Joseph King Fenno) Mansfield was shot through the lungs and died soon after. He was at the head of his troops with sword waving over his head, cheering on his men at the time he received his wound.

During this time the troops under Generals Burnside and Porter had not been idle. They drove the enemy from the line of the Antietam creek on the main road to Sharpsburg, built a bridge, the old one having been burnt, and occupied the opposite bank. The loss here was considerable.

The troops now held both sides of the creek. To get possession of the ridge of hills on the right and left hand sides of the road, from where the rebels were thundering away with artillery, was a task not easily accomplished. General Sykes's brigade, with the assistance of General Sumner, crossed the ridge on the right hand side, after considerable trouble and loss, the rebels running in all directions.

It was now 5 o'clock, and all the enemy's positions had been carried except the one on the left hand side of the road. To perform this duty General Burnside was assigned. The artillery opened and the infantry advanced, and the point was carried at a charge. They were, however, forced to retire before a largely superior force. Knowing that if they lost this ridge a complete rout of their army would be the result, they fought with great desperation.

Darkness now overtook the two armies, and hostilities ceased, as if by mutual consent. The battle lasted from 5 o'clock in the morning till 7 o'clock at night, without a momentary cessation.

The conduct of the troops, without exception, was all that any general could wish. Several regiments of new troops, who were in action for the first time, behaved admirably.

Hundreds of Marylanders were present to witness the battle, which could be seen from many of the surrounding hills. The sharp rattle of fifty thousand muskets, and the thunder of a hundred pieces of artillery, nor the consequent excited movements of such armies is not often witnessed.

It is impossible at this writing to form any correct idea of our loss or that of the enemy, but it is heavy on both sides. Ours will probably reach in killed and wounded 10,000. That of the enemy will not exceed it.

The enemy's dead, which nearly all fell into our hands, were thickly strewn over the fields, laying in heaps in many places.

Our wounded were immediately carried from the field, and the best possible attention given them.

When Gen. Hooker fell, Gen. McClellan immediately proceeded to the right, where he was enthusiastically received, and by his presence added much to our success in recovering the ground lost. He was on the center and on the left as well, anxiously watching the progress of the battle and giving directions as to the manner of attack. He is in his tent to-night for the first time since he left Frederick city.

A Federal wagon train crosses Antietam Bridge.

National Archives

Confederate dead along Hagerstown Road after the battle.

We took some fifteen hundred prisoners during the day, while the enemy obtained but a few.

🙥 *The two-days-in-one accounts that reached Washington nearly two days after the battle may have lacked accuracy and clarity of detail. But they got across the surging ferocity of the struggle, which would go down as the bloodiest single day of the war. It was an endless series of Federal attack and Confederate counter-attack. First it was a cornfield between two woods alongside the Hagerstown road. Then the assault into the westernmost of those woods, on the edge of which was a little white church used by the Dunkard sect. A sunken road farther east became known as "Bloody Lane." A stone bridge a little to the south across Antietam Creek was finally stormed by Burnside's corps in a hail of lead. Despite the piecemeal manner in which McClellan*

Confederate dead after Antietam. Remains of cornstalks are seen at top; it was in this cornfield that the deadliest action took place.

threw his overpowering numbers against Lee, the Confederate lines steadily pressed back closer to Sharpsburg. Lee's shifting of troops from one side of the line to the other to meet each crisis could not go on forever. Finally, in the wane of the afternoon, when Burnside's troops appeared on the verge of smashing through Lee's right, Ambrose Powell Hill's division came up from Harper's Ferry and crushed the left of Burnside's attacking line. That was enough for McClellan for the day. Of a total force of between 75,000 and 87,000—a large portion of which never entered the fight—the Federals sustained more than 12,000 casualties. Lee's army of between 41,000 and 51,000 lost upwards of 11,000. 🙥

(Friday, September 19, 1862)
MOST IMPORTANT
FROM THE SEAT OF WAR.

GEN. McCLELLAN ANNOUNCES
A COMPLETE VICTORY
OVER THE REBELS.

The Enemy Abandon Their Position and Make a Precipitate Retreat, Leaving Their Dead and Wounded on the Field.

HEADQUARTERS ARMY OF THE POTOMAC,
September 19—8:30 a.m.
Maj. Gen. Halleck, General-in-Chief, U.S.A.:
But little occurred yesterday except skirmishing.
Last night the enemy abandoned his position, leaving his dead and wounded on the field.
We are again in pursuit.
I do not know yet whether he is falling back to an interior position or crossing the river.
We may safely claim a complete victory.
George B. McClellan, Maj. Gen.

ANOTHER OFFICIAL DISPATCH
FROM GEN. McCLELLAN.

He Is Driving the Rebels Across the River, into Virginia.

HEADQUARTERS ARMY OF THE POTOMAC,
September 19—10:30 a.m.
Gen. H. W. Halleck, General-in-Chief, U.S.A.:
Pleasanton is driving the enemy across the river.
Our victory was complete.
The enemy is driven back into Virginia.
Maryland and Pennsylvania are now safe.
George B. McClellan, Maj. Gen.

WASHINGTON HOMEFRONT, SEPTEMBER, 1862.

During the week after Antietam, The Star was having mechanical problems on top of the usual difficulties of obtaining accurate news swiftly.

TRIBULATIONS.—Since Monday last the *Star* office has experienced tribulations in the labor of getting new machinery to work satisfactorily, such as were never before undergone in this region, though all at the North, where complicated and at the same time huge machinery is in general use, are accustomed to them. On Monday we put in operation our new rotary four-cylinder press, for the first time, hoping that we should have no trouble with it. But experience proves otherwise.

We find that we require paper with a different run of its grain from that used in our old presses; also a different description of ink; also changes in the machinery connected with our steam engine, to gain the requisite power to drive the press steadily; and, above all, a little practice in our employees in discharging their respective tasks in connection with it; as we prefer to continue our old hands in the pressroom at the expense of a few balks for a few days, to discharging them and importing others from the North who have had experience in the management of the vast machine, which, by the by, occupies a space thirty-four feet long, thirteen broad, and twelve high, and is well nigh as delicate in its joints and complications as a chronometer . . .

A COMMON TERM BEAUTIFULLY DEFINED.—A soldier, in appealing lately to his son to go and fight for the Government and the Union, said: "Perhaps you have never thought what your country means. It is all that surrounds you—all that has brought you up and fed you—all that you have loved. This country that you see—these houses, these trees, those girls who go along there laughing—this is your country. The laws which protect you, the bread which pays for your work, the words you interchange with others, the joy and grief which come to you from the men and things among which you live—this is your country! The little room where you used to see you mother, the remembrances she

Library of Congress

"Burnside's Bridge" over Antietam Creek.

has left you, the earth where she rests—this is your country! You see it, you breathe it everywhere. Think for yourself of your right and duties, your affections and your wants, your past and present blessing; write them all under a single name—and that name will be *your country*. We owe all that we are, and he who enjoys the advantage of having a free country, and does not accept the burdens of it forfeits his honor, and is a bad citizen. Do for your country what you would do for your father and mother. Your country is in danger."

Confederate wounded at an aid station near Keedysville, Maryland.

Library of Congress

ABRAHAM LINCOLN HAD LONG PONDERED A SOLUTION TO the "Negro question," as Abolitionist fanatic John Brown called it before he died on the gallows. Lincoln opposed slavery as a matter of principle. Yet, before the war, he had been willing to preserve the institution, where it existed, if such a policy helped preserve the Union of States. The Abolitionists were constantly pressuring for immediate and unqualified freedom for slaves everywhere in the country. Lincoln knew, however, that a conservative element in the North opposed sweeping and precipitate action. He was aware also that the course urged by the Abolitionists would doubtless offend slave-owners in the border States. And adherence of Maryland, Kentucky and Missouri to the Union was essential if the Union cause were to succeed. One other consideration involved the seceded States where slavery flourished most: the President desired to act in no way that might provoke Negroes to rise against their masters in a bloody slave insurrection.

Lincoln had started seeking cautiously for the right answer early in 1862. He had recommended to Congress in March that some sort of compensated emancipation of slaves be undertaken. Under such a program the Federal Government would pay the slave owners of any State willing to launch gradual abolition of slavery.

By midsummer a new misgiving was troubling the President. Could the Union survive when its armies, in the East at least, were proving to be chronic losers? Lincoln doubted it. He decided that, despite the conflicting views on how, when and under what circumstances the slaves should be freed, he must act boldly. He had to resolve the Negro question in a way that would offend as few Northerners and border States as possible, and win as many friends as possible—overseas as well as at home. He determined to use his Presidential war powers and issue a proclamation. He would proclaim the abolition of slavery in the "rebellious" States, where the economic system depended on slavery. That way he could weaken the Confederacy and brighten the chances of maintaining the Union.

The President tried out a preliminary draft of a proclamation along these lines at a Cabinet meeting in July. Secretary Seward offered one suggestion: the time was not right. Issuing the proclamation at that moment would probably be regarded as a sign of Federal weakness. It might appear that since the Union cause was not being won on the battlefield, the Administration was stooping to a desperate stratagem to gain popular support for the cause. Lincoln tucked the proclamation away to await a season of military victory when he could lead from strength.

The next month he had an opportunity to state his philosophy about the whole issue. Horace Greeley's New York *Tribune* stridently demanded immediate emancipation. The President replied: "My paramount purpose in this struggle is to save the Union, and is not either to save or destroy slavery. If I could save the Union without freeing any slave, I would do it; and if I could save it by freeing all the slaves I would do it; and if I could save it by freeing some and leaving others alone, I would also do that. . . . I have here stated my purpose according to my view of official duty; and I intend no modification of my oft-expressed personal wish that all men everywhere could be free."

On September 22, 1862, he felt the time for his proclamation had come. The battle outside Sharpsburg could hardly have been called a Federal triumph. But Lee's army had been repulsed and was back in Virginia. On that signal date, the complete text of the President's edict appeared at the top of Page One in *The Star*.

LINCOLN PROCLAIMS FREEDOM OF SLAVES

(Tuesday, September 23, 1862)

OFFICIAL.

By the President of the United States
of America.

A PROCLAMATION.

I, ABRAHAM LINCOLN, President of the United States of America, and Commander-in-Chief of the Army and Navy thereof, do hereby proclaim and declare that hereafter, as heretofore, the war will be prosecuted for the object of practically restoring the constitutional relation between the United States and each of the States, and the people thereof, in which States that relation is or may be suspended or disturbed.

That it is my purpose, upon the next meeting of Congress, to again recommend the adoption of a practical measure tendering pecuniary aid to the free acceptance or rejection of all Slave States, so called, the people whereof may not then be in rebellion against the United States, and which States may then have voluntarily adopted, or thereafter may voluntarily adopt, immediate or gradual abolishment of slavery within their respective limits; and that the effort to colonize persons of African descent, with their consent, upon this continent or elsewhere, with the previously-obtained consent of the Governments existing there, will be continued.

President Lincoln's first handwritten draft of the Emancipation Proclamation. A longer, formal proclamation, based on this version, was submitted to Congress January 1, 1863.

That on the first day of January, in the year of our Lord one thousand eight hundred and sixty-three, all persons held as slaves within any State, or designated part of a State, the people whereof shall then be in rebellion against the United States, shall be then, thenceforward free; and the Executive Government of the United States, including the military and naval authority thereof, will recognize and maintain the freedom of such persons, and will do no act or acts to repress such persons, or any of them, in any efforts they may make for their actual freedom. . . .

☞ *The proclamation was in effect an advance notice and a pledge.*

The editorial silence of The Star *regarding the proclamation prompted one of its Washington competitors to jeer. A verbal hassle ensued.* ☞

(Wednesday, September 24, 1862)

THE REPUBLICAN'S ASSAULT ON THE STAR.—*The Republican* of this morning takes occasion to say:

"The *Star* of last evening was as silent as the grave upon the proclamation of the President. It is too much of a courtier and too long habituated to 'kiss the foot that is on the throne,' to be ready to condemn an act done by a President actually in office. It has been a Vicar of Bray too long to do a thing of that kind; at any rate without great deliberation. But while hesitating to condemn the President's action, the *Star* equally hesitates to approve it. That paper enjoys private as well as public patronage; and the proportion of the population of this metropolis which dislikes the President's proclamation is too large to be rashly offended, upon the *Star's* tactics of balancing loss and gain, before determining which side of a question to take."

The *Star* is silent on the subject of the Proclamation, simply and plainly for the reason that whatever doubts we may have as to the wisdom of the policy entered upon by President Lincoln, to urge them now that that policy is a foregone conclusion cannot be advantageous to the national cause. Our great impending danger at this juncture is from divided counsels.

The *Star* "enjoys" neither "private" nor "public patronage," nor does it solicit "patronage" of either. It accords to its customers a fair equivalent for every penny it receives. Hence the so much greater extent of its business than that of the *Republican,* as a glance at the advertising columns of the two will con-

President Lincoln about the time he issued the Emancipation Proclamation. With him is General McClellan.

vince any man that has eyes in his head. The *Star* has never received "patronage" to the extent of a sixpence from the Government under any administration, all of them being directed by law to advertise, as businessmen do their advertising, in the paper of the largest circulation.

We trust that sooner or later our contemporary, the *Republican,* will learn that the journal seeking to live on "patronage" in these *times* is sure to starve; else it will soon draw its own last breath. To be sure, the alleged history of its complication with Peck's defaulting depredations upon the treasury of the State of Maine, with the attempt to blackmail the treasury of the State of Massachusetts for lobbying through the bill to pay for the services of her noncombatant militia in the war of 1812, with its persistent efforts to obtain "patronage" through Congressional action for the restoration of the General Post Office advertising to the journals of Washington, and its hourly button-holing of Departmental functionaries at this time for "patronage," (to enable it to live, while the public, in whose midst it is printed, turn their backs upon it as being a mere echo of abler mischief makers, bent on forcing negro social and industrial equality upon this population,) render it questionable whether it will ever acquire sufficient taste for the true way of making a prosperous newspaper, to do business enough to meet its business obligations as the *Star* does.

(Monday, December 1, 1862)

. . . Is it doubted then that the plan I propose, if adopted, would shorten the war, and thus lessen its expenditure of money and of blood? Is it doubted that it would restore the national authority and national prosperity, and perpetuate both indefinitely? Is it doubted that we here—Congress and Executive—can secure its adoption? Will not the good people respond to a united, and earnest appeal from us? Can we, can they, by any other means, so certainly, or so speedily, assure these vital objects?

We can succeed only by concert. It is not "Can *any* of us *imagine* better?" but "Can we *all* do better?" Object whatsoever is possible, still the question recurs "can we do better?" The dogmas of the quiet past are inadequate to the stormy present. The occasion is piled high with difficulty, and we must rise with the occasion. As our case is new, so we must think anew. We must disenthrall ourselves, and then we shall save our country.

Fellow-citizens, *we* cannot escape history. We, of this Congress and this administration, will be remembered in spite of ourselves. No personal significance, or insignificance, can spare one or another of us. The fiery trial through which we pass, will light us down, in honor or dishonor, to the latest generation. We *say* we are for the Union. The world will not forget that we say this. We know how to save the Union. The world knows we do know how to save it. We—even *we here*—hold the power and bear the responsibility.

In *giving* freedom to the *slave*, we *assure* freedom to the *free*—honorable alike in what we give, and what we preserve. We shall nobly save, or meanly lose, the last, best hope of earth. Other means may succeed; this could not fail. The way is plain, peaceful, generous, just—a way which, if followed, the world will forever applaud, and God must forever bless.

ABRAHAM LINCOLN.

December 1, 1862

And on the first day of the new year, the President formally proclaimed what he had promised that September day just after Antietam.

WASHINGTON HOMEFRONT, SEPTEMBER, 1862.

Washington's reaction to the proclamation came two days later.

SERENADE TO THE PRESIDENT.—The announcement made yesterday of the intended serenade to President Lincoln drew a large gathering at the Executive Mansion last evening. At eight o'clock the band appeared, and after loud calls made for him the President appeared, accompanied by his private secretary, Mr. Hay. He was received with loud cheers, and when silence was restored he addressed the crowd as follows:

Fellow Citizens:—I appear before you to do little more than acknowledge the courtesy you pay me, and to thank you for it. I have not been distinctly informed why it is that on this occasion you appear to do me this honor. I suppose—(An interruption. "It is because of the proclamation." Cries of "good" and applause.) I was about to say, I suppose I understand it. (Laughter and voices, "That you do;" "You thoroughly understand it.")

What I did, I did after very full deliberation and under a very heavy and solemn sense of responsibility. (Cries of "Good," "God bless you," and applause.) I can only trust in God that I have made no mistake. (Cries of "No—all right," "You've made no mistake yet," "Go ahead," "You're right.") I shall make no attempt on this occasion to sustain what I have done or said by any argument. (Voices, "That's unnecessary," "We understand it.") It's now for the country and the world to pass judgment on it, and may be take action upon it.

I will say no more upon this subject. In my position I am environed with difficulties. (A voice—"That's so.") Yet they are scarcely so great as the difficulties of those who, upon the battle-field, are endeavoring to purchase with their blood and lives the future happiness and prosperity of this country. (Applause, long continued.) Let us never forget them. On the 14th and 17th days of this month there have been battles bravely, skillfully, and successfully fought. (Applause.)

We do not yet know the particulars. Let us be sure that, in giving praise to particular individuals, we do no injustice to others. I only ask you, at the conclusion of these few remarks, to give three hearty cheers to all good and brave officers and men who fought these successful battles.

Cheer after cheer was given, when the President bade the crowd good night and withdrew.

The band followed by the crowd then proceeded

President Lincoln reading the draft of the Emancipation Proclamation to his cabinet.

to the residence of Secretary Chase, and after one or two airs had been played that gentleman appeared. Calls were made for "Light, more Light," and Mr. Chase said:

"My friends, all the light you can have this evening will be light reflected from this great act of the President. (Cries of "Good; good. That's light enough!") I understand that you have just paid your respects to the Chief Magistrate of the Republic to assure him that the proclamation which he has recently issued finds echo in the hearts of the American people. (Great Applause.)

No one can rejoice more sincerely, in the belief that the judgment which you have expressed of that act will be the judgment of the whole people of the United States. (Loud applause.) . . .

Gen. C. M. Clay was the next speaker. He said he came there, as well as those before him, to do honor to the great act which would make Abraham Lincoln immortal among men. . . .

(He said) the proclamation will reach the blacks —no barrier will prevent the intelligence from reaching them; that after January 1st, 1863, all slaves of masters who have arms in their hands will be free. (Applause.) He argues that millions of whites in the South were fighting for slave-holders as against their own interests; the proclamation will reach these men and they will discover their interest is ours, and we will invite them to take up arms in defense of our rights. If we win, as we shall, we will place the same hard conditions upon them that we enjoy. He further argued that the manufacturers and commercial men of the North had been catering to the aristocrats of the South. The proclamation is right, and if it is right we will not stop to ask whether it is expedient or not.

He also argued that the proclamation will have a most beneficial effect upon the European governments. . . .

Mc CLELLAN HAD THE "SLOWS" FOR THE LAST TIME. Despite the beseeching from Washington, he permitted Lee's outnumbered and battle-weakened army to escape. For weeks the Army of Northern Virginia lay almost contemptuously in the Shenandoah Valley, within short marching distance of the Federal behemoth. McClellan, instead of following through, puttered on the Maryland shore of the Potomac while his troops, he said, recovered from the "fatigue" of Antietam. What he did not rationalize was the fact that a large part of his force had not even been engaged in the battle, and that thousands of fresh reinforcements had since joined him. In this October lull, "Little Mac" sustained a humiliation that had been visited upon him on the Peninsula. Jeb Stuart's cavalry rode entirely around his immobile army. This time Stuart penetrated Pennsylvania, looting Chambersburg, brushing past the crossroads town of Gettysburg and emerging South of McClellan to recross the Potomac into Virginia. The Federal commander finally bestirred himself toward the end of October and crossed the Potomac himself. On November 7, however, a message arrived from Washington, and the Army of the Potomac was no longer his.

The eternal eeny-meeny-miney-mo of trying to find a winning commander for a brave army tapped Ambrose Burnside this time. Burnside, personally courageous, had shown he could lead a corps. Could he lead an army? Lincoln had his doubts. So did Burnside. The President very likely was becoming fatalistic about the never-ending chore of selecting generals. Just a week before McClellan's removal, Buell had been replaced by William Starke Rosecrans in the West. Here again, Buell had proved to be a victim of the "slows." A few weeks before, he had stemmed the Confederate campaign in Kentucky by showing up in time at Louisville. When his adversary Bragg retreated, Buell followed. The two armies fought to a draw at Perryville, Ky., and Bragg continued his retreat. Washington's patience burst when Buell's "pursuit" crawled. Lincoln liked the looks of Rosecrans as a successor. In the past two months, Rosecrans had repulsed the Confederates at Corinth and Iuka, Miss.

There was still one commander Washington needn't worry about. Ulysses Grant was on the move in upper Mississippi, starting an arduous campaign that would lead to Vicksburg.

The new man in the East knew that prompt and aggressive action was expected of him. Burnside quickly formed a plan to assault Richmond via Fredericksburg. Lincoln and Halleck shied at that. They preferred a route along the Eastern foothills of the Blue Ridge, especially since only half of Lee's army was now in front of Burnside on the upper Rappahannock River. (Jackson was still in the Valley.) Burnside's plan was hesitantly assented to, with the admonition that he hurry. The Fredericksburg crossing of the lower Rappahannock had to be made before Lee could array his army on the heights behind the town. Burnside moved his three "grand" divisions quickly enough, but when he reached the opposite shore from Fredericksburg, delay set in. He had ordered pontoon bridges to facilitate the crossing, but they had not arrived. By the time they did, 10 days later, Jackson's corps had galloped on foot all the way from the Valley, and Longstreet had also moved into position.

None of these portentous developments would materially change Burnside's strategy. He would still pit his 120,000 Federals against Lee's 78,000 entrenched on the heights behind Fredericksburg.

BURNSIDE REPULSED AT FREDERICKSBURG

(Thursday, December 11, 1862)

Telegraphic.

A GREAT BATTLE IN PROGRESS AT FREDERICKSBURG!

Gen. Burnside Heavily Engaged with the Enemy at That Point!

THE BATTLE CONTINUES TO RAGE!

HEADQUARTERS ARMY OF THE POTOMAC,
December 11—9 a.m.

Everything last night was bustle and activity, as to-day was the time fixed for the crossing of the river. During the night the pontoons were conveyed to the river, and the artillery, 143 pieces, placed in position opposite the city. At 5 o'clock this morning the Rebels fired two signal guns, while during the latter part of the night rockets were frequently seen within their lines.

At 5 o'clock the construction of three bridges in front of the city was commenced, and when about completed the enemy opened a murderous fire of infantry from the houses on the river bank. Up to this time not a shot had been fired from our side. The engineers were driven from the bridge and several killed and wounded.

At 6 o'clock Gen. Burnside ordered all the guns to open on the city.

The cannonade, which has continued without interruption up to the present time, is terrible. The city is on fire, and its destruction appears to be certain.

The enemy, about 7 o'clock, opened with their heavy guns from their works; but so far have done no serious injury.

Gen. Franklin constructed his bridge about three miles below the city, meeting with but slight opposition. His troops are now crossing.

The gunboats are now shelling the enemy about fifteen miles down the river, where they have been concentrating their forces during the past two days.

The concentrated fire of our batteries on the city has had the effect of driving back the enemy's infantry, and the work on the bridges has been again commenced.

The troops are all under arms near the river, preparing to rush over as soon as the bridges are completed.

Fredericksburg, Virginia, with the Rappahannock River in the foreground.

Federal troops providing cover for construction of a pontoon bridge across the Rappahannock.

(Second Dispatch.)

HEADQUARTERS ARMY OF THE POTOMAC,
Thursday, Dec. 11—12 o'clock.

On the attempt being made to finish the bridges in front of the city the Rebel infantry again opened their fire. The artillery in position was again opened on the city, the result being that it was fired in several new places. The enemy have used very little artillery up to this time, as it would endanger their own men who are holding the river front. Gen. Burnside has just issued an order to concentrate every available gun upon the city, under cover of the fire of which it is believed the bridges can be finished. The killed and wounded so far do not amount to more than fifty men.

☞ *For the first time in the war, a city was being laid waste. Military necessity was the justification. Brig. Gen. William Barksdale's Mississippians were mowing down Burnside's bridge-builders. The massed artillery on Stafford Heights failed to reduce the Confederate sharpshooting.* ☞

(Friday, December 12, 1862)

FREDERICKSBURG CAPTURED.
THE CONFEDERATE SHARPSHOOTERS DRIVEN OUT.
THE CITY OCCUPIED BY FEDERAL TROOPS.

HEADQUARTERS ARMY OF THE POTOMAC, Thursday evening.—From one to three o'clock but little firing took place, but during this time all the available batteries were placed in position. They now number 176 guns.

At a given signal all the batteries opened on the city. The fire was terrible, but the rebel sharpshooters would not be drawn from their hiding places. The shot and shell went crashing through the houses, in many cases setting them on fire, causing dense volumes of smoke, which, together with the explosion of so large a quantity of powder, almost hid the city from view.

It soon became evident that the bridges could not be built except by driving away the sharpshooters by a bold dash across the river. Volunteers were called for to cross in small boats. The order was no sooner given than hundreds of braves stepped forward, but all could not go. About 100 were selected for the perilous undertaking, and were soon on their way, while the artillery threw a perfect storm of iron on the opposite bank. They soon reached the opposite shore, but not without loss, and with fixed bayonets they rushed upon the enemy, killing several, and taking 101 prisoners, who were safely landed on this side.

At half-past four o'clock two bridges were finished opposite the city, when the troops immediately began to cross over. The enemy were soon driven from the city, back to their line of works.

The two bridges in front of Gen. Franklin's position were successfully laid during the day, but his troops did not cross until the two upper ones were ready. A sufficient force is now on the opposite side of the river to resist any attack that is likely to be made.

The rebels fired but few guns in the morning and none in the afternoon, although their works were in easy range. During the forenoon the rebels burnt the railroad bridge just outside the city.

Between 30 and 40 houses were burnt, mostly .in the business part of the city.

A. Waud—Library of Congress

Officers rallying the Federal troops for the charge up Marye's Heights.

During the day between eight and nine thousand rounds of ammunition were fired by our artillery.

Everything is quiet to-night, but the indications are that a battle will be fought to-morrow.

🔫 What was left of Fredericksburg fell to the Federals, but its capture signified nothing, except that the advance up the slopes against Lee's whole army could begin. The next day would be crucial and, fortunately for newspaper readers, the front was less than 50 miles from Washington and communications were good—for a change. 🔫

(Saturday, December 13, 1862)

MOST IMPORTANT FROM FREDERICKSBURG!

A GREAT BATTLE GOING ON!

Reynolds' Corps Commences the Battle at 9 O'Clock This Morning.

A HEAVY FOG OBSTRUCTS THE VIEW.

(Special Dispatch to the Star.)

HEADQUARTERS IN THE FIELD, Saturday morning, Dec. 13, 11 o'clock.

The battle so long anticipated between the two contending armies is now progressing.

The morning opened with a dense fog, which has not yet entirely disappeared.

Reynolds' corps, on the left, advanced at an early hour, and at 9:15 engaged the enemy's infantry. Seven minutes after, the Rebels opened a heavy fire of artillery, which has continued so far without intermission.

Their artillery fire must be at random, as the fog obstructs all view. Our heavy guns are answering them rapidly.

As the sun gets higher it is hoped the fog will lift.

At this writing no results are known.

Not much infantry has yet become engaged.

A portion of the enemy's cavalry crossed a ford above here, and yesterday were found on our right and rear. A sufficient force, however, has been sent out to meet them.

🔫 At the time this report was sent, only the left of the Federal line was making its assault about a mile downriver from the town. The Federal center was just then preparing to storm the heights on which the mansion of the Marye family was located. 🔫

(Monday, December 15, 1862)

Telegraphic News.

From the Army of the Potomac.

GEN. FRANKLIN'S DIVISION OPPOSED TO SUPERIOR NUMBERS.

A CLOSE AND DESPERATE FIGHT.

GENERAL BAYARD KILLED.

HEADQUARTERS IN THE FIELD, Saturday, Dec. 13, 8 p.m.—The great battle at Fredericksburg, which commenced at sunrise this morning, closed at a quarter past six o'clock this evening. It was desperately fought on the left. We were met by an overwhelming force, but could not be driven back.

At four o'clock Sumner had carried the enemy's first line of works.

166

At five o'clock the fire of musketry was deafening.

At six o'clock the enemy ceased firing, and hostilities ceased altogether, to be renewed in the morning, if the enemy does not abandon his position.

9 p.m.—Among the casualties in the battle of to-day was Gen. George D. Bayard, of the cavalry brigade, killed; Major General (Winfield Scott) Hancock, wounded; Brig. Gen. Kimball, wounded.

The battle was desperately contested, and at the close of the day the advantage appeared to be on our side.

If the rebels do not retreat, to-morrow will witness the bloodiest battle of the century.

To-night reinforcements are being thrown into our weak points, and several regiments that were held in reserve all day have been brought forward to take part in the coming struggle.

Gen. Jo. Hooker will take part to-morrow and will endeavor to pierce the enemy's center.

Gens. Burnside and Sumner are in the best of spirits, and confident that to-morrow will close on a brilliant victory for the Union arms.

The signal fires of the rebels are in full blast, showing that they are also watchful, and are seizing every opportunity to strengthen their lines.

HEADQUARTERS ARMY OF THE PO-TOMAC, Saturday evening, 11 o'clock.—The fog began to disappear, affording an obstructed view of our own and the rebel positions. It being evident that the first ridge of hills in the rear of the city, on which the enemy had their guns posted behind the works, could not be carried except by a charge of infantry. Sumner assigned that duty to French's division, supported by Howard's.

The troops advanced to their work, ten minutes before 12, at a brisk run—the enemy's guns open-ing a rapid fire. When within musket range of the base of the ridge they were met by a terrible fire from the rebel infantry, who were posted behind a stone wall and some houses on the right of the line.

This checked their advance, and they fell back to a small ravine, but not out of musket range.

At this time another body of troops moved to their assistance in splendid style, notwithstanding gaps were made in their ranks by the rebel artillery. When they arrived at the first line they double-quicked, and, with a command of fixed bayonets, endeavored to dislodge the rebels from their hiding place. The concentrated fire of artillery and infantry which they were forced to face was too much, and the center gave way in disorder, but were afterwards rallied and brought back.

From that time the fire was spiritedly carried on, and never ceased until some time after dark.

Gen. Franklin, who commanded the attack on the left, met with better success. He succeeded, after a hard day's fight, in driving the enemy about one mile. At one time the rebels advanced to attack, but were handsomely repulsed with terrible slaughter, and a loss of between four and five hundred prisoners, belonging to Gen. A. P. Hill's command.

Our troops sleep where they fought to-day, and the dead and wounded are being carried from the field to-night. . . .

Of the more than 100,000 Federals who took part in the attacks all along the line, nearly 13,000 were killed or wounded. Most of these fell on the fields below the Marye place, where one division followed another across open ground swept by Confederate musketry and cannon. It was as hopeless as it was heroic, but Burnside stubbornly sent the blue-clad

Federal troops looting Fredericksburg.

waves up the hill all afternoon. Grief-stricken, finally, over the enormity of what he had done, he was barely dissuaded from taking to the field at the head of his old corps and leading a suicide charge. ⚞

(Tuesday, December 16, 1862)
Latest News by Telegraph.
OUR ARMY HAS RECROSSED THE RAPPAHANNOCK TO FALMOUTH!
THE PONTOON BRIDGES TAKEN UP.

The following has been received by the military telegraph, dated Falmouth, Va., Dec. 16, 1862:

"It is raining very fast. The river is rising rapidly. Our troops are all this side of the river. The pontoons are up."

(Wednesday, December 17, 1862)
Latest News by Telegraph.
FROM GENERAL BURNSIDE!

General Burnside sends the following dispatch explaining his reasons for withdrawing from Fredericksburg:

HEADQUARTERS ARMY OF THE POTOMAC, Dec. 16, 1862—6 o'clock p.m.—*Major General Halleck:* The army was withdrawn to this side of the river because I felt the position in front could not be carried, and was a military necessity either to attack or retire. A repulse would have been disastrous to us. The army was withdrawn at night without the knowledge of the enemy and without loss either of property or men.

> A. E. Burnside,
> Major General Commanding.

EDITORIAL.
(Tuesday, December 16, 1862)
MOST IMPORTANT NEWS FROM THE ARMY OF THE POTOMAC.

Elsewhere we publish this afternoon a dispatch from Falmouth announcing that we have crossed our whole force back to this side of the Rappahannock. The hesitation and delay of a forward movement since the great battle of Saturday served to prepare the public mind for this speedy retrograde step.

Does it not suggest unutterable thoughts to the country at large, and especially to the relatives and friends of our slaughtered thousands on Saturday—slaughtered through grave military mistakes somewhere?

Does it not tell most forcibly that the crossing should not have been made at a point from whence we could not advance a furlong without coming under fire of the apparently impregnable works with which the failure to expedite the arrival of the pontoon trains at Fredericksburg up to the time required and agreed on, permitted the enemy to block egress from that town in the direction of Richmond!

If we are ever to overcome the rebellion, must we not have better management than this affair indicates?

Can we hope for the necessary better management before due responsibility is fixed where it belongs, for the delays and strategy which culminated in the terrible slaughter of our country's brave defenders on Saturday last, the inefficiency and impolicy of which are so patent in this speedy retrograde movement?

Will Congress stop wrangling long enough to call for such an exposition of the history of Ben. Burnside's brief campaign, as will render it plain to all where the responsibility justly belongs?

Let this investigation embrace a call for the representations concerning the necessity of having the Azuia Creek railroad repaired long before that was done, and the means of throwing the army across the river long before they were ready, which, it is well known, the late commander of the Army of the Potomac made more than three weeks before he was superseded.

Let it also embrace a call for all the orders which Gen. Burnside has received bearing upon the selection of this point of crossing; and, also, his selection of the point of attack, if any such were given to him. No less thorough investigation will answer for such a case.

WASHINGTON HOMEFRONT, DECEMBER, 1862.

⚞ *Just two weeks before Christmas, the city's school board had reversed an earlier action taking away the traditional Christmas holidays from the kiddies and teachers. There had been a long discussion, duly published in* The Star. *A reader added his own afterthoughts.* ⚞

THE SCHOOLS AGAIN.—*Editor Star:* The action of the School Board, reported Wednesday, is taken by the people as an evidence of returning sanity on the holiday question. But the discussion reveals more clearly what was very well known before, that some schoolmen and some parents still regard public schools as "houses of refuge;" in the apt phrase of Mr. Rhees (a board member)—very convenient receptacles for unruly boys and girls who are troublesome at home and apt to get into trouble on the streets, and are therefore caged in durance, regarded by them either as tolerable or intolerable, and kept in subjection by a hired guard, called by courtesy a teacher. I have known three-year-olds, from a laudable desire to escape the expense of nurses, to be sent to school by persons of similar views. Is it possible that intelligent guardians of public education can have no higher ideal of a true school? If not, cradles should be supplied for the benefit of nurselings, and little vagrants should be subjected to workhouse regulations.

Because one could for a short time endure the most continuous and severe mental application from early morn to starlight, Saturdays included, it does not follow that a board of education should recommend to a city full of children of every grade of mental and physical strength the physiological outrage and absurdity of continuous sessions from one year's end to another.

There need have been no suggestion that the abolition of all holidays was a "Yankee movement." Whatever sins the Yankees may have to answer for (and I have no doubt they are many), they have had schools long enough to see the practical sense and actual necessity of a total cessation of study for at least a quarter part of each year for all school children, if advancement in knowledge or health in body or mind is desired.

The pertinacity with which the old fogy element of the board sought to take a part of Saturday, or an Easter day, or a week or two in July along the borders of dog days, from the expectant children and suffering teachers is amusingly refreshing.

General Ambrose Burnside, who commanded the Federal action at Fredericksburg.

The statement relative to the wages of teachers betrays an ignorance of what is paid to public school teachers in other cities, strangely suggestive of an untraveled experience or a woeful lack of observation. If they would get the schedule of prices for New York, Boston, Chicago, St. Louis, Louisville, Cincinnati, or Jackson or Natchez in Mississippi, (when they had schools there,) or New Orleans, they would discover that many of them pay much higher wages than Washington; and in view of the comparative cost of living, that female teachers are poorer paid here than in any considerable city in the Union, and, without exception, worked longer.

These positions I defy either of the apologists of stupid and everlasting plodding to disprove or gainsay in any degree.

Fair Play

THE CARNAGE BEFORE THE BREASTWORKS OF FREDERICKS-burg left the Federal army sprawled bleeding and exhausted along the opposite bank of the Rappahannock River. Respite was the least they deserved. Besides, winter had come, and the men were due to go into the usual "winter quarters," anyway. Across the river, Lee's troops could do with a bit of cold-weather hibernation themselves. Quiet, that December, settled unprotested over the Eastern armies.

The customary miseries of winter in the valleys of the Missis-sippi, Tennessee and Cumberland Rivers did not deter the combatants.

Federal armies were plodding relentlessly South. As they moved, Confederate cavalry—always a threat—raced north to the Fed-eral rear. Two days after Burnside's disaster, Bedford Forrest began his second raid into Tennessee. Before the month was over, Forrest's 2,500 troopers would capture Lexington, Humboldt, Trenton and Union City in that State, finally to be whipped at Parker Crossroads near Lexington. Forrest could retreat with the satisfaction of having de-stroyed much of Grant's rail communications for the Vicksburg cam-paign. Grant got the idea. He subsequently shifted his supply base from Columbus, Ky., to Memphis, Tenn., closer to the scene of opera-tions. John Hunt Morgan, with a brigade of 1,800, started a raid of his own a week later than Forrest. Morgan, drawing a bead on Kentucky, captured Lexington, Upton, Nolan and Elizabethtown before returning south. Hunt's cavalry left in its wake a wide swath of destroyed rail-roads and bridges.

Notwithstanding Forrest's raid, the Federal drive down the Mississippi toward Vicksburg continued. Sherman's force sailed down the river, escorted by Porter's gunboats, and paused along the way at Milliken's Bend to wreck a few Confederate rails. He had less success in an assault on Chickasaw Bluffs, just upstream from Vicksburg, being bloodily repulsed by Lt. Gen. John Clifford Pemberton, commander of the Confederate Department of Mississippi.

In central Tennessee, Rosecrans was out to show the higher authorities that, in him, they had an aggressive successor to the daw-dling Buell. As head of the new Army of the Cumberland, "Old Rosey" pushed after Bragg's Confederates as if he meant it. He had cavalry troubles en route. Joseph Wheeler, who was not called "Fightin' Joe" for nothing, had chopped up the Federal supply line. Wheeler's raid caused consternation and delay, but Rosecrans pressed forward. The town of Murfreesboro was in sight. On the last day of 1862, 45,000 Federals faced 38,000 Confederates just west of Stone's River.

MURFREESBORO CARNAGE IS INDECISIVE

(Friday, January 2, 1863)

GREAT BATTLE NEAR MURFREESBORO.

The Losses Enormous!

THREE UNION GENERALS WOUNDED!
TWO REBEL GENERALS KILLED!

The following has been received at the War Department from the Government telegraphic superintendent, who is now in the West:

CLEVELAND, OHIO, Jan. 2, 1863.—*Hon. E. M. Stanton, Secretary of War:* The following is just received from Cincinnati, dated Murfreesboro, January 1, 1863:

"Terrible battle fought yesterday.

"The latest from the field is up to noon.

"The rebel center had been broken, and things looked favorable.

"The losses reported are enormous. Generals (David Sloan) Stanley, Rosseau (Clovell Harrison Rousseau) and (John McAuley) Palmer wounded, and the rebel Generals (Benjamin Franklin) Cheatham and (James Edward) Rains killed."

Anson Stager

The initial dispatch was correct in one respect. It was indeed a "terrible" battle. Bragg alone was battlefield commander, although Joe Johnston was head of the Confederate Division of the West. The Federals did not break the rebel center, nor was Cheatham killed. More details were forthcoming.

(Saturday, January 3, 1863)

Telegraphic News.

The Battle at Murfreesboro.

Two Days' Fighting—Greatest Carnage of the War—Defeat of the Confederates.

NEAR MURFREESBORO, Dec. 31.—Our entire army suffered terribly this morning.

Four regiments of regulars lost half of their men, and all of their commanding officers.

The Anderson Troop suffered severely. Majors Rosengarten and Ward were killed, and Generals Stanley, Rousseau, and Palmer were wounded.

Two o'clock, p.m.—General Thomas breaks the rebel center, and drives the enemy the distance of a mile.

We advance the entire line, which Gen. Rosecrans is personally superintending.

The charge of General Negley's division across Stone River in the face of heavy rebel fire.

Library of Congress

One shot killed two of his staff.

The Fifteenth Wisconsin lost seven captains.

Gen'l (James Scott) Negley's artillery is still mowing the rebels in the center.

(Thomas Leonidas) Crittenden's left wing has taken the intrenchments at Murfreesboro.

The rebel guerillas Cheatham and Rains were killed.

———◆———

NASHVILLE, Jan. 2—There has been a terrible battle at Murfreesboro—the greatest carnage of the war. The Federal troops encountered the rebels on the 30th ult. near Stewart's Creek (tributary of Stone's River), when heavy skirmishing took place. The rebels were driven back, and we captured 100 prisoners and killed and wounded a large number. Our loss on this day was seventy killed and wounded.

At daybreak on the 31st the fight was renewed with great fury. Gen. McCook's corps was opposite to Hardee. After desperate fighting, with heavy loss on both sides, McCook retreated two miles. He soon rallied, however, but was again driven back, and at night was four miles this side of the ground occupied in the morning. The fight continued until 11 o'clock p.m., at which time we had maintained our other positions. . . .

🙐 *Both commanders had the same plan of attack: strike the enemy's right. Hardee's and Polk's Confederate corps struck first early December 31. They bowed the lines of "Pap" Thomas and Maj. Gen. Alexander McDowell McCook back in a 100-degree arc, pivoted near Stone's River, before the Federals stiffened and held. From the welter of confused accounts,* The Star, *in one of its curious news story-editorials, distilled this here-is-the-real situation piece:* 🙐

THE GREAT BATTLES AT MURFREESBORO.
THE TURNING POINT IN THE WAR!
Interesting Explanations Connected with It!

The facts received in Washington bearing on the great battles at Murfreesboro, up to 1½ p.m. to-day, we publish elsewhere. Such as they are they furnish ground for the strong hope that the Union cause has gained in them a substantial victory of more importance to its future than any other marking the progress of the war to this time.

The first engagement (a skirmish) took place on the 30th ult. near Stewart's Creek, and on that day we drove the rebels back, with heavy loss of killed and wounded and a hundred prisoners; our loss in killed and wounded being seventy.

The battle was renewed on the next day (the 31st) at daybreak, with great fury, and continued until ten p.m. Its result on that day was as follows. Viz.: McCook's division was substantially beaten, being driven back five miles. At 2 p.m. Gen. Thomas broke the rebel center, driving it the distance of a mile; and Crittenden's left wing took the rebel entrenchments at Murfreesboro. Whereupon Gen. Rosecrans (according to a telegram) advanced our whole line. We apprehend, however, that this may be an error, as another telegram (of the same date) intimates that McCook's division rested that night in the position four miles in the rear, to which it had been driven.

However, on the 1st instant, the engagement was again renewed at 3 a.m., and at 10 a.m. Wood's and Van Cleve's divisions were in Murfreesboro, driving the enemy, *who were in full retreat.*

We thus present the *Star*'s readers a succinct explanation of "the situation" up to the last moment at which (at 1½ p.m. to-day) there is information in Washington from that bloody field. It gives substantial ground for believing that we have gained an important and decisive victory, as heavy as our losses have been. For an idea of these we commend the reader to the telegrams concerning the battles published in other columns of to-day's *Star*.

If, as we now believe, Gen. Rosecrans has signally beaten the great rebel army contending with him for the possession of the Department of the Cumberland he was sent to wrest from them, the importance of his success can hardly be overestimated. It must, if properly followed up, rescue the command of East Tennessee and Northern Georgia from the Richmond authorities, and at the same time greatly strengthen the probabilities of the success of the combined land and water campaign for the rescue from the rebels of the control of the Mississippi river between Vicksburg and Port Hudson—a distance of 190 miles—which has so far enabled them to obtain from Texas the supplies they have drawn from that State, which are of vital necessity to the success of their entire military operations. At this moment Grant, Banks and Porter's fleet are fairly engaged in this campaign.

With the railroad connections of the rebels in East Tennessee and Northern Georgia in our hands, or at our mercy, as the result of a great victory at Murfreesboro, and with the control of the channels of communication (by water and rail) between Texas

Pennsylvania troops charge a rebel artillery position during the battle of Murfreesboro.

and Arkansas and the rest of the States in revolt, as the result of the Grant, Banks and Porter campaigns, Secessia will be fairly divided into three isolated sections, and its military strength well nigh destroyed. Up to that time its strength has resulted for the most part from the facility with which (by its railroad and Mississippi river advantages) it could concentrate its troops and supplies without delay just where they might be needed for the nonce.

With East Tennessee and Northern Georgia and the command of the entire Mississippi river in our hands, this great advantage will be instantly swept away.

The reader will therefore perceive at a glance why we regard the Murfreesboro battles—if they have, as we believe, resulted in a substantial and important Union victory—as of more importance to the good cause than even the reduction of Richmond would be at this time.

Two days later, disjointed reports were still coming in, although the battle was long over. Their total impact was clear: many thousands of men had been killed or maimed. With nearly 13,000 Federal and 12,000 Confederate casualties, this was worse than anything so far.

(Monday, January 5, 1863)
The Battle of Murfreesboro.
THE REBELS IN FULL RETREAT.

LOUISVILLE, Jan. 3.—Telegraphic communications resumed between here and Nashville.

(First Dispatch.)

NASHVILLE, Jan. 3.—It is reported here that Gen. Bragg was killed to-day. There has been fighting all day. Our forces are advancing, and the rebels are falling back across Stone's river.

The following officers were wounded slightly: Col. Miller, Col. Blake, 40th Indiana. Lieut. Col. Neff, Col. Hill, and Captain Pate. Heavy rain all day.

(Second Dispatch.)

NASHVILLE, Jan. 3.—Heavy cannonading to-day until noon. The rebels attacked our left but were terribly repulsed. Very little fighting yesterday. Our forces do not yet occupy Murfreesboro. The rebels attacked and destroyed our hospital building on Thursday. The Richmond army is furnishing rebels strong reinforcements.

(Third Dispatch.)

NASHVILLE, Jan. 3.—There was a spirited engagement at Lavergne, between the Mechanics and Engineers Corps, Col. Innis, and Gen. Wharton's rebel cavalry. The latter was routed with the loss of 33 killed. All the contrabands captured by the rebels on the Federal wagon train were shot. Twenty dead contraband are lying on the Murfreesboro pike. Major Slemmer and Captain King, wounded, and in an ambulance, were captured by the rebels, taken four miles, paroled and thrown out on the road.

Gen. Willich is not killed but wounded and a prisoner.

Yesterday, Gen. Rosecrans took command of the 4th U. S. cavalry, and personally attacked Gen. Wheeler's rebel cavalry, who were cut to pieces and utterly routed.

Capt. Mark, chief of artillery of Gen. Thomas' staff, mortally wounded.

Col. Anderson's dispatch in headquarters, just received, is as follows:—"We have whipped the rebels decidedly, and are at Christina, nine miles south of Murfreesboro, on the railroad."

General Braxton Bragg

(Fourth Dispatch.)

NASHVILLE, Jan. 3.—Col. McKee is reported killed. Our loss of officers is heart-rending. Fighting to-day was resumed at daylight. It closed last evening with terrible slaughter of the enemy.

Up to 5 o'clock the first day's fighting was all our own way, but the right wing fought itself into a bad position.

The third day we repulsed the enemy with terrible slaughter, ourselves sustaining but slight loss.

A merciful lull settled over the battlefield on New Year's Day. But on January 2, Breckinridge's Confederates had a try at the left of the Federal line.

FURTHER PARTICULARS OF THE GREAT BATTLE.

NEW YORK, Jan. 4.—A special dispatch from Murfreesboro, dated Friday evening, 2d inst., states that the rebels were twiced repulsed on Thursday in making fierce attacks on our center and right.

On Thursday night General Rosecrans ordered Beatty's brigade across Stone's river, on our left, which was accomplished.

On Friday afternoon the rebels made a tremendous attack on our center, but were again handsomely repulsed. At the same time they threw an immense mass of infantry against Beatty's brigade, driving it across the river, when Negley's and Davis' divisions went to their aid. A most desperate struggle now ensued, and all the artillery of both armies were brought to bear. Our men suffered terribly but unflinchingly.

At last Negley ordered a charge, when the rebels gave way.

The 78th Pennsylvania Regiment charged home on the 26th Tennessee, capturing its colors. Another regiment charged also, and captured an entire rebel battery. A grand shout of victory arose along the whole line, when General Rosecrans advanced his whole line, the left establishing itself on the east bank of the river; the center holding the enemy's former position, and the right holding its original position of Wednesday. The advantage is with us. The battle will be resumed on Saturday, and all feel confident of victory.

(*Note.*—"The National Telegraph Line" was not working yesterday, being interrupted from some cause, and the foregoing dispatch reached New York via the Buffalo Line. This may account for the fact that no official dispatches had reached Washington last night from Tennessee.—*REPORTER.*)

Breckinridge was beaten back. Contrary to the prediction in the news dispatch, action was not resumed Saturday, January 3. Bragg decided to head farther south in Tennessee. A jubilant dispatch to the War Department from a Federal officer broke the news.

General John C. Breckinridge, former vice-president of the United States and Democratic candidate for the presidency in 1860, commanded a rebel army corps at the battle of Murfreesboro.

GLORIOUS NEWS FROM TENNESSEE!

Splendid Union Victory!

THE REBELS WHIPPED COMPLETELY.

NASHVILLE, 10 a.m., Jan. 5.—*Hon. E. M. Stanton, Secretary of War:* Rebels whipped and driven from Murfreesboro, our forces pursuing. The rebels are retreating in the direction of Tullahoma. The Lord's on our side! The rebels are whipped and the Cumberland is this morning in good boating condition.

ROB'T B. MITCHELL, Brig. Gen'l.

WASHINGTON HOMEFRONT, JANUARY, 1863.

THE NEW YEAR.

The results of the war measures of the Government throughout the past year to re-establish the authority of the Union over the States in rebellion, have not been such as to make this a joyous day to the loyal section of the country. Nevertheless, it behooves all hearty Unionists to cast regrets and doubts behind him, and to redouble the energy and earnestness with which they support the legitimate authorities of the land in the restoration of the Union:—as, if in these dark hours the heart of the country falters, all is lost. The hope for the coming year is that those charged with the prosecution of the war will profit by their last year's experience, aided by the lessons deducible from the seeming so much better management of their so much less available military resources, which has marked the military administration of the oligarchy.

We believe that we surely possess all the necessary resources to speedily crush the rebellion, and that if the mistakes of policy and the errors of omission and commission of the past year be avoided and corrected from this first of January, 1863, the first of January, 1864, will find the authority of the United States established over all the seceded States. Else, there can be little room for hope that the advent of that day will fail to find the contest substantially settled against the right.

The sources from which the needed lessons or counsels of experience may be drawn, are so fresh in the memories of all that we need not particularize

them here. In telling us why we have failed up to this time, they surely teach us how we may succeed hereafter, if we will but heed their warnings.

The great danger ahead is the possibility that a majority of the people of the loyal States may hesitate to sustain the Government's military measures with the heartiness absolutely necessary to secure success. It is useless to attempt to disguise this patent fact. The only possible remedy for this threatening state of things is a display of such military energy and efficiency, and an adherence in future to such moderation of policy as will impress all with the belief that we not only *have* the power to crush the rebellion in due time, but that that power is being wielded to the legitimate end of restoring the Union in fact, as well as in name.

HELP THEM ALONG.—By the burning of Ford's new theater, a large number of people, male and female, have been thrown out of employment; and many of them, by the burning of their wardrobes, have lost their all. A large number of our citizens, sympathizing with Mr. Ford, tendered him a benefit; but he, with characteristic generosity, waived it in favor of his employees. During this and the coming week, entertainment will be given for the benefit of the sufferers; and it is to be hoped that our citizens will respond liberally, and thus aid them to make up, to a slight extent, their losses.

The Messrs. Maeder have tendered to Miss Richings the use of the Washington Theater, and to-morrow night she will take the benefit proffered her by a number of Senators and Representatives. It will be remembered that this complimentary entertainment was to have taken place last night, at Ford's.

LEVEE OF THE SONS OF TEMPERANCE. —Last evening there was a levee of the Sons of Temperance, held in the hall of the new division, Federal City, No. 3, in the large four-story building lately erected on Ninth street, near E. Addresses were made by several distinguished speakers. Mr. J. S. Polar presided.

After a song by the choir present, and a prayer by Rev. Mr. Reed, Senator Willey, of Virginia, was introduced, and in his eloquent manner spoke of the horrors of intemperance. He believed that intemperance was a greater evil than the war. During the last year, from fifty to a hundred thousand soldiers have died from sickness or wounds; while one hundred thousand of our citizens were dying every year from intemperance . . .

Billy Yank at his ease on the north side of the Rappahannock figured he was snug for the winter as the new year began. Well, as snug as any soldier could be in a tent or a log hut, or whatever other material he could scrounge for shelter. Comfort, relative or real, was not to be his that January.

Burnside, the commander who had failed the foot-soldiers so conspicuously the month before, had new plans for action—winter or no. His subordinates were appalled. Some even tattled to Washington. To campaign in mid-winter was unthinkable, they argued. Weather in that season was always a risk. There was always the cold to contend with. Snow was a threat. If not snow, then rain. If neither, then the thaws. One way or another, sooner or later, a dreaded enemy was sure to be on the front—"General Mud." The "general" would be a problem, indeed, since paved roads were virtually non-existent where armies were likely to wage war.

On top of the menace of weather, there was another consideration. The fighting spirit of the Yanks encamped along Fredericksburg's river had sunk dangerously low. They were only several days removed from the bloody futility of assailing an unassailable position. They wondered—not when they would have the next fair shot at Johnny Reb, but what the top brass' next blunder would be. All, of course, at the foot-soldiers' expense.

None of this seemed to concern Burnside. He thought only that his Government wanted a victory—and soon—somewhere between Washington and Richmond. He also had a military disgrace to live down.

In any case, the winter weather had been dry so far. The roads west of Fredericksburg were usable. Perhaps these advantages would hold.

The troops were rallied from their rude shelters early January 20. According to their general's plan, they would march along the river to shallow water, and sweep around the west end of Lee's lines, then onward to Richmond.

The weather was still dry when they left.

BURNSIDE OUT AFTER MUD MARCH

(Thursday, January 22, 1863)

GEN. BURNSIDE'S ADDRESS TO THE ARMY OF THE POTOMAC.

We announced yesterday that Gen. Burnside had issued an important address to the Army of the Potomac, in connection with the resumption of active movements. The following is a copy of his eloquent address:

Headquarters, Army of the Potomac,
Camp near Falmouth, Va., Jan. 20, 1863

GENERAL ORDERS, No. 7.—The Commanding General announces to the Army of the Potomac that they are about to meet the enemy once more.

The late brilliant actions in North Carolina, Tennessee and Arkansas have divided and weakened the enemy on the Rappahannock and the auspicious moment seems to have arrived to strike a great and mortal blow to the rebellion and to gain that decisive victory which is due to the country.

Let the gallant soldiers of so many brilliant battlefields accomplish this achievement and a fame the most glorious awaits them.

The Commanding General calls for the firm and united action of officers and men, and, under the providence of God, the Army of the Potomac will have taken the great step towards restoring peace to the country and the Government to its rightful authority.

By command of Major General Burnside:

LEWIS RICHMOND, Ass't Adj't Gen'l.
Official—EDWARD M. NEILL, Capt. & A.A.A.G.

Burnside's intentions were as stirring as his words. His army started marching as soon as the address was read to them. By afternoon, the skies became overcast, and before dark it was raining. For two or three days, no one away from the front seemed to be sure what was going on.

General Burnside's troops slogging through mud and rain on the abortive campaign that followed Fredericksburg.

A. Waud—Library of Congress

Telegraphic News.
FROM FORTRESS MONROE.
Burnside Moving.

"It is reported and confirmed (say the Richmond papers of the 20th) by the passengers which arrived last night that General Burnside's forces have crossed over the river, and are now above and below Fredericksburg."

THE RUMORS OF A BATTLE.

The Report Probably Unfounded—No Troops Across the Rappahannock on Monday

PHILADELPHIA, Jan. 22.—The *Evening Bulletin* says the *Times'* rumor of a battle near Fredericksburg cannot be true. The passengers that took it to New York must have left Washington at the latest yesterday morning; and if there had been a battle it must have occurred day before yesterday.

This morning the Rev. Jeremiah Shindle, Chaplain of the One Hundred and Tenth Pennsylvania Volunteers, called at the *Bulletin* office. He left the army at Falmouth day before yesterday, with a pass from General Hooker, dated Monday. At that time the troops had not crossed the Rappahannock. He pronounced the rumors untrue, and is a gentleman whose word may be relied upon.

A succession of later reports inferred there was trouble, and hinted what it was.

FROM THE ARMY OF THE POTOMAC.

HEADQUARTERS ARMY OF THE POTOMAC, Jan. 22.—The storm which has been prevailing here for the past three days has moderated, leaving the roads in the worst possible condition. There is at present no indication of a change of wind.

The Army on the Move.
THE RAIN IMPEDES THEIR PROGRESS.
Everything Quiet on Wednesday, and No Signs of a Battle.

(Correspondence of the Philadelphia *Inquirer*.)

NEAR FALMOUTH, Jan. 21.—At last the army moves. Yesterday the order of Gen. Burnside was read to all on parade, and we at once took up the line of march for Dixie.

Where we go first I cannot tell you, but the Rebels know we are moving. It is, however, now too late for them to avert the impending blow. Perhaps ere this, you have heard of our having struck a blow. The storm, last night, was fearful, but it is not yet very cold, and we hope it will not be the means of again saving the Rebel hordes.

Burnside's address to his troops was issued about noon on Tuesday. Immediately afterwards, Franklin's and Hooker's Grand Divisions moved off by the rear of Sumner's Grand Division, seven or eight miles above Falmouth, on the Rappahannock. The rain commenced immediately after they began their march, and they made slow progress.

General Burnside's artillery wallowing in mud and water.

A. Waud—Library of Congress

Yesterday (Wednesday) morning everything was quiet, with no signs of a battle, and no cannonading heard in any direction.

Sumner's Division remains opposite Fredericksburg, without change, but with orders to be ready to move at a moment's notice.

(Saturday, January 24, 1863)

Telegraphic News.

The Army of the Potomac.

The Forward Movement Delayed— Impassable Condition of the Roads.

HEADQUARTERS ARMY OF THE POTOMAC, Jan. 23.—The tempestuous weather since Tuesday last, and the consequent impassable state of the roads, have rendered any advance of the army of the Potomac beyond the Rappahannock a matter of utter impossibility. The same causes so delayed the transportation of the pontoons and heavy artillery to the designated points as to prevent a surprise of the enemy at the points where it was designed to cross. This afternoon the clouds broke away, and the influence of the sun is telling favorably upon the soil.

Several paymasters have already arrived, bring joy to the soldier and relief for their families at home. A delay in the payment of those actively employed may occur.

President Lincoln wanted to find out what was going on, and did.

(Saturday, January 24, 1863)

GENERAL BURNSIDE IN WASHINGTON.

Gen. Burnside is in town to-day, and has had interviews with the President, Secretary Stanton, and Gen. Halleck.

(Monday, January 26, 1863)

Telegraphic.

LATEST FROM THE ARMY OF THE POTOMAC.

The Command of the Army Turned over to Gen. Hooker.

Gen. Burnside's Farewell Address.

HEADQUARTERS ARMY OF THE POTOMAC, Jan. 26.—This morning Gen. Burnside turned over the command of the Army of the Potomac to Gen. Hooker, who came to headquarters camp for that purpose.

As soon as the change became known, a considerable number of superior officers called on Gen. Burnside and took their parting leave with many regrets.

The following is Gen. Burnside's address to the army:

HEADQUARTERS ARMY OF THE POTOMAC, *Camp near Falmouth,* Jan. 26.—General Orders No. 9.—By direction of the President of the United States, the commanding general this day transfers the command of this army to Major General Joseph Hooker. The short time that he has directed your movements he has not been fruitful of victory or any considerable advancement of our lines, but has again demonstrated an amount of courage, patience and endurance that under more favorable circumstances would have accomplished great results.

Continue and exercise these virtues. Be true in your devotion to your country, and the principles you have sworn to maintain. Give to the brave and skillful general who has been identified with your organization and who is now to command you, your full and cordial support and cooperation, and you will deserve success.

In taking an affectionate leave of the entire army, from which he separates with so much regret, he may be pardoned if he bids an especial farewell to his long-tried associates of the ninth corps. His prayers are, that God may be with you, and grant you continued success until the rebellion is crushed.

By command of Major Gen. Burnside:

Lewis Richmond, A.A.G.

It is understood that Generals Sumner and Franklin have also been relieved from the commands of the right and left grand divisions, but the news of their successors has not been divulged, if appointed.

General Burnside, with most of his late staff, has been allowed thirty days' leave of absence. They go to New York.

The mud is fast drying up.

WASHINGTON HOMEFRONT, JANUARY, 1863.

The departure of Southern legislators from the Federal Congress did not mean that quiet had settled over the Hall.

DISGRACEFUL SCENE IN THE SENATE.

While the bill proposing to legalize all the acts of the President of the United States, and others in authority, in suspending the privilege of the writ of *habeas corpus,* was up before the Senate yesterday, Mr. (Willard) Saulsbury, (Democrat) of Delaware, indulged in a style of remark and procedure discreditable to him in the highest degree. After denouncing the President of the United States and the acts of the Administration, he stated that Mr. Lincoln was the weakest man ever placed in high office. He said he had been in conversation with him, and knew he was an imbecile.

Mr. (James Wilson) Grimes, (R) of Iowa.—I think the Senator ought not to be allowed to continue such remarks.

Mr. Saulsbury was admonished by the Vice President that his remarks were out of order, when he proceeded to denounce the President, stating that if he "wanted to paint a despot, he would paint the hideous form of Abraham Lincoln."

The Chair decided such remarks as completely out of order.

Mr. Saulsbury.—Will the point of order be submitted to writing.

The Vice President told the Senator to take his seat; that his remarks were out of order.

Mr. Saulsbury.—I shall not take my seat until I know what I have said that is out of order.

The Vice President said if the Senator did not take his seat he should order the Sergeant-at-Arms to take him in charge.

Mr. Saulsbury.—The voice of freedom is not allowed in the American Senate.

The Vice President.—The Sergeant-at-Arms will take the Senator in charge.

The Sergeant-at-Arms then advanced to Mr. Saulsbury, who refused to go, making a motion to his side pocket, but after some conversation the two walked toward the cloak room, and then Mr. Saulsbury stopping, sat down on the sofa near the west entrance of the Senate Chamber. Mr. Saulsbury was engaged in earnest conversation with the Sergeant-at-Arms, and after talking for a time, took from his side pocket a revolver, which he turned several times in his hands and then replaced. Afterwards he went out with the officer, but returned again in about half an hour, when, after sitting a while in his seat he advanced to the desk near the Speaker's chair and made several attempts to gain the floor; when

Mr. (James Rood) Doolittle, (R), of Wisconsin, called him to order, and read a rule of the Senate which deprives a Senator of the right to speak after having been called to order for contempt of the Senate.

Mr. Saulsbury. Does the Senator from Wisconsin say I am in contempt to any honorable man?

The Chair. (Mr. (Daniel) Clark (Republican of New Hampshire) in the Chair.) The Senator from Delaware will take his seat. He is out of order.

Mr. Saulsbury. Just as I please, and not otherwise.

(Cries of "Order!" from several Senators.)

The Chair. The Senator will take his seat, and the Sergeant-at-Arms will take him in custody.

The Sergeant-at-Arms approached the Senator from Delaware, who refused at first to accompany him, but after some conversation left the Chamber.

After being gone for about half an hour, Mr. Saulsbury returned again, and made several efforts to gain the floor.

The Chair (Mr. Clark.)—The Senator will take his seat.

Mr. (Charles) Sumner. (Republican of Massachusetts.) I rise to a question of order. I understood that the Senator was committed to the custody of the Sergeant-at-Arms, and I see him on the floor now. I am not aware that the order of the Chair committing him to the custody of the Sergeant-at-Arms has been discharged.

The Chair.—The Sergeant-at-Arms will take the Senator in charge.

Mr. Saulsbury.—I should like to see that order executed by any one.

The Senator then took his seat, swearing at Mr. Sumner and other Senators, and muttering inaudibly to the Sergeant-at-Arms, as he approached, but refused to leave. Soon after, he retired to the cloakroom with that officer. After the lapse of considerable time he returned to his seat, when he was conducted from the Senate Chamber. (Apparently for the last time that day, at least.)

TEAMED WITH PORTER'S TIRELESS RIVERBOAT NAVY, Grant's army was beginning to breath hard on Vicksburg, perched high on the east bank of the Mississippi River. The combined forces were also just plain breathing hard: the water-logged condition of the countryside around Vicksburg defied military movement. Grant had been trying since midwinter to get through the bayous, swamps and general muck. After one failure, at Chickasaw Bluffs, to get at the city from the river side, he changed his strategy. He would try to take the city from the land side by circling around it and coming in from the east. Toward this end, he tried two campaigns down the west bank of the river. One of these involved digging a mile-long canal across a neck of land opposite the city to provide a route for supply ships out of range of Vicksburg's guns. That project failed, and Grant gave up on another which involved building roads through 400 miles of Louisiana lowland. The Federal commander then shifted his operations north of the city on the east bank of the Mississippi. One attempt was along the Yazoo River, the other along Steele's Bayou. Both came to nothing. In each instance, Grant was seeking a water-borne supply route that could be protected by gunboats. With five fruitless attempts behind him, he looked south again in mid-April. He marched his army down the west bank of the river well below Vicksburg to a place called Hard Times, La. Porter's gunboats and supply ships then brazenly passed Vicksburg's cannon to rendezvous with the army. On April 30, the fleet carried the troops across the Mississippi to Bruinsburg, and Grant had his base on the east bank at last. During this period, he sought to confuse the Confederates in the area by diversive actions. One was spectacular and highly successful: a raid by Col. Benjamin Henry Grierson at the head of 1,700 cavalrymen. The force swept 600 miles from lower Tennessee to Baton Rouge, La. The havoc played by Grierson's raiders on railroads and other property effectively distracted Confederate attention from Grant's main operation at Bruinsburg.

The Richmond Government had civilian distractions as well, food being not the least of them. In the capital itself, bread riots flared up in early April. So serious was the food shortage that President Davis proclaimed his compatriots should plant edible crops instead of cotton and tobacco, which could neither be eaten or marketed. His Government also worried about the North's preparations to organize Negro troops to fight the armies of their former masters. The Confederate Congress consequently resolved that any white officers captured while leading Negro units would be subject to court martial and possible execution for inciting Negro insurrection.

The Federal Government had a pleasant chore that month: proclaiming West Virginia the 35th State of the Union. There were, of course, civilian aggravations, too. The peace movement seemed to be gaining ground, and one official caused a flurry by taking direct action. This was Ambrose Burnside, recently deposed commander of the Army of the Potomac, now heading the military Department of the Ohio. In that capacity, he sternly decreed that he would not tolerate any expressions of sympathy for the enemy in his department.

And what of Burnside's successor to his old command in the East? "Fighting Joe" Hooker, all vigor and confidence, had a plan for doing in Robert Lee which impressed Washington as a sound idea. It involved swinging the Federal army far west of Lee's entrenched concentration at Fredericksburg, crossing the shallow waters of the Rappahannock and Rapidan Rivers, and falling on the Confederates' supply lines to Richmond. Hooker had even more than the usual preponderance of numbers: 130,000 to 60,000. He would leave a third of these under Maj. Gen. John Sedgwick to threaten Fredericksburg, another third would deliver the main attack from the West, while the balance would be reserved to beef up either wing of the army as needed. In the process, Maj. Gen. George Stoneman with 10,000 cavalry would smash Lee's communications all the way to Richmond. Hooker made his upstream crossings in the last days of April, and his forces were soon sweeping out of the woods past Chancellorsville toward open ground and the Confederate rear.

But Lee had a surprise for Hooker. Instead of fleeing toward Richmond, as Hooker had expected, the Confederate master left a skeleton force at Fredericksburg and smashed headlong into the Federal advance units with the rest of his army. Hooker quickly backed up and consolidated his army around Chancellorsville, a crossroads hamlet. Fighting Joe, now in a strictly defensive mood, arranged his lines facing south, and waited for Lee to use his abundant initiative. As the armies prepared for combat, a blanket of silence cut off the Federal army from the outside world.

LEE WINS CHANCELLORSVILLE; LOSES JACKSON

(Monday, May 4, 1863)

Hooker's Movement upon Richmond.

Chancellorsville, Occupied by Gen. Hooker.

Gen. Stoneman Playing the Mischief with His Cavalry in the Rear of the Rebels.

GENERAL LEE SURPRISED.

We have scrupulously refrained from giving publicity to any of the late movements of General Hooker, and in accordance with what was understood to be the wishes of the Government, did not reproduce what had appeared in the Northern papers. As the *Chronicle* and *Intelligencer* have now given them full ventilation, nothing can be gained by withholding the same information from our readers. While giving these details of what has already transpired, we shall carefully avoid furnishing anything of what is occurring in the present or likely to in the future, calculated to afford any possible information to the enemy, and trust that our contemporaries will be guided by the same sense of duty. In the present encouraging position of affairs we can well afford to wait a short season for the full development of the plans of General Hooker, which have thus far been carried out with such brilliant success. . . .

Here was one of the oddest developments of the war to date. Hooker, in a fever to preserve security, kept even the White House and the War Department in the dark as to the success of his campaign. Not until May 6 would Lincoln himself know the outcome. If, as the Star's *explanation implies, the editors were keeping the news quiet by agreement with the Government, it is obvious that the paper could have published no details on Hooker's fortunes until after the Government received word. Even the New York papers, which had correspondents in the field, were carrying hedging or erroneous reports on Monday, May 4. The stories which the* Star *picked up from other papers and spread over three columns of its first page were long but mostly inexplicit. The only news that stood up was that Hooker's army had crossed to Chancellorsville, and that Stoneman's cavalry was off on a raid toward Richmond. A Philadelphia paper reported under a dateline as recent as May 3 that the "main body" of Hooker's army had crossed the Rappahannock at Fredericksburg—which was certainly not a fact. The* Star, *in short,*

Artillery, manned by Connecticut troops, at Chancellorsville.

A Pennsylvania regiment that suffered heavy casualties at Chancellorsville.

knew something decisive was going on. Just what, was anybody's guess. Things became a little clearer next day. 🔫

(Tuesday, May 5, 1863)
LATEST FROM THE SEAT OF WAR.
The Situation at Fredericksburg and Chancellorsville.
Hooker Retrieves a Check in Splendid Style and Advances a Mile.

Sedgwick, after getting possession of the rebel batteries at Fredericksburg on Sunday, moved out on the plank road towards Chancellorsville some four miles; but encountering a staggering force of the enemy, did not push further in that direction.

On the same day (Sunday), Gibbon's division, of the Second Corps, occupied Fredericksburg and most of the heights.

On Monday morning, about day-break, the enemy suddenly appeared on the extreme heights, on the telegraph road southeast of the plank road, and came forward without much resistance, our force at that point not being of any great strength. This force of the enemy, which rumor announced to be reinforcements, under Longstreet, hastening up from the Blackwater, is believed now to have been only a body of the enemy left down river to oppose our crossing below Fredericksburg.

Some assistance was afforded to our troops over the river by the well-known heavy battery called the "Seven Sisters," planted on the heights of the north side of the Rappahannock about a quarter of a mile below the Fredericksburg and Aquia Creek railroad.

The enemy, however, succeeded in advancing until they occupied all the positions southeast of the plank road, well down to the famous stone wall, which is the first line of battery in the rear of Fredericksburg, east of the plank road, it not being Hooker's plan evidently to make any serious contest for this ground.

Yesterday at three p.m., they held about this position: The enemy occupying all the intrenchments southeast of the plank road, (leading from Fredericksburg to Chancellorsville) and Gibbon all northwest of the same road. He also occupied the city of Fredericksburg. Sedgwick is further out on the plank road, and sandwiched, as it were, between Lee (who is in turn sandwiched between Sedgwick and Hooker) and the rebel force that retook the lower fortifications at Fredericksburg. Sedgwick, however, who is one of the best officers in the service, knows fully what he is about, and has, it is reported, already opened communication with Hooker.

The loss on both sides has been heavy, some estimating it as high as twenty thousand to each army. But experienced Army men hold that the rebels have suffered materially the most, as they have been fought in masses.

The Fight on Sunday Afternoon and Yesterday.

On Sunday afternoon Hooker advanced some distance towards Fredericksburg, met with a temporary check, and fell back, but rallied in splendid style and advanced and held a mile in distance. In this affair Hooker's hospital tents were shelled by the enemy, and it was found necessary to remove the inmates.

In this fight the 2d, 5th and 9th, and two divisions of the 2d corps were hotly engaged; and later in the afternoon the 1st corps also.

The fighting yesterday afternoon, as heard from Falmouth, was mostly musketry. The cannonading ceased about 10 o'clock a.m., but the musketry was continued through the day.

The number of prisoners on both sides, thus far, is believed to be about equal.

Our greatest loss (in prisoners) was in the 11th army corps, Howard's—late Sigel's—which is said not to have behaved well.

The country where Hooker is now operating is undulating, wooded and broken, fully as rough as the Bull Run country, though not cut up by any large water courses. The so-much-talked-of plank road is an old one, out of repair, so far as the planking is concerned, but tolerably well graded.

A noticeable feature of the present fighting is, we are told, in the few stragglers seen. At the time of Sedgwick's crossing to Fredericksburg every man went, and the *elan* of the army as a whole was of the same satisfactory sort.

The present Army of the Potomac is undoubtedly the finest we have yet put in the field, being composed of veterans in every sense of the word, a majority of them having been in as many as six engagements heretofore. In this respect Hooker's army is superior to the Army of the Peninsula, which, up to the time of its grand trial battles, had been in no engagement of consequence, if we except Williamsburg.

Such an army cannot be beaten, and with a commander of the bull-dog tenacity of Hooker, must eventually force the rebels to the wall, no matter how desperately the latter may struggle or how protracted the conflict.

It will occur to the reader at once, from the position of the two armies, that a reverse on either side will be no half-way affair, but overwhelming, and hence we may expect the most sanguinary fighting of the war before the contest is settled.

🙣 *Still no hint of the final outcome—unless the discussion of the troops "elan" and unbeatability might raise a few suspicions. In something like desperation the* Star *turned to Richmond papers as a news source.* 🙣

(Wednesday, May 6, 1863)
THRILLING NEWS FROM THE ARMY!
HOOKER ALL RIGHT!
Stonewall Jackson Is Severely Wounded, and Generals Heth and A. P. Hill Badly Wounded.

We have positive information from General Hooker's army up to yesterday at noon.

The Richmond papers of yesterday, the 5th, contain various dispatches from Lee's army. One of them claims victories for the rebels on Saturday and Sunday last, when they really effected nothing, (as we know well from a dozen different Union sources), though losing enormously in killed and wounded, as the Richmond papers admit.

New battle line forming on the field at Chancellorsville to cover the retreat of the Eleventh Corps.

A. Waud—Library of Congress

This rebel dispatch says that on Saturday Lee drove Hooker out of the Little Wilderness back to Chancellorsville, and on Sunday drove him from Chancellorsville to a position in that immediate vicinity. As the Union accounts of Saturday's engagement, in other columns of to-day's *Star*, explain, the falling back was on the part of Sigel's late (now Howard's) corps, which behaved so disgracefully and was only saved from annihilation by the gallantry of Hooker's original division, under Berry, which checked the enemy's pursuit and drove him back in turn with great loss.

So far as Sunday's change of position is concerned, it was simply a concentration of Hooker's force in a far better position than immediately at Chancellorsville, though very near it. It was effected with small loss to us when compared with the loss sustained by the rebels in assailing us during the movement.

On Monday afternoon, the rebels attacked our left—Howard's corps—and after a desperate engagement, were completely repulsed with great loss. Yesterday forenoon they again advanced against us at the same point, but were able to stand the contest but for fifteen minutes; when they again fell back, repulsed with heavy loss.

Stoneman's expedition proved a great success, indeed. The Richmond papers of the 5th (yesterday) say that his forces played sad havoc with their railroad at Hanover Junction and other points; destroying locomotives and a large amount of other valuable property, and all the railroad bridges to within five miles of Richmond.

Gen. Sedgwick having duly executed his feint below Fredericksburg, has recrossed the river with his force, and we presume is now doubtless carrying out some other portions of Gen. Hooker's plans.

In the Richmond papers mentioned above is a dispatch from Gen. Lee to Jeff. Davis, saying that (the rebel) General (Elisha Franklin) Paxton is killed, Stonewall Jackson severely wounded, and Gens. (Henry) Heth and A. P. Hill also badly wounded.

Another rebel dispatch states that the rebel loss in killed and wounded has been very heavy.

We may add that it is understood here that the position which General Hooker has occupied since moving a short distance from Chancellorsville on Sunday last, is impregnable.

He and his whole army were yesterday morning in the best spirits, and the sentiment of entire confidence in the final result of his admirable strategy and tactics was universal there.

Whether the editors realized it or not, the mention of the "disgraceful" behavior of Howard's corps *and of Hooker's withdrawal to "impregnable" positions (closer to the Rappahannock) gave the tip-off. What had happened was this: Jackson's corps had been detached from Lee's main army, marched rapidly westward through the Little Wilderness across Hooker's front and had fallen savagely on the west flank of the Federal line held by an unsuspecting Howard the evening of May 2. The Federal rout on that wing was marred for the Confederates by heavy losses, which included the wounding of Jackson by his own men. Sedgwick, meanwhile, had advanced on and past the Fredericksburg defenses and was marching toward Chancellorsville, when Lee detached another portion of his army from Hooker's front. These divisions under Maj. Gen. Richard Heron "Dick" Anderson and Brig. Gen. Lafayette McLaws, joined by Early, hemmed Sedgwick's corps against the river and forced it across near Fredericksburg on May 4.*

(Thursday, May 7, 1863)

EXTRA.
Very Important from Hooker's Army.
HOOKER BRINGS OFF 2,500 PRISONERS.

The reader will find elsewhere in to-day's *Star*, an intelligible account of the occurrences near Fredericksburg since Tuesday at noon, to which time we yesterday published all the details at hand.

The storm that commenced on Monday evening and continued throughout Tuesday was at its height yesterday, evidently warned General Hooker—whose movement was necessarily made with only eight days' supplies, carried by the men (which were nearly then consumed), and without trains—of the imminent danger, that unless he promptly sought his camps the elements would put a stop to his operations; the railroad communication with Aquia Creek having been destroyed by the floods for twelve hours at Brook's Station before he determined to recross the river.

In the course of all the fighting throughout Saturday, Sunday, Monday, and Tuesday, the enemy had not ventured a general engagement with his army, only a portion of which was in action at any one time; and no occasion with as great loss as he inflicted upon the rebels. Nevertheless, as it became evident that this greatest storm of the season would surely cut off his supplies of all descriptions, if he remained on the south side of the river awaiting an opportunity, to induce the enemy to risk a general engagement, he evidently had left him the only alternative of returning, for the time being, to where his supplies could readily reach him. . . .

(Friday, May 8, 1863)
CONFIRMATION OF THE NEWS OF THE SAFETY OF STONEMAN'S CAVALRY.

YORKTOWN, Va., May 7, 1863.—Col. Kilpatrick, with the Harris Light Cavalry, 13th Illinois Cavalry, &c., have just arrived at Gloucester Point, having accomplished the object of their mission fully and most gallantly. They pursued the enemy to within three miles of Richmond, and destroyed a large amount of property and bridges.

HEADQUARTERS ARMY OF THE POTOMAC, May 7.—Major Gen. Stoneman's aid-de-camp, Capt. Sumner, is just in. He left his chief this morning, having disarranged all the enemy's railroad communications between this and Richmond, and one party having extended their operations to James River, destroying the canal, &c. Three regiments of the command left his to destroy the railroad bridges across the Chickahominy, with instructions to go into Yorktown.

While daring, and a potential menace to Lee's communications, Stoneman's raid disrupted Confederate army operations not at all. Hooker would probably have found his cavalry vastly more useful around Chancellorsville.

(Friday, May 8, 1863)
Telegraphic.
THE VISIT OF THE PRESIDENT AND GEN. HALLECK TO THE ARMY.

Secretary Stanton Telegraphs to Governor Curtin That the Army Will Speedily Resume Offensive Operations.

HARRISBURG, May 8.—The following dispatch was received this morning by the Governor of Pennsylvania, from Washington:

The President and General-in-Chief have just returned from the Army of the Potomac.

The principal operation of General Hooker failed, but there has been no serious disaster to the organization and efficiency of the Army. It is now occupying its former position on the Rappahannock, having recrossed the river without any loss in the movement. Not more than one-third of Gen. Hooker's force was engaged.

General Stoneman's operations have been a brilliant success. A part of his force advanced to within two miles of Richmond, and the enemy's communications have been cut in every direction.

The Army of the Potomac will speedily resume offensive operations.

Edwin M. Stanton, Secretary of War.

Lincoln's first reaction when he finally heard of Hooker's withdrawal across the Rappahannock: "My God, my God, what will the country say!" He was not prone to blame anyone for the failure, despite his dismay. The Federal army, which sustained 17,000 casualties, had at least inflicted nearly 13,000 casualties upon Lee's army. And one of those lost was the irreplaceable Thomas Jonathan (Stonewall) Jackson, who had stirred up the dust with his foot cavalry for the last time.

(Tuesday, May 12, 1863)
EXTRA.
Stonewall Jackson Not Expected to Live.
GEN'L HAYS (UNION) NOT WOUNDED.

The following dispatch from a gentleman in the position to obtain the latest and most correct intelligence from Richmond, and who would not have sent the following dispatch unless thoroughly satisfied of the truth of the information it embraces:

FORTRESS MONROE, May 12.—I am informed on good authority, that General (Stonewall) Jackson is not expected to live. He was shot by accident (in the engagement at Chancellorsville) by his own men. Gen. Hays is reported (from Richmond) not to be wounded.

General George Stoneman, who led the cavalry diversion on Richmond during the Chancellorsville battle.

LATER.
STONEWALL JACKSON DEAD!

HEADQUARTERS ARMY OF THE POTO-MAC, May 12.—We have Richmond papers of yesterday containing obituary notices of Gen. Jackson, who died Sunday at 3:30 p.m.

(Thursday, May 14, 1863)

General Lee upon the Death of Stonewall Jackson.

HEADQUARTERS ARMY POTOMAC, May 13.—The following general order is published in the Richmond *Sentinel:*

CHANCELLORSVILLE, May 4.—*To Lieutenant General T. J. Jackson*—GENERAL: I have just received your note informing me that you were wounded.

I cannot express my regret at the occurrence. Could I have directed events, I should have chosen, for the good of the country, to have been disabled in your stead.

I congratulate you upon the victory, which is due to your skill and energy.

Most truly yours,

R. E. Lee, General.

HEADQUARTERS ARMY OF NORTHERN VIRGINIA, May 11.— *General Order No. 61.*—With deep grief the commanding general announces to the army the death of Lieut. Gen. T. J. Jackson, who expired on the 10th inst. at 3:15 p.m.

The daring skill of this great and good soldier, by the decree of an all-wise Providence, are now lost to us; but while we mourn his death, we feel that his spirit still lives, and will inspire the whole army with his indomitable courage and unshaken confidence in God as our hope and strength.

Let his name be a watchword to his corps, who have followed him to victory on so many fields. Let officers and soldiers emulate his invincible determination in defense of our beloved country.

R. E. Lee, General.

WASHINGTON HOMEFRONT, MAY, 1863.

☞ *The suspense over the battle of Chancellorsville notwithstanding, an impending sporting event was deemed important enough to deserve special headlines in the local news columns.* ☜

PRIZE FIGHT BETWEEN JOE COBURN AND MIKE McCOOLE.
The American Championship and a Purse of $2,000 at Stake,
Sporting Circles Excited.

The "mill," which has for a long time been the topic of interest in sporting circles, between Joe Coburn, of New York, and Mike McCoole, of the West, was announced to come off this morning at a point on the Philadelphia, Baltimore and Wilmington railroad, near Wilmington. Except among the intimate friends of the combatants, it was not positively known where the fight would take place until within a day or two. In fact it was announced to take place somewhere in northern New York or Canada; but after having turned all eyes in that direction the combatants set their faces southward to bother the police.

Both men have exhibited their power on several occasions, and their respective friends have thus had an opportunity of judging their relative merits. Coburn is well known as a hard fighter, with plenty of science and good "bottom," his best fight occupying over three hours. He is thoroughly posted up on the tactics of the ring and has any amount of gameness, quickness, and fistic skill. McCoole is regarded as the Champion of the West, and though comparatively untried, is nevertheless a dangerous customer to deal with tenderly. He is not so scientific perhaps as his opponent, but has immense endurance, and can stand a fearful amount of "pummeling." He is a very muscular fellow, and his friends are confident of his success. He is 20 pounds better than Joe, and a little taller. He has a long reach, and is said to carry a very dangerous "bunch of fives."

Betting runs high, over $100,000 having been already staked.

Australian Kelly and Johnny Roach are seconds to McCoole, while Ned Price and Jim Gusack do the agreeable for Coburn. Ned Price was one of the men that Joe fought, the battle lasting over three hours, and the selection of such men as above, indicates fair play and a square fight.

A great number of the sporting fraternity of this city left night before last and yesterday for the scene of operations; over three hundred persons leaving here on the trains during the day.

☞ *Mr. McCoole, it was subsequently reported, was "completely used up" by Mr. Coburn after 68 rounds of bloody fist-swinging. Coburn thus became the "champion of the American prize ring," while poor McCoole's "almost lifeless" body was carted off in a wagon.* ☜

THE VICKSBURG CAMPAIGN WAS NOW ON DRY GROUND ON the east side of the Mississippi. Grant's army, far from any supply base either to the north or south, was marching eastward in three columns under "Cump" Sherman, James Birdseye McPherson and John Alexander McClernand. On May 14, shortly after Joe Johnston had taken over the Confederate command at Jackson, Miss., Sherman and McPherson assaulted and captured the city. Two days later, the Federal corps, having doubled back toward Vicksburg, combined at Champion's Hill to defeat Pemberton's army, which had left Vicksburg to join Johnston. Another defeat at Big Black River forced Pemberton to retire to the Vicksburg defenses. Grant had hoped to capture the city quickly, but assaults on the strong entrenchments were beaten off May 19 and 22. Grant then reluctantly settled down to siege tactics.

On the civilian front that month, stubborn Burnside made good his threat. He ordered the arrest of Clement Laird Vallandigham, Democratic politician, for expressing sympathy for the Confederacy in a speech at Mount Vernon, Ohio. The former Congressman, a leader in the Copperhead movement which assailed Lincoln's war policies and agitated for a negotiated peace, was convicted by court martial and ordered confined. The President rescinded the sentence and instructed that Vallandigham be banished to Dixie. He was; and later the Confederacy wearied of his complaints against its policies, and expelled him. Early in June, Burnside figured the Chicago *Tribune* was getting too critical and ordered it shut down. Lincoln swiftly reversed that decision. Indicative of the peace sentiment which was persisting in many quarters in the North was the fact that a few days later Vallandigham was nominated by the Democrats for governor of Ohio.

Unknown to the Federal Government, Lee around this time had reached another decision that spelled trouble for the Army of the Potomac. He would strike north again. The reasons were the same which impelled him to march into Maryland the previous September. A victory would stimulate the peace movement up north, and might at last induce France, if not Great Britain, to recognize the Confederacy. Lee started his troops westward out of Fredericksburg toward Culpeper. Hooker noticed the move, and prodded at the fringes of Lee's army with his cavalry. Maj. Gen. Alfred Pleasonton now was in charge of Hooker's cavalry. At dawn of June 9, less than 24 hours after Jeb Stuart had held a stirring review of his 9,500 Confederate cavalrymen, Pleasonton's 11,000 troopers splashed through the fords of the upper Rappahannock near Brandy Station.

HUGE CAVALRY CLASH AT BRANDY STATION

(Tuesday, June 9, 1863)

Stirring News from the Rappahannock.

A SEVERE BATTLE FOUGHT AT BEVERLY'S FORD THIS MORNING!

The Union Troops Succeed in Crossing the River!

A severe engagement took place this morning between our cavalry and that of the rebels under General Stuart. The locality at which it occurred was Beverly's Ford, of the Rappahannock, five miles above Rappahannock Station, and about the same distance below the Sulphur Springs.

It will be recollected that Stuart has been massing a large body of rebel cavalry around Culpeper Court-House of late, evidently for a raid north and east. Gen. Hooker has of course kept his eye on him, and this engagement is the result. Stuart made an obstinate fight to cross the river, in which purpose he was not only foiled, but our troops drove him from the south bank, which they now hold.

Our belief is that the engagement is progressing, as our force engaged is now on the south side of the river.

No further details of the battle had reached here up to 3 p.m., but we believe that we are strong enough there to drive Stuart out of Culpeper across the Rapidan.

Cars have already been sent up from Kettle Run to Rappahannock Station to bring our wounded to the rear.

Stuart's assignment was to provide a cavalry screen for Lee's army. When Pleasonton struck the compact group, Stuart must still have been enjoying visions of his splendid review of the day before. At any rate, the charging Federals achieved complete surprise.

(Wednesday, June 10, 1863)

EXTRA.

The Greatest Cavalry Battle of the War!

STUART'S PROPOSED RAID CUT SHORT!

FOURTEEN HOURS HAND-TO-HAND FIGHTING!

Yesterday we briefly stated the fact that a severe cavalry engagement was in progress on the Upper Rappahannock as our paper was going to press. We have been able to ascertain the following additional particulars of the battle:

It was known at Hooker's headquarters that Gen. Lee had assembled his cavalry, supported by artillery and infantry, between Culpeper Court-House

E. Forbes—Library of Congress

Action at Brandy Station.

and Beverly's Ford, designing soon to send them upon a raid in this direction, and Gen. Pleasonton was sent with portions of the divisions of our cavalry commanded by Gens. (John) Buford and (David McMurtrie) Gregg respectively, to spoil their sport.

The force under Buford (portions of the 1st, 2nd, 5th and 6th regular cavalry, and the 6th Pennsylvania cavalry) reached Beverly's Ford early on Monday evening, and crossed the river unopposed shortly after midnight. The force under Gen. Gregg (portions of the 8th and 9th New York, 8th Illinois, and 3d Indiana cavalry) reached the ford at midnight, and commenced to cross at 4 a.m. Buford's force, which was on the right, first met the enemy's pickets half a mile south of the ford; when a severe engagement immediately commenced, the rebels being in heavy force and resisting the advance of our troops with continuous hand-to-hand fighting. When Gregg brought his force up to the fight and became engaged, the enemy gradually gave way, disputing every inch of the ground desperately, however.

In this way our men made more than a dozen charges into the midst of the rebel ranks, relying almost entirely upon the sabre, which they used with terrible effect. The enemy, on the other hand, repeatedly charged also, relying on their revolvers for the most part, however. Both sides were repeatedly driven back in the course of the battle; though we succeeded in driving the rebels—Fitzhugh Lee's and Wade Hampton's divisions of cavalry, with artillery, all commanded by Major General J. E. B. Stuart—back to a point about five miles southwest of where their pickets were first encountered, where Pleasonton found the enemy so heavily reinforced with infantry and artillery as to make it prudent to return to this side of the river.

This—the return—was commenced at about four p.m., General Pleasonton bringing off about 200 prisoners, his own wounded, and the bodies of his officers who had been killed in the engagement.

The 6th Pennsylvania cavalry, which was in the advance, under Buford, lost heavily, including six officers killed, wounded or missing. Indeed, Buford's whole force was much cut up. Of the 6th Pennsylvania cavalry, we hear of Captain Davis, killed by a shell; Major Robert Morris, missing; Lieut. Lennig, missing; Lieut. R. Ellis, revolver shot through his leg; and Captain Lieper, cut with a saber.

The 8th New York had the advance under Gregg, and (under the command of Col. Davis, who was killed on the field) after slightly wavering, acquitted themselves with much gallantry. We hear that among

General William Henry Fitzhugh Lee, son of Robert E. Lee, who was badly wounded at Brandy Station.

the casualties of that regiment were Capt. Foote, Co. E, and Lieut. Cutler, Co. A, killed, and Lieut. Reeves, Co. C, and Lieut. Epler, Co. I, mortally wounded.

On the return to this side of the river, the enemy skirmished frequently with our rear guard, doing us no damage to speak of, however.

As yet our loss has not been definitely ascertained.

The number of wounded could not have been more than 200 or 300, we apprehend, as they were sent down here last night on eleven cars, together with the bodies of our officers killed.

The proportion of horses killed on both sides in this almost unexampled hand-to-hand cavalry battle, was very large.

The field, from where Buford and Gregg first became engaged, throughout the whole distance of five miles over which the enemy were driven before getting back to their reinforcements, was strewn with dead and wounded rebels.

The headline was correct. It was the biggest all-cavalry battle of the war—up to then and afterward. For more than 12 hours the fighting surged back and forth between the river and Brandy Station, up and around Fleetwood Hill, where Stuart had his headquarters. Whole regiments went in at a time, and then charged again and again. The Confederates under Brig. Gen. William Edmonson "Grumble" Jones were rammed back in the initial shock. After a touch-and-go situation that grew desperate at times, Stuart rallied and drove the Yankees away. Pleasonton's force sustained around 900 casualties, Stuart's 500, including a son of the commander, Brig. Gen. William Henry Fitzhugh "Rooney" Lee, badly

A good view of history's largest cavalry battle.

wounded. In this action, Federal cavalry came of age, after two years of being outclassed by rebel mounted men. 🔫

(Thursday, June 11, 1863)
The Rebel Raid into Maryland.
THE ENEMY CROSSED AT SENECA THIS MORNING 250 STRONG.

The following has been received at headquarters in this city:

HEADQUARTERS BRIGADE CAMP HEINTZELMAN, *near Poolesville,* June 11, 1863: —Lt. Col. J. H. Taylor, A.A.G.—The enemy's cavalry came across the river this morning, at daybreak, about 250 strong. They dashed rapidly up the tow path, driving in our patrols, and attacked company I, 6th Michigan cavalry, who were on picket at Seneca. Our forces gradually fell back, pursued by the enemy to within three miles of Poolesville. The enemy then retreated to Seneca, burned the camp of the Michigan company and returned down the tow-path and recrossed. We lost 4 men killed, one badly and one slightly wounded. The enemy left on the field 1 lieutenant and 1 man.

A. B. Jewett, Col. Comd'g.

LATER.

The following is from the latest dispatch, and was received at 1:40 to-day:

HEADQUARTERS BRIGADE, CAMP HEINTZELMAN, *near Poolesville,* June 11, 1863. —The enemy remain on the opposite side of the river from Muddy Branch. . . . (it is evident the raid is over.—ED. STAR.)

🔫 *After Brandy Station, what did this little cavalry action at Seneca, Md., North of the Federal City, signify? Robert E. Lee knew, if the Federal authorities didn't.* 🔫

WASHINGTON HOMEFRONT, JUNE, 1863.

🔫 *The war certainly occupied most of the attention of the Federal Government. But there was one local project the authorities were determined to expedite, come what may.* 🔫

THE DOME OF THE CAPITOL.—The Statue of Freedom will not be ready to be raised to its place on the dome of the Capitol by the 4th of July, as was expected. The machinery for hoisting and placing the material of the dome in place is so constructed that only a limited number of pieces can be set per day, and the ratio for the time will not allow for the completion of the work by that date. In the early part of the season, it was hoped to have the dome ready for the reception of the statue by the 30th of this month, but the unusual amount of rainy weather has deferred the work at least two months, and it is now thought, should the weather prove favorable, that the dome will be ready for the reception of the statue by the 1st of September.

As soon as the ornamentation around and below the windows shall have been completed and the covering of the joints of the tiles finished, the machinery for hoisting will be changed, and the work on the lantern commenced. The frame scaffolding for the

General J. E. B. Stuart, rebel commander at Brandy Station.

General Alfred Pleasonton, Federal commander at Brandy Station.

erection of the lantern is completed, and is ready to be put up, and will reach one hundred feet above the present summit. This scaffolding is novel in its form, and is exceedingly ingenious, and will afford a safe means of constructing the lantern and putting up the statue without resorting to braces or guys, as is the case with ordinary apparatus. The scaffolding will reach to a height of over three hundred feet from the ground, and in general appearance will be that of a cage, and it is intended that the lantern of the dome shall be built up inside of this scaffolding.

☛ *It would be months before the dome was installed.* ☛

------◆------

TERRIBLE ACCIDENT.—*Explosion of a Magazine—Twenty Reported Killed and Thirty Wounded.*—About two o'clock this afternoon, this place was startled by a tremendous explosion, which shook the houses in many parts of the city, breaking glass, jarring down plastering, &c. The shock was caused by the explosion of a magazine at Fort Lyon, situated on Ballenger's Hill, on the opposite side of Hunting Creek, about a mile and a half distant.

A gentleman just from the fort, gives a terrible account of the explosion. He reports 20 men attached to the garrison killed, and about 30 seriously wounded. Many of the killed were thrown a great distance in the air, and mangled in a shocking manner. Two men were thrown nearly two hundred yards, and landed on their feet in the fall, without being seriously injured, and walked back to the fort without assistance. Most of the wounded will die. Most of those killed were in the magazine procuring powder for practice on the garrison guns, and as their death was instantaneous, the cause of the explosion can never be known.

One of the men attached to the garrison, says he noticed that two of the men who went into the magazine had pipes smoking.

Every tent within the fort was torn to fragments, and some of the guns dismounted, but the fort was not materially damaged, and before dark will be repaired. Fortunately another magazine of larger size and filled with powder did not explode, although but a short distance from the one demolished.—*Alexandria News.*

Charge of General Buford's troops near Beverly Ford.

Invasion!

To the North, whose armies had been on Southern soil virtually since the commencement of war, the word was as horrible as the experience was novel. Only once before had a Rebel army plunged into loyal territory. That was September of the previous year. But that "invasion" had gone only a few miles into Maryland, and had been stopped with some finality near Sharpsburg.

Now, nine months later, an even stronger army of Confederates under the redoubtable Lee was piercing the Potomac River barrier with seemingly more drive and purpose than before.

Northerners who believed in Union at all cost were fearful. Their fine Army of the Potomac just a short month earlier had received a shocking blow from Lee's Army of Northern Virginia. At Chancellorsville, vastly superior numbers had given way before Lee's ferocious tatterdemalions. The army which lost was the guardian of the Union's fortunes in the East. In addition to the military uncertainty, war-weariness was spreading through the civilian North. This depression of the will to fight was helped along by organized peace-lovers willing to settle for peace without reunion.

One important group may have shared these fears, but didn't show it: the Army of the Potomac. The soldiers, after months of doing things the hard way, had learned to fight in spite of mediocre generalship. But despite the faults of the top brass, the discomforts, the loss of buddies in the ranks, the longing for home, the faint-heartedness at home—these citizen-soldiers of the North were willing to keep on going for a long while. It was a spirit understood and matched by those at the far end of the Yankee gun barrels—gray-clad lads and oldsters who had a Robert E. Lee, if no Abraham Lincoln.

The stalwarts of Yankeedom and Rebeldom marched and steeled themselves for the holocaust. Meanwhile, the headlines in the North grew more hysterical.

Invasion! they cried.

CONFEDERATES PUSH INTO PENNSYLVANIA

(Monday, June 15, 1863)

EXTRA.

Telegraphic.

STIRRING NEWS.

HAGERSTOWN, MD., IN POSSESSION OF THE CONFEDERATES.

The Confederates Move on Chambersburg, Pa.

PHILADELPHIA, June 15.—A dispatch from Greencastle, dated 10:30, reports that our troops were then passing there in retreat from Hagerstown to Chambersburg.

Hagerstown had been evacuated, and all the stores and rolling stock of the railroad removed.

Rumor fixes the rebel force at ten thousand, which is probably an exaggeration.

———◆———

PHILADELPHIA, June 15.—The *Evening Bulletin* publishes the following news from dispatches received at the Pennsylvania Railroad Company:

A dispatch to-day from Bolton Station on the Northern Central Railroad says that Gen. Lyles had retreated from Martinsburg at eight o'clock last evening; that our force at Winchester had probably been captured yesterday, and that the enemy are in force, probably ten thousand strong, at Hagerstown.

The dispatch adds that the danger is great, as the enemy is advancing in heavy force.

A private dispatch from a trustworthy source states that the rebels appeared near Chambersburg this morning, and it is probable that the place has already been occupied by them.

🔫 *The day of this report, The Star gave a prominent spot to President Lincoln's proclamation calling for 100,000 militia from Pennsylvania, Maryland, West Virginia and Ohio to defend their soil until the Federal army under Hooker could reach the new "seat of war." The governor of the State which seemed most directly threatened translated the President's words into action.* 🔫

The Threatened Invasion of Pennsylvania.

Gov. Curtin Calls for Fifty Thousand Troops to Resist the Advance of the Rebel Troops upon the Border.

LEE'S ARMY SAID TO BE APPROACHING IN FORCE.

HARRISBURG, June 15.—Gov. Curtin has issued a proclamation stating that the President has called on Pennsylvania for fifty thousand men, to repel the invasion of the State and urge the men to rush to arms to resist the advance of the rebel troops now threatening our border.

———◆———

PHILADELPHIA, June 15.—The following dispatch has been received by Collector Thomas from Gov. Curtin:

Wm. G. Thomas, Philadelphia:—The President calls for a hundred thousand men for a term not exceeding six months, all the men so raised to be credited to the draft. Lee's army is approaching in force. We must have men immediately to check him. Can you not raise force at once? The men to be equipped and paid by the United States.

A. G. Curtin.

🔫 *The quotas of Maryland and West Virginia were 10,000 militiamen each, Ohio 30,000. In Pennsylvania, Lee's army was penetrating at an alarming rate. But Gov. Curtin was finding it difficult to arouse the populace to the imminent danger.* 🔫

(Tuesday, June 16, 1863)

Stirring News from Pennsylvania!
THE CONFEDERATES AT CARLISLE, EIGHTEEN MILES FROM HARRISBURG!!

PHILADELPHIA, June 16.—The Pennsylvania railroad has received a dispatch that the rebels were within ten miles of Carlisle at noon to-day.

195

Occupation of Wrightsville, Pennsylvania by Lee's troops.

The State House bell in this city will be rung this afternoon.

The people are awakening to a sense of a crisis.

LATER.

Reports from Harrisburg state that the Rebels are at Carlisle, which is but eighteen miles from Harrisburg.

STILL LATER.

Stirring Appeal of Mayor Henry, of Philadelphia, to the People of That City.

PHILADELPHIA, June 16.—The city is alive with excitement. The news of the Rebel advance has caused the most profound sensation.

Intelligence is eagerly looked for from the interior. In view of the pressing emergency, Mayor Henry has issued the following proclamation:

OFFICE OF THE MAYOR,
CITY OF PHILADELPHIA,
12 O'clock Noon, June 16.

Citizens of Philadelphia:

In view of the urgent need for instant action to protect the capital of your State and secure the safety of your homes I do hereby earnestly appeal to all citizens to close their places of business, and to connect themselves without delay with the existing military organization for the defense of the city.

Alex. Henry, Mayor of Philadelphia.

INDIGNANT APPEAL FROM GOV. CURTIN, OF PENNSYLVANIA.

Harrisburg in Danger, and the Philadelphia Militia Fail to Come to the Rescue!

HARRISBURG, June 16.—The following has been promulgated:

TO THE PEOPLE OF PHILADELPHIA.

For nearly a week past it has been publicly known that the Rebels in force were about to enter Pennsylvania.

On the 12th instant, an urgent call was made to the people to raise a departmental army corps for the defence of the State. Yesterday, under the proclamation of the President, the militia was called out.

To-day a new and pressing exhortation has been given to furnish men. Philadelphia has not responded. Meanwhile the enemy is six miles this side of Chambersburg, and advancing rapidly.

Our capital is threatened, and we may be disgraced by its fall while the men who should be driving these outlaws from our soil are quibbling about the possible term of service for six months.

It never was intended to keep them beyond the continuance of the emergency. You all know this by what happened when the militia was called out last autumn (Antietam campaign). You then trusted your government, and were not deceived. Trust it again now.

I will accept men without reference to the six months. If you do not wish to bear the ignominy of shirking from the defense of your State, come forward at once. Close your places of business and apply your hearts to the work. Come in such organizations as you can form.

Gen. Couch has appointed Lieut. Col. Ruff to superintend your organization. Report to him immediately.

A. G. CURTIN.

Which way would the Rebels head—west to the industrial centers or east to the political heart?

(Saturday, June 20, 1863)

EXTRA.

Late Telegraphic News.

A LARGE FORCE OF REBELS SAID TO BE ADVANCING UPON PITTSBURG, PENNSYLVANIA.

Their Pickets Near Uniontown, Fayette County.

Maj. Beazell, U.S. Volunteers, received intelligence from Fayette county, Pa., this morning, that the rebels, in heavy force, were advancing on Pittsburg, Pa., via the National road leading from Cumberland across the Allegheny mountains. Their pickets had reached Grantsville, Md., thirty-eight miles from Uniontown, Fayette county, Pa., on Wednesday evening last.

A pair of headlines breathe panic. One of them introduced the name of a town that will live as long as history is recorded.

(Thursday, June 25, 1863)

THE INVASION!

THE REBELS TEN REGIMENTS STRONG AND A FORCE OF ARTILLERY AND CAVALRY BEYOND GETTYSBURG.

WASHINGTON HOMEFRONT, JUNE, 1863.

The planners of civic affairs were active, no matter how perilous the plight of the Federal Union. If Jeb Stuart had popped into a meeting waving his sabre, he probably would have been ruled out of order until duly qualified to participate.

FOURTH OF JULY.—Two meetings have already been held at the National Hotel, for the purpose of making arrangements for the proper celebration of the coming Fourth of July. A committee of arrangements, embracing the names of Judge Purcell, District Attorney Carrington, Geo. W. Riggs, Lewis Clephane, Samuel Bacon, Thos. Fisher, Hudson Taylor, Dr. Wm. B. Magruder, Rev. Drs. Sunderland and Channing, A. C. Richards and others, has been appointed to raise funds and get up a celebration in every way worthy of the capital of the Nation.

There's nothing like a crisis for relaxation.

Lee's troops encounter the New York Militia in the main street of Carlisle, Pennsylvania. (Confederates are in the foreground.)

The rebel army crossing the Potomac.

PIC-NIC.—The first afternoon and evening picnic of the Washington and Georgetown Passenger Railroad Relief Association will be given on Wednesday, June 17th, at the Washington Park, Seventh street. The gentlemanly conductors of this road will certainly give an entertainment delightful to all who may participate.

☞ *People were taking drinking water for granted in those days, too—even though the city water system was a novelty.* ☞

WATER WASTERS.—The police officers are now under orders to enforce the law to prevent the wasting of the Potomac water. Housekeepers who are in the habit of wasting the water, or allowing it to be wasted by their employees, will be prosecuted according to law. The Superintendent is determined, if possible, to prevent the waste so much complained of, and the police officers will no doubt zealously enforce his orders. The use of the water for children's sports, or allowing it to run in the gutters, will be attended to.

198

LEE'S INVADING ARMY HAD ENTERED THE NORTH BY that safest of all routes, the Shenandoah Valley. Crossing the Potomac at Williamsport, Md., the Confederates tramped into Pennsylvania by way of the Cumberland Valley, the Shenandoah's northern extension. Beyond Hagerstown, Md. and Chambersburg Pa., sections of the army followed the curve of the Cumberland to Carlisle and to the west bank of the Susquehanna River, across from Harrisburg, the State capital. Other units struck due east from Chambersburg, over South Mountain to Gettysburg, and farther on to York and the Susquehanna below Harrisburg. All these advance contingents were part of Jackson's old corps, now commanded by Ewell. As the end of June approached, York had surrendered and paid tribute; the Rebel flag flew over Carlisle, the northernmost point of any Southern invasion, and Ewell's men were poised to strike across the Susquehanna to Harrisburg and Philadelphia.

The other two Confederate corps, Longstreet's and A. P. Hill's, stayed close to Chambersburg while Lee waited for word from his missing cavalry. At that point, the commanding general had no idea whether the Federals had followed him, cut off his supply line, or were stalled around Washington. Lee didn't know that Stuart—a man he relied on more than ever since Jackson was dead—had gone off on one of his fantastic roundabout gallops. The cavalry chief interpreted his marching orders in a way that best suited his nature, and detached his 9,000 troopers from their task of screening the main army and keeping tabs on the Federals. While still deep in Virginia, he headed east and trailed the Army of the Potomac as it moved to catch up with the Army of Northern Virginia. When Lee was in Pennsylvania anxiously looking for him, Stuart crossed the Potomac above Washington and captured a fine prize of Federal supply wagons near Rockville. Thus encumbered, and still headed in the wrong direction, he moved on a few miles west of Baltimore and on into Pennsylvania near Hanover. Riding his men to a frazzle, he had no idea where either army was.

With or without the necessary information, Lee had to make a move. He was on the point of following after Ewell for the Harrisburg strike when, on June 28, a Confederate spy came in with important news: the Federals were approaching the Pennsylvania line north of Frederick, Md. Lee swiftly changed his plans, ordering Ewell to pull back his scattered corps toward the main army. Early on July 1, Ewell's men were hurrying toward Gettysburg.

Three days before, in the bivouac around Frederick, the main Federal army of the East had just received its sixth commanding general since the start of the war. The change surprised no one. A theory had developed that Joe Hooker, after his bungle at Chancellorsville, was hardly the man to lead the troops in an invasion crisis. The responsibility was thrust, instead, upon Maj. Gen. George Gordon Meade. There was no time for formalities. The march northward drove on. On June 30, Meade learned that Lee was pulling his scattered elements together somewhere in southern Pennsylvania. He ordered Maj. Gen. John Buford's cavalry ahead to scout. Maj. Gen. John Reynolds' corps moved out behind Buford. Reynolds had instructions from Meade to keep an eye open for a favored site to do battle, especially in the vicinity of Gettysburg.

LEE'S INVASION STOPPED AT GETTYSBURG

(Thursday, July 2, 1863)

EXTRA.

Late Telegraphic News.

A Terrible Battle!

OUR FORCES SUCCESSFULLY RESISTING.

GEN. REYNOLDS KILLED.

Yesterday at 9 a.m., the rebel corps of Longstreet and Hill attacked our 1st and 11th army corps, under Generals Reynolds and Meade, on the road between Gettysburg and Chambersburg, near the former place, and a battle occurred which was very severe up to last advices from that point.

Though our troops were successfully resisting the attack, our loss had been heavy, including General Reynolds killed.

At four p.m., our 3d and 12th army corps were rapidly moving up to take part in the engagement.

THE GREAT BATTLE IN PENNSYLVANIA.

Up to 3 p.m. to-day we had been unable to learn that the authorities here had received anything official concerning the battle of yesterday near Gettysburg, Pa.; or, indeed, that aught unofficial on the subject had reached Washington in addition to the information up to 4 p.m. of yesterday, published in the first edition of to-day's *Star*. It is evident from that that at that hour the fortune of the day remained undecided. The fact, however, that two more of our army corps were then getting into the fight, while those two that were engaged had successfully held the ground Longstreet and Hill were striving to drive them from, gives us strong hopes that the next advices from thence will indicate a substantial victory for our arms.

Readers had to be content with this slim word from the front on the first day's fighting at Gettysburg. John Reynolds had brought his I Corps up on the run after Buford's cavalry made the initial contact with Confederate Harry Heth's division. Next

General Longstreet's attack upon the Union, left center.

Library of Congress

day there were more details, and the correspondent who filed the story mentioned the difficulty of getting out the news. ✺

(Friday, July 3, 1863)

EXTRA.
The Great Battle Near Gettysburg.
A FURIOUS STONE-FENCE FIGHT.

Desperate Attempts of the Enemy to Retrieve the Fortunes of the Day.

PHILADELPHIA, July 3, 1863.—The *Inquirer* of this morning has the following:

FREDERICK, MD., July 2, 1863.—A severe battle was fought yesterday about a mile and a half north of Gettysburg, Pa., between the 1st and 11th corps of our army, and a large force of the rebel army, supposed to belong to Longstreet's and Hill's corps. The battle commenced about 10 o'clock in the morning. The 1st and 11th corps were advancing on the Chambersburg pike, beyond Gettysburg, where they encountered the rebel pickets, about a mile outside the town. The first intimation of the close proximity of the rebel troops was a shot from one of their advance pickets, which struck Major General John F. Reynolds in the head, killing him instantly.

At the same time Gen. Reynolds was riding at the head of his corps, which was marching along the pike. Major Gen. Doubleday, commanding the third

Rebel dead after Gettysburg.
Library of Congress

division, then took command of the corps. The first division, Gen. (James Samuel) Wadsworth, took position behind a stone fence running through a wheat and corn field, in front of the enemy, at short musket range. The rebels in large force charged upon this division, and compelled it to leave the cover of the fence and fall back some distance after fighting gallantly . . .

Our wounded are at Gettysburg and well taken care of. Our forces at Gettysburg were largely reinforced last night, and the battle will probably be resumed to-day. It is said Longstreet's and Hill's corps were both engaged yesterday, and would be reinforced by Ewell's corps during the night. Gen. Meade is at the front to-day superintending operations. We are in a region without railroads or telegraphs nearer than 30 or 40 miles, rendering the transmission of news difficult.

I have just returned from near Gettysburg, and officers and soldiers from there this morning report that no fighting had taken place up to 10 o'clock, beyond occasional artillery fire. Upwards of 1,000 rebel prisoners passed through Taneytown (Md.) this morning on their way to the rear, Gen. (James Jay) Archer among them.

Gen. Meade will undoubtedly push the enemy rapidly. Our army is in fine condition and will fight well.

✺ *Archer was the first general of the Army of Northern Virginia to be captured after Lee took command.* ✺

LATEST FROM THE BATTLE FIELD!
No Battle Yesterday.
OUR TROOPS CONCENTRATED.
Gen. Meade Selects His Own Position.

Despatches have been received here from our brave Army of the Potomac up to last night. It is announced that Gens. (Francis Channing) Barlow and Schimmelpfenning (Alexander Schimmelfennig) were both wounded and fell into the enemy's hands in the engagement of the day before yesterday. They, with Generals Reynolds and (Gabriel Rene) Paul killed, were the only Union general officers who met with casualties. It is definitely stated, we hear, in the despatches referred to above, that the battle was fought on our part only by the First and Eleventh army corps; while the rebel force engaged against them were believed to embrace two-thirds of Lee's entire army.

202

At the end of the fight, after repulsing the rebels' last attack, General Meade shifted his position to the heights above Gettysburg, where he awaited the coming up of the five other corps of his army that had not participated in the engagement. In that position the enemy had declined to attack him up to last evening, by which time the balance of our troops had gotten up and were duly in line. Lee was at that time concentrating all his troops near by, but ceased manifesting the purpose of renewing the attack which at 4:30 p.m. he seemed about to do. It is judged here that Lee was not attacked yesterday because our troops, as they came up, were necessarily too much fatigued to permit them widely to be thrown into action against an unfatigued enemy. From the tenor of the despatches, it is believed here that if the enemy declined renewing the attack this morning, General Meade would at once engage his whole line.

🔫 *In the first day's fighting on McPherson's Ridge, Seminary Ridge and Oak Hill, the overwhelming number of Confederates pressing in from Chambersburg drove the Federals back toward Gettysburg. As the day wore on, Ewell's corps charged in from Carlisle, and York hit the Federals North of Gettysburg. Caught in the two-way crush, the Federals retreated in near-rout southward through the town. Gen. Paul, though badly wounded, did not die. Later news published July 3 left no doubt the battle was continuing.* 🔫

Telegraphic.

STIRRING NEWS!

A Great Battle Fought Yesterday at Gettysburg Between the Combined Armies of Lee and Meade!

PHILADELPHIA, July 3.—Parties coming here from Gettysburg say that on Wednesday ten thousand of our troops were engaged with thirty thousand of the enemy.

During Wednesday night about seventy-five thousand of Meade's troops came up and took favorable positions, while twenty-five thousand other Union troops were near at hand. The rebels had mainly concentrated near Gettysburg on Wednesday night, and there is little doubt but that the great battle of yesterday would involve every available man of both armies.

General George Meade, Federal commander at Gettysburg.

HARRISBURG, July 3.—From the cannonading heard here late last night it is evident that a terrible battle was fought yesterday.

(Saturday, July 4, 1863)

GREAT AND GLORIOUS NEWS!
The Union Arms Victorious in the Greatest Battle of the Century!

After the last edition of yesterday's *Star* went to press, official despatches reached Washington announcing that one of the most desperate battles of the war occurred on Thursday afternoon from 4.30 until 8.30 p.m., in which our General (Samuel Kosciusko) Zook and the rebel General Barksdale were killed. Prisoners invariably assert that Longstreet was also killed.

We take the following account of this great engagement from a special despatch to the New York *Times,* published in that journal's issue of yesterday afternoon:

At about 4½ p.m. the enemy sent his first compliments by a salvo of artillery, his first shell falling uncomfortably near Gen. Meade's headquarters. From this hour forth to 8½ o'clock occurred by all odds, the most sanguinary and bloody engagement yet chronicled in the annals of the war, considering its short duration.

The artillery attack which was made by the enemy chiefly on the left and centre, was rapidly followed by the advance of his infantry. The third corps re-

Battles & Leaders

The rebel charge on Cemetery Hill.

ceived the attack with great coolness. The Rebels at once made an attempt to get on our flank, and kept moving heavy columns in that direction. This necessitated support which was quickly given by the Fifth corps, the division of Gen. (James) Barnes' being sent to the right and that of Gen. (Romeyn Beck) Ayres (regulars) to the left, with Gen. (Samuel Wylie) Crawford in reserve.

The battle now became terribly fearful. The armies engaged each other at a very short range, and for three long hours the roar of musketry was incessant. I have heard more noises, louder crashes in other battles, but I never saw or heard of such desperate, tenacious fighting as took place on this flank. The enemy would often bring up suddenly a heavy column of men and force our line back, only to be in turn forced back by our own line of glittering steel.

Our gallant columns covered themselves with glory over and over again. They fought a superior force in numbers; the dispositions of the enemy were very rapid, for look where you would on that field, a body of rebels would be advancing. Our dispositions were equally rapid, and the enemy found more than their equal in such gallant veterans as (Daniel Edgar) Sickles, and (David Bell) Birney and (Andrew Atkinson) Humphreys. At 6½ Gen. Sickles was struck in the right leg by a piece of shell and borne from the field. The injury was so great that amputation became necessary, and it was performed successfully, the limb being taken off below the knee.

The struggle grew hotter and hotter, and many of our regiments, small enough before, melted away into almost nothing. The Second Corps was called on for aid, and though its own position was strongly threatened, yet the First Division, formerly General (Winfield Scott) Hancock's, flung themselves into the fight with desperation, and after a long and obstinate conflict, the enemy slowly and sullenly gave way. In this last charge the brigade of General (John Curtis) Caldwell, Second Corps, and that of Col. Sweitzer, from the Fifth Corps, won great honors.

The charges made by our men deserve mention, but want of time forbids. The rebels made frequent attempts to capture our artillery, and at one time had Watson's battery in their possession, but it was retaken in a furious charge by Birney's division.

The battle lasted till fully half-past 8 o'clock, when the enemy fell back to his old position, and left our veterans the ensanguined victors of that field. Our pickets were thrown out, and our lines covered the most of the field, including great numbers of the enemy's dead and wounded. I visited some portions of the line by moonlight, and can bear personal witness to the terrible ferocity of the battle . . .

Place names were understandably lacking in the news accounts. The reporter was trying to describe the fighting in the Federal salient which Sickles had created west of Little Round Top, in front of the main defense line along Cemetery Ridge. Longstreet's Confederates drove Sickles' men back from the Peach Orchard and the Wheat Field and through Devil's Den to Cemetery Ridge. In the course of the fighting, Maj. Gen. Gouverneur Kemble Warren saw that unprotected Little Round Top was being threatened, and ordered troops up to man it. His action probably saved the entire Union position, since the hill was the southern anchor of the line. Longstreet, of course, was not killed. While one column dealt with the second day's fighting, another carried a proclamation by the President.

Congratulatory Address of President Lincoln upon the Brilliant Successes of the Army of the Potomac.

The President has just issued the following congratulatory order:

WASHINGTON, July 4th—10 a.m., 1863.

The President announces to the country that news from the Army of the Potomac up to 10 p.m. of the 3d, is such as to cover that army with the highest honor, to promise a great success to the cause of the Union, and to claim the condolence of all for the many gallant fallen, and that for this he especially desires that on this day He whose will, not ours, should ever be done, be everywhere remembered and reverenced with profoundest gratitude.

(Signed,)   Abraham Lincoln.

It was not until three days after the battle that anything like detailed accounts of the final day's climactic fighting were available for publication— and this under a quiet little headline.

(Monday, July 6, 1863)

ANOTHER ACCOUNT OF FRIDAY'S BATTLE.

HEADQUARTERS ARMY OF THE POTOMAC, July 3.—(Correspondence of the *Associated Press.*)—The decisive battle has been fought to-day and the enemy have been repulsed with terrific loss.

At daylight Lee's right wing batteries opened upon our left, and shortly after those of his centre followed. After half an hour's cannonading, doing but little damage to us, the fire slackened and only occasional shots were exchanged.

Shortly afterward the enemy's left, composed en-

tirely of infantry and sharpshooters, made an attack on our right wing. So suddenly and impetuously was it accomplished, that our skirmishers and front line were driven back from their entrenchments, but by aid of the batteries in the rear and the indomitable bravery of the Twelfth Corps, we regained the first position, capturing a considerable number of prisoners.

Several hours of ominous silence followed the repulse. At 1 o'clock the enemy fired two shots, apparently as signals for the grandest artillery fight ever witnessed on this continent. Before a moment had elapsed it is estimated that at least eighty guns opened upon us. Our batteries returned the compliment with interest. The air seemed literally thick with iron, and for more than an hour it seemed impossible that man or beast could live through it. Strange to say the enemy's accuracy of range, as exhibited on the two previous days, was wanting on this occasion. Most of the shells exploded far in the rear of our front, and generally missing our batteries.

Under cover of this *feu d'enfer*, Lee advanced his columns of infantry from their covers, and made several desperate attempts to carry our lines by assault, but each successive attempt was repulsed with terrible havoc to their ranks.

After an hour's incessant cannonading the fire grew less intense for a short time, but was again renewed for a short time with equal spirit. During this period some of our batteries, whose ammunition had been exhausted, ceased to fire, and on the approach of the reserve batteries, withdrew to the rear.

Confederate dead in the "slaughter pen" at the foot of Little Round Top.

Library of Congress

The enemy only seeing the batteries withdrawn, and mistaking this for a retreat, made a rapid infantry charge up the hill and obtained a position in our line, cutting to pieces and almost annihilating the small infantry supports, but before they had time to rejoice at their imaginary success the fresh batteries poured in a deadly fire of canister and case shot. The infantry reserves joined on the other flank of the gap, charged them and added greatly to their destruction. They were completely surprised, and hundreds threw down their arms and asked for quarter. Nearly the entire brigade of Gen. Dick Garnett surrendered, and Garnett, himself wounded, (mortally) barely made his escape. Longstreet was mortally wounded and captured. He is reported to have died an hour afterward.

About 4.30 p.m. the artillery of the enemy slackened, and had entirely ceased at five, the last shots which they fired being far beyond their original position, and the infantry columns had withdrawn to their covers.

We took upwards of 3,000 prisoners. The enemy captured but few if any of our men.

The rebel prisoners report that Gen. A. P. Hill was killed outright upon the field, and that their officers suffered far greater casualties than in any previous engagement.

So terrific was the enemy's fire that the small house where Gen. Meade and staff were quartered was perforated by several shots. Many of the staff horses were killed around the house. Gen. (Daniel) Butterfield was struck in the breast, and it is feared internally injured by a piece of shell which exploded in the building. Lieut. Col. Joseph Dickinson, of the staff, had his left arm perforated by a flying fragment of shell, and it seemed a miracle that no greater damage was done to life or limb.

Several of our general officers were wounded in the engagement. Gen. Hancock was wounded in the leg. Gens. (John) Gibbon, Warren and (Henry Jackson) Hunt were wounded. In consequence of the excitement and difficulty in ascertaining their locations, the names of many prominent officers, reported as killed or wounded, cannot be ascertained to-night.

Too much credit cannot be given to our batteries, who for hours stood to their guns under a broiling sun, and surrounded by the missiles of death, retiring only to give their position to others when their caissons and limbers were exhausted of ammunition. The infantry engaged also nobly did their duty, and the enemy to-day at their hands have received the greatest disaster ever administered by the Union forces.

All officers award the highest honors to Gen. Meade for the able generalship he has displayed since he assumed command, and particularly for the coolness, decision and energy of this memorable 3d of July. Last night, believing it to be his duty to the cause, to learn how far he should be supported in the approaching conflict, he summoned his corps and division commanders for consultation.

The messenger who brought this letter says we advanced and occupied Gettysburg during Friday night, without opposition. Firing was heard early on Saturday morning, towards Gettysburg, supposed to be our forces pursuing Lee.

☞ *This account reads as if all the fighting were on the same front. The reference to the Twelfth Corps encompasses the crucial fighting that took place at Culp's Hill, northern anchor of the Federal line. The remainder deals with what has become known as Pickett's charge. Longstreet wasn't killed in this one, either, contrary to the report. And here was the welcome word.* ☞

Dead horses around the Trostle House in the salient occupied by General Sickles corps.

CONFIRMATION OF THE NEWS OF THE RETREAT OF LEE TOWARDS THE POTOMAC.

Preparations Made to Intercept His Retreat.

(Correspondence of the *Associated Press*.)

NEAR GETTYSBURG, July 5.—The enemy have retreated towards the Potomac.

Their skirmishers were drawn in last night, and a small cavalry force, probably the rear guard, passed through Emmitsburg this morning about daylight.

Our troops have been engaged all day in burying the dead, relieving the wounded, and collecting arms, many thousands of which belonged to the rebels.

The rebel pontoon bridge at dam No. 4 has been destroyed by our cavalry, almost unopposed, and the cavalry, at last advices, had gone up to Williamsport to destroy the two bridges there.

Other preparations are in progress to intercept Lee's passage of the Potomac, and our army is already in motion. So much time, however, has elapsed since Lee commenced to withdraw from our front, that his advance may have reached Williamsport to cross before we can prevent it.

Lee yesterday paroled about two thousand Union prisoners. They were received by Gen'l Couch.

It is not true, as stated, that Longstreet was captured and died. General Hunt, chief of artillery, was not wounded. Both of these reports were apparently well authenticated and freely believed.

The second Confederate invasion of the North had been repelled. The cost was fearful to both sides: Federal losses, 23,000, and Confederate somewhere between 20,000 and 28,000. Whatever the exact figures for Lee's casualties, they involved troops and officers he could ill afford to lose in a remorseless war of attrition. Despite the talk of pursuit, Meade regarded the prospects as too risky with his weakened though still strong army. Lincoln was troubled by the decision. But at least Lee had been stopped.

WASHINGTON HOMEFRONT, JULY, 1863.

At the height of the critical battle, an anxious President looked to the defense of the Nation's capital.

THE DISTRICT MILITIA ORDERED OUT.

Below will be found the President's order directing Major General George C. Thomas to muster into the service at once eight regiments of the militia of this District for a period of sixty days, unless the exigencies of the occasion shall sooner pass away. Our own belief is that their services will not be needed for more than a week or two, if so long. In the meanwhile, however, prudence certainly counsels their employment; an ounce of precaution always being worth a pound of cure, especially in military affairs.

We are able to assure the public that up to the hour at which we write . . . all the information that has reached here from Pennsylvania indicates that Gen. Meade is succeeding in his operations, and bids fair to use up Lee's army before our patriotic fellow-citizens, upon whom this call has been made, will be able to get a glimpse of a rebel in arms.

We may not inappropriately add that we hear that the names of all liable to service under this Presidential call who fail to obey the order will be promptly reported to the Provost Marshal General, to be dealt with equally promptly according to the military rules, which must necessarily be enforced on such occasions as the present.

Later The Star was able to report with relieved calm the July Fourth Parade.

THE CELEBRATION OF THE FOURTH.— The eighty-seventh anniversary of American independence was celebrated in this city by a general suspension of business; each citizen giving himself up to the observance of the day either on his own hook or by participating in the celebration as conducted by the committee, who, for some time, have had the matter in hand. The burning of "villainous saltpetre," in the shape of fire-crackers, squibs, wheels, rockets, &c., was commenced early on Friday evening (July 3), and continued throughout the greater portion of the night, and the day was ushered in by the explosion of powder in all directions. The day itself was fair and beautiful, and all were prepared to celebrate it in an enthusiastic manner, on account of the sacred memories that clustered around it; but when it began to be whispered about that the rebel army under Lee had been terribly whipped, the excitement became great indeed. But when about ten o'clock, and as the procession was passing along the Avenue to the President's grounds, a bulletin was put out at the *Star's* office, announcing the glorious news, and also the fact of the President's congratulatory order, the enthusiasm went up with a bound. Cheers went up from every throat, and gunpowder explosions sounded louder and clearer than ever before, and a zest unfelt for two years at least was given to every participant in the celebration.

A SIEGE WAS THE LAST THING GRANT WANTED AT VICKS-burg. He had been confident back in May that a quick assault would win the city and free his army for campaigns elsewhere. Three bloody attempts late that month convinced him, however, that direct assault was not the answer. The Confederate engineers had done too thorough a job on the fortifications around the city. He was surprised also by the spirit of the defenders. The Confederates may have been discouraged by their reverses at Jackson and Champion's Hill, and by Joe Johnston's inability to merge his force with theirs. But determination rather than demoralization set in. Grant had no recourse but to harass and starve Vicksburg into submission.

The futile attacks in May had at least given him a chance to clear a piece of deadwood from his army. John McClernand, one of his three corps commanders, had given Grant misleading information which led to the bloodiest of the three assaults. Despite the slaughter that resulted, McClernand later issued a "general order" to his corps hailing its unquestionable bravery and his own highly questionable abilities as a general. McClernand was one of the North's numerous "political generals." It wasn't by coincidence that his congratulatory order found its way back to his political friends in Illinois. Grant would have none of these shenanigans. He bounced McClernand, and replaced him with a talented soldier, Maj. Gen. Edward Otho Cresap Ord.

The preliminaries behind, the Federal army—soon to be 70,000 strong—undertook the grim business of siege. Pemberton had some 25,000 troops to man his nine-mile ring of entrenchments and forts. They were in an eight-square-mile trap. With them was the civilian population of Vicksburg. Alike, they were cut off from outside help by an army on the east and a gunboat fleet on the west. Food and every other supply was limited—even clear drinking water. In a matter of days, troops were on fractional rations and civilians on worse. Sickness took an unsurprising toll. Among the soldiers alone, more than a third were laid low. Bombardment, fierce and unrelenting, from land and water, heightened the misery. Cellars and caves became the natural habitat of citizenry and soldiery.

Boredom was the principal enemy. Grant hated the inactivity. His soldiers detested the trench and dugout life. For the Federal troops it was almost entirely a matter of sitting and waiting in their double line of entrenchments—one line facing Vicksburg, the other facing east where an attack might come from Joe Johnston's green and poorly-equipped army. There were some combat diversions. On June 25, the Federals exploded a mine under one of the Confederate forts. A follow-up infantry charge got nowhere. A week later, when another mine was set off, the infantry wasn't even sent in. The greatest ordeal of the Federals was to sweat out the roar and concussion of the endless cannonade.

Then on July 3, the last day of the battle of Gettysburg far across the continent, a flag of truce appeared on the Vicksburg parapets. Pemberton wanted a parley.

GRANT FORCES VICKSBURG SURRENDER

(Tuesday, July 7, 1863)

EXTRA!
VICKSBURG SURRENDERED!

The following dispatch has this moment been received:

U.S. MISSISSIPPI SQUADRON,
  FLAG SHIP BLACK HAWK.
    VICKSBURG, July 4th, 1863

Hon. GIDEON WELLES,
  Secretary of the Navy,

Sir: I have the honor to inform you that Vicksburg has surrendered to the U.S. forces this Fourth of July.

Very respectfully your obed't serv't,
                    D. D. PORTER,
        Acting R. Adm'l, com'g Miss. Sq'n.

🔫 *Brief as the news flash was, and despite the fact that it was competing with the sensational news from Gettysburg, the fall of Vicksburg received due recognition.* 🔫

(Wednesday, July 8, 1863)

OFFICIAL FROM GEN. GRANT CONCERNING THE CAPTURE OF VICKSBURG.
The Surrender Made Early on the Morning of July 4th.
GEN. GRANT MOVES ON FOR NEW VICTORIES.

A dispatch from Gen. Grant to Maj. Gen. Halleck, dated at Vicksburg at half-past ten in the morning of the 4th of July, states that the enemy surrendered that morning and their troops were paroled as prisoners of war. The movements of his force about to be made are detailed, but not proper for publication at present.

🔫 *Grant's report was received a day later than Porter's in Washington. Both dispatches probably had to be taken by river to St. Louis or Cairo, the nearest friendly telegraph points. In any case, it was all official, and The Star dropped a hint on how military operations might now proceed.* 🔫

The fight in the crater of Fort Hill during the siege of Vicksburg.

Library of Congress

Admiral Porter's fleet running the rebel blockade at Vicksburg.

VICKSBURG.

The surrender of Vicksburg gives us in effect quite a hundred thousand veterans to be instantly employed in other quarters. Gen. Halleck remarked in his speech last night that Grant is already at Port Hudson. We knew a week ago that he had sent large reinforcements to Banks, who have doubtless reached him by this time. That Grant has himself already gone down there illustrates his energy and promptness forcibly.

It is to be presumed that he has already aided Rosecrans, sending him sufficient reinforcements to enable him to take Chattanooga and to destroy the important military manufacturing establishments of the traitors in upper Georgia almost as soon as Port Hudson will be ours. In three months, the surrender of Vicksburg gives us at least one hundred thousand, if not two hundred thousand, additional black troops —many more than sufficient, with a few white officers, to hold every important point, not only on the Mississippi, but west of the Alleghenies, our armies may take ere the termination of this glorious campaign; leaving all our gallant troops now in the field to continue active operations in all directions.

The Navy thumped its own tub, gave due credit to the landlubbers, and supplied some detail on the Vicksburg siege.

(Saturday, July 11, 1863)

Official Report from Admiral Porter Concerning the Capture of Vicksburg.

IMPORTANT PART TAKEN BY OUR NAVY IN THE REDUCTION OF THE REBEL STRONGHOLD.

The following dispatch from Admiral Porter was received at the Navy Department this morning:

U.S. MISSISSIPPI SQUADRON, *Flag Ship "Black Hawk," Vicksburg,* July 4, 1863.—Sir: I have the honor to inform you that Vicksburg has surrendered at last, to the United States forces, after a desperate, but vain, resistance.

That she has not done so sooner has not been for want of ability on the part of our military commanders, but from the magnitude of the defenses which were intended to repulse any force the Government could possibly send there.

What bearing this will have on the rebellion remains yet to be seen, but the magnitude of the success must go far toward crushing out this revolution, and establishing once more the commerce of the States bordering on this river.

History has seldom had an opportunity of recording so desperate a defense on one side, with so much courage, ability, perseverance and endurance on the other, and if ever an army was entitled to the gratitude of a nation, it is the Army of the Tennessee and its gallant leaders.

The Navy has necessarily performed a less conspicuous part in the capture of Vicksburg than the Army; still it has been employed in a manner highly creditable to all concerned.

The gunboats have been constantly employed below Vicksburg in shelling the works, and with success, co-operating heartily with the left wing of the Army.

The mortar boats have been at work for forty-two days without intermission, throwing shells into all parts of the city, even reaching the works in the rear of Vicksburg and in front of our troops, a distance of three miles. Three heavy guns placed on scows, a nine-inch, ten-inch and a one-hundred-pound rifle, were placed in position a mile from the town and commanded all the important water batteries; they have kept up an accurate and incessant fire for fourteen days, doing all the damage that could be done by guns under such circumstances. Five eight-inch, two nine-inch, two forty-two pounder rifles, four thirty-two pounder shell guns, have been landed, at the request of the different Generals commanding corps, from the gunboats, and mounted in the rear of Vicksburg, and whenever I could spare the officers and men from our small complement, they were sent to manage the guns; with what ability I leave to the General commanding the forces to say.

In the meantime I stationed the smaller class of gunboats to keep the banks of the Mississippi clear of guerillas, who were assembling in force, and with a large number of cannon, to block up the river and cut off the transports bringing down supplies, reinforcements and ammunition for the Army. Though the rebels on several occasions built batteries, and with a large force attempted to sink or capture the transports, they never succeeded, but were defeated by the gunboats with severe loss on all occasions. Without a watchful care over the Mississippi, the operations of the Army would have been much interfered with; and I can say honestly that officers never did their duty better than those who have patroled the river from Cairo to Vicksburg. One steamer only was badly disabled since our operations commenced, and six or seven men killed and wounded.

While the Army have had a troublesome enemy in front and behind them, the gunboats, Marine brigade under Gen. Ellet, and a small force under Generals Dennis and Mower, have kept at bay a large force of rebels, over 12,000 strong, accompanied by a large quantity of artillery. Though offered battle several times and engaged, they invariably fled, and satisfied themselves by assaulting half-disciplined and unarmed blacks.

The capture of Vicksburg leaves us a large army and naval forces free to act all along the river, and I hope soon to add to my department the vessels which have been temporarily lost to the service, viz: the *Indianola* and *Cincinnati*.

The effect of this blow will be felt far up the tributaries of the Mississippi; the timid and doubtful will take heart, and the wicked will, I hope, cease to trouble us, for fear of the punishment which will sooner or later overtake them.

There has been a large expenditure of ammunition during the siege. The mortars have fired 7,000 mortar shells, and the gunboats 4,500. Four thousand five hundred have been fired from the naval guns on shore, and we have supplied over 6,000 to the different army corps.

David D. Porter, A. R. Admiral
Commanding Miss. Squadron.

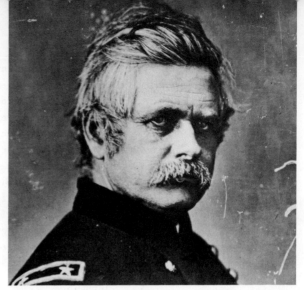

General Edward Ord, one of Grant's most reliable field commanders at Vicksburg.

HON. Gideon Welles, Secretary of the Navy, Washington, D. C.

And Grant stated the acceptable terms on the preliminaries to the Vicksburg finale.

(Monday, July 13, 1863)

The Surrender of Vicksburg.
Official Dispatches to the War Department.

The following was received at the War Department:

NEAR VICKSBURG, July 4, 1863.—*Major General U.S. Grant, Commanding U.S. Forces:* General—I have the honor to propose to you an armistice for blank hours, with a view to arranging terms for the capitulation of Vicksburg. To this end, if agreeable to you, I will appoint three commissioners to meet a like number to be appointed by yourself, as such place and hour to-day as you may find convenient. I make this proposition to save the further effusion of blood, which must otherwise be shed to a fearful extent, feeling myself fully able to maintain my position a yet indefinite period. This communication will be handed you, under a flag of truce, by Major General James Bowen.

Very respectfully, your obedient servant,
Jno. C. Pemberton.

To this General Grant replied, as follows:

HEADQUARTERS DEPARTMENT OF TENNESSEE, IN THE FIELD NEAR VICKSBURG, July 3, 1863.—*Lieutenant General J. C. Pemberton, Commanding Confederate Forces, &c.:*—General:

Your note of this date, just received, proposes an armistice of several hours for the purpose of arranging terms of capitulation, through commissioners to be appointed, &c. The effusion of blood you propose stopping by this course can be ended at any time you may choose, by an unconditional surrender of the city or garrison. Men who have shown so much endurance and courage as those now in Vicksburg will always challenge the respect of an adversary, and I can assure you will be treated with all the respect due them as prisoners of war. I do not favor the proposition of appointing commissioners to arrange terms of capitulation, because I have no other terms than those indicated above.

I am, General, very respectfully, your obedient servant, U. S. GRANT, Major General.

🖎 *Though he sounded firm in his messages to Pemberton, Grant's terms were short of "unconditional." He granted paroles to the captured Confederates, rather than make them prisoners of war. Some in the North criticized this concession, but Grant had decided that thousands of Confederate prisoners would only tie up transportation and troops, and waste time that could be better spent elsewhere fighting the war. For its part, the South considered Pemberton's choice of National Independence Day on which to surrender as something close to treachery. But the Northern-born Pemberton simply had reasoned that if he agreed to give up on July 4, Grant might unbend a little from an "unconditional surrender" frame of mind. Newspaper dispatches, meanwhile, were not confined to official statements. There was human suffering to report, too.* 🖎

ADDITIONAL FROM VICKSBURG.
Terrible Sufferings of the Residents During the Siege.

VICKSBURG, July 5.—Yesterday and to-day have been remarkably quiet, and good feeling prevails. The weather is fearfully warm. Nineteen general officers have been paroled. Two or three days must elapse before prisoners can be sent out to their destination, which is reported to be Talladega, Alabama.

Many are anxious not to be paroled, and wish to take the oath of allegiance, quit the rebel service and be sent north.

Several women and children were killed or injured during the siege, while hundreds of houses occupied by the sick and wounded, have been constantly exposed to our shells. About two thousand five hundred persons have been killed inside the works since the siege began.

The labor performed on the fortifications on both sides has been prodigious. The weight of our artillery has knocked most of their works into undistinguishable heaps.

There were about twelve hundred women and children in the city during the bombardment, who have for the most of the time been obliged to live on dead carcasses, of which there are several hundred more.

Library of Congress

Unloading Union supplies at Vicksburg.

Citizens have not been allowed to draw supplies except in cases of destitution.

Prices of food have been enormous. Five dollars a pound being charged for flour; one dollar a pound for mule meat.

🔫 *However much the suffering on either side, the Union cause had advanced a giant step forward. The Confederacy was severed. The inland sections of the North once again had their outlet to the sea. The Mississippi, Father of Waters, could now flow "unvexed," as President Lincoln remarked.* 🔫

WASHINGTON HOMEFRONT, JULY, 1863.

🔫 *Everyone was elated over the big news from the West.* 🔫

THE SURRENDER OF VICKSBURG!

The news of the fall of Vicksburg the most intense and joyous excitement about the departments, and in fact all over the city. As soon as it became known, the "starry flag" was flung to the breeze at the War and State Departments, and the others quickly followed suit. At the Treasury Department the clerks all hastened to the portico on the east side of the building, just as a military company was passing, and the air was made to resound with cheers. On the east front of the State Department too, a crowd soon collected, and made similar demonstrations of joy.

An order was promptly issued from the War Department for the firing of a grand salute of one hundred guns in honor of the glorious event.

The President, Secretary Stanton, Secretary Welles, and other members of the Government were waited upon by eager circles of friends, tendering their heartiest congratulations over the results so honorable to them, and to those selected by them to execute their plans.

At the *Star* office a bulletin was immediately displayed, and the glorious news, as soon as caught by the crowd, was received with enthusiastic cheers, the army of newsboys adding a big one on their own individual account.

The decisive victories gained at Gettysburg and Vicksburg, coming together must crush the last hope of rebeldom.

🔫 *So elated was* The Star *that it got a little giddy.* 🔫

The two Burgs.
VICKSBURG!   GETTYSBURG!
To whom shall we *Grant* the *Meade* of praise?

🔫 *But important local matters were not forgotten.* 🔫

Public School Examinations.

The Female Grammar School of the First District, Miss Mary P. Middleton, teacher, was examined on Thursday July 2d. . . . There are thirty-three pupils on the rolls of this school; all present. This school is held in Corcoran's Building, on H street, opposite Dr. Gurley's Church. It is one of the finest rooms in the city, and is admirably adapted to school purposes; and it is therefore a matter of regret that it is to be vacated, as it appears that the Government has need of it. On the day of examination the room was tastefully decorated with American flags and evergreens, and we were pleased to notice in attendance a number of ladies, parents and relatives of the pupils. The attendance was not, however, so large as could have been desired, and it certainly is a matter of surprise that parents do not take a more lively interest in these examinations. The classes in grammar and in mental and practical arithmetic were examined rigidly, and the pupils evinced a steady progress, the classes of the present year excelling (it was said) those of last year. There was one thing here, however, in which the pupils might have learned a good lesson from some of the secondary and intermediate schools, viz: in correct and symmetrical formation of figures. This is no small matter, for badly formed letters evince a carelessness on the part of the pupil.

The whole school was examined together in geography. . . . , and so far as it went the examination was a good one, but the short time allowed for the examination of so important a study could not fully develop the improvement of the classes. All, however, gave evidence of a thorough knowledge of the principles of the study. In reading and spelling all the classes were good, and in mental arithmetic, answers to questions were given quickly and were generally correct. The copy-books of the young ladies were all neat and clean, and gave evidence of a steady improvement in penmanship. But the copy-books usually presented for inspection on such occasions are no adequate criterion, for but few pages are written. It would no doubt afford a better opportunity of judging of the improvement and neatness of the pupils if all the copy-books used throughout the year were submitted for examination. . . .

IN THE BURST OF PATRIOTIC ENTHUSIASM THAT FOLLOWED the outbreak of war, both the Confederacy and the Federal Government had been flooded with enlistments. By 1863, the realities of suffering and death on the battlegrounds had reduced enthusiasm to doggedness. Battle tolls required a steady stream of replacements. The North, in addition, needed men to occupy the wide areas gradually being reclaimed by its armies in the South. Conscription was the only answer.

The Confederacy, always at a disadvantage in manpower as well as materials, was the first to pass a conscription act. Through this law of 1862, plus the various calls for volunteers, Dixie succeeded in raising throughout the war an estimated total of one million troops. No matter what means were tried to strengthen the armies, desertions reduced their numbers at an appalling rate. Desertions rose in proportion to the tide of Federal victories. By late 1864, President Davis would grieve that two-thirds of his soldiers were absent from the ranks. By war's end, less than 200,000 Confederate troops would be on hand to surrender.

Absenteeism in the Federal ranks similarly increased as the war dragged on. And reluctance was developing as early as 1862 to respond to calls for volunteers. In August of that year, a new device was tried by the Government: a draft call for 300,000 short-term State militia. As a draft, it failed. The quota was reached only by offering cash bounties to the men who joined up. This disappointing response, plus battle casualties, sickness and absenteeism, necessitated more drastic measures. Consequently, the National Enrollment Act of March, 1863, introduced compulsory military service. Public reception, especially by the male eligibles, was fainthearted. One provision of the law rankled in particular: draftees willing and able to pay $300, or hire a substitute, could escape conscription. What that amounted to, according to a cynical wisecrack of the day, was "a rich man's war, and a poor man's fight." Danger signs were evidenced soon after the law was passed. Coal miners of Eastern Pennsylvania, already economically distressed, felt they were being dragooned to die simply because the wealthy could pay and avoid the risk. Turning to violence, they killed some of their company officials, destroyed property, and otherwise demonstrated that they wanted no part of conscription. Troops and pacification by Government leaders finally brought order. Similar flareups were reported in numerous sections of the North.

Resentment of the draft reached a higher and uglier pitch, ironically enough, on the heels of the North's two greatest victories of the war: Gettysburg and Vicksburg. In mid-July, trouble boiled over in the Nation's biggest metropolis, New York City.

RIOTS PROTEST DRAFT IN THE NORTH

(Tuesday, July 14, 1863)

EXTRA.

FURTHER OF THE GREAT RIOT IN NEW YORK.

The City in Possession of the Mob.

The city has been filled with rumors to-day of terrible doings by the mob in New York city, to the effect that, thirty thousand strong, they had the city in their possession and were burning and destroying on all sides.

The Associated Press, up to this hour, has not furnished one word to-day in relation to affairs there, but the following dispatches have reached here by the *Independent Telegraph line:*

NEW YORK, July 13, 11 p.m.—The post office is closed, and bells are ringing constantly for fires burning in different parts of the city.

The windows of the *Evening Post* are closed.

The U.S. Sub-Treasury is garrisoned by soldiers.

The office of the Associated Press is closed, and all lights in the telegraph offices are extinguished.

The Fifth Avenue Hotel is threatened with destruction by the mob.

A young reporter, named Lawson, of the Philadelphia *Inquirer,* was severely handled and maltreated by a crowd of ragged boys and Irishmen.

It is understood that most of the damage was done in Lexington avenue.

(SECOND DISPATCH.)

NEW YORK, July 14.—12.30 a.m.—The mob has been sensibly diminished by the heavy rain that is now falling.

Two handsome brown-stone-front buildings in Lexington avenue have been destroyed.

The Allerton Hotel is also destroyed by fire.

The negro boarding-houses on Roosevelt street, and several houses occupied by negroes on Cherry street, have been destroyed.

These and several other buildings of lesser note were all burned by the mob.

It is reported that the up-town residence of Horace Greeley has been fired and destroyed.

Cannon have been brought from the Brooklyn Navy Yard, and placed in position to protect the Custom House, the Sub-Treasury, and Post Office.

Cannon firing was heard in the direction of the locality of the first outbreak, about 11 o'clock. No particulars respecting it yet received.

The lower part of the *Tribune* office was torn out by the mob. A strong force is now guarding it. They are said to have six boxes of Sharpe's rifles and ammunition to defend it.

Fire bells have now ceased ringing, and the lower part of the city is now comparatively quiet.

The bulk of the mob appears to be up in the vicinity of Forty-third street.

Several negroes, in various parts of the city, have been severely beaten.

A recruiting center in New York City Hall Park.

It is believed that the rioters will be dispersed before daylight.

STIRRING NEWS FROM THE NORTH!!
A RIOT BROKEN OUT IN HARTFORD!!

SPRINGFIELD, MASS., July 13.—A riot has broken out in Hartford, and troops have been sent here to protect the armory and arsenal.

There is considerable excitement in this city.

☛ There was more than a suspicion that the mobs were carefully organized. Their meetings were planned, their points of attack carefully selected and assaulted. The question was raised: were the peace-at-any-price factions at work? Or were the agitators such northern disunionists as former mayor Fernando Wood of New York? News of the rioting was to jam the columns of The Star *for days. At the very outset the editors gave their appraisal of what was going on. ☛*

EDITORIAL.

(Tuesday, July 14, 1863)

THE RESISTANCE TO THE CONSCRIPTION IN NEW YORK CITY.

The telegraph brings the intelligence that the political teachings of Wood & Co.—the unscrupulous demagogues who would peril the fate of a nation for the advancement of their personal fortunes—have borne their legitimate fruit and a bloody attempt has been made by an armed mob to resist the draft in New York city. A squad of soldiers sent to suppress the disturbance were disarmed and beaten, and some fifteen policemen, including Superintendent Kennedy, were killed, it is reported. The telegraph wires eastward were cut by the mob and trains prevented from leaving in the same direction, and other acts of disorder had been committed.

New York city cannot afford to permit mob law to prevail there twenty-four hours. Her business interests alone make it imperatively necessary that any such scheme of anarchy shall promptly be put down, and we are confident that before this time the supremacy of law and order has been emphatically reasserted in the great commercial metropolis.

Deplorable as the affair is in some aspects of the case, we are not sure but that it will result in good. It must serve certainly, in New York, to unmask the heartless demagogues who, in the name of peace and good will to the rebels in arms, incite ignorant men to assemble in mobs and shoot down their own neighbors.

The easy-going citizens of New York, who treated the mischievous utterances of Wood & Co. with such philosophic indifference as "amounting to nothing," as mere "political clap-trap," find that they *do* amount to something; and that municipal as well as national safety demands that the traitorous demagogues shall have no more rope, unless, indeed, that rope takes the shape of a halter!

So far from hindering the enforcement of the draft, we believe further that this affair will serve to bring out such an expression of public sentiment on the right side, as will have the happiest effect in forwarding the labors of the enrolling officers throughout the country.

At this auspicious juncture, with Lee's defeated army straining every nerve to get out of harm's way, and with the Southern Confederacy cut in twain by the capture of Vicksburg, with the Legislature of North Carolina already moving to bring that State back into the old Union, and with Louisiana, Texas, Arkansas, Georgia and Virginia taking steps in the

Police battle the New York draft rioters outside the *Tribune* office.

same direction, and the hitherto tabooed word "reconstruction" whispered from length to breadth of the bubble Confederacy, with all these encouraging facts in view, we have no idea that the Government's requirement of sufficient men to finish up the good work at once and forever will be defeated by any such attempt to resist furnishing the insignificant quota required of New York city.

☞ Whoever was fanning the flames, resentment was genuine against the conscription law provision that permitted those with money to pay $300 to avoid the draft. The humorist, Artemus Ward, made this sardonic comment: "I have already given two cousins to the war, & I stand reddy to sacrifiss my wife's brother, ruthurn'n not see the rebellion krusht. And if wuss comes to wuss, I'll shed every drop of blood my able-bodied relations has got to prosekoot the war." ☞

THE NAUGHTY BOY GOTHAM, WHO WOULD NOT TAKE THE DRAFT.

Library of Congress

(Wednesday, July 15, 1863)

EXTRA!

From New York.

THE MOB AT WORK AGAIN TO-DAY.

NEW YORK, July 15—10 a.m.—The wires of the *Independent Telegraph Company* east have been cut for several blocks by the mob.

One mob is now in Greenwich street, destroying houses of ill fame and gin mills.

The crowd and excitement continue on the Second avenue, near Forty-third street.

No cars or stages are running.

LATEST!

Gov. Seymour Declares New York City in a State of Insurrection.

NEW YORK, July 15.—Gov. Seymour has issued a proclamation declaring the city of New York in a state of insurrection, and giving notice to all persons that the means provided by the laws of this State for the maintenance of law and order will be employed to whatever degree may be necessary, and that all persons who shall, after the publication of this proclamation, resist or aid, or assist in resisting, any force ordered out by the Governor to quell or suppress such insurrection, will render themselves liable to the penalties prescribed by law.

(Thursday, July 16, 1863)

EXTRA!

THE LATEST FROM NEW YORK.

Collision Between the Military and the Mob.

Between Two and Three Hundred Persons Killed and Wounded.

We are indebted to Mr. Talcott, the enterprising Superintendent of the *Independent Line of Telegraph* for the following:

NEW YORK, July 16.—A very serious collision occurred yesterday, between the military and the Rebels in east 19th street. At one time the military were driven back, but the rioters were repulsed eventually with great loss.

The number injured is estimated at between 200 and 300.

During the day several negroes were caught and hung to the lamp posts.

The *Times* and the *Tribune* are the only papers that have dared squarely to denounce the mob and sustain the conscription law.

There has been no disturbance this morning, as far as we can learn, and many places of business that have been closed up are again open.

Although quiet prevails this morning to a comparative extent, the mob cannot be considered as put down.

Anti-Negro feeling ran high. Aside from lynchings, there were other brutalities around the city, especially in the Negro quarters, where an orphanage was set afire. But the savagery of the mob was aimed in every direction: churches, businesses, individual public officials and, above all, at vested authority. Draft headquarters were a particular target. City police suffered hundreds of killed and wounded. Federal troops, up from the Gettysburg battlefield, were pelted with stones, and finally resorted to firing into the mobs. The extensive gang and hoodlum element of New York gleefully joined the rioters for the fun of looting and mayhem, if nothing else. And Gotham was not the only metropolis involved.

The Riot in Boston.
THE MOB DISPERSED.
Leading Rioters Arrested.

BOSTON, July 15.—All is quiet this morning. Four or five persons were killed last night, and probably a dozen wounded—some of them severely.

The most daring act of the rioters was an attack upon the armory in Cooper street, where a force of militia was stationed. When the mob had beaten down the doors, it was fired upon by a six-pounder, loaded with canister.

This effectually scattered the mob at that point. . . .

The rioters who attacked the gunshops were speedily dispersed by a volley from the revolvers of the police.

The first dragoons appeared at nine o'clock, patroling the streets, and together with the infantry force, overawed all further outbreaks.

The military continue in quarters in sections of the city where the disturbance occurred.

Mayor Lincoln has issued a proclamation warning all riotously disposed persons from further violence, and calling upon all citizens to aid in the preservation of quiet and order. He says the peace of the city shall be preserved at all hazards.

The leading rioters arrested last night are to be proceeded against for burglary and wilful murder.

The mobs ruled New York for three days, but weakened under the threat of army bayonets and the pleas of religious and civic leaders. Peace at last could be reported.

(Saturday, July 18, 1863)

EXTRA!
LATEST FROM NEW YORK.
THE RIOTS THERE SUPPRESSED.

(Special Telegram to the *Star*.)

NEW YORK, July 18, 1863.—The night passed quietly here, and this forenoon so far. There has been no renewal of the disturbances, the mob spirit having been quelled through the fears of the loyal bayonets already assembled to protect public and private rights.

Thousands had been killed or hurt in the uprising. As much as $5 million in property had been damaged or destroyed. The Star was editorially indignant.

EDITORIAL.
(Saturday, July 18, 1863)
The New York "Confederacy" Nipped in the Bud.

Elsewhere we publish a telegram to the *Star* announcing the end of the recent riot in New York. All information from that quarter received up to this time, goes to make it more certain that public opinion is growing there in intensity, against those whom it so unanimously holds responsible for the excesses of the mob—Gov. Seymour, who, in his speech to the miscreants styled them "my friends," and substantially palliated and justified their treason and excesses, and the secession politicians and disloyal newspapers, who, to force peace on the Government with the Union dismembered, have, since the beginning of the war, been maligning the authorities and misrepresenting their acts, and instilling into the minds of the ignorant, cowardly and vicious, the idea that they have a constitutional right to resist the Government's necessary war measures, by violence. That such teachings in such times as the present should result in remitting the lives and property of the citizens of New York, for the nonce, to the mercy of the city's thieves, prostitutes and open and secret sympathizers with the rebellion is so natural that the authors of the mischief evidently make no headway whatever in their efforts to escape the indignation of all surrounding them who have anything to lose by such a reign of terror as that through which the Union's commercial metropolis has just passed.

The violence, in any case, led to one result. The New York City draft was postponed a month. And when it was resumed, thousands of infantry and cavalry from the Army of the Potomac patrolled the streets to keep the peace. There would be further resistance to the draft, but it would be mostly passive. The prosecution of the war proceeded. 🜚

WASHINGTON HOMEFRONT, JULY, 1863.

At a time when Washington was served by only one railroad, something as seemingly minor as a heavy rain could disrupt communications to the North. 🜚

THE EMBARGO.—Paint Branch still runs riot, and several other branches "ain't doing as they'd orter," consequently Washington continues cut off effectually from the outside world, causing a decidedly odd but not agreeable state of things. No mails, no exchanges; the Departments letterless, dispatchless; markets dried up because of the wet, barely six quarts of blackberries at the stalls to-day, and vegetables in proportion; prices of meat up because Paint Branch is up. Nary *"Herld," "Times," "Trybune," "'delphy Inquirer," "Sun,"* or *"Clipper"* on the street.

How many hundreds of thousands of these sheets have accumulated in bundle on t'other side of Paint Branch we know not, but there must be a few.

It is a time of great leisure for the penny postmen, and these indefatigable servants of the public, who, year in and year out, know no rest day or night, now walk the streets like other folks by day, and go to the Canterbury at night if they list, all because Paint Branch is up. A *Star* reporter, who went down into Maryland on Saturday, to see his wife, is supposed to be seated on the north bank of Paint Branch, waiting patiently for the waters of that turbulent stream to simmer down. Mr. Secretary Harvey, of the Council Board, and other mourners, are supposed to be keeping him company in that philosophic attitude.

For shame, Paint Branch!

Eternal vigilance at the city borders often bore interesting fruit. Of course, personal liberties were sometimes flouted outrageously. 🜚

———◆———

A GOOD HAUL.—Yesterday about 7 o'clock p.m., as Officer Cline of the first precinct was going the round of his beat, east of the Anacostia, he noticed three men in a stage coach approaching this city. Suspecting that they were not right, he followed them. The guards at the bridge allowed them to pass, but Cline was not satisfied—and pushed on after them and arrested them. He took them to the Provost Marshal, where they gave their names as H. Hamberger, Moses Mann and Wm. Lutzbacher, all Germans, and claim to be merchants. Upon search $46,000 in Confederate money was found upon them. They are supposed to have been engaged in trading with Richmond, and were returning from a trip. Capt. Todd sent them to the Old Capitol.

———◆———

CONTRABAND ARRANGEMENT UNDER HER PETTICOATS.—The most novel and ingenious contrivance of the war for the smuggling of liquor to soldiers, we found this morning at the office of the Provost Marshal. It is a tiny vessel made to fit the middle portion of the body, and composed of four sections, each of which is capable of holding a gallon and a quarter. This extensive and unseemly bustle gave a certain Mrs. Yett, bound for Alexandria, such huge proportions as to attract the attention of the guard at Aqueduct Bridge. A search was instituted, resulting in the discovery of the above-described piece of mechanism, each section of which was filled to its utmost capacity with "rot-gut" whisky. The *delivery* was borne with fortitude, and the party is doing "as well as can be expected." In addition to the above, Mrs. Yett had on her person fifteen bottles filled with the same chemical.

O ALL THE BRANCHES OF THE SERVICE, NONE COULD remotely match the cavalry for glamor and dash. Romantic aspects aside, cavalry was indispensable to any land operation. It was the eyes and ears of an army. It was the highly mobile arm that could stretch far around the enemy to learn what he was up to, or to smash his supply lines and bases, or frighten him into doing reckless things.

Confederate leaders recognized the value of cavalry in the earlier stages of the war. The Federals were slow to realize or develop its potential. The war in fact would be many months old before Federal foot-soldiers would stop taunting horse-soldiers with ''Who ever heard of a dead cavalryman'' and feel grateful instead.

The Confederates, largely an outdoor people, had plenty of trained horsemen and made the most of them. Cavalry was one means of offsetting the Federal preponderance of infantry. And the Rebel cavalry usually made the most of its opportunities. Outstanding in the East were Jeb Stuart, of course; Wade Hampton, Fitz Lee, Rooney Lee—and that independent operator, John Singleton Mosby, who made guerilla warfare an art.

It was only after the clash of horsemen at Brandy Station that Union cavalry began emerging as a force to be reckoned with under such leaders as John Buford, Alfred Pleasonton, Judson (''Kill-Cavalry'') Kilpatrick, George Armstrong Custer, James Wilson and ultimately Phil Sheridan.

The Confederates in the West had an abundance of expert cavalrymen active from start to finish of the war. There was Bedford Forrest, Joe Wheeler, Jo Shelby and—one of the most effective and devil-may-care of all—John Hunt Morgan.

Morgan's specialty was the long free-wheeling raid far behind the enemy's front. In 1862, he had led three such raids out of Tennessee and all over central Kentucky. In July of that year, in conjunction with Forrest, he threw the Federals advancing on Chattanooga into turmoil by slashing their supply route to shreds. Three month later, he drove into Kentucky all the way north to Lexington, captured that place among others, and destroyed railroads and bridges necessary to the Federal movement on Murfreesboro. In December he was on the prowl again, bagging nearly 2,000 prisoners and destroying two millions' worth of property in the Federal rear.

Now, in July, 1863, Morgan had a more ambitious ride in mind. The peace movement seemed to be gaining momentum up North. Yankees were demonstrating against military conscription. This might be just the time to give the Union summer of discontent a little stimulus.

MORGAN RAIDERS HIT INDIANA AND OHIO

(Tuesday, July 7, 1863)

Invasion Panic at Louisville, Kentucky.

MORGAN RAIDING IN THAT DIRECTION.

LOUISVILLE, July 7, 12:30 a.m.—The alarm bells are now ringing, calling the citizens together for the defense of the city.

Rumors were prevalent all this evening of the approach of Morgan's forces. They were reported at Bardstown this morning and at McPherdsville (Shepherdsville) this afternoon. This force is estimated at from 2,000 to 4,000.

This evening, at five o'clock, the Nashville train, due here at six o'clock, was thrown off the track by guerillas. Our guard of fifty repulsed the assailants. It is impossible at present, owing to the excitement, to obtain further particulars.

☞ *Morgan crossed the Cumberland River at Burkesville and headed in what appeared to be a beeline for Louisville, hitting in succession Columbia, Lebanon and Bardstown. He veered west of Louisville and reached the south bank of the Ohio River at Bradenburg.*

☞ *The various dispatches estimated Morgan's forces at anywhere from 2,000 to 8,000. It is obvious that they were only guessing.* ☞

(Friday, July 10, 1863)

Invasion of Indiana.

Gen. Morgan's Forces Capture Corydan— They are Marching on New Albany and Jeffersonville—Great Excitement.

INDIANAPOLIS, July 9.—Morgan's forces, infantry, cavalry, and artillery, numbering from six to eight thousand, have crossed into Indiana and captured Corydan. Our forces are falling back. The rebels are supposed to be marching on New Albany and Jeffersonville, where large quantities of supplies are stored.

Troops are being organized throughout the State, to be sent forward rapidly. Business is entirely suspended. The citizens are forming companies, and eight have been raised since last night.

It is reported that two citizens were killed at Corydan when the rebels entered the town.

(Monday, July 13, 1863)

The Rebel Raid in Indiana.

They Are Repulsed by the Militia—The Destination of the Main Force.

CINCINNATI, July 12.—Morgan's raid to-night reached within seven miles of the Ohio line.

Some of the bridges on the Ohio and Mississippi railroad, between Cochrane and Mount Vernon, are destroyed.

The rebels also approached the Indianapolis and Cincinnati railroad, near Tummans, where they were met by a regiment of militia and driven back.

This probably was only a small body of the enemy. The main body appears to be making for Aurora and Lawrenceburg.

☞ *The Ohio River crossing was made on two steamboats "requisitioned" from the civilians. The militia, which tried half-heartedly to stop the raiders, were swept aside as the troopers streaked through Corydon, Salem, Vienna, Lexington, Paris, Vernon, Dupont and Summansville. The raiders had a scare when their leader was nearly captured in his sleep at Lexington. By July 12, they were nearing the Indiana-Ohio border.* ☞

General John H. Morgan

Library of Congress

221

(Tuesday, July 14, 1863)

Important from Ohio.
CINCINNATI, COVINGTON AND NEWPORT PLACED UNDER MARTIAL LAW.
Nothing Definite as to Morgan's Whereabouts.

CINCINNATI, July 13.—General Burnside has declared martial law in Cincinnati, Covington and Newport.

Business is suspended until further order. All citizens are required to organize in accordance with the direction of the State and municipal authorities.

There is nothing definite as to Morgan's whereabouts, but it is supposed he will endeavor to move around the city and cross the river between here and Maysville.

The militia are concentrating in obedience to the order of Gov. Tod.

🔫 *The raiders entered Ohio at Harrison on the 13th, and sped through the outskirts of Cincinnati the same night. The Federal pursuers were now beginning to close in, and Morgan found himself in a trap at Bluffington Island, where he had intended to recross the Ohio.* 🔫

General Mosby's guerrillas destroying a Union sutler's train.

Library of Congress

(Tuesday, July 21, 1863)

Official Report of the Capture of Morgan's Gang.
Capture of a Large Number of Colonels, Majors and Line Officers.

The following was received at headquarters to-day:
HEADQUARTERS, CINCINNATI, 10:45 a.m., July 21, 1863.—*Gen. H. W. Halleck, General-in-Chief:* Following just received:

Headquarters U. S. Forces in the Field, Geiger's Creek, 9 p.m., July 20.—Lt. Col. Richmond, A.A.G. —Colonel: We chased John Morgan and his command over 50 miles to-day. After having skirmishing for 6 or 7 miles between the 45th Ohio, of Col. Wolford's brigade, which was in the advance, and the enemy, we succeeded in bringing the enemy to a stand by 3 o'clock this afternoon, when a fight ensued which lasted an hour, when the rebels fled, taking refuge upon a very high bluff.

I sent a flag-of-truce demanding an immediate and unconditional surrender of Morgan and his command. The flag was received by Col. Coleman and other officers, who came down and asked an hour for consultation among their officers. I granted forty minutes, in which time the command—excepting Morgan, who deserted his command, taking with him a very small squad—surrendered. It was my understanding that Morgan himself had surrendered, and learned it was the understanding of Morgan's officers and men.

The number of killed and wounded is inconsiderable. The number of prisoners is between one thousand and fifteen hundred, including a large number of colonels, majors and line officers. I captured between six and seven hundred prisoners yesterday.

I think I will capture Morgan himself to-morrow. I had Col. Wolford's and Jacob's brigades—the conduct of officers and men, without an exception, evinced the greatest gallantry and a high degree of skill and discipline.

(Signed) (James M.) Shackelford, Brig. Gen.

We have strong hopes of being able to capture Morgan and the remaining portion of his force, thus entirely wiping out this band.

A. E. Burnside, Maj. Gen.

🔫 *Morgan lost nearly 1,000 of his men killed, wounded or captured. He managed to escape with about 300 survivors, and continued eastward toward the Pennsylvania border.* 🔫

General Nathan Bedford Forrest

(Saturday, July 25, 1863)
Morgan's Raid in Ohio.

CINCINNATI, July 24.—Shortly after Morgan crossed the Muskingum yesterday, he was attacked by the militia under Colonel Hall, with two pieces of artillery. Fifteen rebels were killed and several wounded. His progress was checked twice by Colonel Hall, but he finally escaped by the way of Cumberland, Guernsey county, which place he left last night at seven o'clock.

This morning he crossed the Central Ohio railroad at Campbell's, but was so closely pursued by General Shackelford that he had not time to do damage beyond burning the depot and tearing up some of the track.

At nine o'clock this morning he reached Washington, Guernsey county, where he did a good deal of damage, plundering, &c.

Shackelford is close behind him.

A courier, arrived from the vicinity of Taylorsville at noon, reports that a squad of about fifty men became detached from Morgan's command when he crossed the Muskingum, prowling around killing stock. A force of three hundred mounted men has been sent after them.

A SKIRMISH WITH MORGAN.

CINCINNATI, July 24.—Major Krouse had a skirmish with the rebels at eleven o'clock this morning, driving them out of Washington.

When last heard from, Morgan was at Winchester, twelve miles northeast of Cambridge, moving towards Steubenville and the Indiana railroad, closely pursued by our force.

The Federal defenders soon could breathe a sigh of relief.

(Monday, July 27, 1863)
The Raid in Ohio.

Morgan Caught at Last—The Whole Command Captured—They Number Only Four Hundred Men—The Rebel Chieftain One of the Party.

CINCINNATI, July 25, 9 p.m.—The latest up to this hour heard from Morgan is that he was eight miles from Steubenville, moving north.

MORGAN'S WHOLE FORCE CAPTURED.

CINCINNATI, July 26.—The following has been received at headquarters:

HEADQUARTERS IN THE FIELD, THREE MILES SOUTH OF NEW LISBON, OHIO, July 26.—*To Col. Lewis Richmond, A.A.G.:* By the blessing of Almighty God I have succeeded in capturing General John H. Morgan, Colonel Chike, (Roy S. Cluke), and the balance of the command, amounting to about four hundred prisoners. I will start with Morgan and staff on the first train for Cincinnati, and I await the General's order for transportation of the balance.

G. M. Shackelford, Col. Commanding.

Arrival of Rebel Prisoners at Cincinnati.

CINCINNATI, July 26.—Nine hundred of Morgan's men were lodged in Camp Chase prison to-day. They will be kept there until the officers of Straight's (Streight's) expedition are released from Libby prison.

Further Particulars of the Defeat of Morgan.

CLEVELAND, July 26.—Major Way, with two hundred and fifty of the 9th Michigan cavalry, forced Morgan to an engagement at three o'clock this morning, a mile from Salonsville (Salineville), Ohio, and routed him, capturing two hundred and forty prisoners. Morgan, with three hundred, escaped, but they were all captured by Shackelford at 3 p.m. to-day, near New Lisbon.

Morgan and his staff are now prisoners at Wellsville, Ohio.

Morgan was confined in the State penitentiary at Columbus as a common criminal. The Union strategy

General John S. Mosby

here was to force the Confederates to release Col. Abel D. Streight from Richmond's Libby Prison. Streight's cavalry raiders earlier that year had been captured on a railroad-smashing foray in Alabama. Morgan took matters into his own hands by escaping from prison that winter. But his raiding days were numbered, and he would never again match his endurance record of averaging 21 hours a day on the march. He would be killed in action before the war ended. 🔫

WASHINGTON HOMEFRONT, JULY, 1863.

🔫 *At the lower end of the social ladder, which was rather heavily occupied in those days, Madame Pauline Meyer was being accused of a certain unpleasantness in her house of pleasure.* 🔫

A MIXED CASE.—Some time ago a soldier visited the house of Madame Pauline Meyer, on Fourteenth street, next to the corner of N north; and the company of the gay damsels proving agreeable he repeated his visits, and upon one occasion lost his watch, a silver one of some value, and no one in the house acknowledged having seen it. Yesterday morning the Madame had a quarrel with her female boarders, and turned them out of the house. They proceeded directly to Sergeant Cronin, of the Fourth

Ward, who had been on the lookout for the watch, and informed him that Madame Meyer had it. The Sergeant, in company with officer Pendle, searched the house, and found the watch, and arrested the Madame and Catharine Chill, a servant, and took them to the Fourth Ward station. Witnesses testified that the servant girl found the watch on the floor and gave it to August Meyer, the reputed husband of the Madame, and the witnesses kept it a secret from the soldier and the police until now. They also charged the Madame and her husband with keeping a bawdy house, and one of them testified that she paid the Madame bed money the night before, and also that she had paid the husband as much as fifty dollars in the last three weeks. Justice Giberson held the man and wife to bail in $300 each for keeping a bawdy house, and the husband separately in $300 additional for the larceny of the watch. The bail was speedily given.

The case being ended, and the proprietors of the house having returned to their dwelling, the witnesses went there in company with some male friends, or "lovyers," and demanded their clothing. The demand created a muss, the result of which was the ornamenting of Meyer's forehead with a knot, with various rays extending from the center, and several smaller protuberances on divers parts of the head, evidently by the application of a billy. Meyer at once went for a warrant to have the parties arrested.

In the meantime, Henry Myers, Mrs. Pauline Myer, and Annie Clark were arrested for disorderly conduct, by Officer Franklin, on the complaint of Mr. Colclazer, and taken to the Second Ward station, where their cases were ruled for trial. . . . The names are written differently on the station house register.

🔫 *And horses as well as people were considered fair game.* 🔫

IN THE WRONG PEW.—Yesterday, while two of Captain Johnson's detectives were crossing the Anacostia bridge, they were stopped by a man who wanted to know if they were riding Government horses, and, after an examination, said that they must be delivered to him. The man's authority for making the arrest was demanded, and he claimed to be one of Col. (Lafayette C.) Baker's detectives, with a roving commission to hunt up Government horses anywhere in Maryland or Virginia. Capt. Johnson's officers conveyed the man to Col. Baker's office, and thence he was committed to the Central Guardhouse, being recognized as an old offender and horse-thief.

LANDMARK VICTORIES HAD BEEN WON FOR THE UNION at Vicksburg and Gettysburg. Then as summer wore on into fall, Sherman ousted Joe Johnston's Confederates from Jackson, Miss., and other Federals captured Little Rock, Ark. There were Union setbacks, too, in that period. The fleet blasted the forts around Charleston harbor, but efforts to occupy the positions got nowhere. Bleeding Kansas was the scene of another blood bath. Late in August the Confederate irregular, William Clarke Quantrill, committed a sickening outrage at Lawrence, murdering nearly 200 "blacklisted" Union men and boys, plundering the town, and destroying more than one million dollars in property.

As far back as June, when the Vicksburg siege was under way and Lee was invading the North, still another theater of war was giving the Lincoln Government concern. This was the middle theater, where General Rosecrans and his Army of the Cumberland were supposedly boxing in the enemy. Rosecrans was spurred, but he was a cautious and deliberate officer. However, he got the Washington hints, at last. At about the time the climaxes were being reached at Vicksburg and Gettysburg, he succeeded in maneuvering Bragg's Confederates out of Tullahoma, Tenn., whence they had retired after the battle of Murfreesboro months before. After Tullahoma, there was another of Rosecrans' long pauses. It took considerable importuning from the War Department before he began to move again on August 15.

The new objective was the important rail center, Chattanooga. Rosecrans undertook another series of maneuvers in the mountains where Tennessee, Alabama and Georgia join borders. His tactics were skillful, and he eased Bragg out of Chattanooga into northwest Georgia. Maj. Gen. Thomas Leonidas Crittenden's corps occupied the city. Three other corps—under "Pap" Thomas, Alexander McD. McCook and Gordon Granger—scattered in various directions. Their general aim was to cut off what was diagnosed as a retreat by Bragg, so they headed generally southward. The Confederate commander, for his part, hoped to fall upon the separate corps as they emerged from the mountain passes. But things went wrong in the lower echelons, and Bragg decided to concentrate and retrace his steps northward toward Chattanooga. He was due to be strengthened momentarily—troops from the lower Gulf States, and Longstreet with parts of his corps from the Army of Northern Virginia. Thus he would be a numerical match for the Federals in a pitched battle.

The opposing commanders spent September 18 shifting their armies in the woods and rugged terrain of the northwest corner of Georgia. Each was trying to locate the other and get organized at the same time for effective battle formations. The first contact was established the morning of the 19th between elements of Thomas' corps and that of Bedford Forrest. It was near the creek the Indians named Chickamauga—"River of Death."

CONFEDERATES HAVE EDGE AT CHICKAMAUGA

(Monday, September 21, 1863)

Telegraphic News.

Great Battle
Near Chattanooga.

**TERRIFIC FIGHT
THROUGHOUT THE DAY.**

Results Indecisive.

CINCINNATI, Sept. 21.—A special to the *Commercial* gives the following account of Saturday's fighting:

The battle opened at 11 o'clock, in the vicinity of Widow Glenn's, on the road leading from McLamore's Cave to Chattanooga. It soon became general, the enemy maneuvering his troops finely.

Early in the action the rebels made an impetuous charge on the famous Loomis Battery, when five out of the six guns were captured. Capt. Van Pelt, commanding the battery, was taken prisoner. At two o'clock the contest became terrific. The roll of musketry was far more continuous and deafening than at Stone River (Murfreesboro). At 2:40 o'clock the division on the center was hard pushed, broke and retreated.

Col. Barnett planted a battery, and soon checked the pursuing enemy, who, in return, was driven in disorder over the same ground. (Jefferson Columbus) Davis' division was driven back with heavy loss.

Every gun of the 8th Indiana battery was captured, when his force rallied, pushed the enemy back, and retook the guns.

(Joseph Jones) Reynolds lost heavily, but stubbornly held his position, driving the enemy, but never leaving his line.

(John McAuley) Palmer, who was overwhelmed, failed to get off his entire battery, and as a consequence, two of his guns were lost.

(Horatio Phillips) Van Cleve, fighting gallantly, lost ground, and being overpowered, failed to regain his position.

Our line was pressed severely, and wavered. The rebels, exulting over the apparent success, made the air resound with cheers. They advanced along the whole line, and when within fire, musketry rolled from right and left, and until five o'clock the fighting was terrific.

The General (Rosecrans) grew anxious. The wounded began to pour in, and the rebels steadily moved up near his headquarters. New forces were opposed to them, and from this time until dark the battle raged with destructive fury.

At dark, the firing having almost ceased, the enemy threw forward fresh troops, and again engaged our right.

The action became general, and until long after dark raged with fury.

The battle thus far is a bloody one. Our loss is very great. Prisoners say some of their regiments are almost annihilated. Both armies occupy the same ground they did when the action began.

We have captured several hundred prisoners, many of whom are from the East. We took ten guns and lost seven.

🙠 *The lines, that first day, were drawn up along the Lafayette-Chattanooga road. Actually, they were formed as the battle progressed, more units hurried to the sound of firing, and those already formed called for reinforcements. The fighting was savage, but neither side gained any great advantage. During the night, Longstreet arrived with his corps and took over the left of the Confederate line, with Bishop Polk in the center and Forrest on the right. The battle was ready for its second day. The headlines were ominous.* 🙠

(Tuesday, September 22, 1863)

LATEST FROM CHATTANOOGA.

Our Loss in Wounded and Prisoners in the Enemy's Hands Less Than 3,000.

DESPERATE BRAVERY OF ROSECRANS' TROOPS.

They Stand Like a Rock.

The following particulars in regard to the operation before Chattanooga have reached this city:

General George H. Thomas, "the rock of Chickamauga."

On Saturday, the 19th, a demonstration was made by the rebels in strong force, which appears to have been repelled by the force under General Thomas, with advantage on the Federal side.

On Sunday the engagement commenced late in the morning. The first gun was fired at 9 a.m., but no considerable firing took place until 10. Previous to 10, General Rosecrans rode the whole length of our lines. Soon after the battle commenced, Gen. Thomas, who held the left, began to call for reinforcements.

At about 12 m. word came that he had been forced to retire to the second line. Reinforcements were then sent to him, and McCook's whole corps, which was on the right and as a reserve in the centre, was sent to his assistance. (Thomas John) Wood, of Crittenden's corps, and Van Cleve, who held the front centre, were also ordered to the left, where the fury of the cannonade showed the rebel force was massed. Their places were filled by Davis and (Phil) Sheridan, of McCook's corps.

But hardly had these divisions taken their places in line, when the rebel fire, which had slackened, suddenly burst out in immense volleys upon the center. This lasted about twenty minutes, and then Van Cleve, on Thomas's right, was seen to give way, but in tolerable order; soon after which the lines of Sheridan and Davis broke in disorder, borne down by the enemy's columns, said to have consisted of Polk's corps.

These two divisions were the only divisions thrown into much disorder. Those of Negley and Van Cleve were thrown into confusion, but soon rallied and held their places, the first on the left and the second on the right of Thomas' corps. Davis and Sheridan, late in the day, succeeded in rallying about 8,000 of their forces and joined Thomas.

Thomas, finding himself cut off from the right, brought his divisions into position for independent fighting—his line assuming the form of a horseshoe, along the crest of a wooded ridge. He was soon joined by Granger, from Rossville, with a division of McCook and (James Blair) Steedman's division, and with these forces firmly maintained the fight until after dark. Our troops were as immovable as the rocks they stood on. The enemy repeatedly hurled against them the dense columns which had routed Davis and Sheridan in the morning; but every onset was repulsed with dreadful slaughter. Falling first on one and then on another point of our lines, the rebels for hours vainly sought to break them.

Thomas seemed to have filled every soldier with his own unconquerable firmness; and Granger—his hat torn by bullets—rode like a lion wherever the combat was the hottest. Every division commander bore himself gloriously; and among them Turchen (John Basil Turchin), (William Babcock) Hazen and Parker (Charles Garrison Harker) especially distinguished themselves. Turchen charged through the rebel lines with the bayonet, and, being surrounded, forced his way back again.

Parker, who had two horses shot under him on Saturday, forming his men in one line made them lie down until the enemy was close upon them, when suddenly they rose, and delivered their fire with such effect that the assaulting columns fell back in confusion, leaving the ground covered with killed. When night fell this body of heroes stood on the same ground occupied by them in the morning, their spirits being unbroken. Their losses are not yet estimated.

Thomas telegraphs this Monday forenoon that the troops are in high spirits. He brought off all his wounded. Of the sick and wounded at Crawfish Spring, including our main field hospital, nearly all had been brought away.

The number of prisoners taken by the enemy will hardly surpass 2,000, besides the wounded, of which not more than 1,000 could have fallen into their hands.

Of rebel prisoners we have already sent 1,300 to Nashville.

Of our losses in artillery, most of them were occasioned because the horses had all been killed.

Thomas retired to Rossville on Sunday night, after the battle had closed.

Rosecrans had issued orders for all his troops to be concentrated with the forces at Chattanooga.

In the last two assaults our troops fought with bayonets, their ammunition being exhausted.

The latest information that has reached this city from Chattanooga last evening, was to the effect that Rosecrans would concentrate on Chattanooga last night. Thomas had been engaged with the enemy prior to 5 p.m. yesterday, and it was therefore questionable if he would be able to reach Chattanooga last night. There were indications that the enemy were contemplating a demonstration on another part of our line last evening.

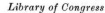 *A mix-up in orders opened a wide gap in the Federal right just as Longstreet's attack began. The Confederates piled through spreading chaos among the Union ranks. The remnants of the line that did not flee toward Chattanooga folded back upon Thomas, who was holding his own on the left. Thomas was beginning to have a deperate time of it when Granger, in reserve three miles away, rushed help to his comrades on his own initiative. Steedman commanded the rescue party, and Thomas, thus bolstered, "stood like a rock" on which the Confederates all but beat themselves to pieces. Not until nightfall, and under Rosecrans' orders, did Thomas withdraw his men to Chattanooga. A brief dispatch from a Southern paper gave an accurate picture of the outcome.*

(Wednesday, September 23, 1863)

REBEL ACCOUNTS OF THE FIGHTING NEAR CHATTANOOGA.

They Admit Heavy Losses in Men and Officers.

FORT MONROE, Sept. 23.—The Richmond *Dispatch* of the 22d instant contains the following:

CHICKAMAUGA, GA., Sept. 20.—After two days' hard fighting, we have driven the enemy, after a desperate resistance, from several positions, but he still confronts us.

The losses are heavy on both sides, especially so in our officers. We have taken twenty pieces of artillery and twenty-five-hundred prisoners.

(The above is signed by General Bragg, and addressed to Adjutant and Inspector General Cooper at Richmond.)

Rosecrans has been heavily reinforced by troops from Grant's army.

The two-day battle claimed a toll of 16,000 Federals and 18,000 Confederates. Rosecrans cooped up his army in Chattanooga, while Bragg's forces entrenched themselves on Missionary Ridge and Lookout Mountain overlooking the city.

General Thomas' men coolly repel the rebel charge at Chickamauga.

WASHINGTON HOMEFRONT, SEPTEMBER, 1863.

🔫 *The musical arts in Washington were many and varied despite the fighting.* 🔫

GERMAN OPERA.—Mr. A. Bergfeld, a gentleman well known in the world of musical management, is in town, arranging the preliminaries for the visit here of the celebrated Anschutz Opera Troupe, consisting of fifteen principal singers and an effective chorus and orchestra. He has engaged the Washington Theater for a series of performances, commencing on the 8th of October.

The leading tenor robusto is Herr Himmer, who has been for several years at the Berlin Opera. The new prima donna for the heavier parts is Madame Himmer Frederici, from the same theater. Both are very fine artists. The soubrette is M'lle Pauline Canisso, from Vienna, who sang with success in Paris last year, and has received high commendation from Rossini and others. There is another soubrette, M'lle Caroline Lang, from Pesth. A singer of the florid style is M'lle Caroline Puckner, from Vienna. The light tenor, Herr Holler, is from the Brunswick Opera.

The first basso is Herr Lorenz Remy, from Vienna, where he was selected by Salvi for the Italian opera. The baritone's name has not been given to us, but he is said to be very fine. M'me Johannsen, and Messrs. Kronfeld, Graff, Weinlich, and others of last year's company, are re-engaged. The orchestra and chorus have been greatly enlarged and improved. A number of operas never played in this country will be produced, including Weber's "Euryanthe," Spohr's "Jessonda," and Gounod's "Faust," which has made such a sensation in London lately.

This troupe created an immense sensation in New York and Philadelphia, drawing crowded houses constantly of both English and German citizens, and, indeed, of all who were capable of appreciating magnificent music.

———◆———

COLUMBIA CORNET AND STRING BAND.—The undersigned respectfully announces to the public, that he is ready to furnish Music for Private Parties, Balls, Pic-Nics, Parades, Exhibitions, etc., with any number of Musicians required, at the shortest notice, by leaving orders at John Iseman's, corner of Pennsylvania avenue and 4th street east.

Henry Iseman.

Major General Gordon Granger, who reinforced General Thomas at a critical moment.

A SERENADE CUT SHORT BY A FLOOD.—This morning, between the hours of 1 and 2 o'clock, a party of gallants took their positions in front of the United States Hotel, and with a variety of musical instruments proceeded to make melody, for the benefit, most probably, of some fair one, who, at that hour, doubtless, was locked in the arms of Morpheus —that is to say, was asleep. "Gentle Annie" was first put through, and then a turn was taken at "Sweet Annie of the Vale." Out upon the night air swelled other favorite tunes, and the serenaders then turned their attention to this "Cruel War," and the time when it should be over. They had got about as far as "How you told me that you loved me," &c., when a window above was heard to open and the party was all agape to receive some sign of recognition from the favorite fair one. They did receive it. Splash, came down a flood of unsavory water from an earthen vessel thrown by some crusty old "cuss," whose slumbers had been disturbed, and who had no soul for music. The "Cruel War" was cut short off, and there was some tall "cussing" among the serenaders. One, in his wrath, pronounced the "fellow who threw that a miserable old devil." However, the baptism had its desired effect. The serenaders moved off. The music ceased and sleepy people rested quietly.

Rosecrans' near rout at Chickamauga, and Meade's failure to pursue and crush Lee's army after Gettysburg, preyed on President Lincoln's mind. But Grant, at least, continued to perform with the determination that was needed to win for the Union. There was also encouragement closer to home. Watching the political tides for a clue to the Northern will to win, the President took confidence in October. That was the month of the gubernatorial elections in Ohio and Pennsylvania. In the Buckeye State, Union candidate John Brough vied with Vallandigham, the notorious peace-at-any-price man. In Pennsylvania, Andrew Gregg Curtin, up for re-election on the Union ticket, faced a man who had once declared "If the Union is to be divided, I want the line of separation to run north of Pennsylvania." Curtin won handily. When Brough, too, prevailed, Lincoln telegraphed the victor "Glory to God in the highest, Ohio has saved the Union."

So it was with relative peace of mind that the President faced a speaking engagement on November 19. The occasion was the dedication of a National cemetery at Gettysburg, where the soldiers who had fallen in that battle the summer before would never be disturbed again. Few around him expected that the President could spare the time to make the customary "appropriate remarks," as had been requested. Besides, the program already boasted perhaps the leading orator of the age, the distinguished Edward Everett of Massachusetts.

Notwithstanding all this, the President had some deep convictions he wanted to express concerning the Nation and the men who fought for it. He would keep his talk short and unobtrusive, in deference to the distinguished guests present. But he could not forego his Gettysburg appointment.

PRESIDENT AT GETTYSBURG DEDICATION

(Wednesday, November 18, 1863)

THE DEDICATION OF THE CEMETERY AT GETTYSBURG.

The opening of the cemetery for the burial of the brave soldiers who lost their lives on the battle-field of Gettysburg, will be celebrated to-morrow, and it will be attended by the President of the United States and heads of Departments, by the Governors of most of the loyal States, and by citizens of the same. Already thousands of people are moving toward Gettysburg, and the city of Washington will be fully represented by a number of our best citizens.

President Lincoln will leave in a special train this afternoon, and while at Gettysburg will be the guest of David Wills, Esq., the Pennsylvania State agent.

The procession is to be formed in the town of Gettysburg, in the morning at nine o'clock, and proceed to the cemetery grounds, where the exercises will take place. The procession will then return to the town.

The exercises will consist of singing and prayer, an address by Hon. Edward Everett, and a dedicatory address by President Lincoln.

Governor Curtin has issued a general order directing, as a mark of respect to the memory of the dead, that the National flag shall be placed at half-mast, from sunrise to sunset, at all armories, arsenals, encampments, and other military posts within the State, and that during the day the several departments of the State government shall be closed.

An invitation is extended in this order to the surviving Pennsylvania soldiers of the war of 1812, and of the war with Mexico, to be present at the celebration.

It would be a bigger affair than anyone had anticipated. Approximately 15,000 spectators converged on the little town for the ceremony at the spot where the center of the Union line heroically stopped the final heroic onslaught of the Confederates. The Star covered the preliminaries as well as the ceremony itself.

(Friday, November 20, 1863)

THE GREAT CELEBRATION AT GETTYSBURG.
An Immense Concourse Present.
SPEECHES BY PRESIDENT LINCOLN AND SECRETARY SEWARD.

The dedication of the Cemetery for the brave soldiers who were slain in the battle of Gettysburg,

The procession from Gettysburg to the cemetery.

induced the attendance of probably as large if not a larger number of people than ever assembled before at any one celebration in this country. The President and his suite reached Gettysburg at 6½ o'clock on Wednesday evening and was greeted at the Depot with much enthusiasm by a large gathering of citizens, who followed him to his lodgings at the residence of David Wills, Esq.

During the evening a large number of persons continued to linger round the residence, eager to see the President, and in hope that he would be induced to make a speech.

Speech of the President.

The Band of the 5th New York Artillery serenaded the President soon after his arrival, in response to which he made the following address:

I appear before you, fellow-citizens, merely to thank you for this compliment. The inference is a very fair one that you would hear me for a little while, at least, were I to make a speech. I do not appear before you for the purpose of doing so, and for several very substantial reasons. The most substantial of these is that I have no speech to make (laughter). It is somewhat important in my position that one should not say any foolish things if he can help it, and it very often happens that the only way to help it is to say nothing at all. (Renewed laughter.)

Believing that that is my precise position this evening, I must beg of you to excuse me from saying "one word."

The President was most enthusiastically greeted, and when he retired, he did so among prolonged applause. . . .

The Celebration.

Thursday morning opened bright and beautiful, and at an early hour the streets of Gettysburg were thronged with the gathering thousands, and the busy note of preparation for the grand demonstration was apparent on all sides. At nine o'clock the military portion of the procession began to assemble on Carlisle street, north of the public square, and the civic portion on York street.

From a tall flag-staff in the center of the square, and on all the public buildings and many private houses, the national ensign was displayed at half-mast, and soon the mournful booming of minute guns smote upon the ear, imparting to the otherwise joyous features of the demonstration a touch of sadness that led the thoughtful to realize that as a nation we must sorrow as we rejoice, for the great deliverance here achieved through the glorious success vouchsafed to our arms by the blessing of a merciful Providence.

At 10 o'clock the procession commenced moving over the route designated toward the Cemetery, in the order already published. The military portion of the procession was headed by a squadron of cavalry, followed by Major Gen. Couch and Staff.

The 5th New York Artillery regiment, from Baltimore, with their fine battery, were next in line, presenting a splendid appearance.

Gen. Schenck and Staff were also present.

The dignitaries on the platform at Gettysburg cemetery. President Lincoln can be seen (arrow) at left.

Next came the Marshal-in-Chief, Ward H. Lamon, Esq., and his numerous staff of aides, wearing yellow and white scarfs with tri-colored rosettes on the breast, and black and white shoulder knots. . . .

Next came the President of the United States, and Secretaries Seward, Usher and Blair, all finely mounted.

The President wore a plain suit of black, and white kid gauntlets. Great curiosity was manifested everywhere to catch a glimpse of the Chief Magistrate.

The remainder of the procession was chiefly composed of various civic bodies.

The head of the procession reached the platform erected in the centre of the cemetery a quarter before noon; but some time was consumed in assigning the different bodies their position round the stand; and it was not until after 12 o'clock that the President and others, assigned to seats upon the platform, were all in their places.

All the arrangements having been finally completed with great order and decorum, B. B. French, Esq., acting as one of the Chief Marshal's Aides, gave the signal, and the solemn ceremonies were commenced by the performance of a funeral dirge by the band, stationed in front of the platform.

Rev. Thos. A. Stockton, Chaplain of the U.S. House of Representatives, then offered a most impressive prayer; after which Hon. Edward Everett was introduced by Hon. B. B. French, and delivered an eloquent address. A dirge was then sung by the Union Glee Club of Baltimore; and President Lincoln then appeared at the foot of the platform and delivered the following dedicatory address:

Four score and seven years ago our fathers brought forth upon this continent a new nation, conceived in liberty and dedicated to the proposition that all men are created equal. (Applause.) Now, we are engaged in a great civil war, testing whether that nation, or any other nation so conceived and so dedicated can long endure. We are met on a great battlefield of that war; we are met to dedicate a portion of it as the final resting-place of those who here gave their lives that that nation might live. It is altogether fitting and proper that we should do this. But, in a larger sense, we cannot dedicate, we cannot consecrate, we cannot hallow this ground. The brave men, living and dead, who struggled here have consecrated it far above our poor power to add or detract. (Applause.) The world will little note nor long remember what we may say here, but it can never forget what they did here. (Applause.)

It is for us, the living, rather to be dedicated here to the unfinished work that they have thus far so

President Lincoln a few days before his speech at Gettysburg.

nobly carried on. (Applause.) It is rather for us here to be dedicated here to the great task remaining before us; that from these honored dead we take increased devotion to that cause for which they here gave the last full devotion; that we here highly resolve that those dead shall not have died in vain. (Applause.) That the nation shall under God have a new birth of freedom; and that Governments of the people, by the people, and for the people, shall not perish from the earth. (Long continued applause.)

It was announced by B. B. French, Esq., that a letter had been received from Lieutenant General Scott regretting his inability to be present on the occasion.

After the ceremonies were concluded a salute was fired by the artillery, and the military portion of the procession reformed and escorted the President to his lodgings, where he was subsequently visited by a large number of persons, and for more than an hour, was the victim of a "hands shaking" that must have tested his good nature to the utmost. The President returned to Washington in a special train, which left

Gettysburg about seven o'clock, and arrived in this city at one o'clock this morning.

The following is a list of the number of soldiers already interred in the Cemetery, with the States they represent:

Maine, 17; New Hampshire, 4; Vermont, 19; Rhode Island, 4; Massachusetts, 139; Connecticut, 12; New York, 158; New Jersey, 22; Pennsylvania, 100; Delaware, 14; Maryland, 15; Ohio, 24; Indiana, 31; Illinois, 3; Michigan, 48; Wisconsin, 21; Minnesota, 24; Virginia, 2; United States Infantry, (Regulars), 19—total, 676. Unknown, 582. Total number, 1,258.

🔫 *By the following March, the last of 3,706 Federal reinterments had been completed. Many of the Union fallen had been sent home for burial. More than 3,300 Confederate dead, buried around the battlefield, were reinterred in the South between 1870–73 by Confederate memorial groups. Accounts of the Gettysburg ceremony appeared in newspapers throughout the North. Papers that had the space carried Everett's oration as well as Lincoln's remarks. Such papers were few—mostly those of the big cities where eight-page dailies were published. To solve its space problem, one Boston daily put out a single sheet supplement, both sides of which were barely enough to accommodate Everett's long-flowing prose, which the speaker had written and thoughtfully provided well in advance. Lincoln's text, as carried by* The Star, *conforms remarkably with the version that has long since been accepted as final.* 🔫

WASHINGTON HOMEFRONT, NOVEMBER, 1863.

A week or two prior to the scheduled ceremony dedicating the cemetery at Gettysburg, Washington theatergoers were being enticed in The Star's *columns.*

AMUSEMENTS.
FORD'S NEW THEATER,
TENTH STREET ABOVE E,

JOHN T. FORD . . . . Manager and Proprietor
(Also of Holiday Street Theater, Baltimore.)

THIS (Friday) EVENING, Nov. 13,
Farewell benefit and positively last appearance but one of
MR. J. WILKES BOOTH.
On this occasion
RICHARD III,
will be presented for the last time.

To-morrow (Saturday) evening, Nov. 14, positively last appearance of Mr. Booth, when will be produced Schiller's great tragedy,
THE ROBBERS
with an eminent cast of characters, new scenery, appointments, etc.

On Monday, Nov. 16, the beautiful and versatile comic actresses,
THE WEBB SISTERS,

will make their first appearance in Washington. Last season at the Holiday street Theater, Baltimore, these young, vivacious and pretty artistes achieved a success unprecedented in that establishment. An engagement originally entered into for two weeks, was prolonged to five in consequence.

———◆———

J. WILKES BOOTH.—Those who imagined that the glory of Ford's must depart with the popular actress who has just finished her wonderfully successful engagement there, have reckoned without their host, as was shown last night.

There can be no doubt that young Booth played Richard to the largest house ever drawn together to see that play (Richard III) in Washington. Every seat, regular or improvised, obtainable in the building was occupied, and hundreds were content to avail themselves of promenade tickets.

J. Wilkes Booth is the youngest of the three brothers—chips of the old block—is barely 24 years of age, and it would be unjust to institute a comparison between him and his sire as remembered at his best (Junius Brutus Booth); but, that he is a performer of singular promise, there can be no question. Personally he does not resemble his father as closely as does Edwin Booth; but he has a fine, expressive face, an eye reminding one of his senior, a good figure, and a voice both forcible and musical.

He was called out at the end of the piece and welcomed with a heartiness that showed he had made his mark. He was well supported by Mr. Charles Wheatleigh, Mr. Pearson, Mr. De Vere, Miss Belle Vaughn, Miss Waite and others of the combination company.

It is worthy of mention that the immense audience at Ford's last night was enabled to make its exit in five minutes' time, owing to the admirable facilities to this end; an important consideration with those who hesitate to visit places of amusement, lest they should be trapped in case of a fire.

To-night Booth appears in Shiel's play of *The Apostate,* a piece in which he is said to be exceedingly effective.

W ASHINGTON AND RICHMOND SEEMED TO REALIZE
simultaneously the desperate importance of Chattanooga, the rail and
road "gateway" to all points south of the Ohio River and east of the
Mississippi. The Confederacy had to occupy it to keep the enemy from
the Deep South. Federal armies needed it to pierce the enemy's vitals.

In mid-September, Longstreet's corps had been detached from
the Army of Northern Virginia to strengthen Bragg's Army of Tennessee. Longstreet arrived in time to help defeat Rosecrans' Army of
the Cumberland at Chickamauga. Less than a week after the shock of
Chickamauga, two corps were detached from the Army of the Potomac
and rushed by rail to reinforce Rosecrans' mauled command, now besieged in Chattanooga. Fighting Joe Hooker, plucked from the oblivion
of Chancellorsville, headed the rescue party from the East. From the
other direction, Grant, under orders, dispatched help from his command
—Sherman's corps—and hastened to Chattanooga to take personal
charge.

One of Grant's first actions was to drop Rosecrans, whose
military conduct since Chickamauga had struck President Lincoln as
"confused and stunned, like a duck hit on the head." Thomas, the
"Rock of Chickamauga," succeeded "Old Rosey." The thing that
alarmed Grant and the Administration most was that Rosecrans had
considered evacuating Chattanooga. His army's back was against the
Tennessee River, his front ringed by Confederate veterans on the
heights of Missionary Ridge and Lookout Mountain. The trapped army
was on short rations. Supply lines by rail and river were blocked. There
was no recourse but retreat. With Grant's arrival, the supply problem
ended. "Baldy" Smith, the chief engineer of the Army of the Cumberland, was given the job of creating a road and bridge route through the
all but impassable Tennessee mud and mountains. "Baldy" delivered.
The supplies soon came slogging through to Chattanooga, and
"Baldy's" road would be fondly remembered as the "Cracker Line."

Their supplies assured, the Federals stayed where they were.
Their numbers swelled, meanwhile. None of this seemed to bother
Bragg. He grew so confident of his fortified heights around the city
that he felt he could spare Longstreet and 20,000 to lay siege to Knox-
ville, occupied for some time by Burnside's Federals. Longstreet's departure still left Bragg with 40,000 manning the impregnable heights
above Chattanooga against Grant's 60,000.

While Bragg sat, Grant perfected his battle plan. Missionary
Ridge, 500 feet high at some points, might be formidable, but Sherman
and his Westerners would try a surprise assault at its northern extremity. Hooker and his Potomac boys would have a go at Lookout Mountain,
1,500 feet high, then strike at the southern end of the Ridge. Thomas
and his Army of the Cumberland—the bitter taste of Chickamauga still
on their tongues—would be ready at the center to create diversions or
take whatever other action might seem in order in front of Missionary
Ridge. The Federal forces were ready on November 23.

U.S. WINS LOOKOUT MT., MISSIONARY RIDGE

(Wednesday, November 25, 1863)

Late Telegraphic News.

Great and Glorious News!!
NORTH SLOPE OF LOOKOUT MOUNTAIN CARRIED BY HOOKER!!

The following dispatches have reached headquarters:

CHATTANOOGA, Tenn., 12 m., Nov. 24, 1863. *Major General Halleck, General-in-Chief:*

Yesterday, at half-past 12, Granger's and Palmer's corps, supported by Howard's, were advanced directly in front of our fortifications, drove in the enemy's pickets, and carried his first line of rifle pits between Chattanooga and Citer's Creeks. We captured nine commissioned officers and about 160 enlisted men. Our loss about 111.

To-day, Hooker carried the north slope of Lookout Mountain, with small loss on our side, and a loss to the enemy of five or six hundred prisoners. Killed and wounded not reported.

There has been continuous fighting from 12 until after night, but our troops gallantly repulsed every attempt to retake the position.

Federal camp beside the Tennessee River near Chattanooga.

Library of Congress

Sherman crossed the Tennessee before daylight this morning at the mouth of South Chickamauga (Chickamauga Creek), and carried the northern extremity of Missionary Ridge.

Our success so far has been complete, and the behavior of the troops admirable.

Geo. H. Thomas, Major General.

Bragg for some reason had installed part of his force in the lowlands at the foot of Missionary Ridge. Thomas' initial assignment was to clear out this nuisance. Why the general chose to file his report with the War Department instead of Grant is one of those military perplexities of the time—unless the commander was too busy to bother with Washington. Grant, in any case, filed his own report a few hours later.

A Great Victory!!
GEN. SHERMAN CARRIES THE END OF MISSIONARY RIDGE!!
Over 2,000 Prisoners Captured.
(Second Dispatch.)

CHATTANOOGA, Tenn., Nov. 24, 6 p.m. *Major General Halleck, General-in-Chief:*

The fighting to-day progressed favorably. Sherman carried the end of Missionary Ridge, and his right is now at the Tunnel, and left at Chickamauga Creek. Troops from Lookout Valley carried the point of the mountain, and now hold the eastern slope and point high up. I cannot yet tell the amount of casualties, but our loss is not heavy. Hooker reports 2,000 prisoners taken, besides which a small number have fallen into our hands from Missionary Ridge.

U. S. Grant, Major General.

The headline writer read a good deal into Grant's terse dispatch. The "tunnel" mentioned was a railroad cut through the north end of the ridge. A later dispatch from the front the same day was well under 24 hours after the actual event—an accomplishment in view of the roundabout telegraphic communications north through Nashville and Louisville, then east to the Atlantic Seaboard.

THE VERY LATEST FROM CHATTANOOGA!!
The Enemy Driven Entirely Off Lookout Mountain!!
Bragg Believed to Be in Full Retreat!

CHATTANOOGA, TENN., Nov. 25—11 a.m.—We have had a brisk engagement this forenoon.

We have driven the enemy entirely off Lookout Mountain, a considerable portion of which they held up to this morning.

We have also taken Missionary Ridge from him this forenoon, and the troublesome rifle pits, in possession of which yesterday's engagement left them at its close.

All firing has ceased for a sufficient time to warrant the conclusion that Bragg has retreated—certainly leaving all the ground and strong points in our possession for which we have been fighting for the last three days!

It is too early yet to enable me to state casualties on either side, which are not yet known.

Our army is in glorious exultation, indeed, over their series of victories.

The stories of the next few days were only slightly less fragmentary, but the keynote was certainly victory. It remained for the Quartermaster General of the Army, Montgomery Cunningham Meigs, who happened to be on the scene, to furnish the most graphic and cohesive account of the battle.

(Saturday, November 28, 1863)

DESPERATE FIGHT FOR THE CREST OF LOOKOUT MOUNTAIN!
A Battle in the Clouds!
Forty Pieces of Artillery Captured on the Summit of Lookout Mountain Alone!
WHAT BRAGG EXPECTED TO DO!

The following satisfactory and graphic report of the battles before Chattanooga has been received at headquarters from Gen. Meigs:

HEADQUARTERS, CHATTANOOGA, Nov. 27, 1863.—*Hon. Edwin M. Stanton, Secretary of War*—Sir: On the 23d instant, at 11:30 a.m. General Grant ordered a demonstration against Mission Ridge to develop the force holding it. The troops marched out, formed in order, advanced in line of battle as if on parade. The rebels watched the formation and movement from their picket lines and rifle-pits and from the summits of Mission Ridge, 500 feet above us, and thought it was a review and drill, so speedy and deliberately, so regular was it all done, as the advanced line proceeded by skirmishers, and at two o'clock p.m. reached our picket lines. They opened a rattling volley upon the rebel pickets, who replied and ran into their advanced line of rifle-pits. After them went our skirmishers and into them—along the center of the line of 25,000 troops which Gen. Thomas had so quickly displayed until we opened fire. Prisoners assert that they thought

Federal troops assault Missionary Ridge in a spontaneous charge, although no orders had been given for the action.

Battles & Leaders

Missionary Ridge as it appeared not long after the incredible Union charge.

the whole movement was a review and general drill, and that it was too late to send to their camps for reinforcements, and that they were overwhelmed by force of numbers. It was a surprise in open daylight.

At 3 p.m. the important advanced position of Orchard Knob and the lines right and left were in our possession, and arrangements were ordered for holding them during the night.

The next day at daylight Gen. Thomas had 5,000 men across the Tennessee and established on its south bank, and commenced the construction of a pontoon bridge about six miles above Chattanooga.

The rebel steamer Dunbar, repaired at the right moment, rendered effective aid in this crossing, carrying over 6,000 men. By nightfall Gen. Thomas had seized the extremity of Mission Ridge nearest the river, and was entrenching himself. General Howard, with a brigade, opened communication with him from Chattanooga, on the south side of the river.

Skirmishing and cannonading continued all the day on the left and center. Gen. Hooker scaled the slopes of Lookout Mountain from the Valley of Lookout Creek, drove the rebels around the point, captured some two thousand prisoners, and established himself high up the mountain side, in full view of Chattanooga. This raised the blockade, and steamers were ordered from Bridgeport to Chattanooga. They had been run only to Kelly's Ferry, whence ten miles of hauling over mountain roads and twice across the Tennessee on pontoon bridges, brought us our supplies. All night the point of Mission Ridge on the extreme left, and the side of Lookout Mountain on the extreme right blazed with the camp fires of loyal troops.

The day had been one of dense mists and rains, and much of Hooker's battle had been fought above the clouds, which concealed him from our view, but from which his musketry was heard. At nightfall the sky cleared, the full moon, the traitor's doom, shone upon the beautiful scene, until 1 a.m., twinkling sparks upon the mountain side showed that picket skirmishing was going on; then it ceased.

A brigade sent from Chattanooga recrossed the Chattanooga creek and opened communication with Hooker.

Gen. Grant's headquarters the afternoon of the 23d, and the day of the 24th, were in Wood's redoubt, except when, in the course of the day, he rode along the advanced line, visiting the headquarters of the several commanders in Chattanooga valley.

At daylight on the 25th the Stars and Stripes were descried on the peak of Lookout. The rebels had evacuated the mountain, and striking Miss Ridge at the Rossville Gap, to sweep on both sides and on its summit. The rebel troops were seen as soon as it was light enough streaming by regiments and brigades along the narrow summit of Mission Ridge, either concentrating on the right to overwhelm Sherman or marching for the railroad and raising the siege. They had evacuated the Valley of Chattanooga, would they abandon that of Chickamauga? The twenty-pounders and four and a quarter rifles of Wood's redoubt opened on Mission Ridge. Orchard Knob sent its compliments to the Ridge, which with rifled Parrotts answered, and the cannonade thus commenced continued all day. Shot and shell screamed from Orchard Knob to Mission Ridge, from Mission Ridge to Orchard Knob, and from Wood's redoubt, over the heads of Generals Grant and Thomas and their staffs, who were with us in the favorable position, whence the whole battle could be seen, as in an amphitheater. The headquarters were under fire all day long. Cannonading and musketry were heard from Gen. Sherman. Gen. Howard marched with the 11th corps to join him. Thomas sent our skirmishers, who drove in the rebel pickets, and chased them into their intrenchments, and at the foot of Mission Ridge, Sherman made an assault on Bragg's right, intrenched on a high knob, next to that on which Sherman himself lay strongly fortified.

The assault was gallantly made, reached the edge of the crest, held its ground for, seemed to me, an hour, but was bloodily repulsed by reserves. A general advance was ordered and a strong line of skirmishers followed by a displayed line of battle some two miles in length, at the signal from his cannon shots from the Headquarters on Orchard Knob, moved rapidly and orderly forward. The Rebel pickets discharged their muskets and ran into their rifle pits. Our skirmishers followed on their heels. The line of battle was not far behind, and we saw the grey rebels swarm out of their long line of rifle pits in numbers which surprised us, and over the hill.

A few turned and fired their pieces, but the greater number collected into the many roads which cross obliquely up its steep face and went on to the top. Some regiments pressed and swarmed up the steep sides of the ridge. Here and there a color was advanced beyond the lines. The attempt appeared most dangerous, but the advance was supported, and the whole line ordered to storm the heights, upon which not less than forty pieces of artillery and no one knows how many muskets, stood ready to slaughter the assailants. With cheers answering to cheers, the men swarmed upwards. They gathered to the point least difficult of ascent, and the line was broken.

Color after color was planted on the summit, while musket and cannon vomited their thunder upon them. A well directed shot from Orchard Knob exploded a rebel caisson on the summit, and the gun was seen galloping to the right, its driver lashing his horses. A party of our soldiers intercepted them and the gun was captured with cheers. A fierce musketry fight broke out to the left, where between Thomas and Sherman, a mile or two of the ridge was still occupied by the rebels. Bragg left the house in which he had held his headquarters, and rode to the rear, as our troops crowned the hill on either side of him. Gen. Grant proceeded to the summit, and then did we only know its height.

Some of the captured artillery was put into position, artillerists were sent for to work the guns, caissons were searched for ammunition. The rebel log breastworks were torn to pieces and carried to the other side of the ridge, and used in forming barricades across it; a strong line of infantry was formed in the rear of Baird's line, hotly engaged in a musketry contest with the rebels to the left, and a secure lodgement was soon effected.

The other assault to the right of our center gained the summit, and the rebels threw down their arms and fled. Hooker coming in favorable position swept the right of the ridge, and captured many prisoners.

Bragg's remaining troops left early in the night, and the battle of Chattanooga, after three days of maneuvering and fighting, was won; the strength of the rebellion in the center was broken; Burnside relieved from danger; East Tennessee, Kentucky, Tennessee rescued; Georgia and the Southeast threatened in the rear, and another victory added to the chapter of "Unconditional Surrender Grant."

To-night the estimates of captures is several thousand prisoners and 30 pieces of artillery. Loss, for so great a victory, not severe.

Bragg is firing the railroad as he retreats toward Dalton. Sherman is in hot pursuit.

To-day I viewed the battle-field, which extends for six miles along Mission Ridge and for several miles on Lookout Mountain. Probably not so well directed, so well ordered a battle has been delivered before during the war. But one assault was repulsed; but that assault, by calling to that point the rebel reserves, prevented them repulsing any of the others.

A few days since, Bragg sent to Gen. Grant a flag of true advising him that it would be prudent to remove any non-combatants who might still be in Chattanooga. No reply has been returned but the combatants having removed from this vicinity it is probable that non-combatants can remain without imprudence.

M. C. Meigs, Quartermaster Gen'l.

🔫 *The most amazing feature of the attack—the charge of Thomas' men up the face of Missionary Ridge—was noted in* The Star *several days later.* 🔫

(Wednesday, December 2, 1863)

THE STORMING
OF MISSIONARY RIDGE.

The storming of the ridge in the great battle before Chattanooga on the 25th is thus described by an officer in a report to the War Department:

"The storming of the ridge by our troops was one of the greatest miracles in military history. No man, who climbs the ascent by any of the roads that wind along its front, can believe that eighteen thousand men were moved upon its broken and crumbling face,

The storming and capture of Lookout Mountain.

unless it was his fortune to witness the deed. It seems as awful as a visible interposition of God. Neither General Grant nor Thomas intended it. Their orders were to carry the rifle pits along the base of the ridge and cut off their occupants, but when this was accomplished the unaccountable spirit of the troops bore them bodily up the impracticable steeps, over the bristling rifle-pits on the crest, and the thirty cannon enfilading every gully. The order to storm appears to have been given simultaneously by Generals Sheridan and Wood, because the men were not to be held back, hopeless as the attempt appeared to military prudence; besides the Generals caught the inspiration of the men and were ready themselves to undertake impossibilities."

⚔ The spectacle of Confederate veterans fleeing in panic before a Yankee charge was given no other explanation at the time. Only Bragg's men knew the lack of confidence they felt in a commander who repeatedly had victory in his hands but refused to grasp it. ⚔

WASHINGTON HOMEFRONT, NOVEMBER, 1863.

⚔ The Federal City was not without labor unrest, despite the requirements of all-out war, and regardless of whether the laborers happened to work for the Government. ⚔

WORKING HOURS IN THE NAVY YARD.— Pursuant to call, a meeting of mechanics and workingmen employed in the Navy Yard was held last night in the hall of the Anacostia Engine House, Navy Yard. There were between three and four hundred persons present.

The Chair stated that the committee appointed at a previous meeting had waited upon the Secretary of the Navy and upon the Commandant of the Yard, and that they had received but little encouragement as to the change desired by them. The committee recommended that the workmen use further measures, and endeavor in a proper manner to persuade the authorities to accord them their rights, and if that course fails they shall unite in a strike and quit work.

Mr. Wm. Ready then made a short speech, and recommended the men to be mild but firm in their actions, and do nothing hasty; but when they did act, to do so only after mature thought, and after taking a stand to adhere to it, and he believed the authorities would soon see the justice of not compelling mechanics and that class to go to work before daylight, and hardly get home again until it was dark. He suggested that it would be well for the meeting to adopt resolutions to be laid before Secretary Welles and Commander Harwood clearly setting forth their demands and what they conceived to be their rights and to await an answer until Monday evening next, when if nothing was done for them they would all quit work on Tuesday morning. But he simply threw this out as a suggestion.

A number of letters from employees of the Charleston and other navy yards were read, to show that all the men went to work there one hour after sunrise and quit at sunset.

Mr. W. H. Harmon then offered the following preamble and resolutions, which were unanimously adopted:

Whereas, we receive the truth that all men have equal rights, especially true, loyal American citizens, and these rights of equality being guaranteed to us by the Constitution, and now being nobly defended by our patriotic brothers in the field, sustaining the great principles of freedom and righteousness by the nation;

And whereas, we, the workingmen of the Washington Navy Yard, are required to work more hours (with no additional compensation) than any other workingmen of other Navy Yards, (as well as other mechanics employed by the Government), while all the necessaries of life are fully one-third higher with us, thereby not only depriving us of our time, but comparatively lessening our ability to meet the ne-cessities of our families, which make us feel as an isolated and uncared-for class, subject to inequality with other employees of the Government;

And whereas we have honorably petitioned the honorable Secretary of the Navy for redress, and have always been met with the statement that the law or act (commonly called the Grimes bill) deter-mines our time and pay, thereby leaving him no power to act, unless outside time and pay in our local-ity would demand it—thereby regulating our time and pay by a few unimportant places of business of Washington city, while the other great cities of the Union, with their enlarged business and growing demands for labor, regulate the prices of the work-ingmen of the country; Therefore,

Resolved, That we again appeal to the honorable Secretary of the Navy and his executive officers for the return of our old and long-accustomed working hours, believing that any law that operates so unequal to a class is inoperative and unjust.

Resolved, That we will use all honorable means for our rights as working men, and pledge ourselves one to the other in good faith to the attainment of that end. . . .

T HE WINTER OF 1863–64 WAS A TIME OF GREAT PREPArations, in both the North and South. Grant's Western army had driven the Confederates safely away from Chattanooga. The Richmond government, alarmed by its fortunes in Tennessee, had replaced Bragg with Joe Johnston; and Johnston was rallying his forces in Northwestern Georgia for the inevitable next Federal advance. Lee and Meade, their respective armies depleted by Gettysburg, were rebuilding on opposite shores of the Rappahannock.

The Northern capacity for war swelled daily. But Washington still worried. That long-sought military crusher was elusive. Until a military victory greater than Gettysburg—nothing short of the conquest of Lee's army—was won, there was danger that the determination of the Rebel would outweigh that of the Yankee. Lincoln in December tried a political gambit to undermine the Southern will to win. He proclaimed amnesty for Confederates who would swear allegiance to the Union. That same month, the Confederate government revealed a weakness in its own ranks. It ended exemptions for those who had been supplying substitutes for their own military service. Two months later, Lincoln countered by issuing another draft call—for 500,000 three-year men. And in the same month the South formed an "invalid corps" equivalent to the organization of disabled Union soldiers who performed non-combatant duties. The South enlisted slave and free Negroes in its war effort at this time.

Despite the nightmares of homefront support, the Confederacy could always count on Robert E. Lee for military leadership. Lincoln had been trying to match this good fortune since the start of the war. By March, 1864, he finally felt that he had found the man for the job of besting Lee and all the Confederacy. A cooperative Congress took care of the technicalities by recreating the post of lieutenant-general.

Lincoln's choice for the new post didn't bear the slightest resemblance to Washington. Ulysses S. Grant was no patrician—but a stumpy, cigar-chewing Midwesterner. He came to Washington by way of Vicksburg and Chattanooga on March 9, 1864.

GRANT NAMED UNION COMMANDER

(Wednesday, March 9, 1864)

PRESENTATION OF GENERAL GRANT'S COMMISSION AS LIEUTENANT GENERAL.

General Grant's commission as Lieutenant General in the Army of the United States was, at one o'clock to-day, formally presented to him by the President, at the Executive Mansion.

This interesting ceremony took place in the Cabinet Chamber, in presence of the whole Cabinet, Gen. Halleck, Hon. Owen Lovejoy, Gen. Rawlins and Col. Comstock of General Grant's staff, the son of Gen. Grant, and Mr. Nicolay, the private secretary of the President.

When Gen. Grant entered the room the President rose and said:

General Grant: The nation's appreciation of what you have done, and its reliance upon you for what remains to do, in the existing great struggle, are now presented with this commission, constituting you Lieutenant General in the Army of the United States. With this high honor, devolves upon you also, a corresponding responsibility. As the country herein trusts you, so, under God, it will sustain you. I scarcely need to add that with what I here speak for the nation, goes my own hearty personal concurrence.

To which General Grant replied as follows:

Mr. President:—I accept this commission with gratitude for the high honor conferred.

With the aid of the noble armies that have fought on so many fields for our common country, it will be my earnest endeavor not to disappoint your expectations.

I feel the full weight of the responsibilities now devolving on me, and know that if they are met it will be due to those armies, and above all to the favor of that Providence which leads both nations and men.

At the conclusion of these brief speeches the President introduced the General to all the members of the Cabinet, after which the company was seated; and about half an hour was spent in pleasant social conversation.

The formalities were awkward. Both the President and the General read their little speeches. Grant's delivery was halting as he read his pencilled scribblings. A soldier, rather than a public figure, he was glad to leave Washington two days later to rejoin his men on the Western front. Sherman had warned him beforehand to avoid the artificialities of the city. But Washington was happy to receive its hero, as this account in The Star *detailing Grant's arrival reveals.*

ARRIVAL IN WASHINGTON OF LIEUT. GEN. GRANT.—The afternoon papers of yesterday having announced that Lieut. General Grant would arrive in Washington in the 5:20 p.m. train, a large crowd assembled at the depot to get a glimpse

Lieutenant General U. S. Grant.

Library of Congress

General Grant and his staff. Grant is seated third from left.

at the "hero of many battles." There was no public demonstration; but at 5:50, when the shrill whistle of the engine announced the approach of the train, a big rush was made to the rear end of the depot.

The General and his son, accompanied by Gen. Rollins (John A. Rawlins), Chief of Staff, and Colonel Comstock, Chief Assistant and Inspector General, occupied seats in a special car, provided by Wm. P. Smith, master of transportation of the Baltimore and Ohio Railroad.

As the party alighted from the car the crowd gave three hearty cheers for Gen. Grant, which the General acknowledged by bowing courteously. Upon the arrival of the party in the hall a company of the Invalid Corps on duty there were drawn up in a line, under command of Lieut. Newber, with arms presented. The General passed through with head uncovered, and upon gaining the street they were ushered into a hack and driven rapidly to Willards' Hotel.

The General reached Willards' without being recognized on the way, his features not being familiar to the public, but had hardly got seated at the dinner table ere the fact of his presence became known, when the Hon. J. K. Moorhead arose and proposed three cheers for the hero of Vicksburg, which were joined in by the three or four hundred people at the table, who arose to their feet simultaneously, the ladies taking part by waving of handkerchiefs.

The guests of the hotel pressed towards Gen. Grant, but Mr. Chadwick stepped forward and an-

nounced that the General had traveled some distance, and that his "rations" were before him, and time should be allowed the General to dispose of them, after which he (Mr. C.) had no doubt Gen. Grant would receive all who called on him.

The General appeared somewhat worn with travel, but has the modest, calm, self-possessed look of the true hero; of light build, with frank, genial face, clear blue eyes, light hair and sandy whiskers, mixed with grey.

📖 *In other columns,* The Star *recounted the events of the preceding night when the general showed up at the White House fatigued by his long train ride from Chattanooga.* 📖

THE RECEPTION AT THE WHITE HOUSE. —The reception last night at the Executive Mansion was overflowingly attended, and it may be truly said the world was fairly represented in the gay assemblage. All the rooms and passages were densely crowded, and but little opportunity was afforded for the display of costumes, but the number of ladies in attendance was quite large, and formed an unusually brilliant feature.

A few moments after 9 o'clock Lieutenant General Grant, in company with his staff officers entered the White House and were presented to the President and Mrs. Lincoln, who received them with warm cordiality, and entered into conversation with their distinguished guests, detaining them in the reception room for some time. Shortly afterwards, General

Grant was escorted into the East Room by Secretary Seward, when a gentleman present mounted a chair and proposed three cheers for General Grant, three for President Lincoln and three for Secretary Seward, which were given with tremendous emphasis. The crowd then made a rush toward the General when it became necessary for him to occupy a standing position upon a sofa, where he remained for an hour or more, receiving the congratulations of the throng who pressed forward to shake him by the hand. The hustling and jostling by parties anxious to get near the General was terrific, and many an unfortunate individual had his corns trod upon.

Among the many notables present were the French and Belgian Ministers; Secretaries Seward, Stanton, Welles; Mr. Fox, Assistant Secretary of the Navy; Mr. Lewis, Commissioner of Internal Revenue; Senators Sherman, Wilson, and Harris; Speaker Colfax, and others of the lower House. Mayor Wallach was also there, together with many of our leading citizens. Among the military men present were Gens. Rollins (Rawlins—*The Star* soon learned how to spell his name), Sickles, Birney, Col. Comstock, Col. Streight, and others.

Mr. and Mrs. Lincoln, as usual, gave a kindly welcome to the visitors. Our lady readers may like to know that Mrs. L. was attired in a heavy white moire antique dress, festooned with narrow white silk ribbon, and wore a rich lace shawl thrown loosely over the shoulders, having upon her head a wreath of flowers.

At a quarter to eleven o'clock the President entered the East Room, accompanied by Mrs. Frederick Seward, followed by Mrs. Lincoln, leaning upon the arm of Gen. Grant, and as they promenaded around the room all eyes were directed towards them.

A detail of Metropolitan policemen were present, and helped to preserve order in the rooms, whilst on the outside of the White House was a squad of cavalrymen, whose duty it was to regulate the arrival and departure of carriages.

🔫 *Elsewhere in the same edition, Grant expressed his feelings in public—a rarity—on the occasion of his arrival in Baltimore, en route to Washington for his latest honor.* 🔫

GEN. GRANT'S RECEPTION IN BALTIMORE.

(Special Dispatch to the Chronicle by *People's telegraph*] Line.)

BALTIMORE, March 8.—Lieutenant General Grant arrived here at noon to-day in the Northern

General John A. Rawlins, Grant's right-hand man.

Central cars, having left Harrisburg this morning. He was met at the depot by a considerable number of soldiers and citizens, though very few were aware of his coming. Four or five officers of his staff accompanied him. The officers of the railroad and George Small, Esq., one of the directors, afforded the distinguished hero and his staff the most courteous facilities at the depot and elsewhere. The General was plainly clad, and seemed anxious to avoid show or parade. There were many, however, on seeing him, went up to shake hands, and gave vent to their feelings by enthusiastic shouts of welcome. The General said, beyond all things he was determined to avoid political demonstrations; his business was with war, while it existed, and his duty was to crush the spirit of treason and save the nation from destruction. When these things were accomplished, as he hoped and believed they surely would be, then it would be time enough for those whose tastes are toward partizanship to indulge themselves. The General and his staff proceeded to Barnum's Hotel, where they partook of refreshments. They departed soon after in the earliest train for Washington.

🔫 *With Grant's elevation, Halleck was eased into a position equivalent to chief of staff of the War Department—actually a key liaison position between the new general-in-chief and President Lincoln. Sherman, at the same time, was named commander of the Western armies.* 🔫

General Grant at his Virginia headquarters.

WASHINGTON HOMEFRONT, MARCH, 1864.

☞ *Those fun-loving—and ingenious—Yanks, making like silent movie comedies long before Mack Sennett's time.* ☞

POLICE ON THE TROT.—About 1 o'clock this morning a young man named Wm. McDonald, who had a whistle similar to those used by the police, took a position on a corner in Hooker's Division (a rough section below the Avenue near Willard's), and sounded the policeman's call. The Second Ward Police answered, and hastened to aid their supposed comrade; but on reaching the corner, he wasn't there. In a few moments the call was sounded at the corner below. Away started the police, but nobody was found at that corner. The police got tired of trotting through the mud and, suspecting something wrong, a strategical plan was layed and the whistler was captured, and for his pains was given lodging for the night in a cell and this morning Justice Clayton fined him $2.

———◆———

"CARELESS BILL" REGULATING A FUNERAL.—Yesterday, two of Capt. Dolan's detectives arrested an individual who gave his name as "Careless Bill," of Company A, 1st regiment Invalid Corps, for assuming command of a funeral procession on the Avenue while in a state of intoxication, and without proper authority. It appears that Bill was not authorized to attend the funeral, but that he assumed the responsibility of walking in advance of the procession, waving his hat, and giving orders. He was committed to the Central guardhouse.

———◆———

ALEXANDRIA AFFAIRS.—A new and ingenious method of smuggling liquor into the city was brought to light on Saturday last, through the efforts of the detectives. For some time past a certain chicken-coop has been observed to have made frequent and regular journeys between this city and Washington on the ferry boats, going up empty and returning well filled with fine fat Shanghais. The poultry traffic has ever been considered an honorable one, and we have not learned what first drew suspicion toward the integrity of the dealer in question, but certain it is that one of those curious chaps employed in this department took the liberty of inspecting the "coop" for the purpose of ascertaining the features of the latest improvements in that species of structure, and his labor was rewarded with the discovery that its bottom was composed of *tin* in the shape of a flat shallow box; and a closer inspection revealed the important item of thirty gallons of old rye contained in the aforesaid box.—*Alexandria Journal, 7th.*

T HE UNION STRATEGY WAS SET: THE HEART OF THE South would be caught in a vast pincers movement. One prong, nominally under Meade but actually under Grant, would tackle Lee's army between Washington and Richmond. The other, under Sherman, would curve deeper into Dixie between Chattanooga and Atlanta, seeking to destroy the Confederacy's other main army under Johnston. The objectives were no longer cities and other geographical places, but the Confederacy's shield, its armies.

There was first some unfinished business west of the Mississippi. In the closing months of 1863, plans had been drawn to pierce inland Louisiana to secure the western section of the State, as well as East Texas, for the Union whose influence was restricted to the coastal area. Around mid-March, Porter, with his inevitable gunboats, teamed with land troops under Banks and began the Red River movement toward Shreveport. Banks' bungling, plus the spirited operations of Confederate Gen. Dick Taylor, at Sabine Crossroads, made the campaign a failure. Low water nearly trapped the river fleet. Only some hasty dam construction to deepen the channels enabled the boats to escape back downstream.

For the main operations, Grant established headquarters at Culpeper, and called in the pugnacious Sheridan to command the Army of the Potomac cavalry corps. He issued another order which indicated that the coming campaigns would be the showdown: no more exchanges of prisoners to replenish the South's dwindling manpower.

Spring, 1864, arrived, and all the contesting armies stirred from their winter quarters. The Army of the Potomac was the first to move. Early in May, 100,000 strong, it began crossing the Rapidan River near the scene of the Chancellorsville disaster one year before. Waiting in the jungle of underbrush and trees were Lee and his 60,000 men of the Army of Northern Virginia.

GRANT DRIVES TOWARD RICHMOND

(Saturday, May 7, 1864)

EXTRA.
STIRRING NEWS
FROM THE FRONT!
FIGHTING GOING ON
NEAR THE WILDERNESS.
Lee's Whole Army in Front
of Meade.

NEW YORK, May 7.—A special dispatch to the New York *Tribune* from Union Mills, Va., says: Wednesday night Warren's headquarters was at the Wilderness; Sedgwick on his right. The general headquarters were at Germania (Germanna) Ford.

Thursday morning the rebels pressed on the pickets, and appeared in strong force on our right.

The 5th New York cavalry, on Orange Court-House road, near Perkin's Tavern, was driven in with severe loss, leaving their wounded on the field. Griffith's division marched forward on the right to feel the enemy's position, but were met by Gen. A. P. Hill, supported by Ewell.

A severe action ensued. We captured 300 prisoners, though it is reported we lost two guns. Hancock marched to the right to connect with Warren's left, resting near Chancellorsville, and was attacked by Longstreet.

Hancock held his position two hours, and half his command suffered severely, inflicting much injury on the enemy. Other developments show Lee's whole force on our front. This being ascertained, Meade ordered the line of battle to be held till morning.

Heavy cannonading Friday morning, when the correspondent passed Kelly's Ford, which leads him to believe we had driven the rebels to their defences, as no heavy guns could be brought into action in our former position.

🌚 *Grant's main line of march was along the Brock road to Spotsylvania. As his columns strung along the road, Ewell's and A. P. Hill's corps assaulted them from the thickets all day, May 5. The Federals held their own, and next day, Hancock's corps began to chew Hill's troops to shreds. Longstreet's corps came to Hill's rescue and almost wrecked Hancock. In the tangle of troops and forest, the Confederates began firing on their own men, Longstreet was badly wounded, and the power went out of the Confederate attack. In his anxiety, Lee rode up at the height of battle to take personal command, but his troops shouted him to the rear and relative safety. The confusion of battle was compounded by forest fires which sprang up in the wilderness. Hundreds of helpless wounded perished in the flames.* 🌚

Federal artillery crossing the Rapidan River.

A portion of the Spotsylvania battlefield.

(Sunday "Extra," May 8, 1864)

OUR WOUNDED, NUMBERING FROM 6,000 TO 8,000, ON THE ROAD TO WASHINGTON!

The Enemy Foiled in His Desperate Attempt to Crush Our Army While Moving!

LEE RETIRING!!

The only official information from the Army of the Potomac is derived from despatches of the Medical Director and Chief Quartermaster to their respective bureaus.

The wounded, numbering from six to eight thousand, have been sent from the battle field to Rappahannock Station, thence to be forwarded to Washington.

A portion of them have arrived at Rappahannock. The Chief Quartermaster has made a requisition for grain for the animals. This imports an advance by General Grant. Gen. Ingalls says, "We have fought two days. The enemy are said to be retiring."

There seems to be no doubt that, although nothing decisive has yet occurred, the enemy has been foiled in his confident expectation of driving General Grant back before his operations could be fully developed, and that Lee has been compelled to give way.

The tactics of the enemy have uniformly been to strike his heaviest blow at the outset, and to this their success has always been owing. This has now failed.

During the present war, as in other instances, a baffled and retiring army soon becomes disorganized. No reason is perceived why this result should not happen to Lee.

🖝 *Neither army could claim victory in the Wilderness. But despite the fact that it had been a stand-off battle and their casualties staggering, the Federal army felt cheered. For when the fighting ended, the troops did not get the accustomed command to retire. Their new general-in-chief immediately ordered them forward instead. The road ahead led to Spotsylvania.* 🖝

(Monday, May 9, 1864)

EXTRA.

More Glorious News from the Front.

GRANT VICTORIOUS ON FRIDAY.

He Captures a "Field full of prisoners."

Lee Retreats 12 Miles, Leaving His Dead and Wounded in Our Hands.

Reports from the front (not official) from parties who left there on Saturday, are to the effect that the result of the fighting on Friday was yet more advantageous to the Union cause than that of Thursday, resulting in Lee's falling back, according to some reports, twelve miles, leaving his dead and wounded in our hands. Grant, according to the same report, has "a field full of prisoners," and had advanced to Spotsylvania Court House.

Fires accounted for many deaths in the Wilderness campaign. Prodigious effort was needed to remove the wounded to safety.

FURTHER.

A verbal message received at General Halleck's headquarters by a messenger from the Army of the Potomac, is to the effect that the battle closed on Friday, the enemy having fallen back twelve miles, leaving his dead and wounded upon the field.

On Saturday at 3 o'clock, Lee's army was in full retreat through Spotsylvania, and when the messenger left, a few hours afterwards, Gen. Hancock was entering the place in pursuit.

🔫 *News reports being about as confused as the fighting itself, it developed that Lee was not in "full retreat" at all. In anticipating Grant's next move, he had simply sped part of his army ahead to Spotsylvania to block the continuing Federal movement south.* 🔫

(Wednesday, May 11, 1864)
Important from the Front.
A TERRIBLE BATTLE YESTERDAY EVENING!
Dispatch from Gen. Ingalls.

We stated in our first edition that a general advance and assault on the enemy was to be made by Grant at 5 o'clock yesterday.

Intense excitement exists in this city to hear the result of the fighting, the cannonading of which was perfectly terrific. The following dispatch is *From General (Rufus) Ingalls, Assistant Quartermaster General, to Senator J. W. Nesmith, of Oregon, dated near Spotsylvania Court House, May 10, at 1 o'clock.*

"We are fighting now and have been all the time. We are 'bursting them up.' Our losses are heavy. We shall make another *general* attack at five o'clock this evening. The world never heard of war before. Tell Orin (my brother) that I am all right, and bound for Richmond."

🔫 *Ingalls' excited dispatch revealed something big was going on—but just what was any reader's guess. These were the Federal attacks of May 9 and 10, first on the Confederate left, then on the center—the breastworks "salient" held by Ewell's men. Two days later, Ingalls' dispatch to his Congressional pen-pal again was the most vivid report in* The Star. 🔫

(Friday, May 13, 1864)
EXTRA.
Great and Glorious News from the Front!
Hancock Achieves a Glorious Victory!!
Capture of More Than 4,000 Prisoners!
CAPTURE OF 25 GUNS!!!

The following despatch has been received by Senator Nesmith from Gen. Rufus Ingalls, Chief Quartermaster of the Army of the Potomac. It brings positive information from the front as late as noon yesterday:

"We have made a ten-strike to-day. Hancock went in at daylight. He has taken over 4,000 prisoners and over 25 guns, and is still fighting. Everybody is fighting, and have been for eight days. We shall hive them this pop, though it may take a day or two more. They fight like devils.

Our losses are heavy. Can't say how many. If Augur's forces were here now we could finish them to-day. Hancock captured Gen'l Ned Johnson and two other Generals, besides lots of lower grades. The old Republic is firm. Bet your pile on it.

Grant is a giant and hero in war; but all our Generals are gallant, and our *men*—the world never had better. Yours, in haste,

Ingalls.

Spotsylvania C.H., May 12, 12m.

Hancock's corps had smashed head-on in the salient, almost achieving a break-through in the Confederate center before being stopped by Brig. Gen. John Brown Gordon's division. The fighting would continue intermittently for another week at Spotsylvania, but the height of the battle had passed—the salient to be known afterward as the Bloody Angle, scene of the most savage hand-to-hand fighting of the war. Immediately beneath Ingalls' near-hysterical report, The Star ran a resounding little dispatch from the commanding general himself.

THE TRUE GRIT.

In a dispatch to the Secretary of War, dated at 8 o'clock Wednesday morning, Gen. Grant says:

"We have now ended the sixth day of very heavy fighting. The result to this time is much in our favor. Our losses have been heavy, as well as those of the enemy. I think the losses of the enemy must be greater.

"We have taken over 5,000 prisoners by battle, whilst he has taken from us but few, except stragglers.

"I propose to fight it out on this line, if it takes all summer."

"This line" of Grant's shifted again on May 20. It was the same side-slipping maneuver to the east and south of Lee's right flank that had got his army through the thickest part of the Wilderness. In 12 days of battle he had suffered 14,000 casualties, including one of his best corps leaders, "Uncle John" Sedgwick. The Confederates lost perhaps 12,000 in killed, wounded and captured. As Grant headed south, so headed Lee—keeping always on the Federal front. While the big armies slugged away in this campaign, Sheridan was off behind Lee on a raid toward Richmond with 10,000 of his cavalrymen.

THE REBEL GENERAL J. E. B. STUART KILLED.

WASHINGTON, May 14, 10.40 a.m.

Major General Dix: An official despatch from General Sheridan, dated at Bottom Bridge, via Fortress Monroe, 13th, states that on the 9th instant, he marched around the enemy's right flank, and, on the evening of that day, reached the North Anna river without serious opposition. During the night he destroyed the enemy's depot at Beaver Dam; three large trains of cars, numbering one hundred; two fine locomotives; one hundred thousand pounds of bacon, and other stores, amounting in all to one million and a half of rebel rations; also, the telegraph and railroad track for about ten miles, embracing several culverts; recaptured three hundred and seventy-eight of our men, including two colonels, one major, and several other officers.

On the morning of the 10th he renewed operations, crossing the South Anna, at Grand Squirrel Bridge, and went into camp about daylight. On the 11th he captured Ashland Station, destroyed here one locomotive and a train of cars, engine house, two or three Government buildings, containing large amounts of stores; also, destroyed six miles of railroad embracing six culverts, two trestle bridges, and the telegraph wire.

A rebel sharpshooter killed at the battle of Spotsylvania.

Library of Congress

251

General "Uncle John" Sedgwick, who was killed at Spotsylvania.

About 7 a.m. of the 11th he resumed the march on Richmond. He found the rebel Gen. Stuart with his cavalry concentrated at Yellow Tavern; immediately attacked him, and, after an obstinate contest, gained possession of the Brock turnpike, capturing two pieces of artillery and driving his forces back towards Ashland, and across the north fork of the Chickahominy, a distance of four miles. At the same time a party charged down the Brock road and captured the first line of the enemy's works around Richmond. During the night he marched the whole of his command between the first and second Railroad and the Mechanicsville turnpike.

After demonstrating against the works, and finding them very strong, he gave up the intention of assaulting, and determined to recross the Chickahominy at Meadow Bridge. It had been partially destroyed by the enemy, but was repaired in about three hours under a heavy artillery fire from a rebel battery. General Merritt made the crossing, attacked the enemy and drove him off handsomely, the pursuit continuing as far as Gaines' Mills. The enemy, observing the recrossing of the Chickahominy, came out from his second line of works.

A brigade of infantry and a large number of dismounted cavalry arriving at this juncture attacked the divisions of Gens. Gregg and Wilson, but after a severe contest were repulsed and driven back behind their works. Gregg's and Wilson's divisions, after collecting the wounded, recrossed the Chicka-

hominy. On the afternoon of the 12th, the corps encamped at Walnut Grove and Gaines' Mills. At 9 a.m. of the 13th (yesterday) march was resumed, and encamped at Bottom Bridge. The command is in fine spirits. The loss of horses will not exceed 100. All the wounded were brought off, except about thirty cases of mortal wounds, and these were well cared for in the farm houses of the country. The wounded will not exceed 250; total losses not over 350.

The Virginia Central railroad bridges over the Chickahominy and other trestle bridges—one sixty feet in length, one thirty feet, one twenty feet, and the railroad for a long distance south of the Chickahominy—were destroyed. Great praise is given the division commanders, Generals Gregg, Wilson, Merritt, and Generals Custar and Davis, Colonels Divine, Chapman, McIntosh, and Gibbs, brigade commanders. All the officers and men behaved splendidly.

HALF-PAST TWELVE, A.M.—A dispatch this moment received from Admiral Lee, reports to the Secretary of the Navy, that Richmond papers of yesterday mention the death of Gen. J. E. B. Stuart, "shot in battle." This, no doubt, happened in the battle with Gen. Sheridan.

Edwin M. Stanton, Secretary of War.

WASHINGTON HOMEFRONT, MAY, 1864.

☞ *If the ladies were getting bored with the war, they could always turn to the ads and shop a bit.* ☜

EXCITEMENT AMONG THE LADIES.—Considerable excitement has been created among our fair friends by Wm. Prince, 381 F street, opposite the Patent Office, in having built and now in use a powerful machine for fluting or crimping the lower portion of ladies' dresses. This trimming is very fashionable, and is taking the place of braiding, so much worn of late. This machine *is the only one in the city,* and ladies can now save the expense of sending to New York or Baltimore to have their work done. Dressmakers will be particularly glad of this.

HEADS THAT REBEL

against the rules of Taste or Beauty, in their color or in the loss of all their color, may be changed in a few moments to any

Beautiful Shade,

by a single application of

Cristadoro's Hair Dye.

The rapidity of its operation, perfect safety, permanent healthful effect, and the exceeding depth and richness of the hues it imparts, distinguish this preparation from all other Dyes in this country or in Europe.

Cristadoro's Hair Preservative

a valuable adjunct to the Dye, in dressing and promoting the growth and perfect health of the hair, and of itself, when used alone—a safeguard that protects the fibers from decay under all circumstances and under all climes. Manufactured by J. Cristadoro, No. 6 Astor House, New York. Sold by all Druggists. Applied by all Hair Dressers.

Ladies' Cloaks and Lace Mantillas
Just Opened.

Paris styles of Ladies' Mantels of every description and prices. Lace shawls, Prints and Mantillas.

Also, Barege, Grenadine, Mozambique and other Shawls of the latest importation.

I have also a large stock of Embroideries, Handkerchiefs, Lace Goods, Veils, &c.

Black and Fancy Silks are bought 50 per cent. less than they can be replaced for at present, will be sold at a small advance.

It will be a great advantage to everyone who is in want of the above goods to examine my stock before purchasing.

S. M. Meyenberg,
(late S. & W. Meyenberg's old stand,)
48 Market Space, under the Avenue House,
between 7th and 8th streets.

SIMULTANEOUSLY WITH THE OPENING OF GRANT'S DRIVE in Virginia, Sherman's equally massive army moved from the Chattanooga defenses and headed southeast. Its route lay along the railroad from Atlanta to Chattanooga. Astride the rails were Johnston's 60,000 Confederates, now whipped back into fighting shape after their rout under Bragg at Missionary Ridge and Lookout Mountain. Under the Federal strategy, there was a secondary goal if Johnston's army escaped destruction somewhere along the line. The capture of Atlanta would mean the loss of still another important rail center in the Confederacy's rickety system.

Sherman's 100,000-man force was divided into three sections: Thomas' Army of the Cumberland, McPherson's Army of the Tennessee, and Schofield's Army of the Ohio. Cavalry would guard the railroad supply line back to Tennessee as the armies advanced. Grant's campaign orders to Sherman called not only for breaking up Johnston's force, but "to get into the interior of the enemy's country as far as you can, inflicting all the damage you can against their war resources."

To stem the nearly two-to-one odds, the Confederates had three infantry corps under Hood, Hardee and Bishop Polk. When the Federals took off from their concentration points in and around Chickamauga Creek valley, the Confederates stood in force at Dalton.

The way ahead was rugged and hilly. It lent itself well to the defense, and Joe Johnston was a master of that art. To readers back home, the news from Georgia would be sketchy for some time to come. The first word, in fact, had to be pried from accounts of more immediate concern to Washingtonians—Grant's campaign.

SHERMAN BEGINS PUSH INTO GEORGIA

(Sunday, May 8, 1864)

DESPERATE FIGHTING ON THURSDAY AND FRIDAY.

Grant Believed to Be Pushing Forward.

Reports received from the front up to 11 o'clock on Saturday morning say that there had been two days severe fighting—on Thursday and Friday—and that it was believed that the enemy was retreating. . . .

Reports from Chattanooga, dated at 5 o'clock yesterday (Saturday) afternoon, say that Sherman was then at Tunnel Hill, the enemy at Buzzard's Roost Gap, and our General, McPherson, was operating against the enemy's communications with Rome through Vilanau and Resacca.

Tunnel Hill drew its name from the railroad line which went through it. Thomas and Schofield were making the direct motions toward Dalton. McPherson, meanwhile, was slipping through passes on to the southwest, already aiming beyond Dalton and Vilanau in the direction of Resaca.

(Monday, May 9, 1864)

Successful Advance of General Sherman.

Rebels Falling Back—Their Dead and Wounded Left in Our Hands—

NEW YORK, May 8.—A special dispatch to the Tribune has reached the Government that Sherman is fighting his way through successfully, and pressing upon Dalton, the enemy falling back and leaving their dead and wounded in our hands. . . .

LOUISVILLE, May 8.—Rumors from Nashville say Johnson has retreated from Dalton to Atlanta.

Sherman's forces have passed Tunnel Hill without opposition, and are outflanking the rebels at Buzzard Roost.

The flanking maneuver by McPherson had worked. The Confederates abandoned Dalton and moved down the railroad to the next sizable town, Resaca. The Nashville rumor was extravagant, but Sherman was moving steadily ahead.

(Monday, May 16, 1864)

HEAVY BATTLE AT RESACA YESTERDAY!

Sherman's Loss Three Thousand in Killed, Wounded, and Missing.

A dispatch received by Gen. Halleck from Gen. Sherman states that a battle occurred yesterday between him and the enemy at Resaca, in which he lost some 3,000 killed, wounded and missing, and the enemy's loss was believed to be much greater. The railroad had been repaired to within seven miles of his position, and everything was progressing most favorably. No further details were given.

General William Tecumseh Sherman

Library of Congress

A baggage train with Sherman's army crossing the Georgia Mountains in a storm.

(Thursday, May 19, 1864)

Further Good News from Sherman.

HE DRIVES JOHNSTON FROM RESACA AFTER TWO DAYS HARD FIGHTING.

Johnston Attempts to Burn the Rail-Road Bridge in His Rear!!

On the night of the 15th of May, Johnston evacuated Resaca after two days fighting, partly burning the railroad bridge. The bridge would be repaired in a few days. The railroad had been repaired as the army advanced from Chattanooga, and railroad trains arrived at Resaca at 6 p.m. of the 16th, with forage for the whole army. The men of the army had been well supplied from the time they left Chattanooga. This is most creditable to the officers of the Quartermaster's Department, including those connected with the military railroads in Tennessee.

Johnston's backward movement continued. It would not halt for another 25 miles. The distance between Sherman and Atlanta was rapidly disappearing.

WASHINGTON HOMEFRONT, MAY, 1864.

All the fighting was not confined to the battlefield. Capitol Hill was witnessing stirring events.

A BLOOD LETTING AFFAIR AMONG CONGRESSMEN.—Since South Carolina and Arkansas have been without representation in Congress, plug musses, free fights, shoulder hittings, &c., among our National Legislators have been rare; but the boarders at the National Hotel were yesterday evening forcibly reminded of the stirring times of past years by a collision between two Congressmen, a Senator and a Representative. It appears that Senator Chandler, of Michigan, and Representative Voorhees, of Indiana, were at dinner at the above hotel and occupied tables near each other. Mr. Chandler was in conversation with a lady and was denouncing copperheads and peace men, in pretty sharp terms; and in order to show her how much he abhorred the latter he stated something to the effect that if he were standing between Heaven and Hell and saw a copperhead in Heaven he would plunge into Hell. Furthermore, that he would not help a copperhead out of Hell if he could, for he believed they were made up of all that was villainous and hellish. He further expressed the conviction that the copperheads and peace men of the North were equally criminal and traitorous as the Rebels with arms in their hands, and more to be dreaded. In the course of his remarks, it is said, he referred incidentally to Indiana or Indianians.

Mr. Voorhees supposed that Senator Chandler was talking at him, and rising from his seat, approached the latter and remarked, "I suppose you meant that conversation for me."

Mr. Chandler responded by asking, "Who are you, sir?"

Mr. Voorhees replied, stating who he was, and accompanied the information by a blow aimed at Senator Chandler. Senator C. retaliated, and the two combatants clinched, and the Michigander was about getting the best of the Hoosier, when a friend of the latter, Mr. Hannegan, (son of the late Senator Hannegan), came to the rescue of his friend with a pitcher, which he broke upon the forehead of Senator C., inflicting a slight wound and drawing blood.

Further fighting was prevented by the bystanders, but not until a few pieces of crockery had been demolished by the belligerents.

Neither party was so much injured but that they appeared at breakfast this morning.

Just two blocks away on the Hill:

A ROW AT THE "ADMIRAL HOUSE."—Wednesday afternoon, a row occurred at a place styled the "Admiral House," on Pennsylvania avenue, near 3d street east. It appears that a soldier took a girl there, who he represented to be his cousin, and called for drinks—it being an ordinary occurrence for females to imbibe there—and she proposed "the Union," which they drank. Two of the servant girls took umbrage at this sentiment, and pitched in, quite a fight taking place between the four; but the servant girls getting somewhat worsted, the reserve was called up—Mr. Rothchild and wife—and a regular knock down and hair pulling ensued, during which the girl with the soldier was cut over the eye, as is supposed, with a knife. The soldier seeing that the odds were against him, made a retreat, getting off with the girl, and reported the facts at the eighth precinct station. He

General Joseph E. Johnston

was directed to Justice Ferguson for redress, who referred him to Capt. Camp, at the Soldiers' Rest; and the latter sent a guard to the house, who arrested Rothchild, the proprietor, and closed it up. Rothchild was committed to the Central Guardhouse. It is believed that the establishment will be permanently closed, as rows are of frequent occurrence there, besides its being a place of resort for women of questionable character. It has been closed three or four times before, while it was known as the "Navy Hotel."

"The hammerer," they were now calling Grant. Heavy losses in the Wilderness and Spotsylvania battles had proved no deterrent to his inexorable advance. Lee's genius and the dogged courage of his army kept the Federals from their prime goal, destruction of the Army of Northern Virginia. But Grant's own determination, backed by an inexhaustible supply of men and material, had prompted Lee to begin fighting a purely defensive war. He had to husband his dwindling manpower and supplies, and defensive tactics based on field fortifications was the best way. Lee could only hope that by sparing his men and exacting the heaviest possible toll of Federal troops, the people of the North might weary of the appalling bloodshed and be willing to settle for a negotiated peace.

With the initiative in his hands, Grant kept slugging forward, always trying to get around the right end of Lee's lines and back into the Confederate rear. As he had at Spotsylvania, Lee anticipated each movement, however. Thus, when Grant slipped east and south from Spotsylvania, he found Lee entrenched and waiting for him at Hanover Junction on the south bank of the North Anna River. The works there being too formidable, Grant moved southeast again, crossing the Pamunkey River at Hanovertown and heading directly for Richmond via Mechanicsville. As he approached Mechanicsville, there was Lee dug in before him on Totopotomoy Creek. In the last days of May, Grant once more tried swinging around the right of Lee's line. When the Federals next looked across open fields at Rebel muskets a few days later, the area to some was as familiar as the enemy muskets. Two years before, McClellan's Peninsula campaign was turned about in these parts so close to Richmond. The battle lines now were drawn near a little crossroads, Cold Harbor.

GRANT SHIFTS LINE AT COLD HARBOR

(Saturday, June 4, 1864)

GREAT BATTLE ON THE CHICKAHOMINY.

The Rebels Driven into Their Entrenchments.

OUR TROOPS WITHIN FIFTY YARDS OF THEM.

The Secretary of War this morning transmitted the following to Gen. Dix at New York:

WASHINGTON, June 4—10 P.M.

To Major General Dix, New York:

Despatches from General Grant's headquarters, dated three o'clock yesterday afternoon, have just been received. No operations took place on Thursday. Yesterday morning, at half-past four o'clock, General Grant made an assault upon the enemy's lines, of which he makes the following report:

"We assaulted at 4:30 a.m. this morning, driving the enemy within his entrenchments at all points, but without gaining any decisive advantage. Our troops now occupy a position close to the enemy— some places within fifty yards—and are remaining. Our loss was not severe, nor do I suppose the enemy to have lost heavily. We captured over three hundred prisoners, mostly from Breckenridge."

Another later official report (not from General Grant) estimates the number of our killed and wounded at about three thousand. The following officers are among the killed: Colonel Haskell, of the 36th Wisconsin; Colonel Porter, 8th New York Heavy Artillery; Colonel Morris, 66th New York.

Among the wounded are General R. O. Tyler, seriously, will probably lose a foot; Col. McMahon, 164th New York; Col. Byrnes, 28th Massachusetts, probably mortally; Colonel Brooks, 53d Pennsylvania.

Edwin M. Stanton, Secretary of War.

There had been preliminary attacks in the vicinity on June 1 as the armies felt each other out. The second day was spent consolidating positions. Grant saw the enemy's position was strong. But Richmond itself was tantalizingly close—within 10 miles. He was also weary of the repeated side-slip maneuver which had marked his campaign so far. He tried the direct frontal assault this time, an effort to smash straight through Lee's lines and pulverize the Confederates with his two-to-one strength.

(Monday, June 6, 1864)

OFFICIAL WAR BULLETIN.

Despatch from General Grant— A Sudden Attack of the Enemy Repulsed—General Grant Reinforced.

WASHINGTON, June 5—1 P.M.

Major General Dix, New York:

A despatch from Gen. Grant's headquarters dated half-past eight o'clock last night, has been received.

Library of Congress

A conference at Massaponex Church, Virginia. At the left, General Grant leans over the shoulder of General Meade to examine a map.

Another view of the council of war held by Grant at the Massaponex Church. Grant is now writing a dispatch while seated at the end of the bench in the center of the picture, directly in front of the double tree.

It states that "about 7 p.m. yesterday, (Friday, 3d June,) the enemy suddenly attacked Smith's brigade, of Gibbon's division. The battle lasted with great fury for half an hour. The attack was unwaveringly repulsed. Smith's losses were inconsiderable.

"At 6 p.m. Wilson, and his cavalry, fell upon the rear of a brigade of Heth's division which Lee had thrown around to his left, apparently with the intention of enveloping Burnside. After a sharp but short conflict Wilson drove them from their rifle pits in confusion. He took a few prisoners. He had previously fought with and routed Gordon's brigade of rebel cavalry.

"During these fights he lost several officers, among them Col. Preston, of the 1st cavalry, killed; Col. Benjamin, 8th New York cavalry, seriously wounded; Gen. Stannard, of the 18th corps, was seriously wounded, yesterday (Friday).

"Our entire loss, in killed, wounded, and missing, during the three days operations around Cold Harbor, will not exceed, according to the adjutant general's report, seven thousand five hundred.

"This morning (Saturday, June 4) the enemy's left wing, in front of Burnside, was found to have been drawn in during the night. . . ."

The real climax of the battle had occurred in the morning. In one hour of assaults, the Federals lost close to 10,000 men. So murderous was the Confederate fire that around 7,000 of these were believed to have been killed or wounded in 20 minutes alone. After the slaughter of the earlier assault waves, many of the boys in blue could be seen preparing for the next attack with a soldier's deepest fatalism— pinning name tags on their uniforms so that their bodies would not go unidentified.

FROM GRANT'S ARMY.

Continued Desperate Fighting—Attack on Warren's Corps Repulsed—Our Lines Advanced.

(Correspondence *Associated Press.*)

HEADQUARTERS, ARMY OF THE POTOMAC, June 3, 9 p.m.—Fighting has been going on nearly all day along the line, but principally artillery, the casualties being quite large. When Barlow's division charged the enemy's works early this morning, he succeeded in getting possession of seventeen guns, besides the prisoners he took, about 250; but not being supported, and subjected to an enfilading fire, he was compelled to evacuate the works he had so gallantly taken and abandon the guns. His loss was very severe, amounting to about eight hundred.

Gen. Warren's corps on the right was attacked this afternoon by a heavy force of the enemy, but the enemy were handsomely repulsed with severe loss.

The 18th corps were engaged in skirmishing most of the day, and made a charge on a portion of the line in their front, but were unable to hold it. They fell back in good order to their former position.

The 6th corps, on the left of the 18th, have been engaged more or less all day, and have suffered a good deal for the past two days. An attack on the left of the 2d corps, supposed for the purpose of feeling our left, was made an hour ago, (8 p.m.), but the enemy was soon driven off. The loss is not known.

A captain of cavalry was captured a day or two ago while trying to rally his men. He was greatly excited and cursed his men at a terrible rate, saying the whole Southern cavalry were worthless, and it was no use trying to fight any more.

Our losses for the last two days at Coal Harbor will number over five thousand in killed and wounded, while the enemy's will be nearly the same.

The change of position to-day has been very little, our advance being about a mile beyond Coal Harbor.

Federal artillery in action at Cold Harbor.

🔫 *Grant soon saw the hopelessness of continued slaughter at Cold Harbor (which The Star incorrectly called Coal Harbor) and called off further attacks. He later admitted it had been a mistake to do battle there in the first place—just as Lee had regretted ordering the final assault on Cemetery Ridge at Gettysburg. Having now run out of maneuvering space and lost his desire to collide head-on with Lee, Grant tried another tactic, reported a week later by* The Star. 🔫

(Wednesday, June 15, 1864)
Official War Bulletin.
OFFICIAL REPORT OF THE MOVEMENT OF GENERAL GRANT TO THE SOUTH SIDE OF JAMES RIVER.

WASHINGTON, June 15—7 a.m.
To Major General Dix, New York:

The movement of the Army of the Potomac to the south side of Richmond, across the Chickahominy river and James river, has progressed far enough to admit of the publication of some general facts without danger of premature disclosure.

After several days' preliminary preparation, the movement commenced Sunday night. The 18th corps, under command of Gen. Smith, marched to the White House, and there embarked for Bermuda Landing. Wright's corps and Burnside's moved to Jones Bridge, where they crossed the Chickahominy, and marched thence to Charles City, on the James river.

Hancock's and Warren's corps crossed the Chickahominy at Long Bridge, and marched thence to Wilcox's, on the James river.

The James river was to be crossed by the army at Powhattan Point.

A dispatch from Gen. Grant, dated Monday evening, half-past 5 o'clock, headquarters, Wilcox's Landing, says that the advance of our troops had reached that place, and would commence crossing the James river to-morrow (Tuesday), and that Smith's corps would commence arriving at City Point that night; that no fighting was reported during the movement, except a little cavalry skirmishing yesterday.

Tuesday p.m., at one O'clock, General Grant was at Bermuda Landing.

In a dispatch from him, dated there, of that date, he says:

Federal mortars being fired over Union troops into the rebel lines at Cold Harbor.

A. Waud—Library of Congress

Barlow's charge during the battle of Cold Harbor.

Our forces will commence crossing James river to-day. The enemy show no signs of yet having brought troops to the south side of Richmond.

Our movement from Cold Harbor to the James river has been made with great celerity, and so far without loss or accident. . . .

🔫 *The movement had been made with speed and stealth, but not quite enough. By the time "Baldy" Smith's lead corps reached the outskirts of Petersburg on the South side of the James, Beauregard, with a handful of troops and citizens, bravely stood between the enemy and the city. He held off Smith's half-hearted assault until reinforcements could be rushed in to man the partly-built trenches. Even with reinforcements, the Confederates on the crucial night of June 15 were still outnumbered five-to-one by the 40,000 Federals on their front. They held long enough for Lee—finally realizing that Grant was present in force before both Richmond and Petersburg—to send adequate help. So began the siege of Petersburg. A Federal force of 35,000 under Ben Butler had actually been posted for more than a month within 10 miles of the city. But Butler, whose movement up the James from Fort Monroe had started when Grant's Wilderness campaign began, had suffered military paralysis after landing at Bermuda Hundred. The force had been easily kept bottled up on a neck of land between the James and*

Appomattox Rivers by another handful of Confederates. 🔫

WASHINGTON HOMEFRONT, JUNE, 1864.

Frightful Explosion at the Arsenal.

A LARGE NUMBER OF THE FEMALE EMPLOYEES KILLED OR FRIGHTFULLY WOUNDED.

Eighteen Dead Bodies Taken Out of the Ruins Already.

At ten minutes of twelve o'clock to-day a terrible catastrophe occurred at the Arsenal, which has cast a gloom over the whole community, and rendered sad many a heart that was buoyant a few moments previous.

While one hundred and eight girls were at work in the main laboratory making cartridges for small arms, a quantity of fireworks, which had been placed on the outside of the building, became ignited, and a piece of fuse flying into one of the rooms, in which was seated about twenty-nine young women, set the cartridges on fire, and caused an instantaneous explosion.

The building in which the explosion took place is a one-story brick, divided off into four rooms, and runs east and west.

Those girls who were employed in the east rooms of the laboratory, mostly escaped by jumping from the windows and running through the doors pell-mell; but those in the room fronting on the east, did not fare so well, and it is feared that nearly all of them were killed by the explosion or burnt to death.

The explosion did not occasion a loud report, the roof being raised from the building about a foot, but the building immediately caught fire and was completely destroyed.

The news of the accident spread like wildfire, and in a few moments hundreds of anxious parents, brothers and sisters flocked to the scene of the disaster, but owing to the confusion no one was allowed to enter or leave the ground.

As soon as it was known the building was on fire the work in all the shops was suspended, and the hands went nobly to work to extinguish the flames and render assistance to those who were unable to escape.

When our reporter left the scene of the disaster nineteen bodies had been taken from the ruins, but they were so completely burnt to a crisp that recognition was impossible.

Ⅰf the confederacy had few resources for conduct-ing land war, it had less for war on the water. It had no navy, except a few gunboats and ironclads it had managed to outfit for river operations. No commercial fleet worthy of the name flew the Confederate flag. And although the Northern navy was little to brag about at the start of war, it was expanded twenty-six-fold to a war's end total of nearly 650 ships of all types. With these the Union Navy forged its strongest weapon, the blockade of Southern ports. The blockade grew tighter as the months passed and the number of Yankee men-of-war increased. Only the fastest of Rebel blockade runners could get through the net. The Confederacy devised a special strategy to ease the stranglehold by sending out the few warships of its own to prey on Yankee commerce. The theory was that the North would get so concerned as to detach warships from the blockade to hunt the raiders.

Yankee shippers did become alarmed. But despite their out-cries, Navy Secretary Welles refused to weaken the blockade to conduct a game of hide-and-seek on the high seas. Faced with this, the shippers lost scores of vessels—250 destroyed or captured by 1865. Their best recourse was to change the registry of their vessels from American to foreign flags for protection from the swift Confederates.

Practically all the damage was done by four raiders: *Sumter, Florida, Alabama* and *Shenandoah*. Capt. Raphael Semmes commanded the first of these until the ship was trapped in Gibraltar in 1862 and the skipper left her for his new command, the *Alabama*. It was the latter that made the most spectacular record. From July, 1862, she prowled the seas for 23 months, the climax of which was a 75,000-mile cruise from the Gulf of Mexico, around the tip of Africa to the East Indies, and back again. In her entire service afloat she sank, burned or captured 69 ships. Stoutly made (in private British shipyards, as were the *Florida* and *Shenandoah*) Semmes' ship was nonetheless bushed at the end of her East Indies run. In June, 1864, she put in at Cherbourg, France, for refitting. Just outside the harbor, the *USS Kearsarge,* Capt. John A. Winslow commanding, waited. It would be two weeks before the people on the other side of the Atlantic learned what happened.

FAMED REBEL RAIDER SUNK OFF FRANCE

(Tuesday, July 5, 1864)

Telegraphic News.

The Pirate Alabama Sunk by the U. S. Steamer Kearsage.

NEW YORK, July 5.—The City of Baltimore has arrived, and reports that the pirate *Alabama* has been sunk by the *Kearsage*. Nine rebels were killed and twenty wounded.

☞ *The source of this "bulletin" was apparently word-of-mouth from passengers aboard a ship just in from Europe. Elsewhere on the same page was another account, part of which was based on hearsay and on European newspapers, in which the encounter created a stir.* ☞

GRAPHIC PARTICULARS OF THE GREAT FIGHT.

NEW YORK, July 5.—Further details, but nothing additional of moment, relative to the *Kearsage* and *Alabama* fight. The whereabouts of the *Kearsage* is doubtful. One rumor places her at Ostend and another at Cherbourg. She landed some wounded men at Cherbourg. It is confirmed that no one was killed on the *Kearsage*. Only three seamen were slightly injured.

Semmes declined a public dinner at Southampton. He has gone to Paris to report to the Confederate commissioner.

Three of the *Alabama*'s officers and six of the crew were landed at Cherbourg from a French pilot boat. Also, several from the British ship *Action*.

Semmes publishes an account of the engagement, in which he says he had nine men killed, and twenty-one wounded. He charges the *Kearsage* with continued firing after the *Alabama* struck her flag. . . .

The following is an extended report of the battle between the *Alabama* and the U.S. gunboat *Kearsage*.

The encounter was witnessed by the English yacht *Deer Hound,* which vessel picked up Semmes and the crew of the *Alabama* and took them to Cowes, and furnished the following details of the affair:

On the morning of Sunday, the 19th (of June), at 10.30, the *Alabama* was observed steaming out of Cherbourg harbor toward the steamer *Kearsage*. At 11.10 the *Alabama* commenced the action by firing her starboard battery, a distance of about a mile. The *Kearsage* also opened fire immediately with her starboard guns. A sharp engagement, with rapid firing from both ships, was kept up, both shot and shell being discharged. In maneuvering, both vessels made complete circles at a distance from a quarter to half a mile.

At 12 o'clock the fire from the *Alabama* was observed to slacken, and she appeared to be making head sail, shaping her course for land, which was distant about 9 miles. At 12.30 the Confederate vessel was in a disabled and sinking state.

The *Deer Hound* immediately made toward her, and in passing the *Kearsage* was requested to assist

Prisoners in the hold of the *"Alabama"* receiving their daily ration of water.

Battles &Leaders

Admiral Raphael Semmes, commander of the *Alabama*.

in saving the crew of the *Alabama*. When the *Deer Hound* was still at a distance of two hundred yards, the *Alabama* sank, and the *Deer Hound* then lowered her boats, and with the assistance of those from the sinking vessel, succeeded in saving about forty men, including Captain Semmes and about thirteen other officers.

The *Kearsage* was apparently much disabled.

The *Alabama*'s loss is as follows: Drowned, one officer and one man. Killed, 6 men; wounded, one officer and 16 men.

Captain Semmes was slightly wounded in the hand.

The *Kearsage*'s boats were lowered, and with the assistance of the French Pilot, succeeded in picking up the remainder of the crew of the *Alabama*.

It is stated that a formal challenge to fight was given by the *Kearsage,* and accepted by Captain Semmes.

According to some accounts, the *Kearsage* sustained considerable damage, her sides being torn open, showing the chain plating.

A dispatch, however, from Cherbourg, where it is presumed the *Kearsage* has arrived, says that she had suffered no damage of importance, and that none of her officers were killed and wounded. Only three seamen were wounded. It says that the *Kearsage* captured 68 of the officers and men of the *Alabama*.

NEW YORK, July 5.—A note from the American Consul at Liverpool, dated the 22d, states that no one was killed on the *Kearsage,* but three of the crew were slightly injured. The vessel was very little injured.

NEW YORK, July 5.—The Paris correspondent of the London *Globe* says the *Alabama* made two attempts to board the *Kearsage,* but her commander outmanoeuvered Semmes, and finally sent a projectile right through the *Alabama*'s boiler.

Then seeing what had occurred, he brought all his guns to bear on the pirate in a concentrated broadside from the starboard, and made a breach four yards in length under her water mark, when she began to sink rapidly.

The gunnery of the Kearsage *was accurate, and her sides were reinforced with chain link which minimized the* Alabama's *shots. Although he didn't say so in his official report published next day, Winslow was more than a little peeved that the British* Deer Hound *made off with Semmes instead of surrendering him to the victor.*

Officers on the deck of the *Kearsarge*.

(Wednesday, July 6, 1864)

Official Report by Capt. Winslow of the Destruction of the Alabama.

Semmes Challenges him to Fight—The Challenge Accepted—Gallant Conduct of the Crew and Officers of the *Kearsage*— The Carnage upon the *Alabama* Dreadful.

The Navy Department has received the following official report from Capt. Winslow, of the *Kearsage:*

U.S. STEAMER KEARSAGE, *Cherbourg, France,* June 19, 1864.—Sir: I have the honor to inform the Department that the day subsequent to the arrival of the *Kearsage* off this port, on the 14th inst., I received a note from Capt. Semmes, begging that the *Kearsage* would not depart, as he intended to fight her, and would not delay her but a day or two.

According to this notice the *Alabama* left the port of Cherbourg this morning at about 9.30 o'clock. At 10.20 a.m. we discovered her, steering towards us. Fearing the question of jurisdiction might arise, we steamed to sea until a distance of six or seven miles was attained from the Cherbourg breakwater, when we rounded to and commenced steaming for the *Alabama.* As we approached her with about 1,200 yards she opened fire, we receiving two or three broadsides before a shot was returned. The action continued, the respective steamers making a circle round and round, at a distance of about nine hundred yards from each other.

At the expiration of about an hour the *Alabama* struck, going down in about twenty minutes afterwards, and carrying many persons with her.

It affords me great satisfaction to announce to the Department that every officer and man did their duty, exhibiting a degree of coolness and fortitude which gave promise at the outset of certain victory.

I have the honor to be, most respectfully, your obedient servant,

J. A. Winslow, Captain.
Hon. Gideon Welles, Sec'ry of the Navy.

U.S.S. KEARSAGE, *Cherbourg, France,* June 20, 1864.—Sir: I enclose herewith the Surgeon's report of the casualties on board this vessel in the late action with the *Alabama.*

Although we received some 25 or 30 shots, 12 or 13 taking effect in the hull, by the mercy of God we

National Archives

Captain John A. Winslow, commander of the *Kearsarge.*

have been spared the loss of life, whereas in the case of the *Alabama* the carnage, I learn, was dreadful.

The ships were about equal in match, the tonnage being the same. The *Alabama* carrying one hundred pound rifle, with one heavy 68-pounder, and six broadside 32-pounders, and the *Kearsage* carrying four broadside 32-pounders, two 11-inch, and one 28-pounder rifle, one gun less than the *Alabama.*

The only shot which I fear will give us any trouble is one hundred pound rifle which entered our stern post and remains at present unexploded.

It would seem almost invidious to particularize the conduct of any one man or officer in which all had done their duty with a fortitude and coolness which cannot be too highly praised; but I feel it due to my executive officer Lt. Commander Thornton, who superintended the working of the battery, to particularly mention him for an example of coolness and encouragement to the men while fighting, which contributed much towards the success of the action.

Very respectfully, your obedient servant,

J. A. Winslow, Captain.
Hon. Gideon Welles, Sec'y of the Navy.

☞ *Of the Confederacy's remaining two raiders,* Florida *would be illegally captured in the neutral port of Bahia, Brazil, within four months, and only the* Shenandoah *would be left to harass Yankee commerce for the duration, mostly in the Western Pacific and the Bering Sea, between Alaska and Siberia, where whalers gathered oil.* ☞

WASHINGTON HOMEFRONT, JULY, 1864.

☞ *In Washington, the main event of the "Glorious Fourth" celebration was the new dedication of a public school. But more attention was being devoted to politics—in particular whether the peace parties or Mr. Lincoln's brand of Republicanism would prevail in the November elections.* ☞

Celebration by the Peace Democrats.

The "National Democratic Association" celebrated the day (July 4) by meeting in their hall opposite the Metropolitan Hotel and marching to the Western Capitol grounds where the meeting was called to order, John D. Clark, Esq., in the chair. The meeting numbered between five and six hundred persons, including quite a number of those who are by no means of the Peace Democracy stripe.

Thomas B. Florence read the Declaration of Independence.

Charles Mason, the President of the Association, followed in a long oration made up mainly of abuse of the present administration. It had done everything, he said, to provoke the ire of the Southern heart. The troubles were now further from a termination than at any previous time. Thousands had been driven from their homes to be destroyed, and still they were calling for "three hundred thousand more."

A change must be made or the nation will not survive. Any change might be for the better; it could not be for the worse. The great object was peace, and if peace were offered on the old terms, (the Constitution as it is), it ought to be accepted, and proud would be the leader of the army of peace. (Applause.) A separation could not be thought of, for where would the Border States go?

Let us attempt a restoration at once. Appeal to our countrymen in the South for the old Constitu-

tion, with such amendments as may be beneficial to all sections. Opposition was to be expected both at Richmond and Washington; but the people, who are the sovereigns, would demand it. If that principle is triumphant in the North, it would prove so in the South, and in this jubilee there must be a general amnesty—the guilty should go free. While the South is responsible for many of the effects of this war, was not the North in a measure to blame? Then let us invite the prodigal to return, and meet him while a great way off, and have the fatted calf killed. (Applause.) Give us once again Union, give us peace. (Applause.) . . .

☞ *While these functions were going on, an ominous cloud appeared on the immediate horizon.* ☞

REPORTS FROM UP RIVER.

Boatmen Report the Enemy to be Crossing at Various Points—Scary Rumors.

Considerable excitement was created in Georgetown this morning by the statements brought in by the boatmen coming down the (Chesapeake and Ohio) canal, who report the rebels crossing the Potomac at nearly every fordable point from Harper's Ferry down to Muddy Branch, this side of Seneca, and less than twenty miles from Georgetown.

The panic-stricken boatmen estimate the rebel force variously from twenty to forty thousand strong, cavalry and infantry!

These reports may be set down as, one and all, the exaggerations of panicky fugitives seeking to make the best possible excuse for their own skedaddling. The river is unusually low, and is fordable at almost all points, and it is not improbable that squads of rebels have crossed in different places on horse-stealing expeditions. Despite the sensation reports via Harrisburg, we cannot see in this rebel demonstration anything more than a movement for plunder by an inconsiderable force of the enemy. . . .

Library of Congress

Alabama, on the right, exchanges fire with the *Kearsarge.*

SHERMAN'S RELENTLESS PRESSURE WAS DRIVING BACK Johnston's outnumbered army. There was nothing precipitate about the retreat. Since the start of the Georgia campaign around Dalton, the Confederate leader had held a series of positions, and had battled to hold some. Sherman, however, was employing the same tactics as had Grant between the Wilderness and Richmond: slipping around the enemy's flanks with superior force. The only alternative to falling back was encirclement, or an offensive that would be foredoomed. Johnston's was an application of the delaying tactics made famous by the Roman general, Fabius. He was trying to buy time and conserve what fighting strength he had for when he might strike a decisive blow at a moment of Federal unwariness. But Sherman, who had a hearty respect for his opponent, refused to get careless. So while the Jeff Davis government fumed, Johnston continued to pull back, abandoning in succession positions at Cassville, Allatoona, Dallas and New Hope Church, Pine Mountain (where Bishop-Gen. Polk was killed in battle) and Kenesaw Mountain. By July 4, entrenched along the Chattahoochee River, the Confederates had only 10 miles more to back up before reaching Atlanta itself.

Grant's vise on Richmond-Petersburg, meanwhile, was tightening to the point that Lee felt daring measures were needed to ease the pressure. He chose "Jubilee" Early for the task. Early had gone to Lynchburg in mid-June to frighten the Federals, under Maj. Gen. David Hunter, away from that key railroad city of Southwestern Virginia. Hunter had fled hastily into West Virginia and out of action. Lee now instructed Early to hurry his little force of less than 20,000 on down the Shenandoah Valley to threaten Washington once more. Possibly the Federal City would scream for some of Grant's men to protect it. By July 2, Early was in Winchester, and in another two days had tramped through Martinsburg and was menacing Harpers Ferry. That town being at last strongly garrisoned, the Rebel raiders by-passed it, marched through the Antietam battlefield, where the first invasion of the North had been stopped two years before, and plowed into Hagerstown and Frederick. There they stopped long enough to requisition $220,000, and headed on south toward Washington.

The capital was frantic by this time, especially after a small and motley Federal force under Lew Wallace was swept aside July 9 at the Monocacy River, only 35 miles away. Sure enough, Grant was ordered to send help from his Richmond army. It still had not come when the Rebels reached Washington's outskirts at Silver Spring.

Not since the War of 1812 had the city been under military attack. *The Star* was crammed with every report available.

CONFEDERATES MENACE CAPITAL

(Monday, July 11, 1864)

EXTRA.

FIGHTING ON THE 7TH STREET ROAD.

Messengers just in report lively skirmishing going on this morning in the vicinity of Fort Massachusetts, (near Clagett's place), some four miles out.

The rebels did not show themselves in large force there, however.

☞ *Fort Massachusetts was also known as Fort Stevens, in honor of Representative Thaddeus Stevens, Radical Republican of Pennsylvania, a power in Congress, and a victim of Lee's 1863 invasion (when his ironworks was destroyed near Gettysburg). Located well within the District Line, its undermanned guns commanded the Seventh Street pike, main road from Washington to Silver Spring and Western Maryland. When Early approached, it was sadly undermanned. There was further cause for alarm.* ☞

TELEGRAPH WIRES CUT BETWEEN WASHINGTON AND BALTIMORE.

(From the *Independent Line*.)

WASHINGTON, July 11, 12.20 p.m.—*Editor Star:* All of our lines have just been cut between here and Baltimore by the rebel invaders.

J. M. Locke.

The Rebel Force in Front of Us—Its Strength and Purpose.

Reports concerning the numbers and purpose of the rebel invading force are confusingly conflicting.

We give elsewhere the opinion entertained by many around us that the rebel force is not of weight sufficient to undertake a serious attack upon the fortifications of Washington, and that it is not their purpose so to do.

Per contra: we have just received the following from a source of great intelligence and reliability, one that has on repeated occasions had the earliest and most accurate information of rebel movements in Virginia. The information received from this quarter is as follows:

The rebel army of invasion marched down the Valley 45,000 strong, including 8,000 cavalry, under command of Major General Jubal Early and Brigadier Generals Breckinridge, Ransom, Imboden and McCausland. Longstreet was at Gordonsville on Tuesday last, with additional forces to join the rebel army of invasion, and the purpose of that army was an attempt at the capture of Washington by a surprise. The Virginia Central Railroad is repaired and running from Richmond to Staunton.

Moseby has 242 men in his command, and expects to have his force increased, the conscripts in Fauquier having the liberty of joining the army or to go into his command. It was Moseby who made the raid

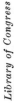

One of the heavy guns at Fort Totten, commanding a sector of the Washington defenses near Fort Stevens.

The heavy guns at Fort Stevens. President Lincoln was under fire on this site.

on Duffield's Station, and the plunder was divided on Friday last at White Plains. Two other companies are organizing for him. At the fight at Aldie, Moseby captured 81 cavalry, killed 20, captured one major, and had with him a 12-pounder in the fight. Kincheloe's command, one company, is operating near Fairfax Court House and the neighborhood of Occoquan.

Jube Early's main mission was to draw Federal troops away from Richmond, in which he had already succeeded. He could play with secondary goals, too. He might capture Lincoln, or Federal gold in the Treasury, or perhaps move through the capital into Southern Maryland to Point Lookout, free the 17,000 Confederate troops imprisoned there, and somehow make it back to safety.

THE PRESIDENT IN THE FIELD.

The President rode to the front in the direction of Tenallytown at about 9 a.m. to-day, accompanied by Assistant Adjutant General Hardie, and a mounted escort. Yesterday he paid a similar visit of observation and inspection. His presence among our gallant troops will doubtless do much to animate and encourage them in the discharge of their duties.

Lincoln's tour of the forts included Fort Stevens, where he calmly viewed the exchange of fire between Rebel skirmishers and Yankee civilians and militia. During this period, Early formed plans for making a full-scale attack, but changed his mind when Fed-

eral reinforcements dispatched from Richmond poured into position. These were, chiefly, Maj. Gen. Horatio Gouverneur Wright's VI corps. But Washington civilians were still being called into the breach.

ARMING THE EMPLOYEES.

This morning arms were given out to the employees of several of the departments, who have organized for the defense of the city. This afternoon the clerks of the Adjutant General's office were drilling in front of Lafayette Square, fully armed and equipped.

(Tuesday, July 12, 1864)

EXTRA.
The Invasion.

The heavy skirmishing in front of Fort Stevens, in the vicinity of the Seventh street road, yesterday afternoon, continued until after dark.

The rebels held a position in the woods, from which they threw out skirmishers, who crept along the ground or fired from behind trees. At one time they succeeded in getting within range of the fort, and their sharpshooters were enabled to pick off our gunners, two of whom were wounded. The rebels used no artillery, but their movements indicated that they were endeavoring to plant a battery to bear on

Fort Stevens, (lately known as Fort Massachusetts), and in order to frustrate their designs the fort threw shells occasionally amongst them. About half-past six our cavalry charged upon them, which had the effect of driving them back some distance. The skirmishing was still kept up, however, and a little after seven o'clock our infantry was brought up and placed in line in front of Fort Stevens, while the cavalry deployed to the right. The object of this movement, or its results, was not known when we left the vicinity of the scene of action last night.

The house of F. P. Blair has not been burned as reported yesterday, the rebels appear to be using it as a hospital, as they were seen to carry some of their wounded into it. The houses of Mrs. Reeves and Mrs. Carberry, on either side of the Seventh street road, were occupied by rebel sharpshooters, who annoyed our troops somewhat. During the afternoon they picked off three of our sergeants, shooting them through the head.

It was found necessary to destroy quite a number of houses on either side of the Seventh street road to prevent them being occupied by the rebel sharpshooters. Among the houses destroyed were Messrs. Richard Butts', Wm. Bell's, J. H. McChesney's, Mr. Shoemaker's, and the house occupied by the family of the late Wm. M. Morrison. Time, however, was allowed the owners of these to remove the furniture, and the road leading to this city was lined with wagons conveying it to a place of safety.

The farmers in the vicinity lost most of their stock, owing, as they said, to our pickets refusing to let the drivers pass through the lines without a permit. The farmers had taken the precaution to drive their stock towards the city as the rebels advanced; but, not being allowed to enter, it fell into the hands of the enemy.

Several citizens, policemen and others, took active part in the engagement, prominent among whom were Augustus Norton, P. McChesney, and Officers Boose and Beale.

A number of our soldiers were overcome by the heat, as were also several citizens, who had walked out to the scene of action to witness the engagement.

Early in the evening thousands of persons could be seen passing out Seventh street by every conceivable means of conveyance, while the road was literally lined with pedestrians. The hills, trees and fences within sight of Fort Stevens were covered with human beings, quite a number of whom were ladies. Quietly seated in a carriage, at a commanding point, was Secretary Seward, viewing the progress of affairs.

Washingtonians still enjoyed a good fight when it was close—shades of First Bull Run! Despite civilian complacency, military authorities continued alarmed.

THE DISTRICT MILITIA CALLED OUT.

Below we give the notification by the Government calling out the militia of the District for sixty days. The citizens of this District have on previous occasions responded to similar calls with an alacrity that won for them the highest commendation, and we are certain that the same will be the case now.

With officers so experienced and competent as Gen. George C. Thomas and Brig. Gen'l Peter F.

On horseback, President Lincoln observes the fighting at Fort Stevens on July 11.

Battles & Leaders

Cattle and plunder taken by Early's cavalry on its march to Washington.

Bacon to organize the militia force, we are confident that it will soon be put in shape to do excellent service:

HEADQUARTERS D. C. MILITIA
WASHINGTON, July 11, 1864.

General Order, No. 1.—Having this day been ordered by the President to call out, for immediate service, the militia and volunteers of this District and specially assigned to the command thereof, the eight regiments of infantry and the volunteer force, including cavalry and infantry, are hereby ordered into the service of the United States for sixty days.

Every available man is wanted immediately, and captains of companies and colonels of regiments will at once notify the men of their respective commands to assemble for muster without delay.

Brig. Gen. P. F. Bacon will personally superintend the details of this order and see that it is promptly executed.

Geo. C. Thomas, Major Gen. Com.

No major battle had developed, but Rebels seemed to be all over the place. With his small force, Early was taking no chances of being surprised by sudden flank attack.

THE DESTRUCTION OF
THE RAILROAD.

The railroad between here and Baltimore has been pretty effectually broken up by the rebels, between Beltsville and Laurel, including the bridge at Laurel.

The rebels appeared on the road about half-past 12 o'clock.

The 10 o'clock train from Baltimore was just missed by the rebels, who were apparently very near the road at the time the train passed this way, as the dust raised by their movement was visible, and the alarm was given to the train about a mile and a half beyond Beltsville. The train came cautiously down to Beltsville, and seeing no immediate signs of the rebels, came on to Washington.

The train had scarcely reached here when the news came that the rebels had struck the road behind them.

We had a considerable picket force at Laurel, and it is possible that the rebel cavalry in their swoop on the road gobbled up this picket, but it is believed that they had time to escape.

The rebels this morning drove in our pickets at Spencerville, eight miles west of Laurel, on the Sandy Spring road, and from this and other indications it would appear that the rebels are swinging a considerable force in that direction.

About one o'clock to-day the rebels were seen in some force in the neighborhood of Fort Lincoln, near Bladensburg.

About eleven o'clock this morning, as a group, consisting of Mr. Duhamel, Mr. Koontz, ticket agent of the Baltimore and Ohio Railroad, Mr. White, ticket agent ditto, and two soldiers were standing on the parapet of Fort Stevens, the two soldiers were simultaneously shot dead by rebel sharpshooters.

Reinforcements were still pouring into Washington. The situation for the Federal City seemed to be well in hand.

(Wednesday, July 13, 1864)

EXTRA.
THE REBELS HAVE DISAPPEARED FROM OUR FRONT!

They Leave Their Dead and Wounded Behind Them!

Reconnoissances made last night and this morning make it plain that the rebels have disappeared from in front of the fortifications of Washington.

They left eleven officers and ninety men in the house of F. P. Blair, sr., at Silver Springs, too severely wounded in the action yesterday to be carried off. They also left their dead of that fight upon the field.

Measures have been taken for their immediate pursuit.

We fear that we are not sufficiently strong in cavalry to make pursuit of much avail, unless our infantry can overtake them through obstructions to their rapid progress placed in their way by other Union forces—those under Hunter, Howe and Couch.

In addition to their work of plundering and devastation, we hear that they have been forcing every able-bodied man they have been able to pick up in Maryland into their ranks; carrying them off with them.

It was not known here (that we can ascertain) at 11 a.m. to-day, to what points or in what precise direction the rebels have withdrawn.

They were moving from the front all night.

Our belief is that they are in full retreat across the Potomac.

LATE AND IMPORTANT!

The Enemy Recrossing the Potomac Near Poolesville—They Drive off 2,000 Head of Cattle.

Information reached here at half-past 1 to-day, by scouts from up river, that the rebels were this morning recrossing the Potomac nearly opposite Poolesville. They were driving before them about 2,000 head of cattle which they had stolen.

Washington's latest tormentors had escaped whole once again. Wright's pursuit lagged. Early's army recrossed the Potomac near Leesburg, Va., and soon was back within the sheltering walls of the Shenandoah Valley. It was still in an aggressive mood.

WASHINGTON HOMEFRONT, JULY, 1864.

The enemy may have been pounding at Washington's back door, but civilian affairs—such as detailed accounts of a city council meeting and the award of scholarship certificates to school children—found their place in The Star. There were, as well, local news items relating to the danger of invasion.

A SUPPOSED REBEL FLAG.—On Saturday last, Capt. Camp, A.W.M. at the Soldiers' Rest, received information that certain parties in the city were preparing a flag for presentation to the advance guard of the rebels when they entered the city. Lieut. Gemmill, of the V.R.C. stationed at that point, proceeded to the house designated, and there found a fine flag, of which is a description, which he took possession of:—Length, three feet; width, about 18 inches; with a white field about 18 inches square, on which are two narrow blue silk stripes running from corner to corner, each stripe having thirteen stars over it (making twenty-six in all), with two stripes, the upper one red, and the other blue. Those having charge of it said that it was intended for a division of the Sons or Cadets of Temperance, but the officers not being conversant with the emblems and flags used in that order, took charge of it, and have referred the matter to the proper authorities.

SUNDAY EXCURSIONISTS BAGGED.—Yesterday morning a number of gentlemen, to avoid the heat and dust of the city, made a visit to the Prince George side of the Anacostia to spend the day in the cool shade of the oaks. Unfortunately they were bagged by the military, who seemed to think the party were loitering around after a suspicious sort and detained until morning. Sunday visits beyond the District lines are not safe at present.

THE COURTS ADJOURNED.—This morning Judge Fisher announced to the Grand and Traverse Juries that he did not suppose their minds were in a condition to try cases, but that, as the city was said to be in imminent danger, every true citizen should be using all his endeavors to assist in its defence. He therefore discharged them until Tuesday, September 6th.

THE WASHINGTON SCARE WAS OVER, BUT THE PROTRACTED nightmare around Richmond had only started. Once his subordinates missed their chance, June 15, to capture Petersburg while its defenses were feeble, Grant had resigned himself to siege tactics. Perhaps Petersburg could be strangled into submission, thus opening the way to encircling Richmond and Lee's army with it. As part of the process, the Federals late in June tried to seize the Weldon Railroad which ran south from Petersburg. After initial success, the attempt was driven off and Grant had to be content with blocking the road which paralleled the rail line, four miles east. Both sides resumed their digging-in operations—which ultimately would extend from a point 10 miles west of Petersburg, almost continuously for 20 miles to Richmond, and ringing that city entirely.

Siege warfare was not new to Grant, but he didn't like it any better now than he did at Vicksburg. As a result, he was receptive to a proposal that came from the commander of a regiment of Pennsylvanians of the coal-mining country. The idea was to undermine a portion of the Confederate fortifications on the eastern outskirts, fill the hole with powder, blow up the works, and charge through the wreckage. Grant was unenthusiastic. He had set off a couple of mines at Vicksburg to no avail. But he approved the suggestion again.

For nearly a month, the Pennsylvanians tunneled away for more than 500 feet. At that point, 20 feet beneath a battery of Rebel artillery, two galleries 75 feet long were extended laterally. On July 23, 8,000 pounds of powder was in and the fuse attached. Seven days later, the fuse was lit.

MINE BLAST LAUNCHES CRATER BATTLE

(Monday, August 1, 1864)

Telegraphic News.
ASSAULT ON PETERSBURG.

Mine Exploded by our Forces—A Terrific Spectacle—The Works Lifted into the Air—Men and Guns Buried in Ruins—Great Artillery and Musket Fire—Rebel Works Assaulted—The Entire First Line Carried—Enemy Completely Surprised—Great Slaughter of the Rebels—Many Prisoners Captured—Movement on the James River.

———◆———

FORTRESS MONROE, July 30.—The mail steamer from City Point has just arrived with important news from Gen. Grant's army. The siege of Petersburg opened in earnest this morning. At daylight we sprang the mine and blew up one of their principal batteries in front of Petersburg, containing sixteen guns, and subsequently carried the outer line of works by assault.

Later.

FORTRESS MONROE, July 30, p.m.—Just as the boat is about leaving for Baltimore your correspondent gathers the following additional particulars:

The explosion took place shortly after four o'clock this morning. It was terrific, and destroyed one of the enemy's strongest fortifications, which, as before stated, contained sixteen guns. The work was rendered a mass of ruins.

Immediately after the explosion the artillery opened with one simultaneous and continuous roar along the entire line of our army.

Up to the leaving of the mail boat at 10 o'clock a.m., two other earthworks had been carried, and also the enemy's entire outer line of entrenchments, and the battle was progressing with great fury.

🔫 *It was no secret either to newspapers readers or the Confederates that a death-dealing project had been under way. An earlier story in* The Star *had mentioned that "the rebels are in momentary anticipation of a 'hyst' from Grant's mines." Lee's troops, in fact, had tried a countermining project of their own. It failed, but so did the Federal follow-up of the explosion. A Negro division had been scheduled to go in first, but that plan was called off at the last minute. A white division went ahead instead, across a field that had not been cleared of obstacles. The Confederates all the while were concentrating infantry and artillery on the mine crater—170 feet long, by 80 feet wide by 30 feet deep. When the Federal charge finally got organized, it foundered in the crater itself.* 🔫

Library of Congress

Federal troops in the trenches around Petersburg.

Powder kegs being placed in the tunnel prior to the explosion.

EXTRA.
Very Important from the Front.
THE FIGHTING AT PETERSBURG ON SATURDAY.

We have the following interesting particulars of the fighting on Saturday in front of Petersburg, obtained from eyewitnesses of the stirring events of the day.

At 2 o'clock on Saturday morning, the arrival of the signal boat at City Point, coming down the Appomattox swiftly and venting its well known and peculiar shrill whistle, indicated to the initiated that something was up. Gen'l Grant rose immediately, and mounting his horse galloped off towards Petersburg to Meade's headquarters, some eight miles distant from City Point. Other parties, anxious to witness the anticipated event, immediately followed as rapidly as possible.

About three o'clock the stillness of the night was broken by an artillery fire, of no great fervor, however, and which, on the surface bore no significance as being anything more than the routine compliments of the morning to the enemy.

About four o'clock, however, the cannonade on our part assumed a vigor that must have warned the Petersburghers and the enemy there congregated that something serious was about to transpire. And about twenty minutes later, something serious *did* transpire in the explosion of Grant's mine, located under the main fort or rather a little to the left of the front of Burnside's position.

Our informants state that the published accounts to the effect that the earth was blown up five hundred feet by the explosion, and that the report "awak-ened Richmond," shaking the earth as by an earthquake for miles away, is all nonsense. The mine was laid very deep, and the explosion, though effective and destructive, was distinguished by none of these pyrotechnic effects given it by the hand of fancy. The earth was thrown up in a brown cloud about one hundred feet, and at the same time a low, rumbling sound was heard, bearing no proportion in weight to the roar of the cannon. The sound of the explosion was not even heard at City Point, and the fact of the explosion of the mine was not known there until the arrival of the train from the front.

A pause of twenty minutes followed upon the springing of the mine before the charge was made by the 9th corps, who then sprang forward to the first line of entrenchments, which was carried, and they then pushed on to the second line, exposed to a murderous enfilading fire from the enemy's batteries. Here it was that the negro troops, who had earned a good name in previous service, and who had asked the privilege of leading the advance, cowered before the terrible fire and fell back in disorder.

Other divisions of the 9th and 10th, however, pushed on, gaining the second line of entrenchments and up to the third and last line, and apparently the day was our own, but here somebody blundered, and, if we may believe report, out troops paused for two and a half hours at this point, waiting the order to assault this third line, giving an opportunity for the enemy to rally their forces and crowd our thinned columns back to their starting point, so that the important advantages gained were snatched from us at the moment when, apparently, Petersburg was won. Our loss was pretty heavy in the fighting between the intrenchments, amounting to 1,000 or 1,500 men. It was reported at City Point when the mail boat left yesterday, that we took 300 prisoners in the rebel intrenchments, and that some 700 of the enemy were killed by the explosion.

The Rebels appear to have been informed as to the direction in which Grant's mining operations were running, as shown by the fact that they had removed 12 of the 16 guns belonging to the fort. . . .

Since writing the above, we have information that the explosion was admirable, realizing all Grant's expectations; but we failed to reap the advantages expected to follow upon it, from the fact that the charge to follow upon it was somewhat delayed, and also to the fact that Ledley's and Turner's divisions, of the 9th and 10th corps, which made it, did not stand up to their work. The report that the negro troops behaved especially bad is not corroborated by our later information, which states that they behaved no worse, at least, than others.

The Negro division had been thrown in as supports, and became entangled with the rest of the force, which tried to drive beyond the crater. For some reason, hundreds chose to stay in the crater and were killed, wounded or captured right there. Federal casualties totaled nearly 4,000 in and around the crater. Grant could well have said "I told you so." But the Confederates lost at least 1,500 in the battle. They could afford such losses far less than Grant. The Petersburg-Richmond siege went on.

WASHINGTON HOMEFRONT, JULY, 1864.

Reckless driving sometimes plagued the city streets, which swirled with horseback riders and horse-drawn vehicles of every sort.

———◆———

ACCIDENT.—Yesterday, about 4 o'clock p.m., as a Government wagon, laden with wagon poles, &c., was passing H street north, a coach, containing a lady and two children, was driven along 5th street. At the intersection of the two streets, the coachman, though near the wagon, undertook to pass ahead of it. The consequence was that the pole of the wagon came in contact with the top of the coach and tore it from the body. The lady and children were alarmed, but not injured. A policeman was about to arrest the coachman, but being told that he was the servant of the British Minister, he declined making the arrest.

Living in the capital of a belligerent also had special hazards.

DWELLING DAMAGED BY THE EXPLOSION OF A SHELL.—During the practice firing from the mortar schooner yesterday afternoon, one of the 13-inch shells exploded prematurely, and a fragment, weighing two and three-quarter pounds, entered the dwelling of Mr. J. R. Miller, residing in West End, causing some damage to the house and considerable consternation among the inmates. One individual, however, lying asleep in the room into which the missile entered, was not disturbed from his nap, though it was deposited in very close proximity to him. Upon the proper representation being made to Gen. Slough, Mr. Miller was promptly reimbursed for the damage sustained to the house and furniture. No blame, of course, attached to the commander of the mortar schooner.—*Alex. Jour., July 29.*

Here was a problem, nobly facted by The Star, *that no one would ever encounter in a supermarket today.*

———◆———

INFAMOUS PRACTICES AT CENTER MARKET.—This morning, a cow dealer at Center Market was hauled up for being guilty of the inhumane practice of tying down the tongues of calves, or muzzling them, to prevent their sucking their dams. Officer Brewer, of the Third Ward, upon hearing of it, went immediately to the dealer and made him remove the muzzles and cords, and at the same time notified him that a second attempt would cause his immediate arrest. All honor to Officer Brewer!

It is about time that the market master should put a stop to this devilish practice of the cow-dealers at Center Market, who, to make the cows show well

Ex-coal miners from a Pennsylvania regiment digging under the rebel lines. The dirt was carried out in boxes.

Battles & Leaders

In the distance can be seen the explosion of the mine under the Confederate lines.

as milkers, keep them unmilked until their udders are swelled nearly to bursting, causing intense suffering to the animals, and sometimes utterly ruining them.

It is about time, also, that the Market Master at Center Market should enforce the law against inhumanity to calves and sheep, tied and thrown upon their backs.

It is impossible to move along the brick sidewalks skirting the Center Market building on a market day, without stumbling at every step over some unfortunate animal closely tied by its four legs, lying on its back strangling, with tongue and eyes protruding, uttering piteous cries, so long as it has strength. It is notorious that they are kept in this position of torture for hours, despite the Corporation ordinance designed to remedy the evil. In no other city, in any civilized country on the face of the globe, would such an inhuman practice be tolerated for an hour.

As soon as he succeeded in running the Mississippi River forts guarding New Orleans in April, 1862, Farragut's attention turned to the fine harbor of Mobile, Ala. The place, he was sure, was ripe for Federal land and sea operations. Its seizure would close, far more effectively than a blockade, the last principal Confederate port on the Gulf of Mexico. But Washington had other plans for its then undersized fleet. Lincoln, characterizing a widespread feeling in the North, was captivated by the idea of capturing Charleston and the harbor that symbolized secession more than any geographical point in the land. Farragut consequently had to wait while the ironclad monitors came off the production lines to be assigned to other purposes deemed more important than Mobile. He waited, in fact, well over two years, maintaining his wearisome blockade watch—a period during which an ironclad sea assault on coveted Charleston failed dismally in early 1863.

All the while, Forts Morgan and Gaines, guarding the narrow entrance to Mobile Bay, were being strengthened. Within the bay, the Confederates under the supervision of Adm. Franklin Buchanan, were building an ironclad fleet of their own. Its designed role was offensive. Buchanan saw it as an attack force to crack the blockade by sailing out and destroying the wooden vessels of the Yankees. The ironclad ram *Tennessee* was to be the spearhead, aided by the gunboats *Selma,* *Morgan* and *Gaines.* As a protective screen, the harbor itself was planted with floating "torpedoes."

Farragut's knowledge of these developments made his own enforced inactivity galling. Finally, late in July, 1864, the admiral got a small quota of four monitors, headed by the *Tecumseh,* Capt. Tunis A. M. Craven commanding. In addition, he readied 14 wooden men-o-war, his old *Hartford,* the flagship, to form the task force that would grab the initiative, reduce the forts and occupy the harbor, thus sealing Mobile for the duration.

In the foggy dawn of August 5, the *Tecumseh* led the way toward the forts, the wooden ships harnessed in twos following close behind. The *Hartford,* back in the line, was conspicuous in that the elderly admiral was up in the rigging, the better to see what was going on. Since Farragut was a victim of gout and vertigo, a thoughtful subordinate had insisted that he be lashed there.

CONFEDERACY LOSES MOBILE BAY

(Saturday, August 6, 1864)

BOMBARDMENT OF MOBILE.

The Forts Commanding the City
Passed by Farragut.

THE REBELS RUN.

NEW YORK, August 6.—A special dispatch to the *Herald* from New Orleans, dated July 30, says information has been received at headquarters that Admiral Farragut had passed Forts Morgan and Gaines, which are supposed to command the entrance to Mobile Bay, and is bombarding the upper line of defences. The Admiral has now six iron-clads. Two more left here to-day.

The bombardment had continued three days, and it was expected that the city would surrender before the close of the week.

General Granger in command of the land forces will occupy Mobile and garrison the forts if success crowns the expedition. . . .

🔫 *This was an odd piece of coincidence—a wholly anticipatory report published the day after the attack. That the plans were well known is indicated by the mention of Gordon Granger's army force, whose role was to invest the forts from the rear. The first report having anything like official status appeared in Washington in the form of a clipping from a Confederate newspaper.* 🔫

(Tuesday, August 9, 1864)

GLORIOUS NEWS!
GREAT NAVAL VICTORY IN MOBILE BAY—SURRENDER OF THE REBEL RAM TENNESSEE—ADMIRAL BUCHANAN WOUNDED AND A PRISONER.

WASHINGTON, Aug. 8, 9 p.m.—The following announcement of the successful operations against Mobile appears in the Richmond *Sentinel* of this date, and has been transmitted by Major General Butler to the President. It was received at seven p.m., August 8, from Headquarters, General Butler, dated three p.m., Aug. 8, 1864.

The deck of the *Hartford,* Admiral Farragut's flagship.

National Archives

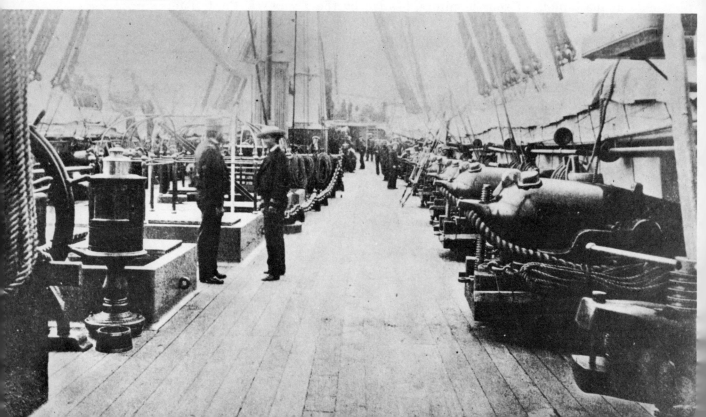

Library of Congress

Admiral Farragut (hand on wheel) on the deck of his flagship.

To His Excellency A. Lincoln, President:

The following is the official report taken from the Richmond *Sentinel,* Aug. 8.

BENJ. F. BUTLER, Maj. Gen.

"MOBILE, Aug. 5, 1864.—*Hon. J. A. Seddon, Secretary of War:* Seventeen of the enemy's vessels (fourteen ships and three iron-clads) passed Fort Morgan this morning. The *Tecumseh,* a monitor, was sunk by Fort Morgan. The *Tennessee* surrendered after a desperate engagement with the enemy. Fleet Admiral Buchanan lost a leg, and is a prisoner. The *Selma* was captured. The *Gaines* was beached near the hospital. The *Morgan* is safe, and will try and run up to-night. The enemy's fleet has approached the city. A monitor has been engaging Fort Powell all day.

"D. H. MAURY, Maj. Gen."

It was over a week before Farragut himself was heard from.

(Monday, August 15, 1864)

From Mobile.

ADMIRAL FARRAGUT'S OFFICIAL REPORT OF OPERATIONS THERE.

Admiral Farragut makes a report to the Department, under date, "Mobile Bay, August 5, 1864," in which he states that on the morning of that day he entered Mobile Bay with the attacking fleet under his command—passing between Forts Morgan and Gaines, and encountering the rebel ram *Tennessee* and three of the enemy's gunboats.

At a few minutes past 7 a.m., Fort Morgan opened, and soon after the action became lively. At 40 minutes past 7 the monitor *Tecumseh* was struck by a torpedo and sunk, going down very rapidly, and carrying with her all of her officers and crew, with the exception of the pilot and eight or ten men, who were saved by a boat that was sent by the *Metacomet.*

The *Hartford* had passed the forts before 8 o'clock, and Admiral Farragut finding himself raked by the rebel gunboats, ordered the *Metacomet* to cast off and go in pursuit. This was done, and resulted in the capture of one of the gunboats—the *Selma.*

All the vessels had passed the forts by 8½ o'clock, but the rebel ram *Tennessee* was still apparently uninjured in the rear of our fleet.

Signal was at once made to all the fleet to turn again and attack the ram, not only with guns, but to run her down at full speed, which resulted in her surrender at 10 a.m.

The rest of the rebel fleet, viz.: *Morgan* and *Gaines,* succeeded in getting back under the protection of the guns of Fort Morgan. This terminated the action of the day.

Admiral Buchanan sent his sword to Admiral Farragut—he being wounded. The wound is a compound fracture of the leg, which, it is supposed, will result in amputation.

An arrangement was entered into by Admiral Farragut and the commanding officer of Fort Morgan whereby the wounded of both fleets, including Admiral Buchanan, were taken to Pensacola.

Our loss in the engagement, as far as heard from, is 41 killed and 88 wounded.

On the rebel ram *Tennessee* was captured 20 officers and say 170 men.

Commodore Porter's mortar boats, their masts camouflaged with branches, being towed into position within range of Forts St. Philip and Jackson.

☞ *With the sinking of the* Tecumseh *and the sighting of suspicious-looking buoys indicating torpedoes in the main approach channel, Farragut had grave doubts. At one point he is said to have muttered, "Oh God, shall I go on?" And then promptly answered his own question by shouting to the skippers of the* Hartford *and* Metacomet, *"Damn the torpedoes! Four bells! Capt. Drayton, go ahead; Jouett, full speed!" The admiral later reported to Navy Secretary Welles that he was fairly sure the torpedos were harmless since they probably had been in the water for a long time. It was a calculated risk that worked.* ☞

(Tuesday, August 16, 1864)

Official Recognition of the Gallant Achievements of Our Navy Before Mobile.

The following has been issued by Secretary Welles:

NAVY DEPARTMENT
WASHINGTON, August 15, 1864

SIR: Your dispatch of the 5th inst., stating that you had, on the morning of that day, entered Mobile Bay, passing between Forts Morgan and Gaines, and encountering and overcoming the rebel fleet, I had the satisfaction to receive this day. Some preliminary account of your operations had previously reached us through rebel channels.

Again it is my pleasure and my duty to congratulate you and your brave associates on an achievement unequalled in our service by any other commander, and only surpassed by that unparalleled naval triumph of the squadron under your command in the spring of 1862, when proceeding up the Mississippi you passed Forts Jackson and St. Phillip, and overcoming all obstructions captured New Orleans, and restored unobstructed navigation to the commercial emporium of the great central valley of the Union.

The Bay of Mobile was not only fortified and guarded by forts and batteries on shore, and by submerged obstructions, but the rebels had also collected there a formidable fleet, commanded by their highest naval officer—a former captain in the Union Navy—who, false to the Government and the Union, had deserted his country in the hour of peril, and leveled his guns against the flag which it was his duty to have defended. The possession of Mobile Bay, which you have acquired, will close the illicit traffic which has been carried on by running the blockade in that part of the Gulf, and gives point and value to the success you have achieved.

Great results in war are seldom obtained without great risks, and it was not expected that the possession of the harbor of Mobile would be secured without disaster. The loss of the gallant Craven and his brave companions, with the *Tecumseh* (a vessel that was invulnerable to the guns of Fort Morgan), by a concealed torpedo, was a casualty against which no human foresight could guard. While the nation awards cheerful honors to the living, she will ever hold in grateful remembrance the memory of the gallant and lamented dead, who perilled their lives for their country and died in her cause.

To you and the brave officers and sailors of your squadron, who participated in the great achievement, the Department tenders its thanks and those of the Government and country.

Very respectfully, &c.,

Gideon Welles, Sec'y of the Navy.
Rear Admiral David G. Farragut, Comd'g
West Gulf Blockading Squadron, Mobile Bay.

The fighting in Mobile Bay. In the center of the picture is the rebel ironclad ram *Tennessee*.

🔫 *With this applause, Farragut's long-delayed ambition was realized. Mobile itself would hold out until the end of the war, but the all-important harbor facilities would be barred for good from further Rebel use.* 🔫

WASHINGTON HOMEFRONT, AUGUST, 1864.

🔫 The Star *and one of its local competitors had a regretful announcement to make—and its nature has the all-too-familiar ring of modern times.* 🔫

NOTICE.—The proprietors of the EVENING STAR and NATIONAL REPUBLICAN, compelled by the unprecedented rise in the cost of publishing newspapers, have to announce that on and after Monday next, the 15th. of August, inst., the charge for their journals served from their offices to subscribers will be 12½ per week; to newsboys to sell again, and to persons served over their counters, three cents per copy. The cost of paper has increased 250 per centum since the commencement of the war, and all the other expenses of their offices have increased from one to three hundred per centum in the same time. . . .

🔫 *The municipal government, too, was having financial problems.* 🔫

WORTHY OF ATTENTION.—On Monday night a communication from the commissioners of the asylum and poor house was transferred to the Board of Aldermen relative to making the asylum and workhouse remunerative by compelling the inmates to labor.

The commissioners say that in the law made for the government of the asylum it is a fundamental principle that employment must be provided for all persons in the asylum capable of any species of labor. In order to carry out the law it is requisite that some one of the commissioners shall be authorized to apply funds appropriated by the corporation for the asylum to purchase raw materials, machinery, tool and implements, and to dispose of all articles made up, wove, spun, knitted, picked, or otherwise prepared.

The commissioners believe this could be done with much advantage to the corporation.

It is 17 years since the law was passed, and it is in effect a dead letter, when if properly carried out $50,000 might have been realized by workhouse la-

Admiral Farragut's flagship engaging the *Tennessee*.

bor. The name of workhouse as applied to the institution is a misnomer and the inmates spend their time in idleness, plotting mischief.

To carry out the recommendations of the Commissioners it will be requisite to have one of them designated to give his whole time to the superintendence of the work, with such additional remuneration as would be proper, and there is no doubt that the Corporation would be largely a gainer by the arrangement.

Not only could a large sum be gained by the labor, but the prisoners themselves would be benefitted by being kept out of idleness. Moreover, it would have the effect to keep away a host of lazzaroni who hate work and patronize the almshouse only so long as they can be boarded and lodged in idleness. This swarm of vagrants have been a terrible burden upon the Corporation, and by putting them to hard work as fast as they reach the almshouse they would hereafter give that institution a wide berth.

The communication of the Commissioners was referred to the asylum committee, which will, we trust, give the matter early attention.

PRESIDENT LINCOLN HAD BEEN NOMINATED BACK IN JUNE
for a second term in the White House. With the passage of months he
grew increasingly pessimistic about the outcome in November. There
had been progress on the battlefronts and at sea. But it was painfully
slow and costly in lives and treasure. The brightest hope of the year,
Grant's Army of the Potomac, seemed stalemated around Richmond
and Petersburg. In Georgia, the Confederate army was still intact, and
although Sherman's men were on the threshold of Atlanta, another
enervating siege and stalemate seemed in prospect. War-weariness in
the North—the South's best hope of victory—consequently was spreading. Even before that likely vote-getter, George Brinton McClellan, was
nominated for President by the Democrats late in August, Lincoln had
penned this despairing message:

"This morning (August 23), as for some days past, it seems
exceedingly probable that this administration will not be re-elected.
Then it will be my duty to so cooperate with the new President-elect
as to save the Union between election and inauguration, as he will have
secured his election on such ground that he cannot possibly save it
afterwards."

What Lincoln's administration needed more than anything
else at the moment was a military victory. Farragut's seizure of Mobile
Bay had been inspiring, but more than the stifling of another Confederate port was needed. The President's anguished eyes turned to central
Georgia.

There, in midsummer, the Confederacy's President Davis was
suffering agonies of his own. Never having got along with his Georgia
commander in the first place, he finally ran out of patience with Joe
Johnston's retreat tactics and sacked him. John Bell Hood took over,
and Confederate action at once became more aggressive. The odds, however, were the same against Hood as against Johnston. From July 20
to the end of August, the Rebels fought for their city from Peachtree
Creek and Ezra Church to Eastpoint and Jonesboro south of Atlanta.

The night of August 29, stores and ammunition in Atlanta lit
up the sky with flame and explosion.

SHERMAN IN ATLANTA, CITY AFLAME

(Saturday, September 3, 1864)

Official War Bulletins.

OUR FORCES IN POSSESSION OF ATLANTA.

A Battle at Eastpoint—Hood's Army Cut in Two.

WASHINGTON, Sept. 2—8 p.m.

Major Gen. Dix, New York:

This Department has received intelligence this evening that General Sherman's advance entered Atlanta about noon to-day.

The particulars have not yet been received, but telegraphic communication during the night with Atlanta direct is expected.

WASHINGTON, September 2, 10.45 p.m.

Major Gen. Dix, New York:

The following telegram from Major General Slocum, dated this day in Atlanta, and just received, confirms the capture of that city:

The Atlanta railroad depot after the flight of the citizens from the city.

Library of Congress

"General Sherman has taken Atlanta. The 20th corps occupies the city. The main army is on the main road near Eastpoint. A battle was fought near that point, in which General Sherman was successful. Particulars not known.

"H. W. Slocum, Major General."

An unofficial report states that in the battle fought near Eastpoint, by Maj. Gen. Sherman with Hood, the rebel army was cut in two, with very heavy loss to the enemy, and that Gen. Hardee was killed. Our loss is not known.

Edwin M. Stanton, Secretary of War.

🔫 *Hood's army evacuated the city the evening of September 1 after having put the torch to whatever supplies they couldn't take with them as they headed south toward Macon. Sherman gave pursuit to Lovejoy, but hesitated to attack the strong Confederate position there. The report of Hardee's death was erroneous. The Star must have regarded the news as too good to be true. Witness this series of reassuring reports from all over.* 🔫

The Entrance into Atlanta.

NASHVILLE, Sept. 2.—General Sherman's advance entered Atlanta this forenoon at 11 o'clock. The whole Federal force will enter to-day.

Early Rumors.

PHILADELPHIA, Sept. 2.—The Philadelphia *Evening Telegraph* has just received a dispatch from a source of the highest credit, dated Marietta Ga., stating that our advance guard entered Atlanta this morning.

LOUISVILLE, Sept. 2.—Brig. Gen. Ewing, commanding the Western District of Kentucky, has just received a telegram from the front, announcing that Gen. Sherman's advance guard entered Atlanta at 9 o'clock this morning. No further particulars.

🔫 *No doubts now. Here was word from the general in-chief, who had been reading Rebel newspapers and listening to other hearsay.* 🔫

Remains of the railroad roundhouse at Atlanta.

(Monday, September 5, 1864)

Official War Bulletins.

FROM SHERMAN.

Atlanta Ours—The Glorious News Confirmed.

WASHINGTON, Sept. 4, 1864

To Major General Dix, New York:

The following telegraphic despatch from Gen. Grant has just been received:

"CITY POINT, Sept. 2.—Hon. E. M. Stanton: I have a Richmond paper to-day. It contains a rumor of a battle at Atlanta, but says that, the War Department having no official information, it declines to form an opinion from the rumors. I have no doubt, however, but Sherman has gained a great success there.

"Before the despatch of last night was received, announcing the occupation of Atlanta by our troops, the fact was known to our pickets. The rebels hallooed over to our men that Sherman had whipped Hood; that the latter had lost forty thousand men, and that our troops were in Atlanta.

"All quiet here.

"U. S. Grant, Lieut. Gen."

Our southwestern telegraphic lines continue down, and this, with a heavy storm that commenced in the afternoon, and is still prevailing beyond Louisville, may damage the lines so as to hinder the arrival of details from Atlanta for a day or two.

Edwin M. Stanton, Secretary of War.

At last, a report from Sherman himself.

WASHINGTON, Sept. 4—8 p.m.

To Major General Dix, New York:

General Sherman's official report of the capture of Atlanta has just been received by this Department.

It is dated twenty-six miles south of Atlanta at 6 o'clock yesterday morning, but was detained by the breaking of the telegraphic lines mentioned in my dispatch of last night.

"As already reported, the army withdrew from about Atlanta, and, on the 30th, had made a break of the West Point road, and reached a good position from which to strike the Macon road, the right (Howard) near Jonesboro, the left (Schofield) near Rough-and-Ready, and center (Thomas) at Couch's.

"Howard found the enemy in force at Jonesboro, and intrenched his troops—the salient within half a mile of the railroad.

"The enemy attacked him at 3 p.m., and was easily repulsed, leaving his dead and wounded.

"Finding strong opposition on the road, I advanced on the left and center rapidly to the railroad, made a good lodgement, and broke it all the way

287

General Sherman (leaning on the cannon) and his staff in a Confederate gun emplacement at Atlanta.

from Rough-and-Ready down to Howard's left, near Jonesboro, and, by the same movement, I interposed my whole army between Atlanta and the part of the enemy entrenched in and around Jonesboro.

"We made an attack on the enemy at Jonesboro on the 1st of September, the 14th corps, Gen. Jeff. C. Davis commanding, carrying the works handsomely, with ten guns and about a thousand prisoners.

"In the night the enemy retreated south, and we have followed him to another one of his hastily constructed lines, near Lovejoy's Station.

"Hood at Atlanta, finding me on his road, the only one that could supply him, and between him and a considerable part of his army, blew up his magazines in Atlanta, and left in the nighttime, when the 20th corps, General Slocum, took possession of the place.

"So Atlanta is ours, and fairly won.

"Since the 5th of May we have been in one constant battle or skirmish, and need rest. Our losses will not exceed twelve hundred, and we have possession of over three hundred rebel dead, two hundred and fifty wounded, and over fifteen hundred well.

"W. T. Sherman, Major General."

A later dispatch from General Slocum, dated at Atlanta last night, 3 p.m., states that the enemy, on evacuating Atlanta, destroyed seven locomotives and eighty-one cars, loaded with ammunition, small arms, and stores, and left fourteen pieces of artillery, most of them uninjured, and a large number of small arms.

Deserters are constantly coming into our lines.

Edwin M. Stanton, Secretary of War.

Lincoln doubtless was more overjoyed than the following account would indicate.

(Monday, September 5, 1864)
OUR RECENT SUCCESSES. RECOMMENDATIONS BY THE PRESIDENT.

The President has issued sundry recommendations and orders in relation to the recent successes by the United States forces at Mobile and Atlanta, from which the following is extracted:

EXECUTIVE MANSION, Sept. 3, 1864.—The signal success that Divine Providence has recently vouchsafed to the operations of the United States fleet and navy in the harbor of Mobile, and the reduction of Fort Powell, Fort Gaines and Fort Morgan, and the glorious achievements of the army under Major General Sherman, in the State of Georgia, resulting in the capture of the city of Atlanta, call for devout acknowledgement to the Supreme being in whose hands are the destinies of nations. It is therefore requested that on next Sunday, in all places of public worship in the United States, thanskgiving be offered to Him for his mercy in preserving our national existence against insurgent rebels, who so long have been waging armed war against the Government of the United States, for its overthrow; and also that prayer be made for the Divine protection to our brave soldiers and their leaders in the field, who have so often and so gallantly perilled their lives in battling with the enemy," etc.

Apparently the fall of Atlanta was still doubted up North for some reason. Under a Louisville, Ky.

Federal wagon train makes a stop on Marietta Street in Atlanta.

dateline of September 8, The Star reported an account in which Sherman patiently recounted in more detail his earlier report to the War Department, and concluded with these words: 🔫

(Saturday, September 10, 1864)

". . . . I am now writing in Atlanta, so I could not be uneasy in regard to our situation.

"We have, as the result of this quick, and, as I think, well executed movement 27 guns, over 3,000 prisoners, and have buried over 400 rebel dead, and left as many wounded that could not be removed. The rebels have lost, besides the important city of Atlanta, stores, at least 500 dead, 2,500 wounded, and 3,000 prisoners; whereas our aggregate loss will not foot up 1,500. If that is not success, I don't know what is.

W. T. Sherman, Major General."

WASHINGTON HOMEFRONT, SEPTEMBER, 1864.

🔫 *Who today has not tasted a soapy brew, had difficulties with a mother-in-law, arrived at a drugstore too late, or squirmed over the high cost of food?* 🔫

SOAP VS. LAGER.—Yesterday, John Schantler, a brewer, lately employed by Herman Richter, near the Navy Yard, was arrested by officer Duvall, on the charge of malicious mischief, and he was taken up before Justice Cull, by whom the case was heard. Schantler had been employed by Richter for about nine months, but a short time since he was discharged. On Saturday last, Richter had turned about $200 worth of lager into a cooler, and it is alleged that the accused maliciously threw soap into the liquid, thereby spoiling it, and it was poured out. The justice, after the case was argued by Messrs. Bradley, jr., for the prosecution, and C. W. Walter for defense, held the accused to bail for his appearance at court.

General Sherman views Atlanta from a Confederate gun emplacement.

289

Remains of the railroad facilities in Atlanta. They were destroyed by the rebels before evacuation.

AN UNFEELING SON.—Mrs. Ann Doudle, 67 years old, was arrested on Monday by officer Skinner, on the charge of disorderly conduct, at the instance of her son, Robert, who it seems is married, and his wife cannot agree with the old woman who lives with them, and the son wishing to get rid of his mother preferred this charge, with the expectation that the mother would be sent to the workhouse, but Justice Boswell couldn't see it in that light, and dismissed the case, giving the son a lecture on filial affections.

A COMPLAINT.—*Editor Star:*—Will you please oblige one of your subscribers by inserting the following in your valuable paper?

"At 10 o'clock p.m., on the 11th inst., I had occasion to procure medicine for a person suffering in-tensely, but though I tried five different Drug Stores on Penn'a avenue, and after almost pulling the bells down at each of them, I could not obtain admission.

"Do these Druggists imagine that medicines are only required by the public during the time they please to keep their doors open?"

WASHINGTON, Sept. 12th.   Justice.

CENTER MARKET TO-DAY.—Beef, best cuts, per pound 30¢; next, 25¢. Veal, 20¢. Lamb, per pound, 25¢. Pork, fresh, 25¢. Pork, corned, 25¢. Bacon, hams, uncut, 30¢; sliced, 35¢. Chickens, per pair, $1. Ducks, per pair, $1.25. Eggs, per dozen, 30¢. Tomatoes, per peck, 50¢. Cymblins, per dozen, 25¢. Apples, per peck, new, 50¢; dried, $1. Potatoes, Irish per peck, 75¢. String Beans, per peck, 40¢.

JUBAL EARLY HAD BEEN DISCOURAGED FROM DOING ANY-thing serious around Washington by a show of greater force. That by no means took the fight out of him. Uncertainty and divided command among his Federal opponents encouraged him instead, after his retreat across the Potomac to Winchester in the Valley of Virginia. Less than three weeks following his departure from Fort Stevens, he was on the offensive again. He drove the Federals from Kernstown, wrecked the railroad yards at Martinsburg, and sent cavalry under Brig. Gen. John McCausland into Pennsylvania, where the town of Chambersburg was burned in reprisal for Federal depredations in the Valley earlier in the year. The Confederates also captured Hancock, Md., and threatened Cumberland farther west.

Early's game was entirely too serious to suit either Washington or General-in-Chief Grant. Despite the main effort around Richmond, something would have to be done about stopping Early and closing the Shenandoah forever as a route of Rebel invasion. Grant summoned his fair-haired boy, Phil Sheridan.

The fighting Irishman was willing. Washington, however, was wary. The War Department thought Early's army equaled Sheridan's 48,000. Sheridan actually outnumbered his foe two-to-one. Based on Harpers Ferry, the Federals showed little aggressiveness until September 19, when they attacked and defeated the Confederates at Opequon Creek near Winchester. Early backed farther up the Valley, only to be whipped again at Fisher's Hill. Thinking the Confederate menace in the Valley was over, Sheridan backed his army down the Valley to the vicinity of Strasburg.

It was a leisurely retreat, devoted to a systematic destruction of the Valley's capacity for supplying Confederate troops or otherwise giving aid and comfort to the Confederacy.

The Federal retreat gave Early renewed confidence. On October 19, after stealthy preparations, he took the enemy by surprise at Cedar Creek.

SHERIDAN CLEANS OUT THE SHENANDOAH

(Thursday, October 20, 1864)

EXTRA.
Another Great Union Victory.
SHERIDAN DEFEATS LONGSTREET!
Forty-Three Rebel Cannon Taken!

Official War Bulletin.
WAR DEPARTMENT,
October 20, 1864—10.45 A.M.

Major General Dix, New York:

A great battle was fought and a splendid victory won by Sheridan over Longstreet yesterday, at Cedar Creek. Forty-three pieces of artillery were captured and many prisoners, among whom was the rebel General (Stephan Dodson) Ramseur. On our side, Generals Wright and Ricketts were wounded; General (Daniel Davidson) Bidwell killed. Particulars, so far as received, will be forwarded as fast as the operator can transmit them.

Edwin M. Stanton, Secretary of War.

General Philip Sheridan

Library of Congress

It was a clear victory, but how Longstreet got into the picture is anyone's guess. Early was in charge all the way. Piecemeal reports received in Washington, meanwhile, gave a cliff-hanging aspect to the battle.

Official War Bulletin.

FULL PARTICULARS OF SHERIDAN'S GREAT VICTORY OVER LONGSTREET.

WAR DEPARTMENT,
WASHINGTON CITY, Oct. 20—10.30 a.m.

Major General Dix, New York:

Another great battle was fought yesterday at Cedar Creek, threatening at first great disaster, but finally resulting in a victory for the Union forces under General Sheridan, more splendid than any heretofore achieved.

The Department was advised yesterday evening of the commencement of the battle by the following telegrams:

"RECTORTOWN, Va., 4 P.M., Oct. 19, 1864.—
"Major Gen. H. W. Halleck, Chief of Staff:—
"Heavy cannonading has recommenced in the Valley, and is now going on.

"C. C. Augur, Major General."

"HARPER'S FERRY, Va., Oct. 19, 1864—6.40 P.M.—*"Hon. Edwin M. Stanton, Secretary of War:* —"Firing at front has been continuous during the day. The direction seemed at intervals to be to left of Winchester, as if at Berry's Ferry. No news from front.

"Jno. D. Stevenson, Brigadier Gen'l."

"HARPER'S FERRY, 8.45 p.m., Oct. 19, 1864. —*Hon. E. M. Stanton, Secretary of War:* The enemy attacked our army with great impetuosity this morning at daylight. The attack was made on left of Eighth Corps, and was at first successful, they capturing some guns, prisoners and wagons. Our line was reformed, and heavy fighting continued through the day.

Sheridan's men moving up the Shenandoah Valley.

"Sheridan, reported at Winchester this morning, went out to the front. The particulars received are not official, and are not favorable, though no serious disaster could have occurred without direct news from Sheridan.

"Respectfully,
"Jno. D. Stevenson, Brig. Gen."

Matters remained in the doubtful state represented by the foregoing telegrams, until this morning, at half-past nine, when the following telegram was received, unofficially reporting the great victory won by Sheridan's army:

"HARPER'S FERRY, VA., Oct. 20, 1864.— *Hon. Edwin M. Stanton, Secretary of War:* News from Sheridan's headquarters at midnight, to the effect that the enemy surprised our forces yesterday morning, driving the command in some confusion this side of Newton, capturing artillery and prisoners.

"Sheridan arrived on the field, reorganized our forces, and drove the enemy beyond Strasburg, capturing, it is reported, forty-three pieces of artillery, one hundred wagons and ambulances, and 2,000 prisoners. Rout of enemy said to be complete. This is not official, but I think reliable.

"J. D. Stevenson, Brig. Gen."

A few minutes later the following official report of his victory was received from Major General Sheridan:

"CEDAR CREEK, 10 p.m., Oct. 19, 1864.— *Lieut. Gen. Grant, City Point:* I have the honor to report that my army at Cedar Creek was attacked this morning before daylight, and my left was turned and driven in confusion. In fact, most of the line was driven in confusion, with the loss of twenty pieces of artillery. I hastened from Winchester, where I was on my return from Washington, and found the armies between Middletown and Newtown, having been driven back about four miles. I here took the affair in hand, and quickly united the Corps, formed a compact line of battle just in time to repulse an attack of the enemy, which was handsomely done at 1 p.m.

"At 3 p.m., after some changes of the cavalry from the left to the right flank, I attacked with great vigor, driving and routing the enemy, capturing according to last report, forty-three pieces of artillery and very many prisoners. I do not yet know the number of my casualties, or the losses of the enemy. Wagon trains, ambulances and caisons in large numbers are in our possession. They also burned some of their trains. Gen. Ramseur is a prisoner in our hands, severely and perhaps mortally wounded.

"I have to regret the loss of General Bidwell, killed, and Generals Wright, Grover and Ricketts wounded —Wright slightly wounded. Affairs at the time looked badly, but, by the gallantry of our brave officers and men, disaster has been converted into a splendid victory. Darkness again intervened to shut off greater results. I now occupy Strasburg. As soon as obtained, I will send you further particulars.

"P. H. Sheridan, Major General."

The battle was fought on the same day (19th of the month), that witnessed Sheridan's victory in September. What forces and their number were opposed to General Sheridan, are not yet reported to the Department, but the boldness, vigor, and success of the attack strongly indicate that a heavy reinforcement had been sent from Richmond, with the expectation of fulfilling Longstreet's boast to smash up

General Sheridan rallying Federal troops after his celebrated ride from Winchester.

Sheridan. Longstreet was known to be in the valley, and had assumed command of the rebel army, and confident hopes of an overwhelming disaster to the Union army were boastfully expressed for several days back by the rebel authorities in Baltimore and Washington.

E. M. Stanton, Secretary of War.

🔫 *The impact of the skillfully planned Confederate attack all but routed the Federals. Sheridan, who had been in Washington conferring with his chiefs, was in Winchester when the potential disaster was reported to him. With characteristic flamboyance, he mounted his horse, Rienzi, and raced the 20 or so miles to the battlefield, rallying his fleeing army as he rode. His personal leadership turned the tide.* 🔫

(Friday, October 21, 1864)

"CITY POINT, VA., Oct. 20, 1864, 8 p.m.—

"*HON. Edwin M. Stanton, Secretary of War:* I had a salute of one hundred guns from each of the armies here fired in honor of Sheridan's last victory. Turning what had bid fair to be a disaster into a glorious victory, stamps Sheridan, what I have always thought him, one of the ablest of Generals.

"U. S. Grant, Lieutenant General."

🔫 *The General-in-Chief had cause for celebration. Never again would the Rebels be a threat in the Shenandoah Valley.* 🔫

WASHINGTON HOMEFRONT, OCTOBER, 1864.

🔫 *Local news at this time spoke of civic improvements. And there were also the overtones of war.* 🔫

BRADY'S GYMNASIUM.—The fine gymnasium in progress of construction for some time for Mr. Brady, of New York Seventh Regiment Gymnasium renown, on Louisiana avenue, between Seventh and Tenth streets, was opened last evening for the inspection of a number of invited guests.

The visitors were some seven hundred in number of the elite of the city, including many ladies, who spent some time very much to their satisfaction in inspecting the superb rooms and apparatus, partaking of a fine collation meantime, and having an opportunity of enjoying the music of the Marine Band.

We have not space to-day to particularize all the notable features of this much-needed health-preserving establishment, but will mention that it is furnished with the following superior apparatus made of the best material: Four ladders each 20 feet long, two sets parallel bars 30 feet long, including poles, rack bars, peg pole, breast poles, horizontal bars, spring-board, batoute board, spool ropes, climbing ropes, single ring, leg machine, flying rings, double rings, stirrup rings, wrist weights, rowing machine, 3 sets pulley weights, flying cord, 220 dumb bells from 2 to 210 pounds, 100 Indian clubs or scepters, vaulting horse, spirometer; and for ladies, wooden dumb bells, wooden rings, wooden wands, small clubs, bags of beans, &c.

Eight hundred lockers with lock and key for members to keep their towel, change of clothing, &c. Four baths with hot and cold water, reading and chess rooms, with daily and weekly papers, books, &c. The gymnasium and its enterprising proprietor, Mr. Abner S. Brady, deserves abundant success.

———◆———

DEATH OF A WASHINGTONIAN.—Henry B. Middleton, son of Robert W. Middleton, Esq., of this city, died on the 29th of last month, at Augusta, Ga., as he was on his way with other paroled prisoners from Andersonville, Ga., to Richmond, where he was to have been exchanged. Mr. Middleton was Master-at-Arms on board of the United States mortar schooner "Dan Smith," and was captured on the 8th of September, 1863, at the storming of Fort Sumter. Mr. Middleton was well-known in the Northern Liberties, and leaves many friends in this city.

THE SCHOOL OF SECESSION.

The *Marlboro Gazette*, of last week, has a long obituary notice of "Lieut. Walter Bowie, C.S.A., who died on Friday, the 7th of October, 1864, from the effect of wounds received in a skirmish in the neighborhood of Sandy Spring," and who is elsewhere spoken of in the same obituary as "possessed of the most admirable and winning traits of character, quickness of intellect, readiness of apprehension, untiring energy, and an abundant capacity for any calling, giving him unusual promise of success in life."

Much of what is said of the deceased is doubtless true, but a sad illustration of what the rebellion is doing for just such young men, is afforded in the fact, stripped of the varnish of friendly eulogy, that young Bowie was killed by a shot-gun in the hands of a Montgomery county farmer, while he, (Bowie), with other C.S.A. young men of "manly and gentle qualities," were endeavoring to beat a retreat, after robbing a country store of its calicoes, needles, and spool cotton!

THE FALL OF ATLANTA, AND SHERIDAN'S CONQUEST AND devastation of the Shenandoah Valley, brought a new and badly needed upsurge of support for Lincoln's administration. Still, the President and the Republican Party leaders were far from convinced that military victories alone meant he would be re-elected in November. They resorted to time-honored methods of vote-getting. Federal patronage was stepped up with a vengeance. Known wrong-thinkers were sacked. To win the support of the influential New York *Herald,* Lincoln named its editor, James Gordon Bennett, minister to France. Postmaster General Montgomery Blair got the ax because of his wide unpopularity with leading Party members. His departure was part of a horse trade in which John Charles Fremont, who had been nominated for the Presidency by the radical wing of the Party, withdrew from the field. In the October state elections in Ohio, Pennsylvania and Indiana, measures were taken to get out as much of the soldier vote as possible, on the theory that the boys who were bleeding for the Union would vote for their old Commander-in-Chief. Sherman went so far as to furlough thousands of Indiana troops from the Georgia campaign to go back home and vote. The Lincoln candidates won. Despite the party efforts and the omens, Lincoln was still worried.

On election day, November 8, 1864, Washington seemed a deserted town, with so many of its residents gone back to the States to vote. Even the White House seemed abandoned by the usual horde of official visitors and individual favor-seekers. Later in the day, Lincoln took up his vigil in the War Department telegraph office just west of the White House grounds. The election returns started clattering in. *The Star* had a special editorial the same day.

LINCOLN RE-ELECTED IN LANDSLIDE

EDITORIAL.

(November 8, 1864)

The Presidential Election.

The day of the Presidential election, an interesting one always to Americans, is made especially so on its recurrence this 8th day of November, 1864, by the deep importance of the issues at stake.

Disguise the fact as politicians may for their own purposes, there is no denying that the fate of the Union depends upon to-day's vote. Shall our leaders in the Cabinet and the field, whose sole purpose is the suppression of the rebellion, and who have so nearly completed the good work, be endorsed and sustained; or shall the reins of government be given (virtually) to those who are plotting not only for a dishonorable abandonment of the contest, but who are scheming for the disruption of the North into petty confederacies on the Jeff Davis plan?

That is the plain issue. Not that there are not patriotic men arrayed on the side of the opposition, but that in the event of the defeat of Mr. Lincoln and the election of General McClellan, the men of the Wood and Vallandigham stripe would be in the ruling spirits, and would dictate the policy of the administration.

The effort to defeat Mr. Lincoln is the last throw of the dice with Jeff. Davis; and the imperative necessity to the Confederate cause of his defeat, is shown in the desperate efforts being made by Davis' agents in the North to carry the election by gigantic frauds, oath-bound conspiracies, border raids, &c., &c.

But all these desperate schemes have providentially been thwarted in season, and have returned to plague the inventors; and to-day all the indications point to an orderly, peaceable election. And with the election so conducted there cannot be a doubt— especially if the fall elections are any index—of the re-election of Abraham Lincoln by a majority that will give joy and courage to loyal hearts everywhere, and cause a corresponding discouragement to the enemies of the Union, North, South and throughout the world.

☞ The next day, a Page One headline in the Star *proclaimed the news. ☜*

The "wigwam" in Evansville, Indiana where Lincoln supporters rallied during the campaign.

National Archives

THE OLD BULL DOG ON THE RIGHT TRACK.

(Wednesday, November 9, 1864)

THE PRESIDENTIAL ELECTION.

Abraham Lincoln Re-elected by an Overwhelming Majority.

Confusion to Copperheads and Traitors Everywhere.

☞ The two-column story that followed gave a state by state tabulation of early vote counts. Another half-column listed the returns from military installations in and around Washington—and the soldier vote was overwhelmingly in favor of Lincoln. More up-to-the-minute news appeared, customarily, on Page Two, showing more firmly the outcome.

LATEST ELECTION RETURNS.
New York All Right, by 10,000 for Lincoln.

NEW YORK, Nov. 9.—The *Tribune* claims New England, Pennsylvania, Delaware, New York, Maryland, Ohio, Indiana, Michigan, Illinois, Wisconsin, Minnesota, Iowa and Kansas for Lincoln. Total, one hundred and nineteen, independent of the Pacific States, which, it says, have probably chosen eleven Lincoln electors. It claims over 10,000 majority in the State of New York, and that a sufficient number of members of Congress are gained in the Union to secure the requisite two-thirds in the House of Representatives for the prohibition of slavery by constitutional amendment.

It makes the New York Congressional delegation stand twenty-two Union and nine Democrats.

The *World* concedes Lincoln's re-election, claiming only New York, Kentucky, New Jersey and Missouri for McClellan, with Pennsylvania, Delaware, Oregon, California and Nevada in doubt, but most likely for Lincoln.

The New York *Times* claims one hundred and thirty-three electoral votes for Lincoln, with a probability of all the remainder, excepting Kentucky, Missouri and probably New Jersey.

☞ It would be several days before the final tally could be made and reported. Lincoln and his new running-mate, Andrew Johnson, a Democrat staunchly loyal to the Union and the Lincoln Administration, garnered 2.2 million votes, a 400,000 plurality over the McClellan-William H. Pendleton ticket. Every State but Kentucky, Delaware and New Jersey went for Lincoln. The electoral vote margin was 212 to 21. Long before the final count was reported, the President was being toasted in Washington. ☞

(Friday, November 11, 1864)

REJOICING OVER THE ELECTION.
Serenades to President Lincoln and His Cabinet.

Last evening, the various Republican clubs, according to the announcement in this paper, formed a procession on Ninth street, and accompanied by several fine bands of music, proceeded to pay a congratulatory visit to President Lincoln and the various members of his Cabinet.

The procession was formed in front of the Union League Rooms on Ninth street, the right being taken by the Giesboro Club, which was preceded by Col. Ekin and the officers of the Cavalry Bureau. This club bore in their line two handsome transparencies, and had with them two bands—one the headquarters band lately from Carlisle Barracks, and the other the band of the third division of Camp Stoneman. They had about 450 men in line, marshaled by Messrs. Prevost, R. Woodburn, and R. Morgan.

The Republican Club (Central) numbering several hundred, marshaled by Messrs. G. H. Plant and T. B. Brown came next, and was followed by the East Washington, which numbered about 500 men under the marshalship of Messrs. Hutchinson, Beron and Dulin. This club had with them two howitzers manned by men of the gunners department of the Navy Yard, which during the progress of the procession were fired at intervals. Healds American Brass Band and a band of field music were with this club.

In this order the procession proceeded up Pennsylvania avenue, large crowds of persons following it, and by the time they reached the President's residence the space in front was blocked up completely, and hundreds of people in their eagerness to get a view of the President and hear what he might say, clambered to every available point of eminence clinging there at no little inconvenience.

After the immense crowd had gathered in front of the White House, several pieces of music were per-

Library of Congress

formed in superb style by the bands, and a spirited salute was fired from the howitzers, and then in response to the loud call from the assemblage, President Lincoln appeared and spoke as follows:

THE PRESIDENT'S SPEECH.

Friends and Fellow-Citizens: It has long been a grave question whether any government not *too* strong for the liberties of its people can be strong *enough* to maintain its own existence in great emergencies. On this point the present rebellion brought our Republic to a severe test; and a Presidential election, occurring in regular course during the rebellion, added not a little to the strain.

If the loyal people *united* were put to the utmost of their strength by the rebellion, must they not fail when *divided,* and partially paralyzed by a political war among themselves?

But the election was a necessity. We cannot have free government without elections; and if the rebellion could force us to forego or postpone a national election, it might fairly claim to have already conquered and ruined us. The strife of the election is but human nature practically applied to the facts of the case. (Voices in the crowd, "That's so!") What has occurred in this case must ever recur in similar cases. Human nature will not change. In any future great national trial, compared with the men of this, we shall have as weak and as strong, as silly and as wise, as bad and as good.

Let us, therefore, study the incidents of this, as philosophy to learn wisdom from, and none of them as wrongs to be revenged.

But the election, along with its incidental and undesirable strife, has done good too. It has demonstrated that a people's government can sustain a national election in the midst of a great civil war. (Enthusiastic cheers.) Until now, it has not been known to the world that this was a possibility. It shows also how sound and how strong we still are. It shows that, even among candidates of the same party, he who is most devoted to the Union, and most opposed to treason, can receive most of the people's votes. (Long-continued applause.) It shows also, to the extent yet known, that we have more men now than we had when the war began. Gold is good in its place, but living, brave, patriotic men are better than gold. (Applause.)

But the rebellion continues; and now that the election is over, may not all, having a common interest, reunite in a common effort to save our common country? (Cries of "Yes," "Good.") For my own part, I have striven, and will strive, to avoid placing

299

Library of Congress

President Abraham Lincoln. His family selected this photo as the best likeness of him.

any obstacle in the way. So long as I have been here, I have not willingly planted a thorn in any man's bosom.

While I am deeply sensible to the high compliment of a re-election, and duly grateful, as I trust to Almighty God, for having directed my countrymen to a right conclusion, as I think, for their own good; it adds nothing to my satisfaction that any other man may be disappointed or pained by the result. (Applause.)

May I ask those who have not differed with me to join with me in the same spirit towards those who have?

And now, let me close by asking three hearty cheers for our brave soldiers and seamen, and their gallant and skilful commanders.

The cheers were given by the vast crowd assembled, and were heartily repeated.

The remarks of the President, so judicious, patriotic and appropriate, were received with tremendous applause by the assemblage, and they lingered as if hoping to hear further from him, and then, with three rousing cheers for "Abraham Lincoln," they took up their line of march to the residence of the Secretary of State. . . .

🔫 *Perhaps it was only the President's gloomy turn of mind, but on election night he recalled a dream that came to him just after his election in 1860. As he lay exhausted on the sofa of his Springfield living-room, he chanced to see his reflection in a mirror on the opposite wall. His image seemed double, and one was paler than the other. When he arose, it disappeared, only to reappear as soon as he lay down again. Troubled, he told his wife about it. Mary Lincoln was unnerved by the vision. She took it as a sign that her husband would be elected to two terms of the Presidency, but would not survive the second. Of more immediate moment, the re-election evoked a sigh of relief from the battlefront.* 🔫

(Friday, November 11, 1864)
Congratulatory Dispatch from Gen. Grant.
He Congratulates the President on a Double Victory.

CITY POINT, Nov. 10, 1864, 10:30 P.M.

Hon. Edwin M. Stanton, Secretary of War:

Enough now seems to be known to say who is to hold the reins of government for the next four years. Congratulate the President for me for the double victory. The election having passed off quietly—no bloodshed or riot throughout the land—is a victory worth more to the country than a battle won. Rebeldom and Europe will so construe it.

U. S. Grant, Lieut. Genl.

WASHINGTON HOMEFRONT, NOVEMBER, 1864.

🔫 *Election day was hardly over, and the returns only preliminary—but some of the more enthusiastic Washingtonians couldn't wait for the next dawn to hail the chief.* 🔫

SERENADE TO PRESIDENT LINCOLN.— About half-past one o'clock this morning President Lincoln was serenaded by a club of loyal Pennsylvanians. Being loudly called for, the President appeared at a window and said:

Friends and Fellow-Citizens: Even before I had been informed by you that this compliment was paid me by loyal citizens of Pennsylvania friendly to me, I had inferred that you were of that portion of my countrymen who think that the best interests of the nation are to be subserved by the support of the present Administration. I do not pretend to say that you who think so embrace all the patriotism and loyalty of the country, but I do believe, and, I trust, without personal interest, that the welfare of the country *does* require that such support and indorsement be given.

I earnestly believe that the consequences of this day's work (if it be as you assure, and as now seems probable) will be to the lasting advantage, if not to the very salvation of the country. I cannot at this hour say what has been the result of the election. But whatever it may be, I have no desire to modify this opinion, that all who have labored to-day in behalf of the Union organization, have wrought for the best interests of their country and the world, not only for the present but for all future ages.

I am thankful to God for this approval of the people; but, while deeply gratified for this mark of their confidence in me, if I know my heart, my gratitude is free from any taint of personal triumph. I do not impugn the motives of any one opposed to me. It is no pleasure to me to triumph over any one. But I give thanks to the Almighty for this evidence of the people's resolution to stand by free government and the rights of humanity.

One troop outfit around the city grew indignant over an erroneous report.

HOW THE SOLDIERS GO.—*Editor Star:* The vote of Co. "K," 150th Pennsylvania volunteers, for President, is as follows:

Lincoln and Johnson, sixty-five, (65), McClellan and Pendleton, none, (0).

I wish this published in your paper as I see it wrongly stated that there was one McClellan vote cast in our ranks.

At the Cliffburn Barracks, the voting of the Pennsylvania soldiers resulted in 44 for Lincoln and 7 for McClellan.

The best in professional entertainment was coming to town.

BENEFIT FOR CHERRY BELLE.—Charming, graceful, piquant, musical Cherry Belle, whose name is fit synonym of her attractiveness, is to have a complimentary benefit at Canterbury [Hall] on Friday next, which will attract all her host of admirers, and these will form a host in themselves. She will appear in her great part of the French Spy, and a fine general bill will be presented on the interesting occasion. We advise all who can to be on hand on Friday, and see and hear this bewitching actress and songstress.

The Cherry Belle blurb appeared as a news item. An adjacent ad, by some coincidence, elaborated on the lady's program, which included such "rich comedy" specialties as "Chair-ology" and "Frangipanni Fitzpoodle," obviously of the stuff to roll 'em in the aisles. And the ghost of a battle passed over the local scene.

TO BE PAID.—It will be recollected that at the first battle of Bull Run a number of carriages, hacks, &c., on the ground were taken possession of by the military, (the occupants who had gone out to see the fight being compelled to walk in,) to bring in the wounded, and while in the service of the Government some of them were damaged or lost. The owners, numbering about 50, have had their claims allowed and are to receive the amounts due them at the Treasury Department.

We understand that the Government, in the settlement of these claims, have allowed $6 per day for hack, horses and driver—the trip occupying three days. Some of the hack owners interested say that they will not receive this money, but will appeal to Congress at the next session, alleging that their teams were so badly used up by the trip that they had to lay by for several days.

Among these claims are also those of parties who had their carriages pressed in service at the second battle of Bull Run.

SHERMAN'S THRUST INTO GEORGIA WAS INVINCIBLE. OR was it? The Rebels under Hood were still an army in being, and they were still long on courage, their strongest asset throughout the war. They still had Bedford Forrest's cavalry far back in the Federal's rear. Where Forrest rode, there rode danger. Even before the Yankees took Atlanta, Forrest was prowling Tennessee, threatening Sherman's slim line of supply. Other Federal forces moved out with specific orders to get the master cavalryman. But he always seemed to be the one on the offensive. At one point he struck his pursuers in a typically brilliant manner at Brice's Cross Roads, midway between Corinth and Tupelo, Miss., and routed their superior numbers. Later, he swept northward to Memphis to throw another scare into Federal authorities.

With Atlanta gone, and Hood's army moving west and north through Alabama, Forrest was called in from his raiding operations and incorporated into Hood's command. For Hood had a counterstroke that rivaled one of Robert E. Lee's for audacity. He would get Sherman off Georgia's back by driving into Tennessee, and perhaps all the way to the Ohio River. With luck, he might even be able to spare part of his army to march eastward from Kentucky or Tennessee, through Virginia, to fall upon the Yankees around Richmond and Petersburg.

Sherman saw the potential threat to his army's rear. But he had no intention of calling off his Georgia push and heading his army back to Tennessee. Instead, he sent back the reliable Thomas, and about one-third of the Georgia force, to thwart Hood's invasion scheme while Sherman resumed his main drive to the coast.

While Thomas busied himself in Nashville whipping together an assortment of green troops and veterans from other theaters, the job of delaying Hood's northward march fell to Schofield, who had about 32,000 troops to hold off better than 50,000 Confederates. Although his army had a couple of nearly disastrous brushes with the enemy—chiefly in the form of Forrest's troopers—Schofield conducted an effective delaying action from Pulaski, Columbia and Spring Hill in southern Tennessee as he fell back toward Nashville and the gathering Federal strength. Hood kept applying pressure, and it was with relief that the Federals, on November 29, reached the prepared defenses of Franklin, less than 20 miles south of Nashville.

THOMAS CRUSHES REBELS AT NASHVILLE

(Thursday, December 1, 1864)

Very Important from the West!

HOOD'S ARMY DISASTROUSLY REPULSED.

A Union Victory Yesterday!

The following highly important and gratifying despatch has just been received here. It illustrates the wisdom of the recent movement of the army under General Thomas, which the gold grumblers and secesh sympathizers construed into a retreat:

FRANKLIN, TENN., NOV. 30, 1864.

Major Gen'l Thomas:

The enemy made a heavy and persistent attack with about two corps, commencing at about 4 this afternoon, and lasting until after dark. He was repulsed at all points, with very heavy loss, probably five or six thousand men.

Our loss is probably not more than one-tenth that number.

We have captured about 1,000 men, including one Brigadier General.

(Signed,)   Schofield.

Hood, on reaching the open ground before Franklin late in the afternoon, had not hesitated. He threw about two-thirds of his army—some 27,000 men—against the Federal entrenchments. Angered by unsuccessful attempts to flank Schofield earlier in the campaign, Hood ordered a direct frontal assault. The battle lasted until well after nightfall, grim determination marking the fighting on both sides.

(Friday, December 2, 1864)

LATER FROM THE SOUTHWEST.

NASHVILLE, Dec. 1.—Parties who arrived from the front, who were witnesses of the battle yesterday, describe the attack of the rebel forces as desperate. Four charges were made upon the Federal line of masked batteries, in a body four lines deep; each time the rebels were repulsed with fearful loss. The fort is on the north bank of the river, opposite the town. Extending up the river, and encircling the town, was a line of masked batteries. Eyewitnesses say this engagement, in desperation and furious fighting, was hardly equalled by the battle of Stone River. Forrest in person was in the field rallying his men.

A rumor is in circulation that he was killed, but it lacks confirmation.

About seven o'clock last night heavy reinforcements reached Schofield, which caused a complete rout of the rebel forces. The city to-day is full of fleeing residents of Williamson and other counties south. They state that Hood is gathering all the horses, hogs, and mules he can find, and sending them South. There is a great panic among the negroes in the counties south of Nashville; large numbers are fleeing to the city for protection.

ANOTHER GREAT BATTLE EXPECTED.

NASHVILLE, Dec. 1.—The Federal forces under General Thomas retired from Franklin last

General James Harrison Wilson, who commanded the Federal cavalry at the battles of Franklin and Nashville.

National Archives

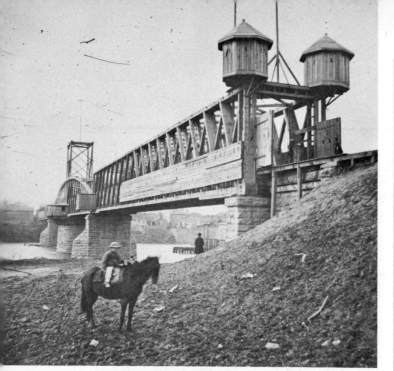

A fortified bridge over the Cumberland River.

night, and have taken a position and formed in line of battle south of Nashville about three miles.

Skirmishing has been going on all day about five miles south of here. Heavy cannonading can be distinctly heard in the city.

No want of confidence is felt by the citizens in the ultimate success of the Federals.

The employees of the Quartermaster's Department are under arms and in the trenches.

One hundred and seven Confederate officers, including one brigadier general, and one thousand prisoners arrived in this city this morning. They were captured last night near Franklin, Tenn.

A great battle may be momentarily expected.

The Federal outer line at Nashville.

DETAILS OF THE CONFLICT.

NEW YORK, Dec. 1.—A special dispatch to the *Herald*, dated Nashville, December 1, 1.40 p.m., says: About noon Wednesday our main army reached Franklin, when Gen. Schofield prepared to give battle. There was very little skirmishing, as Hood's object was to attack us before we had time to throw up defensive works. About 4 o'clock in the evening he commenced advancing on our lines, when the battle opened by our batteries shelling their advance, and some time after, regular cannonading opened along the whole line.

The rebels, who had been protected by the woods, now emerged from cover, and opened with a fierce volley of musketry along our lines, and then charged. For a moment part of our line wavered and fell back before the desperate charge of the enemy. Generals Ruher and Cox, however, rallied their men, and charged the enemy, who had crossed over our abandoned line of works. The rebels were now fighting with the desperation of demons, charging our line furiously, some leaping our works, and fighting hard.

Now was the critical moment, and our generals, rallying their men, swung on the rebel flank, doubling them in the center, where our artillery and musketry mowed them down by hundreds. The tide now turned. Our men, inspired by success, gave a wild huzza, and swept back on the rebel line like an avalanche, hurling the enemy back in the wildest disorder and confusion.

The night was now setting in, and yet we followed up our advantage. What once threatened to be a disastrous defeat was thus turned into a glorious victory. The courage of our officers and the desperate courage of our men was unexampled. Our loss is about seven hundred killed and wounded. We captured over one thousand prisoners and eight battle flags. Two rebel brigadier generals are in our hands. A rebel division general was left on the field mortally wounded. The rebel loss in killed and wounded is estimated at three thousand.

The rebel Generals Cheatham's and Lee's corps were engaged.

The brunt of the battle on our side fell on the 2d division of the 4th corps. Captain Coughlin, of General Cox's staff, was killed, and several regimental commanders and officers killed and wounded whose names are not ascertained.

General Stanley was slightly wounded in the neck, but did not leave the field. General Cox states that one could walk fifty yards on the dead rebels in his front.

The excitement is allayed here by the knowledge of the above facts. Our troops have taken a position in the line works between Nashville and Franklin.

🔫 *The Confederate assault was probably more courageous than the final charge at Gettysburg—if that were possible. The men had to advance across two miles of open field without help from artillery, against a strongly fortified position manned by veterans. The casualty toll was more than 6,000, including six generals killed. Pat Cleburne, one of the best of division commanders, was among the dead. The battle over, Schofield moved his men out of the town and back to Nashville. Weakened though he was, Hood followed, but in front of the Nashville works concluded he lacked strength to attack. His troops dug in just south of the city, while Thomas spent two weeks gathering his own strength and methodically preparing an attack to end all attacks. He was ready with nearly 50,000 effectives in mid-December. On the 15th, he swung his hammer-blow against a force one-half that number. 🔫*

(Friday, December 16, 1864)
Official Report by General Thomas of the Battle before Nashville.
A Brilliant Union Victory!
Fifteen Hundred Prisoners Captured and 17 Pieces of Artillery!
NEARLY THE WHOLE LINE OF THE ENEMY'S EARTHWORKS CAPTURED.

WAR DEPARTMENT, WASHINGTON, D.C., Dec. 16, 1864, 9.15 a.m.

Major General Dix, New York:

The following official report of the battle before Nashville has been received from Major Gen. Thomas:

"NASHVILLE, Tenn., 9 p.m., Dec. 15, 1864.— Attacked enemy's left this morning, and drove it from the river below the city very nearly to Franklin pike—distance about eight miles. Have captured Chalmers' headquarters and trains, and a second train of about twenty wagons, with between eight hundred and a thousand prisoners, and sixteen pieces of artillery. Troops behaved splendidly—all taking their share in assaulting and carrying the enemy's breastworks. I shall attack enemy again to-morrow, if he stands to fight, and if he retreats during night will pursue him, throwing heavy cavalry force in his rear to destroy his trains if possible.

"Geo. H. Thomas, Major General."

🔫 *Thomas had struck both of Hood's flanks and folded them in. The next day, as Thomas had promised, the Federals hit the shrunken Confederate positions with another set of massive blows. 🔫*

(Saturday, December 17, 1864)
EXTRA.
GLORY!!!
VICTORY!!!
Hood Smashed Up and Done For.
GREAT BATTLE YESTERDAY.
General Thomas' Official Report.
THE ENEMY UTTERLY ROUTED.

WAR DEPARTMENT, WASHINGTON CITY, D.C. Dec. 17, 8:35 a.m.

Major General Dix, New York:

The following official report of the great victory achieved yesterday by Major General Thomas and his gallant army, over the rebel forces under General Hood, in front of Nashville, was received this morning. One of the most surprising circumstances connected with this great achievement is the small loss suffered by our troops, evincing, among other things, the admirable skill and caution of General Thomas in his disposition of the battle. In our rejoicings at the defeat of the enemy, thanks are due to the Almighty for His protection to our gallant officers and soldiers in the great conflict they have passed through. The report of General Thomas, and also an unofficial report, containing interesting details, are subjoined.

Edwin M. Stanton, Secretary of War.

"HEADQUARTERS DEPARTMENT CUMBERLAND, *Eight miles from Nashville,* 6 p.m., Dec. 16.—

To the President of the United States, Hon. E. M. Stanton and Lieut. Gen. U. S. Grant: This army thanks you for approbation of its conduct yesterday, and to assure you that it is not misplaced.

"I have the honor to report that the enemy has been pressed at all points to-day in his line of retreat to the Brentwood Hills. Brig. Gen. Hatch, of Wilson's corps of cavalry, on the right, turned the enemy's left, and captured a large number of prisoners—number not yet reported.

Federal troops charge a rebel entrenchment at Nashville.

"Maj. Gen. Schofield's corps, next on the left of the cavalry, carried several hills, captured many prisoners and six pieces of artillery. Brevet Maj. Gen. Smith, next on left of Maj. Gen. Schofield, carried the salient point of the enemy's line with McMillan's brigade, of McArthur's division, capturing sixteen pieces of artillery, two brigadier generals and about 2,000 prisoners.

"Brigadier General Garrard's division, of Smith's command, next on the left of McArthur's division, carried the enemy's entrenchments, capturing all the artillery and troops on the line.

Major General Schofield
National Archives

"Brigadier General Wood's troops, on the Franklin pike, took up the assault, carrying the enemy's entrenchments, in his retreat captured eight pieces of artillery, something over six hundred prisoners, and drove the enemy within one mile of the Brentwood Hill Pass.

"Major General Steedman, commanding detachments of the different armies of the Military Division of Mississippi, most nobly supported General Wood's left, and bore a most honorable part in the operations of the day.

"I have ordered the pursuit to be continued in the morning at daylight, although the troops are very much fatigued.

"The utmost enthusiasm prevails. I must not forget to report the operations of Brig. Gen. Johnson in successfully driving the enemy, with the co-operation of the gunboats under Lieut. Commander Fitch, from their established batteries on the Cumberland river, below the city of Nashville, and of the success of Brig. Gen. Croxton's brigade in covering and returning our right and rear. The operations of yesterday and to-day, although I have no report of the number of prisoners captured by Johnson's and Croxton's command, I know they have made a large number.

"I am glad to be able to state that the number of prisoners captured yesterday greatly exceeds the number reported by telegraph last evening. The woods, fields and entrenchments are strewn with the enemy's small-arms abandoned in their retreat. In conclusion, I am happy to state all this has been effected with but a very small loss to us.

"Our loss probably does not exceed three hundred, and very few killed.

"Geo. H. Thomas, Maj. Gen."

"NASHVILLE, TENN., 9 p.m., Dec. 16, 1864. —During last night Hood withdrew his right from river and took new position covering Hillsboro', Granny White, and Franklin Pikes, which line had been carefully prepared for just this contingency. He was driven from the first line easily, but the second was stubbornly defended, and at last heavily assaulted three times before succeeding.

"It was carried, however, and twenty pieces of artillery, two thousand men, including Gen. Jackson with the remnant of his division, were taken, the enemy forced back two miles, and his army broken into two parts, one on the White pike and the other on the Franklin with range of bluffy hills between them, Steedman and Wood pressing down the latter —A. J. Smith, Schofield and the cavalry down the former. Small arms lay as thick on the contested line as the rebels had stood there.

"Hood can't make another such day's fight while Thomas is in good condition to press him.

"Caught more wagons—can't say number. Everybody, white and black, did splendidly."

🔫 *Nashville ranks with the most brilliantly planned, executed and decisive battles of the war. For the first time, a major Confederate army had been routed, its effectiveness as a fighting force ended. The retreat of Hood's brave remnants, scantily clothed and half-starved, through the freeze and floods back across the Tennessee River; the gallant rear-guard actions by a few against many pursuers, evoked this praise from the man who had smashed them: "Ragged, bloody, without food and without hope (Hood's army was) undaunted, firm and doing its work bravely to the last."* 🔫

WASHINGTON HOMEFRONT, DECEMBER, 1864.

🔫 *There was sport, culture and civic improvement in Washington as befitted the capital of a growing though war-torn Nation.* 🔫

MR. BENSON, of the National Hotel, came up from the Lower Potomac on Tuesday with one hundred and seventy-seven wild ducks, the fourth instalment for this season, which has thus far given six hundred against two thousand five hundred for the entire season last year. In his last remittance there is a good proportion of canvas-backs, which were becoming numerous up to the commencement of the present Indian Summer days, when they suddenly disappeared.

———◆———

ANOTHER WARNING TO CHILDREN.—On yesterday, (the hour of recess,) whilst the pupils of Secondary School, No. 2, First District—Miss H. H. Slater, teacher—were playing bandy, one of them, Wm. Wise, who lives on 11th street, between F and G, was run over by a street car, crushing one of his legs and foot in such a manner that it is feared amputation will be necessary. The teachers of this build-

Nashville as seen from the steps of the state capital.

ing have repeatedly cautioned the children on the danger of playing in the streets.

🔫 *Horse-drawn street cars had been introduced in Washington in 1862. Their average speed was four miles an hour.* 🔫

———◆—◆———

CONCERT BY THE BLACK SWAN.—The renowned colored vocalist known as the Black Swan (Miss E. T. Greenfield) will give her first grand concert on Monday evening, December 5th, at the Fifteenth-street Presbyterian Church, on which occasion she will be assisted by four of her pupils. The concert will be for the benefit of the church, and we trust will be well attended.

———◆—◆———

METROPOLITAN STREET RAILWAY.—It is expected that this road will be put in operation next week from the Capitol to 17th street. Two of the cars have already arrived, and are now at the Baltimore and Ohio Depot. Twenty have been ordered to be placed on the road immediately, and they are rapidly being finished in the shop at Philadelphia. They are of the style, peculiar to that city known as the box car, and are similar in style to those made by Murphy and Allison, running on the Avenue. They are tastefully finished in cream color and green, the sides being of the latter color, and inside are velvet cushions of the same color. Along the upper portion are the words "City Hall, Patent and Post Offices, Willard's, Treasury, War and Navy Departments," and on the sides, in gilt letters, "H and F streets, from 17th to Capitol and Baltimore Depot," while the center of the sides is embellished with ornamental paintings. They are of the usual size, and will seat comfortably twelve on a side.

It is contemplated to run by the last of this week, but iron sufficient to finish the track is not now on hand, and the company may be disappointed for a few days, but they are using every exertion to make good their promise to run the cars by the 10th inst.

I CAN MAKE THIS MARCH, AND MAKE GEORGIA HOWL."
So wired Sherman from Atlanta in October 1864 to his chief in Virginia. He was asking Grant's permission to take the bulk of the Federal army in Georgia from Atlanta to the Atlantic. He was content to let Thomas handle Hood's Tennessee invasion. For himself, Sherman would sever all his communications with the outside world, pack a month's supplies in wagons and knapsacks, and head for Savannah where communications could be re-established through the blockade fleet, under Adm. John Adolph Dahlgren, patrolling the harbor. Other supplies, as might be needed, would be taken from the countryside. Although it was the kind of thing Grant himself had done in his Vicksburg campaign, he was nonetheless taken aback by the risks involved. If Sherman's calculations proved wrong, as Southerners expected, the projected march to the sea might turn into a debacle that would end the war short of union. Grant had faith in his chief lieutenant, however, and assented.

So, for a month, Sherman gathered the necessary supplies for his force of 60,000, ripped out the rail and telegraph lines between Atlanta and the nearest Federal base at Chattanooga, and destroyed Atlanta. On November 16, his army disappeared into Central Georgia, and to Northerners it was as if Georgia had swallowed him. The Union government and its people would not hear from him again—except for accounts in Southern newspapers—for more than a month.

SHERMAN ENDS SEA MARCH; SAVANNAH FALLS

(Tuesday, December 27, 1864)

SAVANNAH TAKEN.
The City Occupied on the 21st.

33,000 Bales of Cotton, 150 Heavy Guns, 800 Prisoners, 190 Railroad Cars, 13 Locomotives, 3 Steamers, and a Large Quantity of Ammunition—Escape of Hardee and His Army—Their Flight Across the River—Rebel Iron Clads Blown Up—The Navy Yard Destroyed—The City Uninjured—Our Flag Waving Over It.

WAR DEPARTMENT,
WASHINGTON, D.C., December 25.

Major General Dix, New York:

A despatch has been received this evening by the President from General Sherman. It is dated at Savannah, on Thursday, the 22d inst., and announces his occupation of the city of Savannah, and the capture of one hundred and fifty heavy guns, plenty of ammunition, and about twenty-five thousand bales of cotton. No other particulars are given.

An official despatch from General Foster to General Grant, dated on the 22d inst., at 7 p.m., states that Savannah was occupied by General Sherman on the morning of the 21st and that on the preceding afternoon and night Hardee escaped with the main body of his infantry and light artillery, blowing up the iron-clads and the navy yard. General Foster enumerates as captured eight hundred prisoners, one hundred and fifty guns, thirteen locomotives in good order, one hundred and ninety cars, a large supply of ammunition and materials of war, three steamers, and thirty-three thousand bales of cotton.

No mention is made of the present position of Hardee's force, which had been estimated at about fifteen thousand (15,000.) The despatches of General Sherman and General Foster are as follows:

"SAVANNAH, Ga., December 22, 1864.

"To His Excellency, President Lincoln:

"I beg to present you, as a Christmas gift, the city of Savannah, with one hundred and fifty heavy guns and plenty of ammunition; and also about twenty-five thousand (25,000) bales of cotton.

"W. T. Sherman, Major General."

🖝 *The army had actually reached the outskirts of the city December 10, and three days later captured one of its coastal forts, thus making contact with the Federal fleet. The troops had left a swath of devastation 50 miles wide and 300 miles long. All*

General Sherman's army entering Savannah on the 21st of December.

public property was destroyed, including that of the capital, Milledgeville. The area was swept clean of food, livestock and material useful to an army on the march. Though discipline was generally strict, hoodlums—"bummers" they were spitefully called—made needless depredations on private property as well. The conduct of the campaign would always be damned by many and justified by many—the latter recognizing the concept of total war. The defenders, with their pitifully outnumbered 13,000 veterans and green militia, could do little to deter the invaders. 🔫

"STEAMER GOLDEN GATE,
Savannah River, 7 p.m., Dec. 22, 1864.

"To Lieutenant General U. S. Grant and Major General H. W. Halleck:

"I have the honor to report that I have just returned from General Sherman's headquarters in Savannah. I send Major Grau, of my staff, as bearer of despatches from General Sherman to you, and also a message to the President.

"The city of Savannah was occupied on the morning of the 21st. General Hardee, anticipating the contemplated assault, escaped with the main body of his infantry and light artillery, on the afternoon and night of the 20th, by crossing the river to the Union causeway opposite the city.

"The rebel iron clads were blown up, and the Navy Yard burned. All the rest of the city is intact, and contains twenty thousand citizens, quiet, and well disposed. The captures indicate eight hundred (800) prisoners, one hundred and fifty (150) guns, thirteen (13) locomotives in good order, one hundred and ninety (190) cars, a large supply of ammunition and materials of war, three steamers, and thirty-three thousand bales of cotton safely stored in warehouses. All these valuable fruits of an almost bloodless victory have been, like Atlanta, fairly won.

"I opened communication with the city with my steamers to-day, taking up what torpedoes we could see, and passing safely over others. Arrangements are made to clear the channel of all obstructions.

Yours, &c.,
"J. G. Foster, Major General."

🔫 *Sherman had been resigned to laying siege to the city. Although the place was fortified, Hardee realized his scraped-together force of 15,000 wouldn't have a chance. In moving out, he headed north through the swamp country. The people of Savannah, for their part, received some advice.* 🔫

Library of Congress

General Hugh "Kill Cavalry" Kilpatrick, commander of Sherman's cavalry on his march to the sea.

(Thursday, December 29, 1864)

NEWS FROM REBEL SOURCES.

The Occupation of Savannah—A Rebel Paper's Appeal—Magnanimity of Sherman.

(From the Savannah *Republican*, Dec. 21.)

TO THE CITIZENS OF SAVANNAH.

By the fortunes of war, we to-day pass under the authority of the Federal military forces. The evacuation of Savannah by the Confederate army, which took place last night, left the gates to the city open, and General Sherman, with his army, will no doubt to-day take possession.

The Mayor and Common Council leave under flag of truce this morning for the headquarters of General Sherman, to offer the surrender of the city and ask terms of capitulation by which private property may be respected.

We desire to counsel obedience and all proper respect on the part of our citizens, and to express the belief that their property and persons will be respected by our military ruler. The fear expressed by many that General Sherman will repeat the order of expulsion from our homes which he enforced against the citizens of Atlanta, we think to be without foundation. He assigned his reason in that case

311

House used as headquarters in Savannah by General Sherman.

as a military necessity. It was a question of food. He could not supply his army and the citizens with food; and he stated that he must have full and sole occupation. But in our case food can be abundantly supplied for both army and citizens. We would not be understood as even intimating that we are to be fed at the cost of the Federal Government, but that food can be easily obtained; in all probability, by all who can afford to pay in the Federal currency.

It behooves all to keep within their houses until General Sherman shall have organized a provost system and such police as will ensure safety to persons as well as property.

Let our conduct be such as to win the admiration of a magnanimous foe, and to give no ground for complaint or harsh treatment on the part of him who will for an indefinite period hold possession of our city.

In our city there are, as in other communities, a large proportion of poor and needy families, who, in the present situation of affairs, brought about by the privations of war, will be thrown upon the bounty of their more fortunate neighbors. Deal with them kindly, exercise your philanthropy and benevolence, and let the hearth of the unfortunate not be deserted by your friendly aid.

WASHINGTON HOMEFRONT, DECEMBER, 1864.

A SALUTE IN HONOR OF THE FALL OF SAVANNAH.

By order of the Secretary of War, a salute of three hundred guns—well charged—was fired at eight o'clock yesterday morning from Franklin Square, in honor of the fall of Savannah, by a battery sent in from Camp Barry, especially for the purpose.

Yesterday morning, at about 6 o'clock, 12 guns went out from the camp of instruction, at the turnpike gate, on the Bladensburg road, to the intersection of Massachusetts avenue and N street, where 200 rounds were fired by them in honor of Sherman's great victory at Savannah.

RIVER NEWS.—The Potomac river is still covered with ice, and the channels are frozen over, although the Government tug Pacific succeeded this morning in cutting her way through two-inch-and-a-half ice from the 7th street wharf to the ice-bound boats off Giesboro Point.

Yesterday afternoon, about half-past three o'clock, the mail boat *Daniel Webster*, Captain

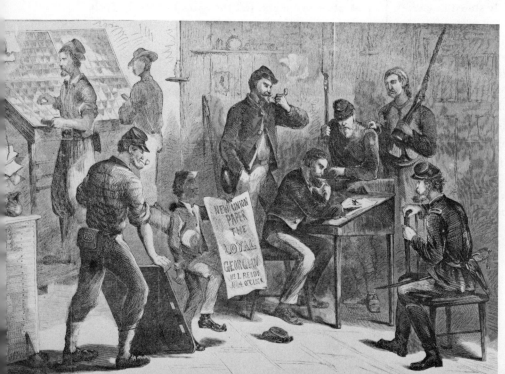

Three days after Sherman's army entered Savannah the occupying forces published the first issue of the *Loyal Georgian* newspaper.

A view of the Savannah waterfront.

Charles Deering, which was caught in the ice off Giesboro on Thursday morning, was pulled out by a tug boat, (after her passengers had walked ashore, among whom was Capt. Wm. Colklesser, Acting Assistant Commissary of Subsistence of the armies operating against Richmond,) but immediately afterwards she ran aground, and is now fast again . . .

———◆———

TERRIBLE SCARE AND GRAND STAMPEDE AT THE GOVERNMENT PRINTING OFFICE.—Yesterday morning, at about 10 o'clock the hot water pipes in the second story of the above-named building burst, causing a loud and rushing noise, something similar to the noise made by blowing off steam from a large steam boiler; when the great number of girls in the room (who are engaged folding documents, &c.,) stampeded, supposing the boiler had burst in the press room, and made a grand rush for the doors, some fainting before they reached it, and tumbling pell-mell down two pairs stairs, which caused an alarm in the composing room, when most of the men ran as manfully as did the girls, and it was with great difficulty that the more self-possessed could prevent some of the panic-stricken males and females from throwing themselves over the stair banisters and from the windows. A couple of men in the composing room applied to earnest prayer for deliverance and many were the embraces and farewells between young and old, male and female, who felt sure they were going into eternity then and there. To make the matter worse, on reaching the pavement the heels of many took an upward flight, in consequence of the ice, and numbers were quite seriously injured, and some had to be taken home in conveyances. One of the compositors was run over by about thirty men and girls before he could gain his feet, and another, in making his way out, broke three of his ribs to the best of his knowledge and belief. Some of the girls lost their underskirts and others their what-do-you-call-'ems; but none would consent to confess proprietorship when some of the gentlemen bashfully inquired for the owners.

The break in the pipe was soon fixed, and all who were able resumed work, rejoiced to find themselves still alive and kicking.

313

W ITH THE CAPTURE OF MOBILE BAY, THE CONFEDERACY had but one port left. That port, Wilmington, N.C., was one too many for the Federal government. There were two reasons for applying the stopper to it. The most obvious was to bring an end to the commerce of blockade-runners which, as late as 1864, still managed to slip in and out through tricky channels past the Federal blockade fleet. The other stemmed from Sherman's arrival at Savannah. Now that Sherman had made it to the sea and his new path led through the Carolinas, the high command decided he might need some help on the way. Wilmington in Federal hands would enable reinforcement by sea. In order to possess Wilmington, its guardian, Fort Fisher, at the mouth of the Cape Fear River, had to be taken.

One of the strongest fortifications built during the entire war, Fisher suddenly was given top priority as a target toward the close of 1864. For the amphibious assault, Adm. Porter was called in from the West, and Ben Butler reassigned from the Virginia theater. Grant, in making the selection of commanders, was enthusiastic about Porter, his Navy teammate in the Vicksburg campaign. He was deeply skeptical of Butler, but Butler had strong political connections. As Grant expected, Butler ruined the whole operation by laggardly timing and a theory that the fort could be seized without a close-in attack.

Porter's outrage and public indignation freed the administration's hands. Butler was dismissed, and a soldier, Maj. Gen. Alfred Howe Terry, named to succeed him. Porter and Terry gave a cooperative performance.

AMPHIBIOUS ASSAULT CLOSES LAST REBEL PORT

(Tuesday, January 17, 1865)

GLORIOUS!!

Fort Fisher Carried by Storm!!

Seventy-Two Guns Captured and Twenty-Five Hundred Taken Prisoners!

The following news, just received by the Navy and War Departments, is glory enough for one day:

FORTRESS MONROE, January 17.

Hon. Gideon Welles, Secretary of the Navy:

The Atlantic is just in from Wilmington.

Fort Fisher and works on Federal Point are in our possession.

The assault was made by the army and sailors on Sunday afternoon, and by 11 p.m. the works were ours.

Losses heavy. Lieuts. S. W. Preston and B. H. Porter, of the navy, are killed.

Our captures are seventy-two guns and about twenty-five hundred prisoners.

Generals Whiting and Lamb, rebels, are prisoners, and wounded.

The Vanderbilt is on her way, with dispatches.

Two fifteen-inch guns were burst on the monitors.

E. T. Nichols, Commander, &c.

The fortifications were mighty, and were manned by 2,500 defenders. But Porter's 60 warships (600 guns) bombarded the position for 36 hours, knocking most of the defending cannon out of action. During and after the bombardment, some 8,000 soldiers, sailors and marines landed and advanced from the land side. Porter was almost rhapsodic in his dispatch to Washington.

The Capture of Fort Fisher.
OFFICIAL DISPATCH FROM ADMIRAL PORTER.
The Army and Navy Hand in Hand in the Glorious Victory.

The following dispatch has been received by the Navy Department from Admiral Porter:

(By telegraph from Fortress Monroe.)

OFF FORT FISHER, Jan. 15, 1865.—*Hon. Gideon Welles, Secretary of the Navy:*— Sir: Fort

Heavy bombardment falling on Fort Fisher, North Carolina, from the Federal ships in the background.

The final assault on Fort Fisher by Federal troops.

Fisher is ours. I send a bearer of dispatches with a brief account of the affair. General Terry is entitled to the highest praise and the gratitude of his country for the manner in which he has conducted his part of the operations. He is my *beau ideal* of a soldier and a general. Our co-operation has been most cordial. The result is victory, which will always be ours when the army and navy go hand in hand. The navy loss in the assault was heavy. The army loss is also heavy.

D. D. Porter, Rear Admiral.

☞ *The fort surrendered January 15. But the assault preparations had been made no easier by the whims of Nature, as the admiral made clear.* ☜

Admiral Porter's Official Report of the First Day's Fight Before Fort Fisher.

The following has been received at the Navy Department:

FLAGSHIP MALVERN, *Off Fort Fisher, N.C.,* Jan. 15, 1865.—Sir: I have the honor to inform you that operations have been resumed against the forts at the entrance of Cape Fear river.

Since the first attack on that place, and the subsequent withdrawal of the troops, I have been employed in filling the ships with ammunition and coal. The difficulties we have had to encounter, no one can conceive. All our work had to be done with the larger vessels anchored on the coast, exposed (you may almost say at sea) to the violent gales that blow here almost incessantly. On these gales the enemy depend to break up our operations. We will see. We

have gone through about the worst of it; have held on through gales heavy enough to drive anything to sea, and we have sustained no damage whatever.

After the troops arrived, the weather set in bad and the gale was very heavy. As soon as it was over I got underway on the 12th instant, and forming the vessels in three lines, with the transports in company, I steamed for Fort Fisher.

On the morning of the 13th, the fleet took its station in three lines, close to the beach, and the boats were sent at once to take off the troops. These were landed, with about twelve days provisions, at two o'clock p.m.

This time I pursued a different plan in attacking the rebel works. I went in the *New Ironsides,* Commodore Radford, leading the monitors *Saugus, Canonicus, Monadnock,* and *Mahopac.*

At 7:30 a.m. the forts opened on them as they approached, but they quietly took up their old position, within 1,000 yards of Fort Fisher, and when ready, they opened their batteries. In this way I tempted the enemy to engage the monitors, that we might see what guns he had, and seeing where they were, be able to dismount them by our fire.

Quite a spirited engagement went on between the fort and the Ironsides and the monitors. It was soon apparent that the iron vessels had the best of it; traverses began to disappear, and the southern angle of Fort Fisher commenced to look very dilapidated.

The guns were silenced, one after the other, and only one heavy gun in the southern angle kept up its fire.

The fire of this gun was not all accurate, as it inflicted no damage on the iron vessels. They were hit though, several times.

By way of letting the enemy know that we had some shell left on board the wooden ships, and did not wish to take any unfair advantage of him by using the iron vessels alone, I ordered line No. 1 (on the plan,) lead by Capt. Alden, of the *Brooklyn* and line No. 2, lead by Com. Thatcher, of the *Colorado,* to go in and attack the batteries. This was done in the handsomest manner, not a mistake was committed except firing too rapidly and making too much smoke.

The heavy fire of the large vessels shut up the enemy's guns at once, and after firing until after dark; the wooden vessels dropped out to their anchorage. The Ironsides and monitors maintained their positions through the night, firing a shell now and then.

They are now lying one thousand yards off the fort, and one of the monitors within seven hundred yards, and the fort does not fire a gun at them, thinking, no doubt, that it is a waste of powder.

The firing from the fleet will commence as soon as we get breakfast, and be kept up as long as the ordnance department provides us with shells and guns.

There is a perfect understanding between General Terry and myself. I believe everything has been done to suit him. I have heard no complaints, and know that we have felt every disposition to help the army along.

A detailed report of our operations will be sent in when we get through. I see no reason to doubt our success. The forts will be used up soon. We have a respectable force landed on a strip of land, which our naval guns completely command, and a place of defense which would enable us to hold on against a very large army.

I will report to you by every opportunity.

I have the honor to be, very respectfully, your obedient servant,

David D. Porter, Rear Admiral.

HON. GIDEON WELLES, Secretary of the Navy, Washington, D. C.

Porter apparently couldn't get over the success of the operation, and the unity of the armed services which had made success possible.

(Wednesday, January 18, 1865)
The Fall of Fort Fisher.
BRAVERY OF OUR SOLDIERS AND SAILORS.
Graphic Account of the Fight.

The following has been received at the Navy Department:

U. S. FLAGSHIP MALVERN, OFF FORT FISHER, Jan. 15, 1865.—*Sir:* I have the honor to inform you that we have possession of Fort Fisher, and the fall of the surrounding works will soon follow. As I informed you in my last, we had commenced operations with the iron vessels, which bombarded while we landed the troops. On the 14th instant I ordered all the vessels carrying eleven-inch guns to bombard the Ironsides—the *Brooklyn* taking the lead. By sunset the fort was reduced to a pulp—every gun was silenced by being injured or covered up with earth, so that they would not work.

On the 15th, General Terry and myself arranged for the assault, and I ordered 1,400 sailors and marines to participate. At daylight, the iron vessels, *Brooklyn,* and eleven-inch gunboats commenced battering the work, while the troops made a lodgment within 150 yards of the fort. At ten o'clock, all the vessels steamed in and took their stations, opening a heavy fire, which was kept up till three p.m., when the signal was made to assault, the soldiers taking the land side, and the sailors the sea face—the ships changing (but not stopping) their fire to other works.

The rebels met us with a courage worthy of a better cause, and fought desperately. About thirty of the sailors and officers succeeded in getting to the top of the parapet, amidst a murderous fire of grape, canister and musketry. They had planted the flag there, but were swept away in a moment. Others tried to get up the steep "pan crupee." The marines could have cleared the parapets by keeping up a steady fire, but they failed to do so, and the sailors were repulsed.

Many a gallant fellow fell trying to emulate their brothers in arms who were fighting to obtain an entrance on the northeast angle, as it appears on our chart.

The enemy mistook the seamen's attack for the main body of troops, and offered a most vigorous resistance there; but I witnessed it all, and think the marines could have made the assault successful.

In the meantime, our gallant soldiers had gained a foothold on the northeast corner of the fort, fighting like lions, and contesting every inch of ground.

The Ironsides and monitors kept throwing their shells into the traverses not occupied by our men, but occupied by the rebels.

In this way our troops fought from traverse to traverse, from 3 o'clock in the afternoon until 10 in the night, when the joyful tidings were signalled to the fleet, we stopped our fire and gave three of the heartiest cheers I ever heard.

It has been the most terrific struggle I ever saw, and very much hard labor. The troops have covered themselves with glory, and Gen. Terry is my *beau ideal* of a soldier and a General.

Our co-operation has been most harmonious, and I think the General will do the Navy the credit to say that this time at least we "substantially injured the fort as a defensive work." General Terry had only a few more troops than we had on the last occasion, when the enemy had only 150 men in the works—this time the works were fully manned, and contained about 800 men at the time of the assault.

It is a great regret to me to see my gallant officers and men so cut up, but I was unwilling to let the troops undertake the capture of the works without the navy's sharing with them the peril all were anxious to undergo, and we should have had the honor of meeting our brothers in arms in the works had the sailors been properly supported. We have lost about 200 in killed and wounded, and amongst them some gallant officers.

I regret to announce the death of Lieut. S. W. Preston and Lieut. B. H. Porter. They were both captured together in the attack on Fort Sumter, and died together in endeavoring to pull down the flag that has so long flaunted in our faces.

David D. Porter, Rear Admiral.

WASHINGTON HOMEFRONT, JANUARY, 1865.

🔫 *Men were still being drafted, no matter how doomed the Confederacy seemed. And things were being done to make the draftee's lot easier.* 🔫

DRAFT MEETING.—The citizens of the Second Ward met last Saturday evening, at German Hall, 11th street, for the purpose of forming an association by which to protect themselves from the coming draft.

Mr. Spaulding, from the committee appointed at the last meeting to draft a constitution and by-laws under which to form an association, reported the following, which was adopted:

The constitution provides that the association shall be called the "Second Ward Draft Mutual Aid Association," and shall be composed of the citizens of the Second Ward, for the purpose of aiding those who may be drafted of its members; the officers to consist of a president, secretary, and treasurer, to serve until the quota is filled. Any one of the ward can become a member by paying twenty dollars initiation fee, and two dollars dues thereafter per week. It provides that any citizen of the ward may become a member by paying not less than five dollars into the fund.

At the time of the first draft, under the late call for 300,000 men, each member drafted and credited to the quota of the ward shall be entitled to an equal division of two-thirds of all the money in the hands of the treasurer, and his membership to cease, the rest of the money to be reserved and the weekly contributions of those members who are not then drafted as a fund for those who may be drafted at a second draft under the call, who will be entitled to two-thirds of the money then on hand, the same rule to apply to all drafts made under the present call: *provided,* the amount received by any member shall not exceed the cost of his substitute at the time he may be drafted. Any member who may be, at the time of any draft, two weeks or more in arrears, shall forfeit his membership in, and all aid from, the association.

🔫 *And the hucksters were trying to make milady's life easier.* 🔫

Interior of Fort Fisher after its surrender.

SHERMAN'S MARCH NORTHWARD FROM SAVANNAH through the swamps of Georgia and South Carolina was anything but easy, even though the Confederate opposition was negligible. However, his troops minded little for they were driving toward the heart of secessionism. The closer they got to Charleston and Columbia, the lighter the Federal invaders' burden seemed to become. If they had made Georgia suffer, South Carolina was going to suffer more. The path the Federal soldiers cut through South Carolina has been likened to that of the Goths through ancient Rome.

Looking southward and all around him in Richmond, President Davis could see doom fast approaching. He agreed to suggestions for a peace conference, but he was a stubborn man, declaring that any peace agreement would have to be predicated on continuing a separate Confederacy. The peace conference held aboard President Lincoln's *River Queen,* February 3, at Hampton Roads, Va., was attended by Lincoln but not by Davis. Just as firmly as the absent President of the Confederacy held to his views, the President of the United States insisted that peace must be predicated on Union of all the States. The conference, naturally, failed.

War remaining the order of the day, Davis made an appointment he might well have made months before. On February 9, he named Robert E. Lee general-in-chief of the Confederate army. Lee, still holding on firmly to his Richmond-Petersburg defenses, proceeded to marshal such resources as the Confederacy had left. The odds seemed hopeless, but Lee was still a fighting general.

Sherman, too, had purpose and capacity to fight. Three days behind the actual event, *The Star* shouted "GLORIOUS NEWS!" about the events in South Carolina.

SHERMAN TAKES COLUMBIA, CHARLESTON

(Monday, February 20, 1865)

SHERMAN'S TRIUMPHANT MARCH.

The Fall of Columbia.

PROBABLE EVACUATION OF CHARLESTON.

WAR DEPARTMENT,
WASHINGTON, February 18, 1865.

Major General Dix:

The announcement of the occupation of Columbia, South Carolina, by General Sherman, and the probable evacuation of Charleston, has been communicated to this Department in the following telegrams just received from Lieutenant General Grant.

EDWIN M. STANTON, Secretary of War.

"CITY POINT, Feb. 18, 1865.—*Hon. Edwin M. Stanton, War Department:* The Richmond *Dispatch* of this morning says Sherman entered Columbia yesterday morning, and its fall necessitates, it presumes, the fall of Charleston, which it thinks likely is already being evacuated.

U. S. GRANT, Lieutenant General.

"CITY POINT, VA., Feb. 18.—*Hon. Edwin M. Stanton, War Department, Washington:* The following is taken from to-day's Richmond *Dispatch:*

"The Fall of Columbia, South Carolina.

"Columbia has fallen. Sherman marched into and took possession of the city yesterday morning. This intelligence was communicated yesterday by General Beauregard in an official dispatch.

"Columbia is situated on the north bank of the Congaree river, just below the confluence of the Saluda and Broad rivers.

"From Gen. Beauregard's despatch it appears that on Thursday evening the enemy approached the south bank of the Congaree and threw a number of

The city of Columbia in flames after occupation by Federal troops.

Library of Congress

The Union flag is planted on Fort Sumter after occupation of the city of Charleston by Federal troops. The city is in flames in the background.

shells into the city. During the night they moved up the river, and yesterday morning forded the Saluda and Broad. While they were crossing these rivers our troops under Gen. Beauregard evacuated Columbia. The enemy soon after took possession.

"Through private sources we learn that two days ago, when it was decided not to attempt the defence of Columbia, a large quantity of medical stores, which it was thought impossible to remove, were destroyed. The female employees of the Treasury Department had been previously sent off to Charlotte, N. C., a hundred miles north of Columbia. We presume the Treasury lithographic establishment was also removed, though as to this we have no positive information.

"The fall of Columbia necessitates, we presume, the evacuation of Charleston, which we think likely is already in process of evacuation.

"It is impossible to say where Sherman will next direct his columns. The general opinion is that he will go to Charleston and establish a base; but we confess we do not see what need he has of a base. It is to be presumed he is subsisting on the country, and he has had no battle to exhaust his ammunition.

"Before leaving Savannah he declared his intention to march to Columbia, thence to Augusta, thence to Charleston. This was uttered as a boast to hide his designs.

"We are disposed to believe that he will next strike at Charlotte, which is a hundred miles north of Columbia, on the Charlotte and Columbia railroad, or at Florence, S. C., the junction of the Columbia

and Wilmington and the Charleston and Wilmington railroads, some ninety miles east of Columbia.

"There was a report yesterday that Augusta had also been taken by the enemy. This we do not believe. We have reason to feel assured that nearly the whole of Sherman's army is together at Columbia, and that the report that Schofield was advancing on Augusta is untrue.

"Removed.

"The Charleston *Mercury* of Saturday announces a brief suspension of that paper, with a view to its temporary removal to another point. This is rendered necessary by the progress of military events, cutting it off from the mail facilities for distributing its paper to a large portion of its subscribers, while the lack of transportation renders its supply of paper precarious.

"Semmes has been made a rear admiral, and will take command of the James river squadron."

U. S. Grant, Lieut. Gen.

No attempt was made to defend the State capital. In fact, the 40,000 Confederates—mostly untried militia—who opposed the Union forces, had been uncertain whether the Federals would strike Columbia or Charleston. The Rebels gathered, consequently, between the two cities, where they were in a position to help neither. Most of Columbia was destroyed by fire. Did the Yankees apply the torch, or did the flames spread from fires started by the Confederates to keep supplies from Sherman's hands? The Federals, in any case, battled the flames, and Sherman later turned over quantities of food to the stricken populace. The predictions concerning Charleston's fate proved well-founded, as reports in a follow-up story the same day showed. 🔫

GLORIOUS NEWS!
CONFIRMATION OF THE EVACUATION OF CHARLESTON!
Official War Bulletin.

WAR DEPARTMENT,
February 20, 1865, 12.40 p.m.

Major General John A. Dix, New York:

The evacuation of Charleston by the rebels is announced in the following telegram just received from Gen. Grant.

E. M. Stanton, Secretary of War.

CITY POINT, VA., Feb. 20.—*Hon. Edwin M. Stanton, Secretary of War:* The following dispatch just received.

U. S. Grant, Lieut. General.

The Richmond *Examiner* of to-day, just received, says Charleston was evacuated on Tuesday last.

(Signed,)   G. Weitzel, Major General.

🔫 *The sources for details of the news of Charleston's fall were highly unofficial, but had an authoritative sound.* 🔫

(Tuesday, February 21, 1865)
Particulars of the Evacuation of Charleston.

THE REBELS FIRE THE CITY.
Six Thousand Bales of Cotton Burned.
THE REBELS BLOW UP THEIR IRONCLADS IN THE HARBOR.
The Union Flag over Charleston and All the Forts.

NEW YORK, Feb. 21.—The steamship *Fulton,* Captain Norton, from Port Royal and Charleston Bar on the 18th at 6 p.m., arrived here this morning.

Purser Tim McManus furnishes us with the following memoranda:

Charleston was evacuated by the enemy on the night of the 17th, leaving the several fortifications uninjured, besides 200 guns, which they spiked.

The evacuation was first discovered at Fort Moultrie, in the morning, at 10 a.m. Part of the corps stationed on James Island crossed over and took possession of the city without opposition. The upper part of the city was on fire.

The blockade runner *Cyrene,* just arrived from Nassau, fell into our hands, and two others which were expected to run out on the night of the 18th.

Charleston in ruins.

Library of Congress

The first flag over Fort Sumter was raised by Captain Henry M. Bragg, A.D.C. on General Gillmore's staff, having for a staff an oar and boat hook lashed together.

The houses in the lower part of the city were completely riddled by our shot and shells.

The wealthy part of the population have deserted the city, and now all that remains are the poorer classes, who are suffering from a want of food.

It was reported at Hilton Head that the left wing of Sherman's army had reached midway on the Charleston and Augusta Railroad, and that the rebels in consequence had evacuated Branchville and fallen back on Orangeburg. A movement had been made by the force under General Hatch which resulted in the capture of six pieces of artillery, which the rebels had abandoned. The carriages were destroyed.

Previous to the evacuation, the enemy fired the upper part of the city, by which 6,000 bales of cotton were burned, and it is supposed that two-thirds of the city would be destroyed before the flames could be subdued.

A fearful explosion occurred in the Wilmington depot, cause unknown, by which several hundred citizens lost their lives. The building was used for commissary purposes, and was situated in the upper part of the city.

Admiral Dahlgren was the first to run up to the city, where he arrived about two o'clock p.m.

Gen. Q. A. Gillmore followed soon after, in the steamer *W. W. Colt,* and had an interview with General Schemmelfinnig, he being the first general officer in the city, and for the present in command.

It is supposed that Beauregard evacuated Charleston in order to concentrate and give Sherman battle.

The remains of the two iron clads were found which the enemy destroyed by blowing them up previous to the evacuation.

The Savannah *Herald* contains no news of a military character.

A fire at Hilton Head destroyed the office of Captain Pratt, ordnance officer, and at one time greatly jeopardized a building containing large supplies of ammunition, but it fortunately escaped.

🖙 *Quincy Adams Gillmore was the commander on Morris Island, where the opening guns of the Civil War had been fired four years before on the Fort Sumter relief ship,* Star of the West. *The Federals under Gillmore had occupied the island for more than a year, periodically bombarding Fort Sumter and Charleston itself to no especial effect. Gillmore finally was able to give Washington official word.* 🖙

Full Confirmation of Our Glorious Successes at Charleston!
THE CITY SURRENDERS TO GEN. GILLMORE ON SATURDAY.

WAR DEPARTMENT,
Washington D.C., 2 p.m., Feb. 21, 1865

Maj. Gen. John A. Dix, New York:

This Department has received the official report of Major General Gillmore announcing the surrender of the city of Charleston, S. C., to the United States forces under his command at 9 o'clock Saturday morning, the 18th inst. Among the captured property are two hundred pieces of good artillery and a supply of fine ammunition. The enemy burned their cotton, warehouses, arsenals, quartermaster's stores, railroad bridges, two iron-clads, and some vessels in the ship-yard.

E. M. Stanton, Secretary of War.

🖙 *With these desperate developments in South Carolina, Lee quickly made an appointment preparatory to a final showdown in North Carolina and Southern Virginia. Joe Johnston was brought out of military limbo to face Sherman.* 🖙

WASHINGTON HOMEFRONT, FEBRUARY, 1865.

🖙 *The capital, sensing final victory over the horizon, found cause for cheer at every hand.* 🖙

DEPARTMENT OF STATE,
WASHINGTON, February 21, 1865.

The Department Buildings will be illuminated on the night of Washington's birthday in honor of the recent triumphs of the Union.

By order of the President:

William H. Seward.

MEED OF HONOR TO BRAVERY.

First Lieutenant and Adjutant Thomas P. Gere, 5th Minnesota veteran infantry, to-day presented the War Department, by order of Major General Thomas, seventeen battle-flags, captured in the battle of Nashville, on the 16th of December last, and in the actions that immediately succeeded that brilliant victory, during the pursuit of the rebel forces under Hood.

THE REBEL ARMY
MELTING AWAY.

The dissatisfaction existing in the rebel army becomes more apparent every day, through the numerous desertions. Yesterday morning one hundred and eighteen deserters arrived here from City Point, a large number of whom belonged to the 25th Virginia regiment.

FOR THE USE OF THE
PRESIDENT AND HIS CABINET.

The steamer *River Queen* (formerly General Grant's headquarters boat) has been detailed for the use of the President and the members of his Cabinet. The *River Queen* has been assigned a berth at the 7th street wharf, where she will await orders.

THIS 22ND.—This anniversary of the birth of Washington is a gala day here indeed. Flags are flying from all quarters, public buildings and private, and the vessels in the river are gay indeed with bunting. At noon the salute ordered by the Secretary of War to be fired in honor of the restoration of the flag of the Union over Fort Sumter woke the echoes from all the environs of Washington, as the long line of circling fortifications thundered forth their several responses to the call. The occasion attracted crowds to the southern facade of the Treasury Extension, the Capitol roof, tops of hotels and other prominent points.

The illumination to-night in honor of the recent Union triumphs will undoubtedly be very brilliant, as not only the government buildings will be lit up but the City Hall and private residences.

ABRAHAM LINCOLN WAS WEARY FROM THE OVERWORK of four years. He was 30 pounds underweight, and looked older than his 56 years. His health had become a matter of public concern. But while he could see more years of deep trouble ahead, events in March, 1865, had given him an inner serenity.

Federal armies were driving the last of Confederate opposition before them, not only in the Carolinas but in Alabama as well. Grant's pressure on Richmond and Petersburg was unremitting, and he was bunching his military muscles for a colossal offensive. As March opened, Lee had tried to forestall the inevitable with a bid to organize a military convention in which peace could be negotiated. Lincoln ordered the offer spurned. The end of resistance was too near to sacrifice his avowed goal by agreeing to a negotiated peace short of it.

March 4 approached, and the President was ready to start his second term. Washington was prepared to make the occasion a glorious one, and *The Star* reported it in a continuous story occupying more than five columns of its precious space—on that day, well over half the news content of the entire paper.

LINCOLN URGES NO MALICE
AT INAUGURAL

(Saturday, March 4, 1865)

☞ *In* The Star's *presentation, virtually all of page 2 was one continuous story, still written in the old-time chronological style.* ☞

THE INAUGURATION.

This 4th of March, 1865, opened rather disagreeably, especially to the eyes of those designing to take part in the procession, and who did not relish having their "fancy fixin's" spoiled by drenching rain and mud-bath combined. The night had been drizzling, and this morning, about 6 o'clock, a heavy gale sprang up from the south, lasting but for a few minutes, but doing considerable damage, uprooting shade trees, &c. It was followed by brighter skies during the morning, but as the day wore on it became pretty certain that the manhood of the processionists was to be tried by a march of considerable discomfort.

EITHER MUD OR DUST.

Four years ago, on the occasion of the inauguration, the weather was dry, and tornadoes of dust swept through the streets. Commissioner Blake then had a large force of men at work the night preceding the inauguration removing the dust from the avenue between the White House and Capitol. This year the streets were covered with a thick coating of mud, carrying out the saying that Washington alternates from dust to mud or *vice versa*.

THE PERILS OF THE DAY.

The Engineer Corps, it is reported, made a survey and took soundings of the avenue, for the purpose of determining the practicability of laying pontoons from the Capitol to the White House, but it was found that the bottom was too soft to hold the anchors of the boats, and the project was abandoned. The police were careful to confine all to the sidewalks who could not swim. At some of the shallow crossings, a steady stream of people were passing throughout the day, some of whom dashed out into the avenue in the most reckless manner, but fortunately no one is believed to have been lost.

THE CITY LAST NIGHT.

The day, yesterday, which had been rather disagreeable under foot, closed rather threateningly over head with driving mists and black skies, rendering it an unpleasant job for new arrivals to pick their way through the muddy streets of a strange city in discouraging quest of lodgings. Carpet-bagged and blanket-strapped strangers were bolting in every direction in a dazed hap-hazard sort of way, and a good many of them found their way to the brilliantly lighted and comfortably warmed Capitol as if with an eye to quartering there for the night.

In the course of the evening the course of the firemen's procession lit up the fog of the avenue with a curious sort of silvery haze. A somewhat similar atmospheric effect on a grander scale was observed over the Capitol building, the great roof lights over the two houses in session illuminating the heavens with a brilliant halo seen for miles away in the country. An inspiring effect was produced by the manner in which the national flag floating over the Capitol was thus emblazoned, every fold in the glorious ensign being brought out in radiant relief.

Within the Capitol curious crowds vibrated between the two Houses, now interesting themselves with the bustle, confusion and noisy whirl of the House proceedings, and anon taking a sedative by listening to the tranquil debate of the Senate upon the question whether the Smithsonian trust fund interest should or not be paid in gold; and if so, what about the Indian annuities.

Mr. Lincoln was at the Capitol during the night attending to official business, as was also most of the Cabinet. Mrs. Lincoln was also there during the evening as a spectator of the busy proceedings. . . .

THE CROWD.

Up to this morning the number of strangers arriving in the city was not so large as was the case four years ago, when the excitement in regard to the inauguration of President Lincoln and the anticipation that some foul play might be attempted by secession gangs to prevent the President elect from taking his seat, caused an extraordinary rush to this city some days in advance of the inauguration. On this occasion large numbers who proposed to come, in order to avoid the difficulty of getting lodgings, deferred coming until the day of the inauguration itself, and for their accommodation extensive arrangements were made by the different railroad companies in the way of running special trains. Numbers from a distance stopped over night in Baltimore, arriving here by the morning trains.

RUMORS OF THE DAY.

So important a day could not well pass without its due proportion of rumors, and amongst these was one that "something was going on," indicating that trouble was anticipated from some undeveloped quarter. Rumor had it that all the roads leading to Washington had been heavily picketed for some days, and the bridges guarded with extra vigilance, as if on the watch for suspicious characters. Also,

that the 8th Illinois cavalry had been rushed out from Fairfax C. H. on an active scouting expedition, as if in search of some of the same suspicious characters. Also, that an undue proportion of "ornary looking cusses" in grizzled costume were to be seen upon the streets, indicating something portending. But as the day wore on in tranquility Dame Rumor took a back seat and was heard no more. . . .

NOW AND THEN.

Four years ago the preparations were of a far more warlike character. The city was filled with rebels who proclaimed their sentiments boldly in the streets, and hinted violence to the Executive. National airs were hissed down in public places of amusement, loyal men were assaulted on the avenue, and cheers for Jeff Davis were of common occurrence. For some time previous to the inauguration there had been threats of bloodshed on that occasion, and the military authorities taxed their brains for devices to prevent any such catastrophe. Every preparation was made for fighting. The volunteer organizations in the procession were supplied with cartridges, sharpshooters were posted at convenient

President Lincoln delivering his address at his second inaugural.

spots along the avenue and on the roofs of buildings, and at the market house a small force of infantry was posted for the support of the riflemen in that vicinity. Gen. Scott, with Magruder's and Fry's batteries, were at the corner of Delaware avenue and B street, ready for action, the gunners and drivers remaining at their posts throughout the ceremonies. Gen. Scott, in the meantime, kept his scouts busily occupied visiting all parts of the dense crowd and watching for the first indication of trouble. The day, however, passed off quietly, but the feverish anxiety of that morning and the certainty of terrible bloodshed following any riotous demonstration, created impressions on the minds of those who were present that probably will never be erased.

The commandant (Magruder) of one of these batteries referred to left Washington a few days after, and subsequently was made a General by the rebels.

THE AVENUE.

Pennsylvania avenue, about the time of the starting of the procession, presented a brilliant appearance indeed, despite the unpleasant weather. Thousands of people occupied the sidewalks and the windows and balconies of private and public buildings. The long colonnade of the Treasury Building bore an immense freight of human beings, and the west front of the Capitol was similarly loaded.

The State Department attracted much attention by its brilliant display of gracefully draped flags; as did the War Department by its display of flags and also of arches, and other decorations of evergreen.

The national flag in some shape, mammoth or miniature, was to be seen at every available point along the avenue, and upon the various carriages, cars, harness of horses, &c., on the streets, giving an exceedingly lively appearance to the scene.

AT THE WHITE HOUSE.

As early as nine o'clock a crowd began to assemble in front of the White House, on Pennsylvania avenue, and in a short time both sides of the street were completely jammed up by those eager to see the President, but they were disappointed in doing so, as he was called to the Capitol early this morning to sign a number of important bills passed by both houses of Congress yesterday and last night, where he remained, and consequently was not in the procession, as was expected. At five minutes to eleven o'clock, Marshal Lamon, and a number of United States marshals acting as his aide, entered the east gate of the enclosure leading to the President's mansion, for the purpose of escorting the President out and assigning him to his position in line. At this time it was first discovered that the President was at the Capitol, when Marshal Lamon immediately detailed Marshal Millard, of Philadelphia, and Marshal Murray, of New York, to escort Mrs. Lincoln through the crowd to the Capitol. Mrs. Lincoln then entered her carriage, in company with Senators Harlan and Anthony, and passed out the west gate of the enclosures of the White House, under escort of the Union Light Guard, and drove in advance of the procession to the Capitol.

AT THE CAPITOL.

Early this morning the grounds surrounding the Capitol assumed an animated appearance, and rapidly filled up with visitors, determined on securing favorable positions. A line of guards were posted about the steps of the eastern front, (all other entrances being closed,) who permitted none to pass except those provided with tickets of admission. The doorway leading from the steps to the Senate chamber was completely invested by ladies awaiting the hour for their admission; and approach from the outside being impossible, a skillful flank movement by the *Star* reporter on a neighboring window became necessary, and resulted in his triumphant occupation of the reporter's gallery. A number of the Metropolitan Police were stationed at various angles of the corridors, and a few of the Capitol police posted at the bronze doors between the House and the old Hall of Representatives, prevented all from passing over to the Senate from that side unless provided with the necessary pass.

The Senate Chamber was arranged at an early hour for the ceremonies. Within the arc formed by the desks around the front of the Vice President's chair, elegant cushioned arm chairs were placed and cane seats sandwiched between the widely separated chairs of the Senators, while sofas and settees filled up the rear. The proceedings of the Senate were quite uninteresting, and about 10 o'clock, on motion of Mr. Powell, the doors of the galleries were opened to the ladies. The rush and scramble for seats was characteristic of the gentle sex, and from that time until the Senate adjourned the confusion rendered the proceedings inaudible. At 11 o'clock the galleries were filled, with no room for more, presenting terraces of variegated hues that vie in beauty with the finest effects of the rainbow.

The time slipped wearily away to the outsiders,

President Lincoln, in a picture taken two days after his inaugural, on the balcony of the White House.

patiently waiting in the mud and rain, while inside the Senate vainly endeavored to transact business, with loud and repeated but unsuccessful calls of the presiding officer upon the ladies to preserve order in the galleries. Vice Admiral Farragut entered the Senate Chamber and quietly sat down in one of the back seats. Next came Major General Hooker, and Major General Bartlett, and others, while the attaches of the several foreign legations, "some gorjus for to see," leisurely sauntered into their gallery.

At fifteen minutes before twelve Vice President Hamlin escorted the Vice President elect to the desk, and soon after the Cabinet appeared, followed by the Supreme Court of the United States.

The President was seated in front of the Secretary's table, and the Committee of Arrangements on the left. Vice President Hamlin, the Chief Justice and Associate Justices of the Supreme Court were seated on the right of the Chair, the Diplomatic Corps on the right of the Chair, next to the Supreme Court, heads of Departments on the left of the Chair. . . .

Members of Congress, and members elect, entered the Senate Chamber by the main entrance, and occupied seats on the left of the Chair.

Vice President Hamlin, in a brief farewell address, feelingly alluded to his connection with the Senate as its presiding officer, and after referring to the brilliant future of the Republic, concluded by wishing all a safe and happy return to their families.

Vice President Johnson followed, referring to his elevation from the ranks as an illustration of American privileges, and proceeded at length upon the subject of the subordination of Presidents and Secretaries to the will of the people, at the conclusion of which the oath of office was administered to him by Vice President Hamlin, the Vice President elect taking the bible in his hand and elevating it before the audience, exclaiming, "I kiss this book before my nation of the United States."

Vice President Johnson, after some further remarks, then took the chair, and calling the Senate to order, administered the oath to the Senators elect to the 39th Congress, after which the body repaired to the east front of the Capitol.

Meanwhile the threatening clouds had dispersed, and the sun lighted up the "pomp and circumstance of glorious war" in the parks most cheerfully, and brightening with its beams the snow white dome and upturned faces of the throng, a well accepted omen of the better days just dawning on the country. As the President, followed by the imposing cortege that had filled the Senate Chamber, stepped out from among the columns of the eastern portico, and in his unassuming way came into full view of the throng, a loud, long and enthusiastic cheer welcomed him, with many repetitions, that seemed as though they would not be checked, even by the expectation for the inaugural. Finally the tumult subsided, the privileged visitors to the Senate Chamber clustered on the porticos and at the windows, and in the universal hush, the President addressed the people as follows:

Fellow-Countrymen: At this second appearing to take the oath of the presidential office, there is less occasion for an extended address than there was at the first. Then, a statement, somewhat in detail, of a course to be pursued, seemed fitting and proper.

Now, at the expiration of four years, during which public declarations have been constantly called forth on every point and phase of the great contest which still absorbs the attention and engrosses the energies of the nation, little that is new could be presented.

The progress of our arms, upon which all else chiefly depends, is as well known to the public as to myself; and it is, I trust, reasonably satisfactory and encouraging to all. With high hope for the future, no prediction in regard to it is ventured.

On the occasion corresponding to this four years ago, all thoughts were anxiously directed to an impending civil war. All dreaded it—all sought to avert it. While the inaugural address was being delivered from this place, devoted altogether to *saving* the Union without war, insurgent agents were in the city seeking to *destroy* it without war—seeking to dissolve the Union, and divide effects, by negotiation.

Both parties deprecated war; but one of them would *make* war rather than let the nation survive; and the other would *accept* war rather than let is perish. And the war came.

One-eighth of the whole population were colored slaves, not distributed generally over the Union, but localized in the southern part of it. These slaves constituted a peculiar and powerful interest. All knew that this interest was, somehow, the cause of the war.

To strengthen, perpetuate, and extend this interest was the object for which the insurgents would rend the Union, even by war; while the Government claimed no right to do more than to restrict the territorial enlargement of it.

Neither party expected for the war the magnitude or the duration which it has already attained. Neither anticipated that the *cause* of the conflict might cease with, or even before, the conflict itself should cease.

Each looked for an easier triumph, and a result less fundamental and astounding. Both read the same Bible, and pray to the same God; and each invokes His aid against the other. It may seem strange that any men should dare to ask a just God's assistance in wringing their bread from the sweat of other men's faces; but let us judge not, that we be not judged. The prayers of both could not be answered—that of neither has been answered fully.

The Almighty has his own purposes. "Woe unto the world because of offences! for it must needs be that offences come; but woe to that man by whom the offence cometh." If we shall suppose that American slavery is one of those offences which, in the providence of God, must needs come, but which, having continued through His appointed time, He now wills to remove, and that He gives to both north and south this terrible war, as the woe due to those by whom the offence came, shall we discern therein any departure from those divine attributes which the believers in a living God always ascribe to Him?

Fondly do we hope—fervently do we pray—that this mighty scourge of war may speedily pass away. Yet, if God wills that it continue until all the wealth piled by the bondman's two hundred and fifty years of unrequited toil shall be sunk, and until every drop of blood drawn with the lash shall be paid by another drawn with the sword, as was said three thousand years ago, so still it must be said, "The judgments of the Lord are true and righteous altogether."

With malice toward none; with charity for all; with firmness in the right, as God gives us to see the right, let us strive on to finish the work we are in; to bind up the nation's wounds; to care for him who shall have borne the battle, and for his widow, and his orphan—to do all which may achieve and cherish a just and lasting peace among ourselves, and with all nations.

At the conclusion of the address, the procession was formed and moved towards the Executive Mansion, President Lincoln accompanied in his carriage by his son, Master "Tad" Lincoln, and Senator Foster, of Connecticut. Next followed the carriage of Mrs. Lincoln, who was accompanied by Senator Anthony, of Rhode Island, then the carriage of Robert Lincoln, and next two of the Foreign Ministers, succeeded by the civic procession.

THE MILITARY ESCORT.

The military escort, consisting of the First Brigade Veteran Reserves, Lt. Col. Johnson, a section of the 4th U.S. artillery, Lieut. King, and a squadron of the 16th New York cavalry, Capt. Leary, all under command of Col. Giles, made a fine appearance, and added much to the attractiveness of the procession. . . .

THE POLICE.

Thirty policemen, headed by Superintendent Richards, were detailed to form across the avenue in front of the procession, for the purpose of clearing the way, and another squad was detailed to form a line on each side of the avenue. The police arrangements were admirable, and the men deserve much credit for the manner in which they carried out their orders. A force was also held in readiness at headquarters, subject to orders.

MOUNTED MILITARY PATROL.

Col. Ingraham detailed a strong mounted military patrol, who were posted at the intersections of the various streets crossing the avenue to prevent vehicles from getting in the way, and to assist the police. In this way the avenue was kept clear of obstructions, and the procession moved along in perfect order.

PHOTOGRAPHIC.

Among the incidents of the day were the operations of the eminent photographers, Gardner, of 7th street, and Brady, of the avenue, taking pictures of the specatcle at the Capitol. The photographs are superb, and will preserve to the future a life-like and remarkably spirited presentation of the scene. Brady also made a group picture of all the members of the House of Representatives, a work of art unsurpassed by any similar undertaking.

CLOSING OF THE DAY.

The day will close in an appropriate manner with a public reception at the White House by the President and Mrs. Lincoln, for which the most extensive preparations have been made, similar to those of New Year's day, in anticipation of a large crowd.

WASHINGTON HOMEFRONT, MARCH, 1865.

☞ *Editorially, The Star, in its Inauguration Day issue, wished the President Godspeed.* ☞

EDITORIAL.
(March 4, 1865)
President Lincoln's Second Term.

Since the inauguration of George Washington no similar event has so stirred the popular heart of the country where that is loyal to the principles of free government, as this inauguration of President Lincoln for a second term. This means, unmistakably, that the people with comparatively few exceptions, emphatically approve the policy and measures by which he is suppressing the rebellion, and have universal confidence in his energy, capacity and patriotism, as the result of their experience with him at the head of American public affairs during the past four most trying years of our brief national lifetime. We submit, to those who reflect, that this so remarkable display of popular approbation of our country's Chief Magistrate, means neither more nor less than an overwhelming endorsement of the new "departure" in the course of our national policy— of our public affairs—into which the so widespread treason of the times, now happily gasping in death throes, has precipitated the country. We need hardly remark that the rebellion has already worked an entire revolution in the public mind with reference not only to the rights and duties of the States, but concerning the obligations which the citizen owes to the State and National Governments, respectively. In the same manner have civil commotions repeatedly worked revolutions in the popular readings of English constitutional and other laws, more than once affecting changes without resorting to scratch of pen, which have amounted to well-nigh an entire reconstruction of English rights, if not of English society. All these eventful transitions have resulted fortunately for the British nation; increasing and strengthening English liberty, and amazingly furthering the material prosperity of the English people and the power of the English State in the affairs of the world. We see no reason to doubt that the revolution in our own government, which the rebellion is so swiftly working, as explained above, will fail to operate as beneficially for us as a nation.

THE INAUGURAL OF PRESIDENT LINCOLN.

The *Star* was the first city paper to present Mr. Lincoln's inaugural address to the public; and our power press was kept busy for a long time supplying the eager demand for it.

In pithy brevity, sagacity and honesty of purpose, the address is Lincolnian all over.

GEN. GRANT RECEIVED A DISTINGUISHED VISITOR AT HIS City Point headquarters where the James and Appomattox Rivers join 10 miles from Petersburg. It was the President of the United States. Workworn and careworn though he was, Lincoln sensed climactic events.

Not that the Rebels were yet whipped, by any means. Just a day or two before his arrival, Joe Johnston's army gave Sherman's mighty invaders an unpleasant surprise. Turning on the Federal host, Johnston fought a savage three-day battle at Bentonville, N.C., before resuming his orderly retreat toward the mountains to the west and near the Virginia border.

Gen. Lee was planning a surprise or two for Grant in his theater of war a little to the north. Lee's troops were almost starving in their trenches around and between Petersburg and Richmond; only shreds of clothing warded off the bitter cold. And though they must have realized that the Confederacy's cause was lost, the bulk of the army had a personal cause they had no intention of abandoning: Robert E. Lee. Knowing this, Lee designed a new campaign. It involved dodging out the back doors of both cities—the western sector as yet free from Federals—and joining Johnston. Together both armies might turn on Sherman and, whipping him, retire to the mountains to hold Grant at bay indefinitely. The hope for success was forlorn, but if the plan worked, Northern war-weariness might lead to negotiated peace after all. Besides, anything was better than sitting in the Virginia trenches waiting for the next Federal blow to fall.

The first step would be to try a major diversion on the east front before Petersburg. The attack called for a breakthrough at Fort Stedman and disruption of the military railroad that ran behind it to supply the Federal lines below the city. This would result in Grant's calling in reinforcements from the western end of his lines. Most of the 60,000 Confederates could then abandon both Petersburg and Richmond with little molestation and head for the mountains.

But the attack on Fort Stedman failed. And Grant counterattacked immediately after. With Sheridan's cavalry now in from western Virginia, Grant dispatched it and other overwhelming forces to the westernmost extremity of the Petersburg front around Five Forks. On April 1, the Confederates under Pickett were crushed. The victory led Grant to order a general assault all along the lines the next day. Unit by unit, the Confederates collapsed. A. P. Hill, the soldier revered by both Lee and Jackson, died in this fighting. Petersburg was going fast, Lee informed his government Sunday, April 2. Evacuation began immediately.

SOUTH'S CAPITAL FALLS; CITY BURNING

(Monday, April 3, 1865)

GLORY!!!

HAIL COLUMBIA!!!

HALLELUJAH!!!

RICHMOND OURS!!!

Lee's Retreat Cut Off!

WAR DEPARTMENT,
WASHINGTON, April 3, 10.45 a.m.

Major General Dix, New York:

LATER.

It appears from a dispatch of Gen. Weitzel, just received by this Department, that our forces under his command are in Richmond, having taken it at 8.15 this morning.

Edwin M. Stanton, Secretary of War.

🔫 *Maj. Gen. Godfrey Weitzel, engineer and commander of the XXV Corps, was a 29-year-old* *Ohioan, who had served before the war under Beauregard, building Federal forts in the South. The uncontested entry of Richmond was, of course, the crowning glory of his career. And if any bulletins had official status, the next one was it.* 🔫

PETERSBURG OURS!

OFFICIAL WAR BULLETIN.

WAR DEPARTMENT,
10 A.M., WASHINGTON, April 3, 1865

Major General J. A. Dix, New York:

The following telegram from the President, announcing the evacuation of Petersburg, and probably of Richmond, has just been received by this Department.

Edwin M. Stanton, Secretary of War.

CITY POINT, VA., April 3d, 8:30 A.M., 1865. —*Hon. Edwin M. Stanton, Secretary of War:* This morning, General Grant reports Petersburg evacu-

Before evacuating Richmond, the rebel army set fire to the city.

View of flame-gutted houses in Richmond. The capital building stands at the center on the heights.

ated and he is confident Richmond also is. He is pushing forward to cut off, if possible, the retreating army.

A. Lincoln.

☞ *The retreating Confederates had put the torch to the Richmond warehouses and ammunition stores over the protests of the municipal government and some officers. A stiff wind spread the fires.* ☞

THE LATEST!
RICHMOND ON FIRE!!!
WEITZEL ENDEAVORING TO EXTINGUISH THE FLAMES!!

Capture of an Immense Number of Guns!!

PRESIDENT LINCOLN GONE TO RICHMOND!!

WAR DEPARTMENT, 12 Noon.

Major General Dix:

The following official confirmation of the capture of Richmond, and announcing that the city is on fire, has just been received by this Department.

Edwin M. Stanton, Secretary of War.

———◆———

CITY POINT, VA., April 3, 1865, 11 a.m.— *Hon. Edwin M. Stanton, Secretary of War:* Gen. Weitzel telegraphs as follows:

We took Richmond at 8.15 this morning. I captured many guns. The enemy left in great haste. The city is on fire in one place, am making every effort to put it out. The people received us with enthusiastic expressions of joy.

General Grant started early this morning with army toward the Danville road, to cut off Lee's retreating army, if possible.

President Lincoln has gone to the front.

T. S. Bowers, A.A.G.

☞ *Lincoln, at grave personal risk, toured the flame-ravaged city on April 4. Army deserters and the hoodlum element roamed the streets unfettered by civil authority. In all likelihood, most of the "enthusiastic expressions of joy" came from the Negro population and the beneficiaries of whisky supplies that had gone undestroyed in the confusion of evacuation. West of the two cities, the Federal pursuit was on in full cry.* ☞

(Tuesday, April 4, 1865)
Later from General Grant.

MORE GLORIOUS NEWS!!!
GENERAL SHERIDAN PICKING UP THE REMNANT OF LEE'S ARMY BY HUNDREDS!!!

Probabilities of Capturing Most of the Retreating Rebels!!!

Capture of Locomotives, Cars and Railroad Material!!!

THE ENEMY FLYING IN THE WILDEST CONFUSION!!!

WASHINGTON, D. C., April 4, 1865, 11.15 a.m.

Maj. Gen. Jno. A. Dix, New York:

The following particulars dated at City Point, April 4th, 8 a.m., give the latest information received from Richmond.

The Tredegar ironworks in Richmond, the South's largest armaments plant.

Gen. Weitzel telegraphs from Richmond that of railroad stock he found there twenty-eight locomotives, forty-four passenger and baggage cars, and one hundred and six freight cars.

At 3.30 this morning, General Grant, from Sutherland Station, ten miles from Petersburg, towards Burksville, telegraphs as follows:—"General Sheridan picked up twelve hundred prisoners to-day, and from three to five hundred more have been gathered by other troops.

"The majority of the arms that were left in the hands of the remnant of Lee's army now scattered between Richmond and where his troops are. The country is also full of stragglers; the line of retreat marked with artillery, ammunition, burned or charred wagons, caissons, ambulances, &c."

Edwin M. Stanton,
Secretary of War.

☞ *Details of the plight of the stricken city began to come north. The fire had destroyed more than half of the waterfront area and about a fourth of the entire city.* ☞

INTERESTING FROM RICHMOND.

The Extent of the Fire— The Business Part of the City Entirely Destroyed—The Whig a Loyal Paper.

Advices from Richmond down to Tuesday morning have been received, and give a deplorable account of the condition of Richmond. On Sunday afternoon, before the evacuation, Mayor [Joseph] Mayo and the City Council ordered all liquor to be destroyed. Heads of barrels were knocked in and the contents emptied into the streets, and bottles of liquors that had commanded fabulous prices were broken on the curbstones. As a consequence the rebel rear guard became intoxicated and ungovernable, and a terrible scene of pillage and ruin ensued. The stores were plundered of jewelry, clothing, confectionery, &c., and the whole city was in tumult with riotous proceedings. Great damage was done by the explosion of the magazine, against which it is said

The residence of Confederate President Jefferson Davis in Richmond.

that General Breckinridge earnestly remonstrated, but General Ewell, to whom the work of destruction had been intrusted, was inflexible. Among the victims to the explosion were all the inmates of the almshouse, close by, who were at the time sound asleep in bed. The damage done by the fire is enormous, all the business part of the city, bounded by Main street and the river and 7th and 15th streets, being destroyed. Burning shingles were carried to other parts of the city, setting fire to houses, and it is estimated that not less than eight hundred buildings were burned. Among them are the Mechanics Institute, used by the War Departments, the Henrico County Court House, the old State Court House, the *Enquirer* office, *Dispatch* office, and the press rooms of the *Examiner,* Haxall's celebrated flour mills, Crews and Smith's tobacco manufactories, and nearly all the banks. The flames were finally arrested by blowing up the (negro) Trader's Bank, by order of Gen. Shepley, who, upon entering the city, assured the inhabitants of protection, and appointed Lieut. Col. Manning Provost Marshal. A force of white troops are encamped on Capitol Square, and Gen. Devins has his headquarters at the Governor's House. The colored troops are feasted by the negro population in the most extravagant manner, and are lords of the city. The Richmond *Whig* was to have been issued again Tuesday morning, by its proprietor, assisted by a former editor, having given pledges to offer a hearty support to the Union cause. The hotels are all virtually closed, owing to the scarcity of food, and the restaurants, with one or two exceptions, were all destroyed by fire.

Washington's wharves were especially busy with traffic from Richmond and Petersburg. And the traffic in the other direction also bustled.

FROM THE FRONT.
More Prisoners Brought In.
Destruction of Cotton by the Rebels.

The mail steamer James T. Brady arrived here this morning from City Point, bringing up fifty captured rebel officers, also the men of Gregg's rebel battery, which was captured entire; also a rebel brigade band, which enlivened the trip with some excellent music. This band, which numbers eighteen instruments, marched into City Point at the head of five thousand prisoners on Tuesday, playing "Dixie."

The sutlers, photographers and others doing business at City Point and Bermuda Hundred have moved up to Petersburg, which already begins to assume a business aspect. Our troops have gained the confidence of the citizens, who express themselves greatly gratified as well as surprised at the kind treatment they have received. The merchants begin to feel perfectly secure, and have opened their stores.

Besides the large quantity of tobacco destroyed by the rebels at Petersburg, they burnt eight cotton warehouses, containing over $11,000 worth of cotton.

The rebel General A. P. Hill was killed at Fort Mahone in a fruitless effort to rally his men. He was

A general view of the Richmond ruins.

Library of Congress

The first Federal wagon train enters Petersburg after the city's evacuation.

buried at Petersburg, with hurried military honors, on Sunday, previous to the evacuation of the place by the rebels.

The work of removing the obstructions in the James river is progressing rapidly, and it is believed that some of our smaller class vessels will be able to go up to Richmond by the end of the week.

All of the rebel prisoners received at City Point up to Tuesday have been sent to Fortress Monroe and Point Lookout. They number about 12,000, but others are still being brought in. . . .

🔫 *Other prisoners were being brought in, but the flow of prisoners would stop soon.* 🔫

EDITORIAL.

(Tuesday, April 4, 1865)

The Beginning of the End.

It strikes us as eminently appropriate that Grant and his glorious gallant army should have taken Richmond without the firing a gun in the immediate work by any other portion of our troops. The great result vindicates his generalship and his army's efficiency past all denial, if there remained any to doubt either, in view of the difficulties of his arduous and long protracted task.

The time has now arrived when serious efforts at peace will be made. Such Southern public men as Alexander Stephens, Judge Campbell and W. W. Holden—sincere Union men at heart—will doubtless at once take the initiative in the desired negotiations based on immediate and absolute submission to the Government's lawful authority. Our impression is that Governor Vance, of North Carolina, will no longer hold out against the Union sentiment of that State, and that Governor Brown, of Georgia, will not

be behind hand in bringing his State back into the Union.

The readers of the *Star* will remember that we have steadily maintained that whenever relieved from the pressure of the (late) Richmond despotism, the people of the South might be relied on to evince a thousand fold more attachment for the Union than was generally believed in the loyal States. We expect to witness such manifestations from that quarter in that way as will astound the country; speedily satisfying all of the truth of what we know well. Viz: that the rebellion was but the result of a well-contrived and boldly-executed conspiracy, in instantly enslaving the instruments (population) with which it essayed to work out its purposes, much more than half of whom have at no time sympathized with the end and aim of its crimes, and three-fourths of whom will now gladly accept a return to the Union without slavery, in preference to adherence to the fortunes of the most diabolical cabal with which God ever cursed the world.

WASHINGTON HOMEFRONT, APRIL, 1865.

THE NEWS—THE GLORIOUS NEWS.

As we write, Washington city is in such a blaze of excitement and enthusiasm as we never before witnessed here in any approachable degree.

The thunder of cannon; the ringing of bells; the eruption of flags from every window and housetop; the shouts of enthusiastic gatherings on the streets, all echo the glorious report, RICHMOND IS OURS! ! !

The first announcement of the fact made by Secretary Stanton in the War Department building, caused a general stampede of the employes of that establishment to the street, where their pent-up enthusiasm had a chance for vent in cheers that would assuredly have lifted the roof from that building had they been delivered with such vim inside.

The news caught up and spread by a thousand mouths, caused almost a general suspension of business, and the various newspaper offices, especially, were besieged with excited crowds.

The *Extra Star,* containing the official bulletin of Secretary Stanton, giving confirmation of the good news reported, was speedily issued, and then followed such a rush for copies as surpassed anything in our newspaper experience. The demand seemed inexhaustible, in fact, and almost beyond the power of our lightning press to supply; and the foreman, in despair, at last shouted to the engineer to "run the engine without the governor." Even with this acceleration of speed, it seemed impossible to supply the eager demand.

Scenes at the War Department—Remarks of Secretary Stanton.

The rumors of the capture of Richmond attracted a crowd about the War Department this morning, and the first confirmatory intelligence being greeted with great cheering, hundreds of people rushed to the spot, and in a few moments filled the park in front of the War Department, nearly obstructing the street.

There were loud calls for the Secretary, who appeared in answer to the call.

Mr. Secretary Stanton, exhibiting great emotion, spoke as follows:

Friends and Fellow-Citizens: In this great hour of triumph, my heart, as well as yours, is penetrated with gratitude to Almighty God for his deliverance of this nation. (Tremendous and prolonged cheering.) Our thanks are due to the President, (cheer,) to the Army and Navy, (cheers,) to the great commanders by sea and land, (cheers,) to the gallant officers and men who have periled their lives upon the battle field and drenched the soil with their blood. (Great cheers.)

The Secretary then presented to the vast assemblage Willie Kettles, aged fourteen years, an operator in the military telegraph office, as the person who received the dispatch [announcing the fall of Richmond], and the first person to receive the great and glorious news, (cheering and cries of "Have him speak," "Let us hear him," &c.) Willie said he "couldn't speak, he felt so."

Following upon the remarks of Secretary Stanton the assemblage pressed forward to take him by the hand and express to him their warm congratulations over the glorious result to the attainment of which his labors had contributed so much.

Vice President Johnson, who was recognized in the crowd, was loudly applauded, and addressed the assemblage with some stirring remarks.

SCENES AT THE STATE DEPARTMENT.

A large crowd subsequently collected in front of the State Department, and called out Secretary Seward, who, after the cheers had subsided, addressed the assemblage as follows:

"I thank you, fellow-citizens, for remembering me in this hour of the nation's prosperity and triumph. (Cheers.) I suppose you have become converts at last, however much you may have differed from me heretofore to my great doctrine, that the war is to be brought to an end, and to a triumphant end in 90 days. (Great laughter and cheers.) I have stood four years upon that platform. (Shouts of laughter.) I always thought that a patient who despaired of life for 90 days was not likely to live for four years. . . .

"What shall I tell John Bull? I will tell him that cotton is to be had cheaper by paying duties to the United States than by running the blockade, and tell him to tell Lord John Russell that this is a war for freedom, for the rights of man and for Union, not a war for empire; and therefore if he is only just and right in his treatment towards the United States, Canada is safe as long as she prefers the Queen of England for her sovereign to a union with the United States of America. If you agree to these messages, I believe I will jot them down, and I think that they will satisfy the world that the true principle of government is for every nation to take care of itself, and let every other nation take care of itself, and the true motto peace and good will to all mankind."

SALUTE.

A salute of eight hundred guns—three in honor of the fall of Petersburg and five in honor of the capture of Richmond—was fired from the corner of 14th and M streets by order of the War Department, by batteries E and F of the 2d United States artillery, and battery H of the 14th Pennsylvania artillery, from Camp Barry, under the direction of Brigad'r Gen'l Hall.

A salute of one hundred guns was also fired from the battery on the Navy Yard wharf.

G EN. LEE'S ARMY WAS NOW RACING AGAINST TIME AND exhaustion. The relative security of the trenches around Petersburg and Richmond was lost. The Confederates, 40,000 tattered but fighting spirits, were in open country marching westward at utmost speed before the Federals could cut them off. For his part, Gen. Grant's job was to head off his canny adversary and prevent a juncture of the two surviving Rebel armies. His pursuit of Lee consequently was swift, powerful and relentless.

Lee's first goal was Amelia Courthouse where a supply train bearing desperately needed rations was supposed to meet his near-starving troops. On the rendezvous date, April 5, the train was not there. Sheridan and other forces were close—seven miles away at Jetersville to the southwest. Lee pushed on toward Farmville where supplies could be brought in by rail from Lynchburg, the next likely spot for a stand by his army. But Lynchburg was more than 60 miles from Amelia Courthouse. And in their strung-out line of march the Confederates were prey to constant flanking attacks. Particularly vulnerable was the tail of the column commanded by Ewell. At Sayler's Creek, a tributary of the Appomattox, the Federals caught up with Ewell's command and parts of others—a total of about 10,000 troops. On April 6, Ewell turned and fought the last pitched battle of the war.

LEE ARMY STAGGERED AT SAYLER'S CREEK

(Friday, April 7, 1865)

GLORIOUS.

Great News!

GREAT BATTLE YESTERDAY!

SHERIDAN ATTACKS AND ROUTS LEE'S ARMY!

THE LAST ACT IN THE DRAMA!

Dispatches from President Lincoln, Gen. Grant and Gen. Sheridan.

WAR DEPARTMENT,
WASHINGTON, D.C., April 7, 1865—10 a.m.

Major General John A. Dix, New York:

General Sheridan attacked and routed Lee's army yesterday, capturing Generals Ewell, [Joseph Brevard] Kershaw, Button, [Montgomery Dent] Corse and many other general officers, several thousand prisoners, and a large number of cannon, and expects to force Lee to surrender all that is left of his army. Details will be given as speedily as possible, but the telegraph is working badly.

Edwin M. Stanton, Secretary of War.

Ewell's men had won some gains along the Sayler's Creek line, but they couldn't last. The Federals swarmed over them from all sides. Close to 8,000 prisoners were taken, including a previously unheard of bag of Confederate officers. The name of "Button" mentioned in the dispatch probably resulted from the faulty telegraph transmission. This officer was Eppa Hunton.

WAR DEPARTMENT,
WASHINGTON CITY, D.C., 11 a.m.
April 7, 1865.

Major General Dix, New York:

The following telegrams announcing the victory won yesterday by Major General Sheridan over Lee's army has just been received by this Department.

Edwin M. Stanton, Secretary of War.

CITY POINT, 8.35 a.m., April 7.—*Hon. Secretary of War:*—At eleven fifteen yesterday at Burkesville Station General Grant sends me the following from General Sheridan.

(Signed.) A. Lincoln.

APRIL 6, 11.15 P.M.—*Lieutenant General Grant:* "I have the honor to report that the enemy made a stand at the intersection of the Burk's Station road

The high bridge over the Appomattox River, across which the Confederate army retreated from Richmond and Petersburg.

Confederates surrendering after the battle of Sayler's Creek, just east of Appomattox.

with the road upon which they were retreating. I attacked them with two divisions of the 6th army corps, and routed them handsomely, making a connection with the cavalry. I am still pressing on with both cavalry and infantry. Up to the present time we have captured Generals Ewell, Kershaw, Button, Corse, De Barr [Dudley McIver Du Bose] and Custis Lee [George Washington Custis Lee, Robert's eldest son], several thousand prisoners, fourteen (14) pieces of artillery, with caissons, and a large number of wagons. If the thing is pressed I think Lee will surrender.

(Signed) "P. H. Sheridan.
Major General Commanding."

———◆●◆———

CITY POINT, 9 A.M., April 7, 1865.—*Hon. E. M. Stanton, Secretary of War:* The following further just received.

A. Lincoln.

———◆●◆———

"BURKESVILLE, VA.—*To A. Lincoln:* The following telegrams respectfully forwarded for your information.

"U. S. Grant, Lieutenant General."

———◆●◆———

"SECOND ARMY CORPS, 7:30 P.M., April 6. —*Major General A. S. Webb:* Our last fight, just before dark, at Sailor's [Sayler's] Creek, gave us two guns, three flags, considerable numbers of prisoners, 200 wagons, 70 ambulances, with mules and horses to about one half the wagons and ambulances.

"There are between thirty and fifty wagons in addition abandoned and destroyed along the road, some battery wagons, forges and limbers.

"I have already reported to you the capture of one gun, two flags and some prisoners, and the fact that the road for over two miles is strewn with tents, baggage, cooking utensils, some ammunition, some material of all kinds, the wagons across the approach to the bridges, it will take some time to clear it. The enemy is in position on the heights beyond with artillery. The bridge partially destroyed and the approaches on other side are of soft bottom land. We cannot advance to-morrow in the same manner we have to-day.

"As soon as I get my troops up a little—we are considerably mixed—I might push a column down the road and deploy it, but it is evident that I cannot follow rapidly during the night.

(Signed) "A. A. Humphrey, Maj. Gen."

Meade, who commanded the northern wing of the pursuing army, also was heard from.

———◆●◆———

MEADE'S HEADQUARTERS, 10 p.m., April 6, 1865.—*Lieut. Gen'l Grant:* At daylight this morning I moved the 2d, 5th, and 6th Army Corps along the Railroad in the direction of Amelia Court House soon after moving reliable intelligence was received that the enemy was moving toward Farmville. The direction of the 2d and 5th Army Corps was immediately changed from a northerly to a northwesterly direction, and the directing corps (the 2d) moving

342

on Deatonville, and the 5th, heretofore in the centre, moved on the right of the 2d, and the 6th facing about and moving by the left flank, taking position on left of the 2d. It was understood the cavalry would operate on the extreme left. The changes were promptly made, the 2d Army Corps soon becoming engaged with the enemy near Deatonville, driving him by right across Sailor's Creek to the Appomattox.

"The 5th army corps made a long march but its position prevented its striking the enemy's column before it had passed. The 6th army corps came up with the enemy about 4 p.m., and in conjunction with the 2d on its right and cavalry on its left, attacked and routed the enemy, capturing many prisoners, among them Lieut. Gen. Ewell and Gen. Curtis Lee. I transmit dispatch both from Gen. Humphreys and Wright, which, in justice to these distinguished officers and the gallant corps they command, I beg may be sent to the War Department for immediate publication. It is impossible at this moment to give any estimate in the casualties on either side, or of the number of prisoners taken, but it is evident to-day's work is going to be one of the most important of the recent brilliant operations.

"The pursuit will be continued as soon as the men have a little rest. Griffin, with Fifth Army Corps, will be moved by the left, and Wright and Humphreys continue the direct pursuit as long as it promises success.

"G. G. Meade, Major General."

☞ *Promising success, the pursuit was pushed with ll vigor.* ☜

WASHINGTON HOMEFRONT, APRIL, 1865.

☞ *The news from Virginia all but filled the pages of the Star. However, there was room for an extensive ccount of a cabinet member's mishap.* ☜

THE ACCIDENT TO SECRETARY SEWARD.

In our third edition yesterday, we announced a erious accident happening to Secretary Seward. It ppears that the Secretary, with Miss Fannie Seward and Mr. Frederick Seward, started from his residence on 15½ street, near Pennsylvania avenue, for the purpose of taking a drive, and when on Vermont avenue stopped to take in Miss Titus, who was to accompany the party. When Miss Titus entered the carriage the driver got down from his box to shut the door, (at the same time holding the reins,) but experienced considerable difficulty in doing so. The horses becoming restive, Mr. Frederick Seward attempted to grasp the reins to assist the driver, but failing to do so, he jumped from the carriage to stop them, but fell, and somewhat bruised himself. Before Mr. Frederick Seward could regain his feet the horses broke away from the driver, he being unable to regain his seat; and when the horses suddenly turned into H street, Secretary Seward attempted to get out of the carriage, but fell violently to the ground, bruising his face severely, and badly fracturing his right arm just below the shoulder blade. The horses continued running, and when turning into the yard adjoining Mr. Seward's residence one of them fell, which stopped the carriage, when the ladies alighted in safety.

The Secretary was immediately picked up in an insensible condition and conveyed to his residence, where the fractured limb was braced, Surgeon General Barnes, Dr. Verdi and Surgeon Morris attending him.

The driver was not killed, as at first reported, but was somewhat injured.

The fracture of the limb is a bad one, but Mr. Seward's injuries are not considered dangerous, we are most happy to state.

The news of the accident to Secretary S. caused much excitement last night, as it was at first feared it might prove fatal, and the general feeling that his loss would be irreparable to the country was mingled with the feeling of high personal regard entertained for him by all in this community.

PS.—We regret to learn since writing the above that Secretary Seward's injuries are more serious than was at first supposed. On examination this morning, the attending physician discovered a fracture of the right jaw. The operation of setting it was very painful, but since it is bandaged, the Secretary feels more comfortable.

At 3 o'clock this afternoon he was comparatively easy, and there seems every reason to believe that he will soon be in a way of convalescence and able shortly to resume the functions of the office he fills with such distinguished ability.

THE DISASTER AT SAYLER'S CREEK, COUPLED WITH THE sheer physical inability of other hundreds of troops to keep going any longer, had reduced Gen. Lee's command to less than 30,000. He plowed ahead toward Lynchburg anyway, in a nightmare of flank attacks and rear-guard actions, two of which took place at the High Bridge crossing of the Appomattox and then Farmville, a few miles further west, on April 7. The Confederates at least found a supply train at Farmville. There was barely time to eat one meal before the westward push continued.

The objective this time was Appomattox Station and nearby Appomattox Courthouse, where more supplies would be waiting. Gen. Sheridan, whose cavalry had been pacing the pursuit, figured on this and spurred his troopers forward to reach Appomattox before Lee. He succeeded. One division headed by Custer captured the supplies at the station despite brief Confederate resistance, and hurried on to Appomattox Courthouse. The Federals got there first, too, and although they were attacked by Lee's advance units, more Federals were coming up from all directions. The date was April 9, and Lee saw that his position was utterly hopeless.

LEE SURRENDERS TO GRANT

SURRENDER OF LEE
AND
HIS WHOLE ARMY!

GRANT'S TERMS ACCEPTED!

All the Arms, Artillery, and
Public Property Turned over
to Our Government.

OFFICERS AND MEN PAROLED.

The Officers Allowed Their Side
Arms and Horses.

LEE'S ARMY
PERMITTED TO RETURN HOME.

Grant Wishes to Spare Life.

LEE DESIRES THE RESTORATION
OF PEACE.

A Grand Salute to Be Fired in
Every Part of the Union.

WAR DEPARTMENT,
WASHINGTON, D.C., April 9, 1865, 9 p.m.

Major General John A. Dix, New York:

This Department has just received official report of the surrender, this day, of General Lee and his army to Lieutenant General Grant, on the terms proposed by General Grant. Details will be given as speedily as possible.

Edwin M. Stanton, Secretary of War.

The surrender terms were made by Lee and Grant in the home of Wilmer McLean, who had moved from Manassas nearly four years before to escape the war. Grant forwarded the notes which the two commanders had exchanged prior to their personal encounter early in the afternoon of April 9.

HEADQ'RS ARMIES OF UNITED STATES,
April 9, 9.40 p.m.

Hon. Edwin M. Stanton, Secretary of War:

General Lee surrendered the army of Northern Virginia this afternoon, upon terms proposed by myself. The accompanying additional correspondence will show the conditions fully.

U. S. Grant, Lieutenant General.

APRIL 9, 1865.—*General:* I received your note of this morning on the picket line, whither I had come to meet you, and ascertain definitely what terms were embraced in your proposition of yesterday. With reference to the surrender of this army, I now request an interview in accordance with the offer contained in your letter of yesterday for that purpose.

Very respectfully, your obedient servant,

R. E. Lee. General.

*Lieutenant General U. S. Grant, Commanding
United States Armies*

APRIL 9, 1865.—*General R. E. Lee, Commanding Confederate States Army:* Your note of this date

General Grant and General Lee meet at Appomattox Courthouse.

Library of Congress

is but this moment, 11.50 a.m., received, in consequence of my having passed from the Richmond and Lynchburg road to the Farmville and Lynchburg road. I am at this writing about four miles west of Walter's Church, and will push forward to the front for the purpose of meeting you. Notice sent to me on the road where you wish the interview to take place, will meet me.

Very respectfully, your obedient servant,

U. S. Grant, Lieutenant General.

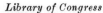

APPOMATTOX C.H., April 9, 1865.—*General R. E. Lee, Commanding C.S.A.:* In accordance with the substance of my letter to you of the 8th instant, I propose the surrender of the Army of Northern Virginia, on the following terms, to wit:

Rolls of all the officers and men to be made in duplicate; one copy to be given to an officer designated by me, the other to be retained by such officers as you may designate. The officers to give their individual paroles not to take arms against the Government of the United States until properly exchanged, and each company or regimental commander sign a like parole for the men of their commands. The arms, artillery, and public property to be packed and stacked, and turned over to the officers appointed by me to receive them. This will not embrace the side arms of the officers, nor their private horses or baggage. This done, each officer and man will be allowed to return to their homes not to be disturbed by United States authority so long as they observe their parole and the laws in force where they may reside.

Very respectfully,

U. S. Grant, Lieutenant General.

HEADQUARTERS ARMY NORTHERN VIRGINIA, April 9th, 1865.—*Lieut. General U. S. Grant, Commanding United States Armies:*—General: I have received your letter of this date, containing the terms of surrender of the Army of Northern Virginia, as proposed by you. As they are substantially the same as those expressed in your letter of the 8th inst., they are accepted. I will proceed to designate the proper officers to carry the stipulation into effect.

Very respectfully, your obedient servant,

R. E. Lee, General.

The following is the previous correspondence between Lieutenant General Grant and General Lee, referred to in the foregoing telegram to the Secretary of War:

CLIFTON HOUSE, VA., April 9, 1865.—*Hon. Edwin M. Stanton, Secretary of War:*—The following correspondence has taken place between General Lee and myself.

There has been no relaxation in the pursuit during its pendency.

U. S. Grant, Lieutenant General.

Federal soldiers pose in front of the courthouse at Appomattox.

APRIL 7, 1865.—*General R. E. Lee, Commanding C.S.A.:*—General: The result of the last week must convince you of the hopelessness of further resistence on the part of the Army of Northern Virginia in this struggle. I feel that it is so, and regard it as my duty to shift from myself the responsibility of any further effusion of blood, by asking of you the surrender of that portion of the Confederate army known as the Army·of Northern Virginia.

Very respectfully, your obedient servant,

U. S. Grant, Lieutenant General.
Commanding Armies United States.

———◆◆◆———

APRIL 7, 1865.—*To Lieutenant General U. S. Grant, Commanding Armies of the United States.*—General: I have received your note of this date. Though not entirely of the opinion you express of the hopelessness of the further resistence on the part of the Army of Northern Virginia, I reciprocate your desire to avoid useless effusion of blood, and, therefore, ask the terms you will offer on condition of its surrender.

R. E. Lee, General.

———◆◆◆———

APRIL 8, 1865.—*General R. E. Lee, Commanding C.S.A.:* General—Your note of last evening in reply to mine of the same date, asking conditions on which I will accept the surrender of the Army of Northern Virginia, is just received. In reply, I would say that peace being my first desire, there is but one condition I insist upon, viz:

That the men surrendered shall be disqualified from taking up arms against the Government of the United States, until properly exchanged. I will meet you, or designate officers to meet any officers you may name for the same purpose, at any point agreeable to you, for the purpose of arranging definitely the terms upon which the surrender of the Army of Northern Virginia will be received.

Very respectfully, your obedient servant,

U. S. Grant, Lieutenant General.

———◆◆◆———

APRIL 8, 1865.—*General:* I received at a late hour your note of to-day, in answer to mine of yesterday. I did not intend to propose the surrender of the Army of Northern Virginia, but to ask the terms of your proposition. To be frank, I do not think the emergency has arisen to call for the surrender of this army, but as the restoration of peace should be the sole object of all, I desire to know whether your proposal would tend to that end. I cannot, therefore,

The McLean house. General Lee signed the surrender papers in a room on the first floor.

meet you with a view to surrender the Army of Northern Virginia; but as far as your proposition may affect the Confederate States forces under my command, and tend to the restoration of peace, I should be pleased to meet you at 10 a.m. to-morrow, on the old stage road to Richmond, between the picket lines of the two armies.

Very respectfully, your obedient servant,

R. E. Lee, General,
Confederate States Army.
Lieut. Gen. U. S. Grant, Commanding United States Armies.

———◆◆◆———

APRIL 9, 1865.—*General R. E. Lee, Commanding C.S.A.:*—General: Your note of yesterday is received. As I have no authority to treat on the subject of peace, the meeting proposed for 10 a.m. to-day could lead to no good. I will state, however, General, that I am equally anxious for peace with yourself, and the whole North entertains the same feeling. The terms upon which peace can be had are well understood. By the South laying down their arms they will hasten that desirable event, save thousands of human lives, and hundreds of millions of property not yet destroyed.

Sincerely hoping that all our difficulties may be settled without the loss of another life, I subscribe myself, very respectfully,

Your obedient servant,

U. S. Grant, Lieutenant General.

General Lee leaves the McLean house after signing the surrender papers.

🔫 *The McLean House parley began with both generals reminiscing about their days with the old army in the Mexican War. Lee was resplendent in his full dress uniform; Grant was mud-spattered and in his plain blue battle clothes. As the details were settled, Lee was impressed with Grant's generosity, particularly his permission to the men to keep their horses and mules for working their farms. "This will have the best possible effect upon the men. It will be very gratifying and will do much toward conciliating our people," Lee remarked. Back in Washington, War Secretary Stanton was beside himself with official joy.* 🔫

———◆———

WAR DEPARTMENT,
WASHINGTON, D.C., 9.30 P.M., April 9, 1865.

Lieutenant General Grant:

Thanks be to Almighty God for the great victory with which He has this day crowned you and the gallant army under your command! The thanks of this department, and of the Government, and of the people of the United States; their reverence and honor have been deserved, and will be rendered to you and the brave and gallant officers and soldiers of your army for all time.

Edwin M. Stanton, Secretary of War.

WAR DEPARTMENT,
WASHINGTON, D.C., April 9,—10 P.M.

Ordered: That a salute of two hundred guns be fired at the headquarters of every army and department, and at every post and arsenal in the United States, and at the Military Academy at West Point, on the day of the receipt of this order, in commemoration of the surrender of General R. E. Lee and the Army of Northern Virginia, to Lieutenant General Grant and the army under his command. Report of the receipt and execution of this order to be made to the Adjutant General, Washington.

Edwin M. Stanton, Secretary of War.

🔫 *Jeff Davis and the Confederate cabinet were at this time at Danville—the new "capital"—about 50 miles south of Appomattox. Davis still hoped to continue resistance somewhere, somehow. The Star editorially heaped as much contempt upon Davis as it did praise for Lee.* 🔫

EDITORIAL.
The End of the Rebellion.

The thrilling intelligence buzzed about Washington at a late hour last night of the surrender of Lee and the army of Northern Virginia was fully and officially announced at daylight this morning by the thunder of artillery and the joyous ringing of bells.

With this surrender perishes the last hope of the rebels and their sympathizers, who have pinned their faith upon Lee, and despite defeat and disaster to their cause, culminating in the loss of Richmond, have yet talked of the successive surrenders of vital points by the rebels as profoundly "strategic," with a view to concentrating the rebel armies at some interior point, where they could bid defiance indefinitely to the Union forces.

But even the New York *News* will hardly be able to hold the surrender of Lee and his army up to its readers as "a blessing in disguise" for the Confederacy or a "masterly piece of policy" on the part of the Confederate leaders. When Lee, the wisest and bravest of the Confederate leaders, sees no ray of hope for the Confederate cause, and voluntarily lays down his arms to prevent the further and futile effusion of blood, the most credulous optimist amongst his followers must accept his judgment as decisive.

We may expect now to hear at any moment of the surrender of Johnston and his army, and that of the scattered remnants of the Confederate military organization throughout the South will follow, as soon as the news of the capitulation of their military chief is known. Could Jeff Davis be assured of the safety of his neck *he* too would surrender, but unpleasant doubts on that point, in view of his great crimes, will doubtless cause the conscience stricken arch-traitor to seek the desperate chance of a skulking exit from the country he has ruined.

His destiny—even if spared to die a natural death—is not to be envied, loaded as he will be with the curses and contumely of his countrymen, and deepest and most bitter, of his own deluded followers.

But we turn to more pleasant subjects—to the certainty of speedy PEACE; of the re-establishment of our glorious Union, in all its integrity; the return of our brave soldiers to their families and their peaceful occupations; the resumption of suspended industrial and commercial pursuits, and the starting out of the country on a new term of prosperity, with a new title to respect among the nations of the world.

Three days after the surrender, the remains of Lee's Army of Northern Virginia spattered through the mud on their last march to lay down their arms. John Brown Gordon led the column. Close behind was the remnants of the old Stonewall Brigade. Arrayed beside the road were two brigades of the Army of the Potomac. A Federal bugle sounded. The Federal troops snapped their weapons to the salute as their defeated but unbeaten foe slogged into memory. There remained a final touching aftermath.

(Monday, April 17, 1865)

Latest from Richmond.

FROM THE RICHMOND WHIG OF SATURDAY.

Farewell Address of Lee.

We have the Richmond *Whig* of Saturday. . . . [It] has the following:

General Lee's Farewell Address to the Army of Northern Virginia.

We publish below Gen. R. E. Lee's farewell address to the remnant of the Army of Northern Virginia on the occasion of the surrender of it to Gen. Grant at Clover Hill. We trust the authenticity of which we can vouch, having received it from an intelligent and veracious Confederate soldier who was present at Gen. Lee's headquarters when it was read, will convince of their error all persons of Secession proclivities who have hitherto, in face of all the facts, refused to credit the surrender of the Army of Northern Virginia.

HEADQUARTERS ARMY NORTHERN VIRGINIA, April 10, 1865.—*General Order No. 9.*—After four years of arduous service, marked by unsurpassed courage and fortitude, the Army of Northern Virginia has been compelled to yield to overwhelming numbers and resources.

The Army of Northern Virginia lays down its arms before long lines of the Army of the Potomac.

John Chapin—Library of Congress

I need not tell the survivors of so many hard-fought battles, who have remained steadfast to the last, that I have consented to this result from no distrust of them; but feeling that valor and devotion could accomplish nothing that could compensate for the loss that would have attended the continuation of this contest, I have determined to avoid the useless sacrifice of those whose past services have endeared them to their countrymen.

By the terms of agreement, officers and men can return to their homes, and remain there until exchanged.

You will take with you the satisfaction that proceeds from the consciousness of duty faithfully performed; and I earnestly pray that a merciful God will extend to you his blessing and protection.

With an unceasing admiration of your constancy and devotion to your country, and a grateful remembrance of your kind and generous consideration of myself, I bid you an affectionate farewell.

(Signed) R. E. Lee, General.

WASHINGTON HOMEFRONT, APRIL, 1865.

A Day of Jubilee.

As we write, the streets are filled with crowds of people, almost wild with excitement over the great and glorious news of the surrender of Lee. The various Departments have been promptly closed in honor of the day, and the stream of clerks turning out swells the tide on the streets. A large procession of Navy Yard men on jubilee to-day are passing up the street, accompanied by bands of music and a well-served howitzer, and other similar demonstrations of popular feeling are showing themselves in all quarters.

This morning, Assistant Secretary of the Treasury Field gave holiday to the clerks of that department; and they immediately started in procession to the President's House, in front of which they sang the "Star Spangled Banner" and "Old Hundred" with electric effect, and then passed on to the War Department shouting the stirring words and air "Rally Round the Flag Boys!"

The Secretary of War having been called for, after repeated and urgent demands, appeared before the enthusiastic crowd that thronged the halls and stairways of the War Department building. He was received with vociferous cheering, but asked to be excused on account of his health from making any

remarks. He, however, begged to introduce Major General Halleck.

The General was received with hearty cheering, and although evidently surprised by the strategy of the Honorable Secretary, addressed the throng as follows:

"Always ready as I am to obey the orders of my superior officer, the honorable Secretary of War, I hardly think he will go so far as to require me to become a stump speaker. (Laughter, cheers and cries of 'The people require it,' 'It is a military necessity,' &c.) Stump speaking, my friends, is something in which I have never indulged. I can only say that our congratulations and thanks are due to Gen. Grant and our brave generals and soldiers in the field for the great victory announced this morning and for the blessing of peace, of which it is the harbinger."

His Honor, Mayor [Richard] Wallach, was discovered in the crowd, and being loudly called for, replied in a few appropriate words, saying that his heart was too full for utterance, and that he was gratified, to observe from their bright looks and happy faces, that they felt as they should feel on such an occasion.

Richard Wallach was the brother of The Star's *editor. He had been first elected in 1861.*

More Enthusiasm.
SERENADE TO PRESIDENT LINCOLN.
HIS SPEECH.
The Tune of "Dixie" Fairly Captured, He Says.

At the Navy Yard this morning, the workmen were promptly on the spot at bell ring, but on account of the news their hearts were too full to allow them to go to work, and after answering to their names they procured martial music and marched in the Yard, paying their respects to the Commandant, Commodore Montgomery, who addressed them in appropriate patriotic language. They also waited on Master Morris, who addressed them, and on Captain Jeffers, of the Ordnance, who was too much indisposed to make a speech. The procession then proceeded to the flag staff on Virginia avenue, where an impromptu meeting was held, and a salute from two howitzers, in charge of Mr. John W. Thompson, was fired.

Rev. Mr. Sipes was introduced, and made a short address, saying that the spirit of kindness should now actuate the people, and they should be grateful to Almighty God especially for this last bloodless victory. He urged that they should each prepare to welcome back the erring brothers in the same spirit the father welcomed back the prodigal son.

By this time there were nearly two thousand persons assembled, and under the lead of Mr. Sipes all united in singing, with impressive effect, the doxology, "Praise God from whom all blessings flow." Mr. John Smith then, from the stand, sang the "Flag of our Union." Nine cheers and a tiger were given for the Union.

Headed by the Marine Band, the line was formed under the direction of Mr. J. C. Dulin and marched up Pennsylvania avenue, Lincoln Hospital Band being also in the procession. Mr. Thompson, with the howitzer corps, kept a short distance in front of the procession and fired at intervals, while a wagon containing a number of young men carrying a transparency labelled, "This flag shall never be surrendered to traitors," and "Shoot the first man who dares to pull down the flag," together with a number of flags, was also in the procession.

They first visited the residence of Secretary Welles, on H street, but he not being at home they proceeded to the Executive Mansion, where they were joined by a large crowd with which was the Quartermaster's Band, and after a salute had been fired by the howitzers, several national airs been played by the bands, followed by loud and prolonged cheering, the President made his appearance amid tremendous applause. After order was restored he spoke as follows:

SPEECH OF THE PRESIDENT.

I am very much rejoiced, my friends, in the fact that an occasion has occurred so pleasurable that the people find it impossible to refrain from giving vent to their feelings. (Applause.) I suppose that arrangements are being made for a formal demonstration either this or to-morrow evening. (A voice—"That's too late.") Should such a demonstration take place I of course will be expected to respond, if called upon, and if I permit you to dribble all out of me now, I will have nothing left to say on that occasion. (Laughter and applause.)

I observe that you have a band of music with you. I propose having this interview closed by the band performing a particular tune, which I shall name. Before this is done, however, I wish to mention one or two little circumstances connected with it.

I have always thought that "Dixie" was one of the best tunes I had ever heard. Our adversaries over the way, I know, have attempted to appropriate it, but I insist that on yesterday we fairly captured it. (Applause.) I referred the question to the Attorney General and he gave it as his legal opinion that it is now our legal property. (Laughter and loud applause.) I now ask the band to favor us with its performance.

The band immediately complied amid the cheers of the crowd.

The procession proceeded to the War and Navy Departments, and several national airs were performed, accompanied by salutes by the artillery.

PRESIDENT DAVIS OF THE LATE CONFEDERACY WAS IN A wagon train nearing Greensboro, N. C., in his flight from Danville on April 14. Nearly 500 miles away, in Washington, President Lincoln, in a serene mood now that the Union cause had prevailed, was preparing to attend a play at Ford's Theater.

His day had started early as usual—7 a.m. One of his first chores was to call a cabinet meeting for 11 a.m. Grant, in town for a brief visit, attended the session at the President's request. Though he had not yet heard from Sherman on the expected surrender of the Confederate army in North Carolina, Lincoln said he was sure the capitulation would come soon. He had had a dream the night before, he told his official family. It was the same dream he had dreamt before on the eve of three Union victories. In it a strange ship could be seen sailing rapidly toward a dark vague shore.

The President then discussed the reconstruction of the South. He praised Lee and his troops who had fought so bravely for the cause they believed in. He fretted some about those radical Congressmen who preached hate and retribution. He wanted no persecution, not even of the Confederacy's ringleaders. It would be better all around if they simply got out of the country on their own volition. With that the meeting broke up; and Grant begged off attending the theater that night with the Lincolns. The general and his wife were anxious to get to New Jersey to see their sons.

A carriage ride with Mrs. Lincoln in the afternoon, another succession of White House visitors, and the Lincolns were ready—a little tardily—for Ford's Theater. Their guests in the Presidential box were Maj. Henry Reed Rathbone and his fiancee, Miss Clara Harris—one of Washington society's more acceptable couples. When the party arrived shortly after 8 p.m., the performance halted, the audience burst into tumultuous welcome and the pit orchestra played "Hail to the Chief."

The President solemnly acknowledged the cheers, then settled back in his oversized rocking chair. The houselights dimmed, and the play resumed.

THE PRESIDENT ASSASSINATED

ASSASSINATION OF THE PRESIDENT.

Attempted Murder of Secretary Seward and Sons.

DESPATCHES FROM SECRETARY STANTON.

WAR DEPARTMENT.
WASHINGTON, D.C., April 15—1.30 P.M.
[A.M.]

Major General John A. Dix, New York:

Last evening, at 10.30 p.m., at Ford's Theater, the President, while sitting in his private box with Mrs. Lincoln, Miss Harris, and Maj. Rathbun, was shot by an assassin who suddenly entered the box. He approached behind the President. The assassin then leaped upon the stage, brandishing a large dagger or knife, and made his escape by the rear of the theater. The pistol ball entered the back of the President's head. The wound is mortal. The President has been insensible ever since it was inflicted, and is now dying.

About the same hour an assassin, either the same or another, entered Mr. Seward's house, and, under pretense of having a prescription, was shown to the Secretary's sick chamber. The Secretary was in bed, a nurse and Miss Seward with him. The assassin immediately rushed to the bed, inflicting two or three stabs on the throat, and two in the face. It is hoped the wounds may not be mortal. My apprehension is that they will prove fatal. The nurse alarmed Mr. Frederick Seward, who was in an adjoining room, and hastened to the door of his father's room, where he met the assassin, who inflicted upon him one or more dangerous wounds. The recovery of Frederick Seward is doubtful.

It is not probable that the President will live through the night.

Library of Congress

President Lincoln, four days before his death.

Gen. Grant and wife were advertised to be at the theater this evening, but the latter started to Burlington at six o'clock last evening.

At a Cabinet meeting, at which Gen. Grant was present to-day [yesterday] the subject of the state of the country, and the prospects of speedy peace was discussed. The President was very cheerful and hopeful, spoke very kindly of Gen. Lee and others of the Confederacy, and the establishment of Government in Virginia All the members of the Cabinet, except Mr. Seward, are now in attendance upon the President. I have seen Mr. Seward, but he and Frederick were both unconscious.

E. M. Stanton, Secretary of War.

☞ *The play had just entered the third act when the dull sound of a shot was heard in the Presidential box. Without realizing what was going on, Maj.*

The Presidential box at Ford's Theater. Lincoln was seated in the right-hand section.

Rathbone grappled with the intruder and was savagely slashed in the arm. As the man leaped from the box to the stage, the spur on his left boot caught in a regimental flag draped on the box front. He landed awkwardly. Further accounts filled in details of the chaotic events. ✒

ASSOCIATED PRESS ACCOUNT.

President Lincoln and wife, together with other friends, last evening visited Ford's Theater for the purpose of witnessing the performance of the American Cousin. It was announced in the newspapers that Gen. Grant would also be present, but that gentleman, instead, took the late train of cars for New Jersey. The theater was densely crowded, and everybody seemed delighted with the scene before them.

During the third act, and while there was a temporary pause for one of the actors to enter, a sharp report of a pistol was heard, which merely attracted attention, but suggesting nothing serious, until a man rushed to the front of the President's box, waving a long dagger in his right hand, and exclaiming *"Sic Semper Tyrannis,"* and immediately leaped from the box, which was of the second tier, to the stage beneath, and ran across to the opposite side, thus making his escape, amid the bewilderment of the audience, from the rear of the theater, and, mounting a horse, fled.

The screams of Mrs. Lincoln first disclosed the fact to the audience that the President had been shot, when all present rose to their feet, rushing toward the stage, exclaiming, "Hang him!" "Hang him!"

The excitement was of the wildest possible character; and, of course, there was an abrupt termination of the theatrical performance.

There was a rush towards the President's box, when cries were heard, "Stand back!" "Give him air!" "Has any one stimulants!" &c.

On a hasty examination it was found that the President had been shot through the head, above and back of the temporal bone, and that some of the brain was oozing out. He was removed to the private residence of Mr. Peterson, opposite to the theater, and the Surgeon General of the Army and other surgeons sent for to attend to his condition.

On examination of the private box, blood was discovered on the back of the cushioned rocking chair in which the President had been sitting, also on the partition and on the floor.

Ford's Theater.

A common single barrelled pocket pistol was found on the carpet.

A military guard was placed in front of the private residence to which the President had been conveyed.

An immense crowd was in front of it, all deeply anxious to learn the condition of the President. It had been previously announced that the wound was mortal, but all hoped otherwise.

The shock to the community was terrible.

At midnight the Cabinet, with Messrs. Sumner, Colfax, Farnsworth, Judge Cartter, Gov. Oglesby, General Meigs, Major Hay, and a few personal friends, with Surgeon General Barnes and his medical associates, were around his bedside. The President was in a state of syncope, totally insensible, and breathing slowly, the blood oozing from the wound at the back of his head. The surgeons were exhausting every possible effort of medical skill, but all hope was gone. The parting of his family with the dying President is too sad for description.

The President and Mrs. Lincoln did not start to the theatre, till fifteen minutes past eight o'clock. Speaker [Schuyler] Colfax was at the White House at the time, and the President stated to him that he was going, although Mrs. Lincoln had not been well, because the papers had advertised that General Grant and themselves were to be present, and, as General Grant had gone North, he did not wish the audience to be disappointed. He went with apparent reluctance, and urged Mr. Colfax to go with him; but that gentleman had made other engagements, and with Mr. [George] Ashmun, [Representative] of Massachusetts, bade him good-bye.

When the excitement at the theatre was at its wildest height, reports were circulated that Secretary Seward had also been assassinated.

On reaching this gentleman's residence a crowd and a military guard were found at the door, and, on entering, it was ascertained that reports were based upon truth.

Everybody was so much excited that scarcely an intelligible account could be gathered. . . .

It is believed the injuries of the Secretary are not mortal, nor those of either of the others, although both the Secretary and the Assistant Secretary are very seriously injured.

Secretaries Stanton and Welles, and other prominent officers of the Government, called at Secretary Seward's house to inquire into his condition, and hearing there of the assassination of the President, proceeded to the house where he was lying, exhibiting, of course, intense anxiety and solicitude.

War Department, Washington, April 20, 1865.

$100,000 REWARD!

THE MURDERER

Of our late beloved President, ABRAHAM LINCOLN,

IS STILL AT LARGE.

$50,000 REWARD!

will be paid by this Department for his apprehension, in addition to any reward offered by Municipal Authorities or State Executives.

$25,000 REWARD!

will be paid for the apprehension of JOHN H. SURRATT, one of Booth's accomplices.

$25,000 REWARD!

will be paid for the apprehension of DANIEL C. HARROLD, another of Booth's accomplices.

LIBERAL REWARDS will be paid for any information that shall conduce to the arrest of either of the above-named criminals, or their accomplices.

All persons harboring or secreting the said persons, or either of them, or aiding or assisting their concealment or escape, will be treated as accomplices in the murder of the President and the attempted assassination of the Secretary of State, and shall be subject to trial before a Military Commission and the punishment of DEATH.

Let the stain of innocent blood be removed from the land by the arrest and punishment of the murderers.

All good citizens are exhorted to aid public justice on this occasion. Every man should consider his own conscience charged with this solemn duty, and rest neither night nor day until it be accomplished.

EDWIN M. STANTON, Secretary of War.

DESCRIPTIONS.—BOOTH is 5 feet 7 or 8 inches high, slender build, high forehead, black hair, black eyes, and wears a heavy black moustache. JOHN H. SURRATT is about 5 feet 9 inches. Hair rather thin and dark; eyes rather light; no beard. Would weigh 145 or 150 pounds. Complexion rather pale and clear, with color in his cheeks. Wore light clothes of fine quality. Shoulders square; cheek bones rather prominent; chin narrow; ears projecting at the top; forehead rather low and square, but broad. Parts his hair on the right side; neck rather long. His lips are firmly set. A slim man. DANIEL C. HARROLD is 22 years of age, 5 feet 6 or 7 inches high, rather broad shoulders; otherwise light built; dark hair, little (if any) moustache; dark eyes; weighs about 140 pounds.

GEO. F. NESBITT & CO., Printers and Stationers, cor. Pearl and Pine Streets, N. Y.

Library of Congress

An immense crowd was gathered in front of the President's house, and a strong guard was also stationed there, many persons evidently supposing that he would be brought to his home.

The entire city last night presented a scene of wild excitement, accompanied by violent expressions of indignation, and the profoundest sorrow. Many persons shed tears.

The military authorities have despatched mounted patrols in every direction, in order, if possible, to arrest the assassins, while the Metropolitan police are alike vigilant for the same purpose. The attacks, both at the theater and at Secretary Seward's, took place at about the same hour—ten o'clock—thus showing a precented plan to assassinate these gentlemen.

Some evidence of the guilt of the party who attacked the President is in possession of the police.

Vice President Johnson is in the city, and his hotel quarters [Kirkwood House] are guarded by troops.

2½ A.M.—The President is still alive, but is growing weaker. The ball is lodged in his brain, three inches from where it entered the skull. He remains insensible, and his condition is utterly hopeless.

The Vice President has been to see him, but all company except the Cabinet, his family, and a few friends, are rigidly excluded.

Large crowds still continue in the street, as near to the house as the line of guards allow.

☞ The ball entered behind the President's left ear and lodged behind his right eye. The attending physicians knew almost from the start that the wound was mortal. ☜

THE DEATH OF THE PRESIDENT.

At 22 minutes past seven o'clock the President breathed his last, closing his eyes as if falling to sleep, and his countenance assuming an expression of perfect serenity. There were no indications of pain, and it was not known that he was dead until the gradually decreasing respiration ceased altogether.

Rev. Dr. Gurley, (of the New York Avenue Presbyterian Church,) immediately on its being ascertained that life was extinct, knelt at the bedside and offered and impressive prayer which was responded to by all present.

Dr. Gurley then proceeded to the front parlor, where Mrs. Lincoln, Capt. Robert Lincoln, Mr. John Hay, the Private Secretary, and others, were waiting, where he again offered prayer for the consolation of the family.

The following minutes, taken by Dr. Abbott, show the condition of the President throughout the night:

☞ At this point, one-fourth of a column gave periodic reports of one line each of the President's pulse and respiration counts starting with entry "11 o'clock —Pulse 41" and ending with "7—Symptoms of immediate dissolution" and "7.22—Death." ☜

Surrounding the death bed of the President, were Secretaries Stanton, Welles, Usher, Attorney General Speed; Post Master General Dennison; M. B. Field, Assistant Secretary of the Treasury; Judge Otto, Assistant Secretary of the Interior; General Halleck, General Meigs, Senator Sumner, F. R. Andrews, of N. Y.; General Todd, of Dacotah; John Hay (Private Secretary); Gov. Oglesby, of Illinois; General Farnsworth, Mrs. and Miss Kenny, Miss Harris, Captain Robert Lincoln, son of the Presi-

The funeral procession down Pennsylvania Avenue.

dent, and Drs. E. W. Abbott, R. K. Stone, C. D. Gatch, Neal [Leale], Hall and Leiberman. Secretary McCullough remained with the President until about 5 o'clock, and Chief Justice Chase, after several hours attendance during the night, returned again early this morning.

SPECIAL CABINET MEETING.

Immediately after the President's death a Cabinet meeting was called by Secretary Stanton, and held in the room in which the corpse lay. Secretaries Stanton, Welles and Usher, Post Master General Dennison and Attorney General Speed present. The results of the Conference are as yet unknown.

War Secretary Stanton took over with his customary energy and, using a back room of the Peterson House, opened his mercifully brief regime as the Nation's head. Searchers went out in every direction, save the one taken by the assassin across the Navy Yard Bridge across the Anacostia into Southern Maryland. In the frenzy of intemperate action, citizens were arrested wholesale; witnesses were brought into the House while the President still breathed, and their testimony taken under oath in a one-man inquisition; ugly mobs roamed the streets threatening and assaulting "suspects," preying on anyone who may have shown the slightest secessionist leanings. Stanton had immediately concluded the assassination was a conspiracy by the Rebel government, and his view was widely shared. The War Secretary did take one respite from his frantic quest for the killer. When Lincoln had breathed his last, Stanton standing near reverently intoned: "Now he belongs to the ages." Soon after, bells began tolling and guns booming in a dirge throughout the city and the Nation.

REMOVAL OF THE REMAINS TO THE WHITE HOUSE.

Shortly after nine o'clock this morning the remains were placed in a temporary coffin, under the direction of Mr. Frank Sands, and removed to the White House, six young men of the Quartermaster's Department carrying the body to the house.

An escort of cavalry, (Union Light Guard,) under the command of Lieut. Jamison, accompanied the remains, which were followed by Generals Augur, commanding Department of Washington; Rucker, Depot Quartermaster; Col. Pelouze, of the War Department; Capt. Finley Anderson, A.A.G., Hancock's corps; Captain D. G. Thomas, Clothing Depot; Captains J. H. Crowell and C. Baker.

The solemn procession moved slowly up 10th street to G, and thence to the White House, the large crowd present along the route standing uncovered. Immediately on the guard being removed a rush was made towards the house occupied during the night by the President, remaining about the entrance for some time.

SECRETARY SEWARD

and sons are much better to-day.

Inauguration of Andrew Johnson as President of the United States!

At an early hour this morning, Hon. Edwin M. Stanton, Secretary of War, sent an official communication to Hon. Andrew Johnson, Vice President, that, in consequence of the sudden and unexpected death of the Chief Magistrate, his inauguration should take place as soon as possible, and requesting him to state place and hour at which the ceremony should be performed. Mr. Johnson immediately replied that it would be agreeable to him to have the proceedings take place at his rooms in the Kirkwood House, as soon as the arrangements could be perfected.

Chief Justice Chase was informed of the fact, and repaired to the appointed place in company with Secretary McCulloch of the Treasury Department, Mr. Attorney General Speed, F. P. Blair, Sr., Hon. Montgomery Blair, Senators Foot of Vermont, Ramsey of Minnesota, Yates of Illinois, Stewart of Nevada, Hale of New Hampshire, and General Farnsworth of Illinois.

At 11 o'clock the oath of office was administered by the Chief Justice of the United States in his usual solemn and impressive manner.

Mr. Johnson received the kind expressions of the gentlemen by whom he was surrounded, in a manner which showed his earnest sense of the great responsibilities so suddenly devolved upon him, and made a brief speech, in which he said:

"The duties of the office are mine; I will perform them—the consequences are with God.

"Gentlemen, I shall lean upon you; I feel that I shall need your support. I am deeply impressed with the solemnity of the occasion and the responsibilities of the duties of the office I am assuming."

Mr. Johnson appeared to be in remarkably good health, and has a high and realizing sense of the

The death of four of the conspirators. From left to right the executed are: Mary Surratt, Lewis Payne, George Adzerodt, and David Herrold.

hopes that are centered upon him. His manner was solemn and dignified, and his whole bearing produced a most gratifying impression upon those who participated in the ceremonies.

It is probable that during the day President Johnson will issue his first proclamation to the American people.

THE CABINET MEETING YESTERDAY.

At the Cabinet meeting yesterday, which lasted over two hours, the future policy of the Government towards the Southern States, and especially towards Virginia, was discussed, the best of feeling prevailing. It is stated that it was determined to adopt a very liberal policy, as recommended by the President.

It is said that this meeting was the most harmonious held for over two years, the President evincing throughout that magnanimity and kindness of heart which has throughout characterized his treatment of the rebellious States, and which has been so illy requited on their part.

One of the members of the Cabinet as he left the chamber, remarked to a friend he met at the door that "the Government is to-day stronger than it has been for three years past."

THE PRESIDENT'S LAST WRITING.

The last writing done by President Lincoln was addressed to Hon. George Ashmun in reply to a request of the latter for an interview.

The message was written on a card, on the President's knee, in his carriage, about quarter-past eight, just as he was starting for the theater. The note was as follows:

"Allow Mr. Ashmun and friend to come to me at 9 a.m. tomorrow.

"April 14, 1865.   A. Lincoln."

🖚 *Two days later,* The Star *published its first news illustration.* 🖚

358

The Fatal Ball.

Below we give a diagram of the fatal ball that killed Mr. Lincoln, taken from actual measurement showing its exact dimensions:

It will be seen that it is of murderous size. It is now pretty well established that the pistol was loaded with two balls, the other of which passed through the box door. The fact of the fracture of the door is thus explained. It is certain that the pistol was held close to the head of the President, from the clear aperture made through the skull, and thus that the assassin must have been in his immediate vicinity.

☞ *With Lincoln gone, the strength of the government would indeed be exerted in a most terrible way. The forces of vengeance would hold the upper hand. Moderation and a constructive reconstruction would have to fight a rear-guard action for 12 long years before sanity could regain control in the North.* ☞

WASHINGTON HOMEFRONT, APRIL, 1865.

☞ *Many Washingtonians were tempted to attend the theater that Good Friday when they read this ad in The Star:* ☞

(Friday, April 14, 1865)

FORD'S NEW THEATRE.
TENTH STREET, above Pennsylvania avenue.

BENEFIT and Last Appearance of
MISS LAURA KEENE.
THIS (Friday) EVENING, April 14, 1865:

When she will appear as FLORENCE TRENCH-ARD, in the celebrated comedy of

THE AMERICAN COUSIN,

from the original manuscript of Tom Taylor, as played at Laura Keene's Theater, New York, for upwards of three hundred nights.

She will be supported by J. C. McCOLLUM, JOHN DYOTT, HARRY HAWK, &c.

To-morrow, Benefit of MISS JEANIE GOUR-LAY, when will be presented the great drama, illustrative of Southern Life, Southern Scenes, and Southern Homes, entitled THE OCTOROON.

The talented young tragedian,
EDWIN ADAMS
Is engaged for twelve nights only, and will appear
MONDAY, April 17.

☞ *And according to a news item in another column, added attractions were slated—clearly telling any reader that the President would attend the theater.* ☞

City Items.

FORD'S THEATRE.—"Honor to our Soldiers." A new and Patriotic Song and Chorus has been written by Mr. H. B. Phillips, and will be sung this evening by the Entire Company to do honor to Lieutenant General Grant and President Lincoln and Lady, who visit the Theatre in compliment to Miss Laura Keene, whose benefit and last appearance is announced in the bills of the day. The music of the above song is composed by Prof. W. Withers, Jr.

☞ *"Local news" the day Lincoln died was assassination, arrests and the search. And at last the authorities had an identity they could connect with the slaying.* ☞

(Saturday, April 15, 1865)

Additional Details of the Assassination.
MILITARY MOVEMENTS.

As soon as the news reached Gen. Augur's headquarters that the President had been shot, the military of this department was ordered out, and in a few moments the city was encircled with pickets, they being stationed at a distance of about fifty feet apart. Cavalry was placed upon all the roads leading from Washington, and mounted men and military detectives proceeded to scour the country in every direction with orders to arrest any suspicious parties that they might find.

J. Wilkes Booth the Assassin.

Col. Ingraham, Provost Marshal of the defenses north of the Potomac, is engaged in taking testimony to-day, all of which fixes the assassination upon J. Wilkes Booth.

Judge Olin, of the Supreme Court of the District of Columbia, and Justice Miller are also engaged to-day at the police headquarters on 10th street in taking the testimony of a large number of witnesses.

Lieut. Tyrell, of Col. Ingraham's staff, last night proceeded to the National Hotel, where Booth had been stopping, and took possession of his trunk, in which was found a colonel's military dress coat, two pairs of handcuffs, two boxes of cartridges and a package of letters, all of which are now in the possession of the military authorities.

One of these letters, bearing date at Hookstown, Md., seems to implicate Booth. The writer speaks of the "mysterious affair in which you are engaged," and urges Booth to proceed to Richmond and ascertain the views of the authorities there upon the subject. The writer of the letter then endeavors to persuade Booth from carrying his designs into execution at that time, for the reasons as he (the writer) alleges the "Government here had its suspicions aroused."

The writer of the letter seems to have been implicated with Booth in the "mysterious affair" referred to, as he informs Booth in the letter that he would prefer to express his views verbally; and then goes on to say that he was out of money, had no clothes, and would be compelled to leave home as his family were desirous that he should dissolve his connection with Booth.

This letter is written on note paper in a small neat hand, and simply bears the signature of "Sam."

THE POLICE REPORT

that about eleven o'clock two men were seen rapidly riding into Maryland, by way of Anacostia bridge. A knife, answering the description of that flourished by Booth on the stage, was picked up this morning on F street, between 8th and 9th, and turned over to the police. At a late hour last night, a horse, with a saddle and bridle, was also taken up in the street by a soldier, and identified by the owner as the animal hired by one of the men.

This morning, Edward Spangler, a livery man, who held the horse of Booth when the latter rode up to the theater, and a boy named Peanut John, were arrested by the Third Ward police, and are now in custody. Peanut John asserted that Booth sold the horse he usually rode, and purchased another, a small bay horse.

John Surratt, of Prince George's county, Maryland, is said to be the man who cut Mr. Seward, but as yet no clue to the direction he took, unless he went with Booth, has been obtained.

SUSPENSION OF TRAVEL.

At 12 o'clock last night, orders were received at the River Transportation office, directing that no vessels be allowed to take their departure. The Alexandria and Washington ferry boats have ceased running for the present.

To-day no one is allowed to leave the city by rail, conveyance, or on foot, and the issuing of passes from the headquarters of the Department of Washington has been suspended by Gen. Augur.

One extraneous item did creep in.

TORCH LIGHT PROCESSION.—The torch light procession of the arsenal employees last evening in celebration of the national flag again over Fort Sumter was a very fine affair. The procession was composed of about two thousand persons, including two companies of the 9th regiment Veteran Reserves, under Captains West and Knower, and preceded by a fine band, attracted great attention. . . .

The very day President Lincoln was planning to spend a relaxing evening in the theater, Joe Johnston had sounded out Sherman on possible arrangements for surrendering the Confederate army in North Carolina. Sherman had just reached Raleigh from Goldsboro, marching his army of 80,000 under earlier orders to knock the Confederates out of the way and make for Danville. During the two days prior to Lincoln's assassination, both generals had learned of Lee's surrender. Johnston at the time was around Durham's Station, west of Raleigh, with an effective force of 21,000, but he realized further resistance was hopeless.

Word of the armistice took three days getting to Washington. The Capital, prostrated by Lincoln's death, scarcely took notice. The columns of *The Star,* crammed as they were with the news of the assassination and the hunt for the murderer, afforded only one paragraph for the news from North Carolina.

LAST CONFEDERATE ARMY SURRENDERS

(Monday, April 17, 1865)

Reported Surrender of Johnston.

It is reported that information has been received from North Carolina, to the effect that Johnston had communicated with General Sherman, asking what terms would be given upon his surrender, and that Sherman had replied by offering the same as those accepted by Lee. When last heard from, Sherman was approaching Raleigh, and the surrender of Johnston's forces was then expected to take place at any time.

Latest reports, courtesy of a steamboat, a Richmond competitor, and a Mr. Smith.

(Saturday, April 22, 1865)

LATEST FROM RICHMOND.
Surrender of Johnston's Army.

We are indebted to Captain Young and Mr. Smith, of the mail boat *James T. Brady,* for copies of the Richmond *Whig* of yesterday, from which we glean the following items of interest:

THE SURRENDER OF JOHNSTON'S ARMY. —Advices from Newbern, N. C., on the 13th inst., state that Gen. Sherman had received a flag of truce from Gen. Johnston, asking for terms of surrender. Gen. Sherman replied that he would tender him the same terms as were granted by Gen. Grant to Gen. Lee's army. There seems to be no reason to doubt that Johnston has surrendered, the event taking place about the 13th or 14th inst., in the neighborhood of Smithfield, before which place, at last accounts, Gen. Sherman was lying. Smithfield is about midway between Raleigh and Goldsboro. Before the receipt of this news the general impression here was that Johnston had retreated in the direction of Charlotte, N. C., and had perhaps reached that point. It would now seem that he has made no movement since the surrender, wisely determining, perhaps, to regulate his efforts according to the result of military operations in Virginia. He is said to have been strongly intrenched at Smithfield. . . .

War Secretary Stanton finally took time out from his intense hunt for Lincoln's assassin to give some attention to developments in North Carolina.

Library of Congress

General Joseph Johnston surrendering to General Sherman near Greensboro, North Carolina.

SHERMAN.

Johnston Offers to Surrender.

Sherman's Terms Disapproved— Jeff Davis Likely to Escape.

WAR DEPARTMENT
WASHINGTON, D.C., April 22—10 P.M.

Maj. Gen. Jno. A. Dix, New York:

Yesterday evening a bearer of despatches arrived from General Sherman. An agreement for a suspension of hostilities, and a memorandum of what is called a basis for peace, had been entered into on the 18th instant by General Sherman with the rebel General Johnston, the rebel General Breckinridge being present at the conference. A Cabinet meeting was held at 8 o'clock in the evening, at which the action of General Sherman was disapproved by the President, by the Secretary of War, by General Grant, and by every member of the Cabinet. General Sherman was ordered to resume hostilities immediately, and he was directed that the instructions given by the late President, in the following telegram, which was penned by Mr. Lincoln himself at the Capitol, on the night of the 3d of March, were approved by President Andrew Johnson, and were reiterated to govern the action of military commanders.

On the night of the 3d of March, while President Lincoln and his Cabinet were at the Capitol, a telegraph from General Grant was brought to the Secretary of War, informing him that General Lee had requested an interview or conference, to make an arrangement for terms of peace. The letter of General Lee was published in a message of Davis to the rebel Congress. General Grant's telegram was submitted to Mr. Lincoln, who, after pondering a few minutes, took up his pen and wrote with his own hand the following reply, which he submitted to the Secretary of State and Secretary of War. It was then dated, addressed, and signed by the Secretary of War, and telegraphed to General Grant:

PRESIDENT LINCOLN'S INSTRUCTIONS.

WASHINGTON, March 3, 1865, 12 P.M.—
Lieutenant General Grant: The President directs me to say to you that he wishes you to have no conference with General Lee, unless it be for the capitulation of General Lee's army, or on some minor or purely military matter. He instructs me to say that you are not to decide, discuss, or confer upon any political question. Such questions the President holds in his own hands, and will submit them to no military conferences or conventions. Meantime you are to press to the utmost military advantages.

Edwin M. Stanton, Secretary of War.

The orders of General Sherman to General Stoneman, to withdraw from Salisbury [N. C.] and join him, will probably open the way for Davis to escape to Mexico or Europe with his plunder, which is reported to be very large, including not only the plunder of the Richmond banks, but previous accumulations. They hope, it is said, to make terms with General Sherman or some other southern commander, by which they will be permitted, with their effects, including the gold plunder, to go to Mexico or Europe. Johnston's negotiations look to that end.

After the Cabinet meeting last night, General Grant started for North Carolina, to direct operations against Johnston's army.

Edwin M. Stanton, Secretary of War.

The agreement reached by the two military commanders on April 18 was in the nature of a peace convention that touched on political and military matters beyond the scope of their immediate commands. What the Washington government demanded was simply a surrender of Johnston's army.

MORE GOOD NEWS!

Surrender of the Whole of Johnston's Army.

TERMS THE SAME AS ACCORDED TO LEE.

WAR DEPARTMENT
WASHINGTON, April 28, 3 p.m.

Major General Dix, New York:

A *despatch* from General Grant, dated at Raleigh, 10 p.m., April 26, just received by this department, states that:

"Johnston surrendered the forces in his command, embracing all from here to the Chattahoochie, to Gen. Sherman, on the basis agreed upon between Lee and myself for the Army of Northern Virginia."

Edwin M. Stanton, Secretary of War.

The James Bennett house in which General Johnston surrendered.

WASHINGTON HOMEFRONT, APRIL, 1865.

While Sherman's knuckles were being rapped for showing anything resembling lenience toward the South, a local item appeared in The Star *reflecting the hate motif all too clearly.*

❦

NOT HERE.—The report that Dr. Cornelius Boyle, who acted as rebel Provost Marshal at Gordonsville, had returned to this city, seems to have originated in the fact that another Dr. Boyle, an Assistant Surgeon in the rebel army, had arrived here on parole. It was indeed not so easy to believe that he would voluntarily return to the city toward which he has shown so much hate.

The Alexandria *Journal* says of him:

"Not ten days ago the same Major Boyle refused to parole Lieutenant Gover and some thirty-five of his men, all members of the Loudoun Rangers. Although he was aware of Lee's surrender, in a conversation with the Lieutenant he stated that he never would submit to return and live under the United States Government, that the South had hardly commenced to fight yet, and when it did show its full strength it would not be many days until its independence would be gained."

Other ex-Washingtonians who went South at the outbreak of the rebellion and took up arms have now returned here under parole, claiming that this is their home, and instead of hiding their heads in shame, they wear an air of insolent swagger and seem to expect to be received with open arms.

Their claim that Washington city is their home is a piece of impudence which should be promptly set aside in the start. In leaving Washington to take up arms in the rebel cause they abjured all rights of citizenship here, and whatever claim they have to citizenship is in Virginia, and most, if not all, of them, have, we hear, exercised the right of suffrage in that State during their four years' stay there.

Now, when the rebellion has played out, they find it convenient to claim Washington as their home, and expect to step at once into the enjoyment of all the privileges of the most loyal citizens.

They will learn, however, two things: one that they will not be allowed to elect Washington as their home, and the other that the moment that their parole is out, *i.e.,* that they are declared exchanged, they will be subject, if found about here, to the penalties of treason.

PRESIDENT LINCOLN'S REMAINS HAD REACHED FINAL RE-pose in Springfield, Ill., after a long train ride. President Johnson's stout fight against the hate-mongers and power-grabbers of the North—those bent on a harsh peace for the South—had just begun. This was May, 1865—a month which also saw the surrender of the remnants of the Confederate army in Alabama, Mississippi, Florida, Arkansas, and Texas—where the last land engagement of the war was fought near Brownsville. The Confederacy's fleeing President Davis was captured, near Irwinsville, Ga. And the *Stonewall,* latest Confederate man-of-war to come off British ways, was surrendered before it had a chance to fire a shot at the foe it was designed to fight.

The shooting war, in short, was over on all fronts—except one. This was the watery battlefield of the Confederate cruiser *Shenandoah.*

The *Shenandoah,* Capt. James Iredell Waddell commanding, aimed its sail and screw-driven prow across the Atlantic Ocean in Oc-tober, 1864. At the time, it was the only Confederate sea raider of any consequence afloat. Its plan of action was to sail across half the world to Australia, northward up the West Pacific to an entirely new hunt-ing ground, the sea between Russian Siberia and Alaska fished by American ships out of New England for whale oil.

Waddell's ship was, of course, thousands of miles from the nearest source of news. Unaware of the surrenders back home, he went about his work in businesslike fashion.

WAR OVER, REBEL SHIP FIGHTS ON

(Monday, August 28, 1865)

More Work of the Pirate.

EIGHT MORE WHALERS DESTROYED—OTHER VESSELS SEEN BURNING.

CHICAGO, August 26.—A San Francisco telegram of the 3d inst. says the following vessels have been destroyed by the pirate *Shenandoah:*

Herman, J. Howland, Nassau, Brunswick, James Mundy, Waverly, Martha, and *Congress,* all of New Bedford.

The *Favorite,* of Fairhaven; *Covington,* of Warren, and the *Neil and James Mundy* were bonded to carry the seamen belonging to the vessels destroyed to San Francisco.

All the foregoing vessels were captured in the vicinity of Behring's Straits. The last seen of the *Shenandoah* she was steering south, and towards Lawrence Bay. The *Neil* saw other vessels burning after leaving the pirate. The crews of the vessels were captured and plundered of everything valuable.

No dates are mentioned in the dispatch with the inland dateline. But the Shenandoah's *skipper recorded that on June 28 he attacked and destroyed "nine Yankee whalers" in the Bering Sea. It was not until the news of this sally was circulating in the United States that Capt. Waddell heard from a British ship that the war was over. Nearly three months would elapse before the country knew he had learned that the war was over.*

(Monday, November 20, 1865)

Telegraphic News.

From Europe.

The Pirate Shenandoah.

NEW YORK, November 20.—The steamships *City of London* and *New York,* from Queenstown on the 9th, have arrived at quarantine.

The pirate *Shenandoah* arrived in Mersey on the 6th and surrendered to the guard ship *Donegal,* and is now in the hands of the naval authorities.

Capt. Waddell states that the first information he received of the close of the war was on the thirteenth of August from the British war vessel *Barraconta,* and that he immediately consigned the *Shenandoah's* guns to the hold and steered for Liverpool.

The *Daily News* says the Americans may be inclined to say it was only fitting that her end should be as British as her origin; but the *News* cannot help asking how the *Shenandoah* was enabled to pursue her course without the least interruption from the American navy. Can it be possible that the expectation of recovering compensation for losses resulting from her depredations from England that made the American Government less eager for her capture. If the world should come to that conclusion, it would be one of the strongest practical arguments against the admission of such liabilities as Seward is now endeavoring to establish against England. It is stated that Waddell sent a letter to Earl Russell. Contents unknown.

The Confederate steamer *Shenandoah.*

The American flag is raised over Fort Sumter by General Robert Anderson who was in command there when the war began four years before.

The *Star* says that if the vessel be claimed by America there is no reason for refusing the request. . . .

🔫 *The liabilities that State Secretary Seward was seeking to pin on Great Britain amounted to millions of dollars worth of American shipping destroyed during the Civil War by the three Confederate raiders,* Florida, Alabama *and* Shenandoah. *Basis of the claim was the fact that the three ships had been built in Britain and outfitted by British firms, while Her Majesty's government looked the other way. These were to become known as the "Alabama Claims." An international court eventually awarded the United States $15.5 million damages, which Britain paid. The Star, meanwhile, huffed editorially at the London* News. 🔫

EDITORIAL.

The London *News* asks, apropos of the arrival of the pirate *Shenandoah* in the Mersey, "how the *Shenandoah* was enabled to pursue her course without the least interruption from the American Navy?" For the simple reason that every British port was a shelter for her and her fellow-pirates, and that the twenty-four hours start permitted her by "neutral"

Britons enabled her, as it did the *Alabama* and the others, to slip away and escape successful pursuit. Should the "next war," or any other war, ever call into requisition American steamer privateers to the disadvantage of British commerce, we opine that Great Britain will have a livelier time, even, in overtaking them than we have had with the fast-sailing rebel pirates.

🔫 *Next day another ship from England docked, and Americans could be positive that the shooting aspects of the Civil War were at last over.* 🔫

(Tuesday, November 21, 1865)

Later from Europe.

The Pirate "Shenandoah" Handed over to the American Authorities—Her Crew Unconditionally Discharged.

HALIFAX, Nov. 21.—The steamship *China,* with Liverpool dates to the 11th and 12th, has arrived. The *Shenandoah* has been handed over to the American Consul, and will be sent to New York. Her captain and crew have been unconditionally discharged.

WASHINGTON HOMEFRONT, NOVEMBER, 1865.

🔫 *Signs of the late war could still be seen in Washington.* 🔫

HANDSOME RESIDENCE.—The building on the corner of 16½ and I streets, formerly owned by Elisha Riggs, Esq., adjoining the residence of Geo. W. Riggs, the banker, has been purchased by Mr. Knapp, who amassed a princely fortune during the war in the business of casting cannon and projectiles for the government. It is one of the most complete and elegant dwellings in the District. He designs making it his permanent residence.

SALE OF GOVERNMENT BEEF CATTLE AND WHISKY.

To-day was the day set apart for the opening of the sealed proposals for the purchase of 500 head of beef cattle, belonging to the Commissary Department, but the bidders failing to properly comply with the conditions, none of the proposals were considered, and the cattle will therefore be offered at public auction tomorrow, at Alexandria, and sold to the highest bidder.

The Commissary Department has also on hand about 60,000 gallons of whiskey, which will be offered at public sale about the 2d of December.

DONATION TO THE UNITED STATES.

Yesterday, Secretary McCullough received from the executors of a deceased Indiana farmer, a $1,000 ten-forty bond, which the deceased had bequeathed to the Government to be applied towards the payment of the national debt.

🔫 *After Lincoln's assassination, the government had bought Ford's theater for $100,000, with the idea of converting it into an office building.* 🔫

FORD'S THEATRE.—Mr. Dunbar, the contractor for the work of transforming Ford's Theatre to subserve its new purposes, has finished his job and delivered the building into possession of the Government. It will be remembered that the price specified in the contract was $28,500, which makes the property now stand at $128,500. The work seems to have been done in a solid, substantial manner. The structure, it is well known, was entirely divested of all its interior finish and furniture, leaving nothing but four naked brick walls and the roof. It is now divided into three stories, with a spacious skylight in the centre. The three floors or stories, into which the structure is now divided, are composed of brick and iron, and finished in the usual mode of fire-proof buildings. The upper two stories consist of galleries extending around the four sides of the building and lighted from above.

Epilogue:

ANOTHER KIND OF CIVIL WAR

The last shots had been fired, but another form of Civil War would continue for twelve years: the era known as the Reconstruction —perhaps the blackest chapter in the Nation's history.

The shooting war had deeply seared both North and South. The Union had suffered around 360,000 dead of 2,200,000 combatants. Confederate losses had been proportionately even greater—close to 258,000 dead of an estimated million soldiers and sailors. In terms of casualties, the Civil War remains the costliest of all this country's conflicts. The loss in property damage and treasure, moreover, ran to tens of millions of dollars.

The North, with stronger resources to begin with, could withstand its losses. In fact, the great industrial upsurge that had mushroomed to prosecute the war, provided the base on which the world's leading industrial power would be founded. The North, further, had bloodily established two fundamentals: the United States was an "indestructible Union composed of indestructible States"; chattel slavery would not be countenanced within its limits.

For its part, the South at the end of war was prostrate physically, spiritually and economically. The bulk of the white population despaired, especially because of the sudden reality of emancipated Negro slaves. Most of the freedmen, through no fault of their own, were illiterate. To hordes of these former slaves, freedom meant no more than escape from work and responsibility.

Circumstances in the South cried for the central government's help and understanding. But power politics, practiced by the Radical Republicans controlling the Federal Congress and other places of influence, plus a black spirit of vengeance, would prevail.

Lincoln had planned a conciliatory policy designed to lead to a genuine reconstruction of the old Confederacy. But even during his lifetime, the radicals of his Party had plotted obstacles. With the death of the master politician, diplomat and humanitarian, chances for a constructive approach disappeared. Andrew Johnson, the slain President's successor, tried to carry out the Lincoln concept. Johnson, a man of high courage and convictions concerning the Union, the Constitution and Southern reconstruction, would almost wreck his public career on the rocks of the radical opposition. As it was to turn out, he stood no chance for re-election. The Radicals, by virtue of bayonets and sweeping Negro suffrage in the South—as well as demagoguery in the North—would sweep the distinguished general, Ulysses S. Grant, into office in 1868. The eight-year administration of the hapless Grant would be blackened by continuation of the mailed fist policy toward the South, and corruption in every quarter.

The Nation would survive this trauma, too, and grow with a vigor and swiftness never before witnessed on the earth. As the Nation flourished—outside its dark closets in the South—so would Washington and Journalism and *The Star*.

The war had transformed Washington into the Nation's Capital in more than name. From being a cockpit of war, it became a peacetime center of far-reaching power. City growth began to take forward strides. In the 1870s, with *The Star* as press champion, far-sighted men would bulldoze a public works program into existence, doing away with mud and dust to lay the groundwork for the city of today. The present commission form of government, answerable to Congress and the White House, would be established during this period.

The war had also brought about a metamorphosis in Journalism. Before the Civil War, Agent Lawrence A. Gobright of the *Associated Press* had noted that, during a period of six weeks, he was the only correspondent in Washington after an adjournment of Congress. The war brought significance to a Washington dateline. Afterward, Mr. Gobright noted, the press was always "efficiently and respectably represented," whether or not Congress was in session. About the country, too, the interest in national news had swelled, leading the Western *Associated Press* to challenge the right of the *Associated Press* lords in New York to skimp with news to which Western readers felt they were entitled. This was a conflict not to be finally resolved until the modern *Associated Press* was established to give readers, anywhere, all the news.

INDEX